GW00368101

AUSTRALIAN SCREEN

General Editor: Sylvia Lawson

Legends on the Screen

National Film Archive

'No beauty comparable to the Americans': Arthur Tauchert in *The Sentimental Bloke*

Legends on the Screen

The Australian Narrative Cinema 1919-1929

JOHN TULLOCH

Currency Press • Sydney
The Australian Film Institute

First published in 1981
by Currency Press Pty Ltd,
87 Jersey Road, Woollahra,
N.S.W. 2025, Australia
and
The Australian Film Institute,
P.O. Box 165 Carlton South,
Victoria 3053, Australia.

National Library of Australia card number
and ISBN 0 86819 057 8 (paper)

Computer set in Garamond by Meredith Trade Lino Pty Ltd,
Burnley, Victoria
Printed by Colorcraft Ltd, Hong Kong

General Editor's Preface

Fifteen years ago, 'Australian film' was the name of a well-recognised vacancy, a barren tract where (so they told us) there had once been quite a deal of tough and struggling growth. Using the rhetoric of cultural nationalism, a few polemicists began to draw attention to the area as a site requiring re-occupation. There was some shooting from the fox-holes, most of it aimed at politicians, some at the vendors for the international film market.

Most of the guerrillas there were cinéastes. In the neighbouring country of television, more orderly and less pretentious troops worked away producing police series and commercials, less tantalised by the pains and promises of contemporary cinema. Without them, re-establishment of the feature film industry would have been even more difficult, if not impossible. Through the late 1960s, television drama staked out some territory it could hold. The cinéastes continued to make the films they could make on starvation budgets: formal visual experiment, small-scale narrative, political animation. The Experimental Film Fund began operations in 1970; the Australian Film Development Corporation, brought into existence by lobbying and fortunate political accidents, in 1971.

At the same time, histories of the country's early film production began to be told and re-told, both in print and on film. Raymond Longford, who had gone down fighting at the end of the silent period, became — perhaps too easily — a symbol for the struggles of the present. The processes of production, consumption, and enquiry set in train during those years have continued through the 1970s with considerable struggle, argument and turbulence in every area — the bureaucracies, the market, the fragmented majority and minority audiences. This series attempts to respond to those processes, to recognise Australian film and television as sets of institutions, texts, and practices.

It responds also to a clear demand for information, as well as analysis, both from within Australia and outside it. This demand arises not merely because the film and television material is suddenly there to be discussed, but also because it is being produced and received in a time when our ways of thinking and talking about film, television and culture in general are all under challenge and revision. The series attempts to take up, and work in terms of, the new questions being asked about the relations of text and context, art and industry; story, society and culture; screen and audience.

Further, the first retrievals of Australia's film-making past have shown that in its particular colonial/post-colonial circumstances, the chancy and changing conditions of production have borne so vitally on all filmic expression that they must be taken as marking the major boundaries of the field of enquiry. Australia, in so many senses an outpost of Britain, is still, as part of the world film/television market, a colony of Hollywood as well, and the story of its film production is very much part of the history of Hollywood's global dominance. Questions about style and authorhip take their places in that context; we are not, therefore, making books which can be called by the names of individual film-makers. At the same time, the story of domination is necessarily also a story of resistance; such real authorship as we might discover will be about resistance as much as about the individual working of styles and materials.

For those reasons, the first books in the series concern the richest early period of production, so far as the survival and salvaging of its films allows their re-reading; and the related story of the shifting relations of government and film, since those relations, by default and otherwise, have set the conditions in which films could be made or not made, seen or not seen, for half a century. Forthcoming texts — some primarily research tools, some essays in historical enquiry and analysis — will consider Australian television drama, documentary production, the position of women both in production and representation and the problems and issues of the re-established commercial industry. We hope to follow these with work on the avant-garde, on political cinema, and particularly with some examination of the relations between black Australians and film-making, both within and outside the category of ethnographic film.

In all this we are trying to make books for the use of concerned film-consumers, and film-users who may or may not be, formally, students; and for film-workers in the industry, the market, journalism and education: in fact for all those, not least the audiences, involved in the production of meaning with and through film and television.

Sylvia Lawson
Griffith University
December 1980

To Rowan

By the same author:

Conflict and Control in the Cinema: a reader in film and society (ed.)

Chekhov: A Structuralist Study

Contents

Illustrations

VOL. 1, No. 14. JULY 19, 1919.

The Picture Show

PUBLISHED WEEKLY.

Registered at the General Post Office, Sydney, for transmission by post as a Newspaper.

CURRENT NEWS OF THE WORLD

PEACE CELEBRATIONS TO-DAY.

TRIUMPH OF RIGHT OVER MIGHT.

WANTED—AN AUSTRALIAN NATIONAL SENTIMENT.

To-day the entire British Empire will celebrate the signing of Peace. It will be a day of jubilation and thanksgiving for the triumph of Right over Might.

Five years ago to-day was held that fateful secret meeting of the Kaiser and his Ministers in Berlin to compound their plot against civilisation. There were little ripples that showed some scheme was afoot, but even the British diplomats in Berlin in their wildest guess did not reckon on the action that Germany ultimately took.

Might went out with blood-red hands to plunge the world into war. The blood-red hand remains, but Might has departed, leaving a once great nation but an impotent shell of its former self.

It remains with us to keep the menace of Might away for ever. It can be done by co-operation of all classes and by the raising in Australia of a steadfast national sentiment, as against the electioneering political catch-phrases which have been flung at us during five years of war under a patriotic cloak.

A true patriotism must arise to-day. It must be fostered in every man, woman and child in every home and in every school.

Either that, or perhaps in another few years a new menace, a more terrible war and—who knows what?

A GIRL'S LOVE TRAGEDY.

Big Sensation in Chicago. Thaw Case Recalled.

The city of Chicago has been startled by a trial as sensational and full of human interest as the famous Thaw case of years ago.

Norma Cook, a beautiful eighteen-year-old girl, has faced an alternative such as few women have been called upon to meet. She has been compelled to stand in the witness-box and either send her own father to the electric chair or besmirch her own good name and that of her fiancee, whom her father murdered.

Norman Cook, the accused, was a man of 48. He represented one of those unfortunate types who, with age growing on, find themselves without money, and without prospects other than those which the marriage of his beautiful daughter to some wealthy magnate presented. He had resolved on the latter, and resented her the girl's love for William Bradway, a moderately prosperous business man. Cook strove to kill the love that existed between the pair. He protested with them both; most strenuously with Bradway, whose money did not come up to his expectations. He failed, and in the end murdered Bradway.

There was only one possibility of saving him from a murderer's doom. He could plead the unwritten law. That plea had been strongly advanced, and when Norma Cook tearfully entered the witness-box she faced a terrible alternative. The whole court hung in expectation on her words.

Slowly and softly she gave her evidence. It was against her own father. She loved the dead, she hated the living, and she herself had done no wrong. Filial duty made her shield her father as much as possible; self-respect restrained her

Preface

'Australian narrative cinema': the words describe a field of enquiry; they also suggest certain key systems, and these have been guiding principles for the analysis which follows. 'Australian': we need to deal with the feature which the film trade of 1919, and many critics thereafter, took to be especially local — the opposition of bush against city; and yet which as a myth can be traced to global economic patterns. 'Narrative': we need to consider some of the cross-cultural codings by means of which these value systems became public entertainment — through historically grounded forms (that is by way of melodrama as narrative) and the intersection of these forms with the growing taste for 'realism'. 'Cinema': we need to locate these films within the constraints of production, and consider the distinction between cinema as trade and cinema as industry in terms of the one-way international flow of film forms, values of practice, institutions and content which we now call media imperialism.

These were the parameters of my study, and I intended at first to write equal chapters on each area. However, in researching and in the early writing, this balance changed. The general editor of the series insisted from the beginning that the story of Australian production still had to be told. As I researched trade sources I found myself becoming as interested in the differences within the film industry as in the similarities. This was not for the anti-theoretical reasons for which many historians cling to the notion of 'human' difference, but because it is only by tracing the subtly differing location of different film-makers that one can begin to see the complexity of codes through which media imperialism has worked. Many historical movements were taking place contemporaneously — of audiences from tin sheds to picture palaces; of popular entertainment from theatrical to film melodrama; of the control of entrepreneurial outlets into fewer hands, many of them foreign; of the hardening of earlier cinema pioneers into 'generalissimos' of the trade; of Australian populism and nationalism within concepts of 'civilisation' and 'progress' coined elsewhere; of growing pressure-group and parliamentary intervention.

These and other developments intersected in complex ways to create the values practised in the Australian film market and industry which allowed for a whole spectrum of modes whereby the individual film-maker was assimilated, compromised or rejected. The rejection and failure of Raymond Longford, for example, has generally been theorised on the basis of a crude 'American imperialism' model. But the acceptance of his *The Dinkum Bloke* by Paramount and the rejection of *Fisher's Ghost* cannot be explained unless we locate these films in relation to a number of developments — for instance, the rising parliamentary agitation against American distributors, the Australian exhibition circuits' desire to tap a 'better class' market, the 'immorality' campaigns against the cinema in both the United States and Australia which led to exhibitors rejecting 'gruesome' and 'repulsive' subject matter, the growing organisation of Australian exhibitors as an occupational group and the attempts by the less organised film producers to meet this problem. All of these movements have to be understood in the last instance in terms of Hollywood's developing global domination. But each, when set in motion, had a limited degree of autonomy and a time scale of its own. Together, they formed a complex set of mediations between Hollywood and Australian producers which could generate quite different fortunes for film-makers in slightly different situations, or even for the same film-makers at different times.

Hence my original idea of a chapter on the film industry expanded to consider the varying modes of construction (and destruction) of Australian film-makers by the Hollywood-dominated film trade. I have written chapters, or extensive sections of chapters, on each of the major film-makers — not because I had any idealist notion of autonomous auteurist creativity, but because this seemed to me the best way to point to some of the *systematic* complexities, of differences within continuity, within the trade and the production industry. The decision to 'tell the story' through the narratives (of individual rise and fall) of film-makers has a number of advantages. It has let me show how media imperialism developed through a number of mediations: professional backgrounds of the film-makers and the trade moguls, their consequent notions of popular entertainment, their differing formal preoccupations, their varying attitudes to Australian history and the bush legend, their notions of modern audiences, of cinema as institution, of social 'progress' and other social issues. It also allows me to consider in some detail the film-makers' own interpretations of events (which have led to some of Australian cinema's more abiding legends) and to sift through the evidence where the answers are not clear. I have preferred to leave the interpretation of details open to the reader. But by and large I counterpose between theories of personal vendetta and global manipulation my own view of a system working normally (that is, for most of the time without malicious intention) against the interests of Australian film producers but, at least for a time, in favour of those who rose from being Australia's earliest cinema pioneers to being generals in the exhibition and distribution field.

Nonetheless, a more complete examination of the film industry of this period has still to be written. This again would need to take account of the differences within continuity — differences, for instance, in the trade location of acceptable 'independent' exhibitors like Bill Howe and Bill Szarka and less acceptable ones like H.D. McIntosh, between the compliant exhibitors' associations (like that of New South Wales) and the less compliant ones (like that of Queensland), and the very real differences between suburban and major circuit exhibitors which made them shifting allies in the disputes with distributors which it was the task of the various professional organisations and trade press to obviate, explain away or deny. More broadly still, the cinema needs to be located within the pattern of a dependent economy, the orientation of that dependence in terms of Britain or the United States, the effect of this on tariff legislation and the complicating factor of tensions between Commonwealth and State rights, etc.

There has not been space for this; nor for the section on Australian film as narrative which I had hoped to include. Some chapters incorporate narrative analysis, particularly chapter 11, where I have attempted an introductory textual analysis of Barrett's *The Breaking of the Drought* and the first few sequences of his *A Girl of the Bush* (since this analysis has been generated by the sequential development of the films, its logic will be better followed by close juxtaposition with the film 'texts' themselves). But a more developed understanding of narrative, and of the specificity of melodrama as narrative (a natural corollary to the analysis in chapter 11), must wait for another book.

The value of an approach to Australian film as narrative can, however, be mentioned here in part. In the first place, an approach through narrative avoids the 'high culture – low culture' assumptions of critics who reject most of Australian cinema as beneath consideration. Instead, it locates these films firmly within popular culture and finds that what some critics reject as simplistic and crude amount, in fact, to quite complex and sophisticated developments of basic popular cultural models. Secondly, the isolation of a basic narrative 'grammar' in films over a given period would have the advantage of allowing us to describe both continuity and change in formal and structural rather than auteurist-psychological terms, since by means of it we could see variations within a paradigm and begin to ask questions about the way those variations work. It seems to me that an analysis of this nature is the only way of avoiding a simplistic listing

April 18, 1928. EVERYONES Page Twenty-five

QUEENSLAND MOTION PICTURE EXHIBITORS' ASSOCIATION

C. ROSE (Vice President), H. THOMPSON (President), R. STEPHENS (Vice President)

"Others call them the Bolsheviks of the Business!

"WHY? Because they use their show sense; they can't be bluffed. They judge the audience value of every special and every service; they see exactly what each picture is worth at the box-office; they make exhibition their BUSINESS; they know more about pictures than the men who try to sell them. Buy on merit.... pay on performance! That's the way they work.

"BOLSHEVIKS? Rot! They're such shrewd, hard-fighting showmen that all over Queensland other Exhibitors seek their advice. And do they know what the future means? You bet! THAT'S WHY THE PRESIDENT AND BOTH VICE-PRESIDENTS OF THE QUEENSLAND EXHIBTORS ASSOCIATION HAVE BOOKED FOX 100 PER CENT.

* * * *

"IN these ad-itorials I've told you I thought 'Mother Machree,' 'Loves of Carmen' and 'Sunrise' were three of the biggest hits that ever came to Australia. Now I've just seen another ....'Four Sons'! Only Fox could make it; and if any other company can produce a box-office knock-out to beat it this year, I'll be the first to tell you RIGHT HERE, IN THE ADVERTISING SPACE I'M PAYING FOR MYSELF!"

S. S. Crick

Managing Director, Fox Film Corp. (Aust.) Ltd.

Everyones 18 April 1928, p.25

The Queensland Exhibitors' Association more than once refused to toe the trade line — for instance on block booking and on total opposition to entertainment taxes. Hence the interesting ambivalence of this attempt to sell Fox films.

of films by chronology, director and anecdote, and because I have not had space for it here, only a few films have been analysed.

The ones I have chosen for extended analysis — *The Sentimental Bloke*, *The Kid Stakes*, the Barrett films — by now form the major part of an increasingly familiar pantheon of Australian 'art' films. But I have not chosen them for that reason — or at least only indirectly so. These were the films which I personally found most stimulating among the whole corpus, causing me to ask questions as to why this should be so, and leading on to questions about narrative subversion, about texts splintering between adopted modal forms, and about the success of other texts in disguising ideological preoccupations by very precise use of traditional allegorical forms.

Inevitably, with these principles of selection and limited space there are omissions. The films, and the production constraints surrounding them, of Jack Wells, Kenneth Brampton, Charles Villiers, P.J. Ramster, Arthur Sterry, Roy Darling, Phil K. Walsh, Stuart Whyte, George Palmer, A.G. Harbrow, Vaughan Marshall, Dunstan Webb and Arthur Higgins receive little mention. They deserve a monograph to themselves in terms of generic and narrative conventions, and the economic–ideological location within the trade of 'mushroom' companies, 'quota quickies', and so on. I have left out most in the way of plot synopses, partly to reduce the length of the book, and partly because the filmography by Andrew Pike and Ross Cooper (*Australian Film 1900–1977*, Melbourne 1980) deals fully with this area, film by film. I had intended to include a chapter analysing the McDonagh sisters' films which, together with those of Longford and Barrett, I find most interesting in terms of formal and ideological complexity. But, given the limitations of space and the knowledge that the McDonaghs' films will be discussed extensively in the work being done by Lesley Stern and Julie Rose on women in the cinema for the Australian Screen series, I chose to omit this analysis also.

Finally, I would like to thank Sylvia Lawson as editor of the series for her initial guidance and continued provocation to thinking and presentation; Derek Barton for his skill and time in editing the work; Julie Rose, Philip Bell and Katharine Brisbane for reading and giving helpful advice; the staff of the National Film Archive, especially Kate McLoughlin, for arranging screening facilities, providing frame enlargements and for continuous help and courtesy throughout my research; the Mitchell Library for further assistance; Elsa Chauvel and Jack Tauchert for permission to reproduce stills; and David Liddle for his photographic work on the trade journals.

John Tulloch
September 1980

Photoplayer 30 June 1923, cover

Pictures of opulence and seduction: the stylistic gesture of the photoplay magazine

PART ONE

After the War, the Construction of Peace

Picture Show (i) 19 April 1919, p.21; (ii) 2 August 1919, p.13

Replacing war gloom: Gaby Deslys with her 'delightful frocks' gives Australian women 'a new interest in life'; while Irving and Bennetto draw 'self-respecting mothers from the wash-up dish' in *Does the Jazz Age Lead to Destruction*.

1

1919, *A Sentimental Bloke* and a *Picture Show*

Nineteen nineteen was only superficially a year of peace. The First World War ended officially in July. But in Europe socialist revolution seemed to threaten the world capitalist order, and many allied soldiers and sailors were simply transferred from one front to another to help contain it. Returning Australian soldiers found a country haunted by the spectre of socialism after the great strikes of 1916 – 17 and the Labor movement's campaign against military conscription. In 1919 returned soldiers clashed openly with 'Bolsheviks' in Brisbane, and with trade unionists in many cities over the issue of employment preference for war heroes. Nineteen nineteen was to be the costliest year for strikes since statistics had been kept, with a loss of over six million man days. In addition to these troubles the world influenza epidemic, which caused far more deaths than the Great War, reached Australia. As people took to wearing masks around the streets of Sydney, some saw the 11,500 Australian 'flu deaths as a foretaste of a more ominous future. Morality, too, seemed under threat. Women were outstripping men as divorcees in the highest marriage break-up rate ever. Sexual mores were said to have been loosened by the war, and as women began to dress, smoke and dance more daringly, people looked for a cause and found it in alcohol and the cinema.

Of all these unnerving events, only the 'flu epidemic and the charge of immorality caused serious mention in the cinema trade press. The trade, normally hostile to government 'interference', now called for government compensation for those in the business 'to keep body and soul together' while cinemas were closed during the epidemic. The trade press criticised the government for closing the picture theatres for seven weeks, and blamed the newspapers for sensationalism in fanning the 'flu panic as a replacement for war gloom. This, it felt, was biting the hand that fed them, since newspapers grew fat on cinema advertising. Other unprovoked aggression was coming from censors and 'wowsers', particularly those 'of the bench and the Church' who were blaming the cinema for every sexual seduction and vicious crime. Throughout 1919 the cinema trade responded actively to the charge. Films were 'really for the good of the kids' because although

© M.L. THE SLAVE.

Picture Show 11 October 1919, p.1

VOL. 1.—No. 26. OCTOBER 11, 1919.

The Picture Show

PUBLISHED WEEKLY.

Registered at the General Post Office, Sydney, for transmission by post as a Newspaper.

CURRENT NEWS OF THE WORLD.

Russia's False Czars.

Pretenders to Throne Worry Bolsheviks.

TWO "CZARS" IN ONE VILLAGE.

This interesting article on affairs in Russia is reprinted from the "Chicago Tribune," for which it was written by Julius Ostman, foreign correspondent.

History repeats itself. Lenin's special commission for suppressing counter-revolution, that lively bloody assize which under the Lett Peters and the Pole Derzhinski sentenced 5,000 innocent Russians to death, has sent out a circular warning its provincial myrmidons to watch out for the sham Czar Nicholases, sham heirs to the throne Alexises, and sham grand dukes and grand duchesses who may claim the Romanoff crown.

The situation is perilous, hints the commission. Not only are unnumbered counter-revolutionaries boldly fostering monarchism and czarism in the abstract, they have begun to discover plausible pretenders to the throne—ordinary citizens, lawyers, doctors, and students, who claim that they are Nicholas, escaped from his Ekaterinburg gaol, or his son, or some of the more presentable grand dukes who have escaped abroad, who are actually either hiding in Russia or have perished in the Peter and Paul fortress.

Keep Country in Unrest.

"The monarchists," says the special commission, "are not dangerous in themselves; but the pretenders keep the countryside in unrest, and encourage the counter-revolutionary ferment." And it mentions that particularly in the northern province of Olonetz, several pretenders have appeared, posing as the martyred Nicholas II., and that on one occasion even two Nicholas II.'s appeared, so that the bewildered peasants took three weeks to decide which was a real czar and which was a fraud.

Pretender Appears.

Naturally when Nicholas II. and his 14-year-old heir perished so obscurely in Ekaterinburg that doubt exists as to whether they are dead at all, pretenders were bound to arise. The first arose while Nicholas was undoubtedly alive. This was in the late summer of 1917.

Nicholas, his empress and his five children were then safely interned in the damp governor's palace in Siberian Tobolsk. The revolt of ex-Army Commander Korniloff against Kerensky's government set the monarchists, who were already encouraged by the nation's growing disgust with Petrograd's weakness, thinking. And a pretender rose. He appeared in the Siberian city Omsk, now headquarters of the anti-bolshevik government; was rejected by the monarchists there as a fraud, and made east for Krasnoyarsk, with the aim, people say, of not declaring himself to be Czar Nicholas till he reached Vladivostok.

Looked Like Czar.

In Vladivostok he hoped to get aid from the monarchist refugees in Japan. On the way through Krasnoyarsk, the most violently Red city in all Siberia, his likeness to Czar Nicholas attracted attention, and the cry spread that the traitor Kerensky had released the czar. And now the pretender was in a queer position. He had to deny that he was Nicholas. Nobody in Krasnoyarsk knew that he had posed as a czar in Tomsk, but his likeness was so extraordinary that no one would believe his vows that he was an apothecary of German origin from Moscow.

The bolshevik council of deputies kept him in prison for a week, and then—doubting whether he was the czar, but to prevent misunderstandings—knocked him on the head.

'vice is inherited, it remains for training in the child's early years to make or mar it'[1], and cinema, as well as keeping children 'from the perils of the streets', elevated their minds by awakening 'argumentative faculties'. As for women's morality, the trade press made a major feature of the Australian film, *Does the Jazz Age Lead to Destruction* to prove to 'maiden aunts' and 'sainted ladies' that grandmas and 'self-respecting mothers sighing over the washing-up dish' could throw themselves into the 'world wonders' of modern entertainment with 'small damage to the morals'.[2] Indeed, even women's nudity on the screen was 'absolutely free from all traces of immodesty'. Cinema was 'the most advanced form of modern art', and artistic nudity worked for the 'entertainment and elevation' of a free and mature civilisation held back too long by 'long-whiskered wowsers'. 'Only the prurient-minded will find anything wrong with the nude — the artistic nude — on the screen'. Yet 'the pursuit of the nude' had 'become a fetish' with the censors who had snipped nude sequences out of D.W. Griffith's *Intolerance* and the Annette Kellerman film, *The Daughter of the Gods*.[3]

Apart from these few defensive postures, the cinema trade was determinedly optimistic in 1919. The trade press claimed that 'Dispelling Gloom' was the prerogative of the cinema, and a crucial task in economic reconstruction. Chaplin and Fairbanks would bring 'tears of laughter in the place of tears of misery', and Gaby Deslys' 'delightful frocks' would give Australian womenfolk, 'so weary of sticking at home, a new interest in life'.[4] The cinemas, 'far from being a menace to the community' were the contemporary way 'of cheering-up the picture-going patrons'. This was good for business too, since 'it has been proved' that when 'people are happy they spend money; when they are gloomy the tendency is to sit at home and think desperately about prevailing conditions . . . We claim then that when our theatres disgorge their crowds of happy smiling people they are fulfilling a national service which besides having a great mental benefit on the public, results also in keeping our trade conditions running briskly along'.[5]

The troubles at home were converted into a future of smiling faces and prosperity. As for the troubles abroad, where the trade press mentioned them it was mainly to wish them away. Stories of Lenin's 'bloody assize' and of bomb throwers in Berlin were juxtaposed with photographs of 'artistic nudes'.[6] It was thought by 'persons who know Russia and the susceptibilities of its illiterate population to crazes' that the peasants would soon flock to a 'first class' royal pretender who would overthrow 'the whole system of bolshevism'.[7] And in Germany where revolutionary violence was said to be the result of hunger and the 'indigent criminal classes' there was good news too. 'It is no exaggeration to say that American food beat Bolshevism in Germany'.[8] There was also news of violence in Britain, caused in the opinion of the trade press by blacks stealing white girls for wives while the Tommies were away, and fanned by 'the white man's natural objection to the black'.[9] However, if racial violence seemed to be accepted as a fact of nature, class conflict was wished away with a fervency that betrayed considerable unease among the cinema capitalists. The trade press was full of stories in 1919 which denied class lines: the Princess of Connaught who married a commoner at Westminster Abbey; the baronet floor-scrubbers and millionaire gun-swabbers in the British army; the Spitalfields basket-maker who had become professor of Italian at Cambridge University; the American millionaire 'Joe Duke' who wore moleskins and hauled logs.

Conflict was wished into the past. Germans were said to be converting guns into farming tools. The battlefields had 'put aside their dark shroud of death' giving 'themselves up to the glories of France's summer'.[10] The historic sites of war were now populated with 'summer flowers', 'industrious peasants', 'new homes built among the ruins', and hotels provided by 'New York and Paris capitalists' to serve the new business enterprises and tourist trade. Schemes for 'housing the workers' in England and New South Wales were proclaimed; as was the Australian plan to collect £100,000 in 'Relief of the Sick Poor'. These were said to be great opportunities 'for all classes to get together — to understand one another — to make for that greater, finer, better Australia'.[11] Each 'deserving, incapacitated soldier' should be provided with a new home which later could become 'a garden of refuge for any poor wharfie or unfortunate who gets ousted in the industrial battle of life'.[12]

On the day of the peace celebrations in July 1919, the trade press proclaimed the 'Triumph of Right over Might', but warned that 'Might' could only be kept at bay 'by the co-operation of all classes' and a 'true patriotism'. 'Either that, or perhaps in another few years a new menace, a more terrible war and — who knows what?'[13] The optimistic belief was that this unnamed — and unnamable — class struggle would never happen. 'A Gleam of Light' was shining beyond the troubles of war, conflict and epidemic. All these unnerving occurrences would 'smooth themselves out, leaving a bright, rosy future'.[14] Wonderful picture palaces would be built, which would bring harmony as well as wealth to the nation. For here 'all classes' would truly come together: the cinema would no longer be purely a worker's entertainment. And in the year ahead some sixty-eight million Australians would pour into its darkened auditoria.

The Sennett Beauties are the Choicest Peaches Ever Picked

Centre: Alice Lake. Upper Left: Harriet Hammond. Right: Marie Prevost. Lower Left: Phyllis Haver. Right: Marie Prevost.

Business Manager:
ALBERT E. LAKE.

Managing Editor:
W. ST. CLAIR ANDERSON.

Assistant Editor .... Reg. A. Long
Art Editor .... Harry Julius
Melb. Representative ...... J. L. Anderson
Artists .... Smith & Julius
Blocks by .... Bacon & Co.

Published at 17 Bond St.,
Sydney, by the Proprietor.
CARTOON FILMADS LIMITED.

Managing Director:
ALBERT E. LAKE.

Directors:
J. L. ANDERSON (Melbourne).
HARRY JULIUS (Sydney).

Secretary: J. A. LAKE.

Half-yearly subscription, 8/8. Yearly subscriptions, 17/9. Post free anywhere in Australia or Papua. Remittances by Postal Note, Post Office Order, or Cheque. Exchange to be added to all Cheques, etc.

MELBOURNE OFFICE ... 67 Queen St.
SYDNEY OFFICE .... 17 Bond St.
BRISBANE OFFICE .... Courier Bldgs.
Advertising Rates on Application.
Advertising Representatives:
S. E. BROWN. F. MORAND.
Telephones:
Sydney .... City 4518
Melbourne .... Cent. 453

"Advance Australia."

FROM the shell-torn slopes of Gallipoli to France's fields of stubborn contest Australia's sons have set the world ringing with the echo of a new personality—the personality of the Australian fighter. Out of the cradle of war Australia has earned the right to take her place among those whose manhood can boast a distinctive character of its own.

The methods of those fighting sons of Australia were characterised by certain peculiarities now known and eulogised by all the nations, and graven on the pages of history.

Aggression, determined impetuosity, fair play, cheery fortitude and unrelenting tenacity, these constitute qualities that have become household words coupled with the name of Australia the world over.

The care-free but indomitable charge at Lone Pine—the clearing of those murderous ridges at Pozieres—the hundred and one dashing affrays of the lone individual units that nightly made the ebony blackness of "No Man's Land" the grim school-house of a nation of fighters.

These men have made the name of Australia the personification of a fighting spirit, saturated with dash and permeated with stubborn aggression. The grim spectre of war became to them a gay game of noble sport, and all the qualities moulded on those fields of fierce conflict have created a new individuality for every Australian.

The war is over, but the ever-present war of commerce looms up before the world. It is accentuated to more fiery competition by the steeping of the sons of the nations in the fierce whirlpool of racial antagonism during those four long years of fire-swept agony in the cockpit of Europe.

Just as war of 1919 became revolutionised to the extent of seering poison gas and vivid liquid fire, spurred by the spirit of military progress, so commerce of 1919 must awaken to the fact that 1919 methods must be used in order that commercial success be attained.

Australia, therefore, having proved the fighting dash of her sons in the great world war, must to-day turn those same qualities to the forwarding of the interests of her commercial supremacy.

A Future Australian Industry.

IN the opinion of this paper there is no greater field for Australian enterprise than the motion picture industry.

Most of the leading men in the big exchanges, and those, too, who own and control the large theatres, are men who have gone through the hard road of experience. They, in most cases, began their careers with nothing to rely upon but their own brains and their steady determination to get on. And just those same qualities of aggression, impetuosity, fairplay and fortitude which characterised our Australian fighters in the field, have placed them in the proud positions they hold to-day.

Field of Production in Australia.

In the field of production, however, the men who are carrying on the fight for recognition, are still in the pioneering stage.

Among them are those who will some day rank as the great producers of future Australian productions. For these men will succeed when a definite and organised policy of Australian production becomes an established fact.

One of the greatest fields yet to be established is the production of scenarios.

All over the world at the present time there is an acute dearth of scenarios of the right kind, and it is very possible that Australia is the least-touched field of any. In the future we hope a great writer will come to the top, who will be able to create the atmosphere of the Australian bush. Some student of the pen and screen will dig from the pages of Australian history an "environment," and will educate the world to the romance of Australia, as so many great authors have done in America.

There can be no doubt of the great work these men have done in their magnificent creations of the fast riding, dare-devil, two-gun West.

Surely from the atmosphere of the days of the early gold rush, and the scores of other like pages of our past, some Jack London or Zane Grey could find magnificent material for a new field of romance.

The "Picture Show's" Sphere.

SO much remains to be done, and this paper is actively setting out with the policy of actively supporting the efforts of every branch of the Australian industry. This will be the cheapest and best paper of its type published in Australia, and it will maintain the policy of an absolutely unbiassed organ.

To every man with the interests of the Motion Picture at heart, it extends the "glad hand," and offers a true and sincere friendship.

It will not, however, be drawn into the vortex of personal prejudice, believing that, if it should permit itself to be thus mis-used, it would become only a stone in the path of progress, instead of the great factor of encouragement which is the principle on which is based the production of this paper.

With the hope that it will prove an inspiration to every Australian who loves the "movies," and that the host of good things that it holds for the future will brighten the hours of leisure and unfold the pages of that great and fascinating romance, the progress of the Australian Motion Picture, we commend to you—"The Picture Show."

A Sentimental Bloke and the *Picture Show*

In April 1919, Raymond Longford, who was to become Australia's leading director, had just finished *The Sentimental Bloke*. The same month saw the birth of the only trade journal dedicated to the cause of Australian film-making, the *Picture Show*. This chapter is about the coming together of these events, and the messages they offered, separately and together, for the future of the Australian film industry.

One of *Picture Show*'s earliest editorials, together with its facing page of American nymphette stars, is shown on p. 31. The juxtaposition reveals immediately the impending problem of Australian cinema: the paradox involved in attempting to project the pioneering bush legend through a heavily capitalised, Hollywood-dependent industry. The magazine does not admit the paradox, but even so, it is forced to employ a series of oppositions in order to handle it:

1. The traditional pioneering spirit of initiative, individualism and enterprise is opposed to the great modern juggernaut of war with its mass-produced, totally impersonal and insidious poison gas.
2. Pioneering 'dash' is represented on the editorial page as the active *male* spirit, heroic throughout Australian history. It is juxtaposed with the passive, fetishised celluloid objects offered to us as women in the era of the Hollywood monopolies. *Picture Show* frequently carried such photographs of stars and starlets, side by side with editorials of spirited 'masculine' exhortation, and by and large they fall into one of three versions: the 'come-hither' glance; the clenched knee, pulled down skirt 'come and get me'; and the leisure time relaxation with open thighs or raised skirt. They all represent women as commodities, as they were defined by the monopolies that created them.
3. The 'still in the pioneering stage' qualities of Australian production are opposed to the dignity of the great distribution houses and exhibition circuits which have 'made it' into the modern civilised world.
4. The call for films of the days of personal enterprise and pioneering endeavour based on authenic bush scenarios is juxtaposed with the fetishised leisure patterns of modern capitalism — the cinema, the beach, the beach-in-the-cinema — which these Sennett 'beauties' represent. They are the 'choicest peaches', ready for men's picking in that leisure time they stand for, which is separated out from the time of men and women's labour. The paradox emerges: how to reconcile those ladies of the facing page with the generic woman of Australian cinema, the independent woman who *labours* in the bush, whose 'femininity' is normally covered with shapeless

riding clothes, and yet is so often played by an imported American star — Eva Novak, Yvonne Pavis, Brownie Vernon (we note the similarity of her photograph in *Picture Show* with that of the central Sennett beauty)? Sometimes the bush girl heroine was even written by an American scenarist, like Bess Meredyth.

5. Finally, the self-consciously pioneering gesture of *Picture Show* itself in making this stand for Australian production was opposed by, and ultimately crushed by, journals on either side of it which were based on bigger, and currently more viable markets. On the one hand, representing 'film as art', and drawing on a powerful 'high culture', British-Imperial orientated constituency, there was *Stage and Society* which absorbed *Picture Show* at the end of 1923. But this happened only because *Picture Show* was by then losing its trade market to 'film as commerce' journals which represented the interests of the American distributors and big cinema circuits. *Everyones*, and later the *Film Weekly*, were to forge ahead under the trade identity. Something of that defeat of the early *Picture Show* spirit is marked by the gap between the emphasis on the making of *The Sentimental Bloke* in the first issue and the main feature of its last — 'Making Love: Valentino Tells How'.

Picture Show was conscious of some of these oppositions, but saw none of them as irreconcilable. If we look carefully at the editorial we can see a principle of blurring and blending at work which, in each case, changes oppositions into continuities. The poison gas war becomes *economic* war which, though huge and fierce, is justifiable because it ensures the 'spirit of progress' for the 'commerce of 1919'. Hence, that pioneering fighting dash turns into entrepreneurial spirit, engaged in the juggernaut world of international commercial empires. It is in this *modern* commercial world also, the one which produces those celluloid beauties and peaches, that Australia's film exchange and theatre circuit directors belong. But because they too were once pioneers, hawking their wares through country and outback, there is no contradiction at all for *Picture Show* in looking for pioneering bush themes to play in their picture palaces. *Picture Show* proposes a *continuity* between those earlier times and these modern civilised days of 1919, which makes it endlessly possible for *other* pioneers — here the Australian producers — to also 'make it' by drawing on the same qualities of 'aggression, determined impetuosity, fair play, cheery fortitude and unrelenting tenacity'. Nor, of course, was there a complete opposition between the early and late *Picture Show*: the gap between Longford's film and Valentino's love life is narrowed by the fact that the magazine *always*,

Brownie Vernon Says: "Glad to Meet You."

rican screen tively identi- Carroll-Lucas l by a special he Picture escapes , de- ologue, with piration.

I hope I'm ty.'' These ard Brownie ncerely hope the last; I 's sweet and going ahead

lown to get vnie (yes, I ersonal, but ntifully, and ikely to go en she reads find her in apartments; en I arrived already oc- interesting Lucas wait- famous hus- at and hat. back to his ne time, he to Bob Dor- h regard to e made that s "Snowy" king-up. I Vernon (yes, then), but seen. Mr. do you do— ve—see you th and dis- so quickly ldered.

y'' assured hat. Moves busy man.'' e to every- n opportun- addition to , a wonder- fellow, Mr. taste in

up,'' said iss Vernon some tests he sun will ence for a

Picture Show 27 September 1919, p.16

HERE'S A SMASHING NEW ANGLE FOR SHOWMANSHIP!

An opportunity to "play up" one of the most sensational real-life stunts ever perpetrated by a real live girl. And she is an Australian!

You remember how Lotus Thompson, the beautiful Australian, in order to attract the attention of Movie Producers to her acting ability, and to dissociate her beautiful limbs from their minds, actually poured acid on her legs so as to disfigure them—and give her Art a chance.

The Press of the world rang with the news of the daring gesture!

"LOTUS OF THE LIMBS"

they called her! Then Universal gave her her big chance. And now, at last, Lotus is a full fledged star—making screen history in the powerful Universal Feature.

Lotus Thompson

in

"The Yellowback"

This Block is available to the Showman who wants to put this picture, this star, this stunt OVER to a tremendous Box Office success!

Get the real sensation "dope" on Lotus in America. Her "rise" to ballet girl, her fall to obscurity because directors could not see further than her beauty—her sudden leap into the limelight—and then her great triumph—the Contract with Universal to Star!

"The Yellowback" is a knockout winner — if you go after it!

Film Weekly 14 April 1927, p.9

Star as commodity: Australian actress Lotus Thompson in Hollywood poured acid on her limbs as a protest against having her legs used in films and attributed to other actresses. Ironically, this 'stunt' gave her the publicity to begin a film career.

Picture Show 3 May 1919, p.12

Business Manager:
ALBERT E. LAKE.
Managing Editor:
W. ST. CLAIR ANDERSON.
Sub-Editor .... Reg. A. Long
Art Editor .... Harry Julius
Melb. Representative .. J. L. Anderson
Artists .... Smith & Julius
Blocks by .... Bacon & Co.
Published at 17 Bond St., Sydney, by the Proprietor.

CARTOON FILMADS LIMITED, Proprietors.
Managing Director:
ALBERT E. LAKE.
Directors:
J. L. ANDERSON (Melbourne).
HARRY JULIUS (Sydney).
Secretary: J. A. LAKE.

Half-yearly subscription, 8/8. Yearly subscriptions, 17/4. Post free anywhere in Australia or Papua. Remittances by Postal Note, Post Office Order, or Cheque. Exchange to be added to all Cheques, etc.

MELBOURNE OFFICE .. 67 Queen St.
SYDNEY OFFICE ...... 17 Bond St.
BRISBANE OFFICE .... Courier Bldgs.
Advertising Rates on Application.
Advertising Representatives:
S. E. BROWN. F. MORAND.
Telephones:
Sydney .... City 4518
Melbourne .... Cent. 453

"The Picture Show" Wins Through.

OUR returns on the first issue of "The Picture Show" tell a very gratifying story of the manner in which our efforts have been endorsed by the general public. We always knew that the urgent need for a publication of this description would carry it through if its materialisation were brought about in the right way.

This we have set out to do, and with a justification for success more than evidenced in the support given us by the people of Australia in our first issue. In the first place we contracted with our printer to print 15,000 copies, and before the week finished we found it necessary to print a SECOND EDITION of an extra 4,000! This surely is a triumph for a new paper, and is the expression of endorsement given by the picture public on the merits of our efforts.

We intend to go on building up rapidly on the foundation we have laid, until we reach the standard of "second to none," and it is to the interests of every film supporter in our country that this should be so, for upon the success of our enterprise hangs the success of most other branches of the Australian industry.

How the American Press Cornered the Australian Field.

THE war has given the Americans, as in most other fields, dominance of the film industry. Nearer home in Australia it has done so very largely through the efforts of its Press. There were practically no other countries sending photoplay magazines to this country in competition with the Americans. Therefore the flooding of our market with the photoplay literature of this one country means that our people hear about the photoplay of that country only.

You have never heard of the stars of France, Italy, Norway, and the rest, for the past four years, not only because of the war but also because these countries were without any vehicle with which to distribute their activities in the Motion Picture world. Do not imagine for one moment that the industries of Italy and Norway have been absolutely paralysed in the same way as has been that of France, for this is not the case, and there is only one reason why you have heard nothing about them, and that is because the American Press saw to it that you heard only about American films and American stars. Now that the war has come to an end, however, we are once more compelled to take up the threads of our industry where we left off. You want to hear about ALL film and not the films of one country only, and it is only through an unbiassed paper of your own that this can be done.

"Infatuation," Gaby Deslys' first film produced in France since the signing of the Armistice, will prove to the picture-going public that productions of even finer technique than those turned out by the Americans can be had through the outside market.

The Case of Australian Production.

IN the last two issues of our paper, we have featured the doings of Australians in the film world at home and abroad, and we have received many letters from readers who have expressed their surprise that Australians have been so actively engaged in the film business, and so little has been known about their activities to date. The same reason can be given for this lack of knowledge of Australian efforts. One of the greatest drawbacks of production of films in Australia to-day lies in the fact that the flood of American publicity can always smother its operations from the general public, but it is a vital thing for all Australians that this should not be the case, as in building up our own industry we are all the time helping to substantiate Australian capital.

The articles on the "Sentimental Bloke" and "A Day at the Studio" in our last two issues, together with that on the art of Mr. Gerald Harcourt in the present issue, are instances of production activities which are vital to all Australians but which never could have reached you through American periodicals.

We will continue the policy of keeping you in touch with the doings of our own people, and in this way know that we are performing a great national duty in helping to place Australian filmdom in a sphere of high efficiency.

with perhaps less emphasis and articulation, peddled Hollywood gossip. But the real difference appears when we note that in its last year *Picture Show* virtually stopped covering Australian production news, there were no more exhortations on its behalf in editorials, and the magazine talked strictly the talk of 'the trade'.

The irony of that early independent gesture is underlined in the second editorial reprinted here (p. 37). *Picture Show* was aware that the United States dominated the film industry, as it did the sphere of 'photoplay magazines' which was of particular interest to the new Australian film journal. But, true to its *laissez-faire* capitalist beliefs, it felt the answer was simply to make the *public aware of the market*. Monopoly was the enemy, but unfair monopoly within a market economy; 'profiteering', not the nature of monopoly capitalism itself. Belief in the possibility of an equal market interchange between producers and consumers was the strong premise behind *Picture Show*'s *raison d'etre* as a *professional* journal. As with the ideal of all professions in the period of market capitalism, this journal believed it should link the scattered parts of the film empire, and so it was that 'upon the success of our enterprise hangs the success of most other branches of the Australian industry'.

Yet there *was* a conflict. No doubt a continuity existed, in terms of the generation of capital, between the tents and tin sheds and the picture palaces; but there was also a parochial — pioneering against cosmopolitan — commodity contradiction which was to become an important one, thematically as well as in production, in the years ahead. And nowhere was this contradiction for *Picture Show* illustrated more clearly than in its presentation of the new Australian film, *The Sentimental Bloke*, based on C.J. Dennis's popular poem and starring Lottie Lyell and Arthur Tauchert.

We can see this contradiction in operation if we look at five *Picture Show* photographs of Lyell as Doreen on pp. 40, 42-43:

(i) *Picture Show*'s cover of 25 October, 1919;
(ii) Doreen, the Bloke and their baby (25 October);
(iii) Doreen and the Bloke (25 October);
(iv) Doreen and the Bloke on the beach (19 April, 1919);
(v) Doreen and the Bloke (November, 1919)

The Picture Show *cover*

This is a photograph of Lyell produced to fit a certain stylistic gesture — that of the genre of 'photoplay magazine' covers. It is a picture of opulence and seduction: Lyell here is elevated to the position of 'star' (by the mere fact of being placed, in line with American stars, on the *Picture Show* cover; and by the signification this particular photograph carries). The qualities of this image are:

Isolation: a woman taken out of her environment and interaction to become a desired object, inviting possession with her gaze. This is not Lottie Lyell; but nor is it anyone else. It is a star; a commodity.

Opulence: the woman, taken from her environment, is placed in another, surrounded by flowers which at once complete a double enclosure within the frame, and at the same time signify abundance in the 'feminine' way — flowers, traditionally a gift from men to women, a stage in the sequence from *seeing* the displayed woman to possession of her. There is another sign of opulence: the knotted working-class scarf we see in image (v) has become the fur wrap of a star. The fur was worn by Lottie in the film: we see it again in image (iii). But there it is worn casually, and is merely one sign among many others of clothing, posture, gesture, expression and action which convey the awkwardly lower-middle-class Doreen. On the cover it is elevated to a much greater significance because it takes up nearly half the static image of the *star*. Wrapped entirely round the woman, hiding her breasts, nestling the seductive gaze, it connotes sexuality and affluence. It is a sign of stardom, and of what Hollywood stardom implies: inaccessibly desirable sexuality. Within the still image it generates its own narrative, one so very different from that of *The Sentimental Bloke*: the seductive commodity; the male gaze; the flowers, a gesture of exchange for the removal of the fur wrap; possession.

Australian-ness: all context having been removed, the image tries to locate this special Australian occasion nonetheless. The lettering anchors the image, tells us — this is Lottie Lyell/'Doreen', star of *The Sentimental Bloke*; graphics bring us 'Australia' and, indicative of the conventional cliché of it all, by the arrow through a heart, *The Sentimental Bloke* is labelled as the genre 'love story'.

Doreen, the Bloke and their baby

Now we see Lottie Lyell in a frame enlargement from the film, showing Doreen, the Bloke and their son. Context (an organic one, of family and bush authenticity) has been restored.

Family: the isolation of a commodity has been replaced by the eternal, near-holy, trinity of the family.

Labour: Australian-ness is located as country labour, on which is based

Registered at the G.P.O., Sydney, for Transmission by Post as a Newspaper.

The Picture Show

Incorporating The PILOT

OCTOBER 25, 1919. FOURPENCE WEEKLY.

(i) Lottie Lyell — elevated to stardom

25 October 1919

The Picture Show

Incorporating The PILOT

RIL. 19, 1919 PRICE FOURPENCE

Inside : MARY PICKFORD CONTRACTS INFLUENZA!

19 April 1919

(ii)

(iii)

(ii), (iii) *Picture Show* 25 October 1919, pp.9,7

(iv)

(v)

(vi)

Lottie Lyell and Arthur Tauchert as Doreen and the Bloke in *The Sentimental Bloke*. (vi) Lottie Lyell directing *The Blue Mountains Mystery* with cameraman Arthur Higgins and Raymond Longford.

Picture Show (iv) 19 April 1919, p.8; (v) November 1919, p.29; (vi) 1 November 1921 p.30

that

Sittin' at ev'nin' in this sunset land
Wiv' 'Er in all the world to 'old me 'and,
A son to bear me name when I am gone . . .
Livin' an' lovin' — so life mooches on.

Simplicity: opulence inviting possession is replaced by the simplicity of an achieved relationship. Sexuality is contained within the family, and wealth is now spiritual wealth, contained within a simple checked dress. There is nothing particularly contradictory in this shift from 'commodity-star' to 'holy mother' in the cinema. Or at least there is, only if we consider both in the context of the images as *produced* for consumption: as cover of the *Picture Show*; as sequence in the film, *The Sentimental Bloke*. Then we can begin to see in the film image an 'unfeminine' awkwardness, an unmotherly and 'un-star-like' Lottie Lyell which helped to generate the creative fusion of actress and part. Now we see a much greater closeness between this image of Lottie Lyell and the one of her as director (*Picture Show*, November 1921), than between the former and the *Picture Show* cover. Once again the isolated 'star' is replaced by a woman in a family; in this case a 'family' of film-makers who shared a few good years, professionally together: Raymond Longford, Lottie Lyell and Arthur Higgins. And in this family the woman is, uniquely, neither passive nor inferior. This is Lottie Lyell, co-director, and Lottie Lyell, actress, who *re-worked* and made play on theatrical and cinematic conventions in *The Sentimental Bloke*, rather than being passively reproduced by them. Returning to the film via this new juxtaposition of images we may realise that this, above all, is the quality of *The Sentimental Bloke*; that whatever the conventionality of the ending (the bush, the family, etc.), there was this same equivalence — in the shared awkwardness, in the determination, to re-work conventional narrative types — between Tauchert and Lyell.

Doreen and the Bloke

It is hard to describe in words what the quality of this equivalence is, which for instance makes the Lyell image of (iii) so different from the *Picture Show* cover, even though the expression of the eyes, the tilt forward of the mouth and the tilt up of the eyes seem almost identical. It is carried even more forcefully in image (iv), which was sensibly used in the advertisement for the film. What we do know is that it was precisely this equivalence between Tauchert and Lyell which caused opposition to their films from First National in America, and was described by Gayne Dexter of First National, and later *Everyones*, as being 'barren of beauty', a 'national ugliness' and, in the more professional-sounding term, a major aspect of

(i)

(ii)

(i) *Film Weekly* 10 February 1927, p.59; (ii) *Everyones* 19 January 1927, p.43

Signs of stardom: isolation, opulence, inaccessible sexuality. (i) Fox star Nancy Nash and (ii) Australian star of *For the Term of His Natural Life,* Jessica Harcourt.

LOUISE LOVELY (Fox).

(i)

(ii)

(iii)

Stars, flowers, gestures of exchange: (i) Louise Lovely, Australian Hollywood star; and (ii) Eva Novak, American star of *For the Term of His Natural Life* and *The Romance of Runnibede.* (iii) Local businessmen quickly latched on to *Picture Show's* criteria for stardom.

(i) National Film Archive; (ii) *Picture Show* 20 September 1929, p.14

Picture Show (i) 1 January 1922, pp.20,21; (ii) 1 November 1922, pp.12,13; (iii) *Everyones* 18 August 1926, p.3

Attempts to beat a 'national ugliness'. *Picture Show's* local star competition, with (i) the American models and (ii) the Australian winners. (iii) Scourge of Australian screen 'ugliness', advertising manager of Union Theatres, Selznick Pictures and First National — and later editor-in-chief of *Everyones,* Robert J. (Gayne) Dexter.

'inferior production values'. What they wanted in America, and what *Picture Show* tried to give them by organising star contests among its readers, is clear from the advice on star selection given by Hollywood experts Anita Loos and John Emerson, and in the choice of winners of the *Picture Show* Screen Contest which Emerson and Loos also judged. Men were to have the 'rounded face, fair skin devoid of hollows and lines, high forehead and expressive eyes' of Hollywood superstar, Charles Ray; women were to have the large eyes, fine skin, small mouth, fine teeth, straight nose, exquisite chin and 'piquant expression' of the American star, Constance Talmadge. The editors of *Picture Show* chose their young Australian winners accordingly; but these were not the qualities of Tauchert and Lyell.

To explain their qualities, as they were produced in *The Sentimental Bloke*, we need to look at least at two things: the narrative structure of C.J. Dennis's poem, *Songs of a Sentimental Bloke* and its conversion into Raymond Longford's film; and Longford's use of actors in the context of the historical development of screen types.

Narrative Structure

In Dennis's poem, 'inauthentic' life is presented as one of cyclical zenith and decline. Thus we have:

1. the paradigm case of the Sun which, full of bravado, swaggers to his noon-day zenith as captain of his 'push'*, only to sink into decline and defeat at the hands of night; and,

2. the allegorical case of the play-within-the-poem as Romeo moves from early romance to marriage and double death.

But we also have:

3. the opening of the poem which gives us the sensations of spring, the perennial working-class male resort to 'tart', followed by the Bloke's self-disgust; and finally,

4. the promised narrative development of the poem from the Bloke's desire to give up the 'push' for marriage and the monotony of respectable bourgeois life. Thus the early narrative paradigm is from an initial situation of potential and yearning, through the zenith of attainment, to the final defeat of aspiration which marks the text's potential closure.

* The Push: a band of street rowdies.

	Potential		*Attainment*		*Defeat*
1.	Dawn	→	Zenith	→	Night
2.	Romeo's romance	→	Marriage	→	Double death
3.	Spring yearnings for love	→	Tart	→	Disgust
4.	Desire to escape the working-class ghetto	→	Marriage	→	Bourgeois monotony

But it should be noted that this includes two allegories:
(a) the Sun swaggers among his 'push' like the Bloke when drunk, until, overweight and flabby with easy living, 'the Bloke'/the Sun declines in defeat and is deserted by his friends:
(b) Romeo/the Bloke, a brawler, is reformed by a good woman's love, but is lured away to disaster by Ginger/'Mick Curio'.

However, the potential of a tragic resolution, carried by the repeated narrative design and double allegory, is cut off by Uncle Jim's gift which transports the Bloke and Doreen to a magical new land in the country. The role of the 'donor' in narrative has traditionally been to confer magical gifts: a magic sword, a flying horse, the gift of invisibility and so on, which enable the hero to win. Yet it is a victory he always deserves because of some innate quality. So it is in Dennis's poem. Uncle Jim gives Bill the farm because 'I likes yer ugly phiz'. That quality of ugliness in Bill is, as Uncle Jim makes clear, one of 'no frills' directness in getting things done: it is essentially this quality that makes him rebel against the conventions of both working-class 'push' and bourgeois respectability. Bill is oppressed by nice middle-class social distinctions: starched collars, china dogs, 'Willie'. But he is equally dissatisfied with the closed working-class world — of easy women, drink, two-up and 'stoushin' Johns' — which separates him from the lower-middle class: 'The sorter skirts I dursn't come too near'.

Each narrative sequence of zenith/decline also represents a class pattern. The tragi-comedy of that working-class aimlessness which leads to gaol is paralleled by that of the middle-class blinkered striving which led to the death of Doreen's father when he fell from a hay cart. In the first half of the poem, Bill believes both class trajectories to be irredeemably matters of fate. Of his 'push' depravity he grumbles, 'I s'pose it's 'ow a man is built', and on meeting Doreen's Ma, he assumes all romances must end trapped in bourgeois monotony.

Yet he also has the quality of seeing through these conventions. His 'Wot's in a name' aside, which prefigures his disgust with Ma for trying

(i)

(i) National Film Archive; (ii) *Picture Show* 1 February 1929, p.5

(ii)

(i) Hero meets Donor (*The Sentimental Bloke*)
(ii) Gilbert Emery as Ginger Mick

to hide his working-class 'vulgarity' by changing his name to Willie, is generated in the play sequence. For Doreen, 'Billo' is as good a name as 'Romeo', and for Bill, Ginger Mick is as good a romantic hero. As he realises, class denominations merely seek to hide basic similarities, and 'romance' (as in *Romeo and Juliet*) or 'vulgarity' (in the life of Ginger Mick) are labels applied by élites to their lives and the lives of those below them. C.J. Dennis was himself the 'writer bloke' he mentions in his poem, seeking to make the Bloke and Mick contemporaneous heroes in the current working-class location. In a number of ways his poem bares the 'artificial' class pretensions of that theatre, which called itself 'legitimate' in order to raise itself above the cinema: by Bill's recognition of the class-labelling as between upper-class 'valler' and the 'degraded broots' of the 'push'; by the working-class participation of 'put in the boot', arguably returning Shakespeare to his original cross-class location; by the repeated device of punctuating, 'high-culture' expressions of tragedy with moments of bathos:

> 'Dear love', she sez, 'I cannot live alone!'
> An, wif a moan,
> She grabs 'is pockit knife, an' ends 'er cares . . .
> 'Peanuts or lollies!' sez a boy upstairs.

As Bill distantly understands that class, not fate, determines his conventional world, so he becomes more open to change — and therefore to Uncle Jim's gift. 'Fate me foot', he says of Romeo's zenith and decline; and it is not so much fate (Uncle Jim's gift) as his own labour, and the toughness developed in back-street living, which allows his success on the land. Uncle Jim notes that continuity of the land and back-street, while also noting: 'Yeh'll 'ave to cut the luxuries o' town'.

Avoidance of the realities of class conflict by a retreat from town to bush was a central device of Australian silent cinema, and there can be no denying the conservatism of the country family 'organic' bliss and the passivity of 'I wasn't built to play no lofty part' at the end of *The Sentimental Bloke* as poem. But before rushing too quickly into a glib interpretation, it is well to recall not only the enormous success of both poem and film with the Australian working class, but also the fact that the agrarian utopianism it represents *had*, not so long before, been a genuinely radical as well as working-class ideal, aimed against the land monopoly of the squatters. As the historian G.L. Buxton has argued, in the last quarter of the ninteenth century Australia's strong rural unions gave a pragmatic political content to the beliefs of utopian radicals that all men could make their homes in rural areas, and that dissipation would cease with inequality.

'Then would every man sit on his verandah or under his fig tree smoking his pipe in contentment while the vine brought forth her fruit and the wilderness blossomed as the rose'.[15]

Buxton's description of the nineteenth-century rural dream is so close to the ending of *The Sentimental Bloke*, as both film and poem, as to make us pause to think about the *differences* between this and other back-to-the land narratives.

(i) Conventionally in Australian 'bush' films, class differences are displaced on to a city–bush dichotomy, and class exploitation is transferred into the parasitic dependence of the city on a work-healthy country (see Chapter 10). In *The Sentimental Bloke*, despite the familiar contrast of 'country life ain't cigarettes and beer', that urban depravity is given a *class* location within a system, seen as inauthentic, of stratification and institutionalised life. Somehow, the poem asserts, neither set of people should live like this. The strong class foregrounding of the first half of *The Sentimental Bloke*, together with its demystification as narrow and stultified, is the basis for the optimism of the ending, and further, it is the physical quality of working-class labour which provides for country success. The appeal to human cooperation at the end and the rejection of mercenary profit is of course a matter of the heart, not of class-consciousness. That is the sentiment of *The Sentimental Bloke* — and given the middle-class positions of Dennis and Longford, we could hardly expect otherwise.

(ii) If conventional class mores are demystified, so too are conventional narrative heroes — here represented by the swaggering sun, the bold hero of the 'push', Romeo of Verona, and the ambitious middle-class owner of a corn store, Doreen's father. At best, these early heroes of the narrative could achieve no more than an anarchic working-class depravity, or else the stifling middle-class conventionality of Ma's china dogs. Each is defined as a closed and stifling location. Heroes of an *ascribed* class position are thus empty and circumscribed heroes. Their narrative fate is predictably the same: striving, zenith, and then fall.

From this kind of fate (the bourgeois 'responsibility' of 'Investin' in a mar-in-lor an' wife') to that quite different trinity of the ending:

> Wiv' 'Er in all the World to 'old me 'and
> A son to bear me name when I am gone

is a change not only of geography and style of interaction, but of narrative paradigm too. 'The Sentimental Bloke' has begun with spring yearnings for something in life that is missing, and has ended 'in the sundown of yer day', with an evening contentment, 'watchin' . . . yerself again, grown nobler in yer son'. It is a narrative closure which, with its cyclical pattern and emphasis on human continuity against short-term hardships, has an epic quality. The gift which the donor offers is, then, more than a piece of land, but rather this continuous life-force, a permanent cycle of betterment to replace the zenith-and-decline narrative pattern which trapped the earlier heroes. Life still 'mooches on', but now located within a more hopeful (because more spiritual) narrative dimension.

And yet the hero and heroine, Bill and Doreen, are very far from being 'epic' figures. They are frail, easily trapped by the greater power of standard class conventions, susceptible (in Bill's case) to any authority figures who come along — the 'push', the police, Ma, Uncle Jim, the midwife. They are also, however, tough, combining between them a puritan ethic and a lower-class rejection of urban middle-class conventions. In this sense, Uncle Jim simply presents them with the gift of their own best qualities. The 'charm' which so many people see in the original Longford *Sentimental Bloke* has, I think, a lot to do with these qualities; or, to put it another way, to the tension between the weakness and vigour which marks the equivalence of Bill and Doreen, and also to the placing of this unstereotypical combination in an epic location.

The central quality of the poem is thus in the relation between ambivalent characters and complex narrative moves. Simple, bold characters of Snowy Baker dimensions crash to defeat and death, while the tough (*and* meek) inherit the earth. This central structure, in which the tough are also small and *made* weak by the oppressiveness of huge impersonal forces, is brought out with more economy in Longford's film than it is in the poem and is lost completely in Frank Thring's later sound version. In the first place this is because of the acting *personae* of Tauchert and Lyell, which fulfil this complexity of character in a way that Dennis admitted he never dreamed possible. Secondly, while Thring turns the poem into 'cinema' by avoiding its wordy metaphysics altogether (for instance the important stanza about the Sun and his 'push') and replacing it with highly conventionalised cops-and-robbers narrative motivation, Longford uses a variety of cinematic means of compression to replace whole stanzas without defeating their narrative significance. For example, the Sun/Moon stanza is cut to its barest outlines: the sun swaggering out, the moon replacing it. But each of these images in the titles is associated with a different version of the Bloke in Longford's film. The swaggering sun introduces, to a bold musical score, the loquacious bravado of the hero of the 'push' who accosts Doreen in the street and is snubbed. The ascendant moon introduces in contrast the more discreet, gentle Bloke, accompanied by a cautious sound

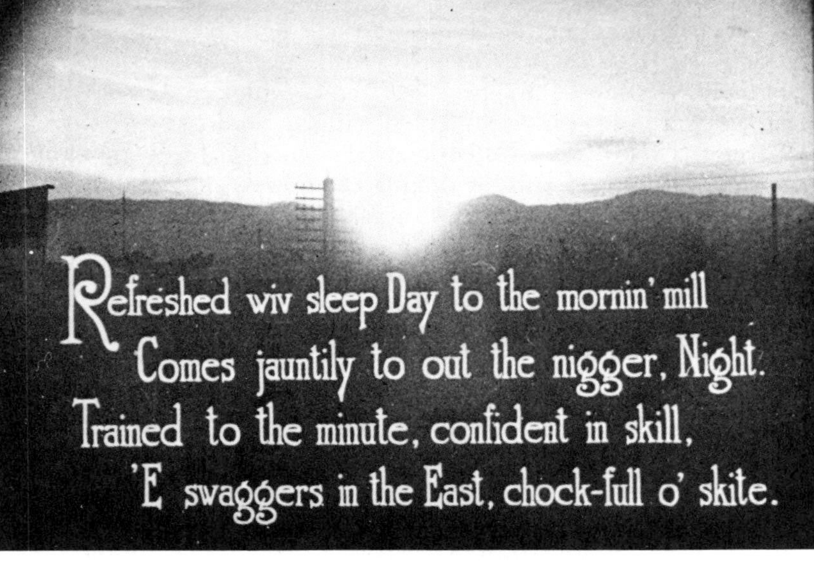

National Film Archive

track. Bravado forgotten, he arranges a chaperoned meeting, is tongue-tied, and politely 'dips 'is lid'.

Similarly, the stanza of spring love and the Bloke's distance from a 'better class' of girl is conveyed, almost without words, as we have a sustained shot of the Bloke isolated in the Botanical Gardens fumbling to make a cigarette, titles of birds singing and flowers, followed by a brief shot of elegant women in white with parasols, before we return him to Woolloomooloo. Again, the 'wots in a name' debate around Romeo is omitted (though taken up later with 'Willie') and the meaning conveyed with extreme economy by the contrast between the melodramatic Shakespearean actors and the 'realism' of *visual style*, as well as the naturalistic acting and 'Put in the boot', 'Peanuts or lollies' titles which accompany it.

In some cases this reduces the overt class comparison (which comes out just as strongly by suggestion). In other cases Longford emphasises it more powerfully, since much of the ameliorative 'spiritual' quality of Dennis's last lines is omitted, with a corresponding foregrounding of the future depending on the Bloke's 'own two hands'. By compression in the Shakespeare sequence, and by *adding* scenes on other occasions (such as Bill's dream of a fight for Doreen on the cliff edge played in a stagey, melodramatic style), Longford's self-conscious irony at the expense of less talented fellow film-makers like Beaumont Smith, mediates the class message. I say mediated rather than replaced, because these sequences pointed in a self-reflexive manner to Longford's own achievement in carving out an Australian cinema, against both the American version as represented by Smith *and* the 'snob' and 'toff' class attitudes of the 'legitimate' stage.

Development of Screen Types

The sequence of Bill alone in the Gardens is crucial, too, in understanding the Longford style and his handling of actors. The class isolation of the hero of the poem is here conveyed without flourish or strident emphasis in the contrast of the very brief shot of the women he 'dursn't touch' and the quite lengthy shot of him alone, picking up paper, rolling tobacco and drawing a minor contentment with his achievement. It is a picture of isolation without mawkishness, which conveys in the same moment the simple competence of this man. As Uncle Jim says in the poem, 'You got a look . . . like you could stay'. The lines are not in the film because Tauchert had already conveyed them, by gesture and timing. Once Longford had selected his actors, he had confidence in them. A feature of his style is an unostentatious camera observing an actor (Tauchert and his cigarette), an actress (Lyell pasting labels on pickle jars) or both together (Tauchert and Lyell on a boat, with lollies), in a prolonged shot with hardly any 'business'. This is what distinguished Longford most from melodramatic directors like Beaumont Smith, and it is something the trade never understood in its attempts to link the 'pioneering' work of these two men. The 'human touch' that critics note is especially conveyed by this mode of directing, the use of prolonged close-up never slowing the pace of the film, partly because Longford uses it so expressively (in contrast to the purely mechanical and less frequent close-ups in Snowy Baker's films, used almost entirely to introduce 'types' for the first time, or for wooden reaction shots), and partly because of the frequent changes of camera angle and distance of shot with which his close-ups are intercut.

The main things noted about Longford as a director at the time were his calmness and openness to actors and the characteristic which caused even the trade to distinguish him from Beaumont Smith — the length of time which he took in production, which extended to months in contrast to Smith's few weeks. Longford especially took time over the writing of scenarios (with Lyell) and the selection of actors. His performers were never 'mere' commodities. It was their 'human' qualities that were always noted in reviews. The British *Kine Weekly* said of *The Sentimental Bloke*: 'It is so perfect that at times we are almost tempted to think that the 'types' portrayed are genuine people, and that the Kid, the Bloke, 'Er, the Straw'atted Loon (sic) and many others, are not players at all, but men and women of the slums, who, by some miracle performed by a master-producer, have been enabled to enact their lives before the camera'.[16] And it contrasted the film with the big American features which 'cost hundreds of thousands (vide publicity) to make and employ 'stars' whose smiles are stereotyped, whose every action is directed and stage-managed'. In Australia, *Picture Show* said, 'One has only to think of Ray Longford's successful films to realise that it was in their human qualities that they excelled. *The Sentimental Bloke* went right to the heart of Australians, and has been praised the world over. It is human through and through. So, in a different way, was *On Our Selection*. So, too, is *Rudd's New Selection*'[17] and the English *Bioscope* said of *The Sentimental Bloke*: 'Intensely human narrative . . . acted quietly and naturally by players who perfectly embody the types they represent'.[18]

Longford was known as the director concerned, par excellence, to find the 'correct types' and to resist all outside influences in the casting of his films. *Picture Show* noted that for

> *Rudd's New Selection* he has assembled the best set of back-block types possible . . . 'Average actors', he says, 'are useless for screen work. When you have them in a picture, the general opinion of the production is, 'Oh, yes, it's good. The acting is splendid, but — it's not real'. A big secret of picture producing is getting the players to realise that what they must study is not "How to act in pictures", but "How not to act in pictures". I want real types — men and women who are human. I don't want the people who think they should drop anchor in front of the camera and make pretty faces".[19]

Explaining his method of directing *On Our Selection*, Longford said,

> I'm making an Australian picture and I want the people in it to be real Australians. Now your average Australian is the most casual person under the sun; so if I put the players through their parts over and over again, worrying them, striving to perfect them, they might do good work, but they wouldn't look like Australians. They'd merely be actors, perfectly conscious that they were acting. My way is let them know the action I want, and allow them to go right ahead with it. For a picture like *On Our Selection*, in which it is absolutely necessary that the characters look natural, I think that's the best course.

So for the part of Cranky Jack, in *On Our Selection* he looked for a long time for a man with the 'eloquent language, backed up by forceful gestures . . . hair, whiskers, wrinkles and all'[20], and eventually found them in a carter at Circular Quay, Sydney, who had never acted before. And after some weeks of searching he found Arthur Tauchert for his 'Bloke' playing in blackface in a minor vaudeville act.

But it would be wrong to assume from this that Longford's success was in roving streets to find 'natural' types. His major actors in these films — Arthur Tauchert, Lottie Lyell, Tal Ordell, Gilbert Warren Emery, J.P. O'Neill, Walshe, Esmond, Reid — had very considerable stage experience. In 1921, *Everyones* commented that the success of Hollywood films depended to a large extent on a pool of necessary 'types' who were readily available and put back on the shelf when not used, whereas in contrast Australian film-makers who had, of necessity, to draw on supporting actors from the stage, should make use of their versatility. One thinks immediately of Tauchert, Ordell and Emery, all of whom were used in a variety of roles by other directors. But only Longford used this vaudeville versatility within the *one* part, allowing for a psychological density, complexity of motivation and consequent 'realism' that was almost entirely missing in the films of his peers. Longford's skill was in mixing old stagers like O'Neill, who had fifty years on the boards behind him, with complete newcomers, while still maintaining a balance between the parts. Beyond this, it was in his blending of melodrama with naturalism, for example in the performances of Lyell, which expanded the conventional concept of 'type' to something quite new.

What this, of course, suggests is that the concept of 'type', despite the conventions of the trade, was not static but developing historically. As Richard Dyer, author of *Stars*, has argued, various writers on the cinema have noted a development among heroes during the twenties from 'ideal' to 'typical' ways of behaving;[21] and a growing density of character. There was a growing concern for social themes (*Fury*, *Mr Deeds Goes to Town*) as compared with the great chases and superhuman rescues of the past. Heroes were no longer 'essences' representing good or evil, but were individual and psychologically credible. Both of these developments are strongly marked in *The Sentimental Bloke* (as compared with, say, the superhuman antics and two-dimensional characterisation of a Snowy Baker film). The fact is that Longford was developing these characteristics some ten years before film historians have generally noted their appearance — around 1930.[22] Some, like Richard Schickel, have put the change from 'ideal' to 'realistic' hero down to the naturalistic qualities of sound: 'A godhead is supposed to be inscrutable . . . It is enough that his image be present that we may conveniently worship it'; to which Alexander Walker added, 'Once they had dialogue on their lips, the once-silent idols suffered a serious loss of divinity'.[23] Others, like Edgar Morin, taking the same date (circa 1930) as symptomatic of the change, argued that it occurred because the cinema was moving in a more middle-class direction.[24] Cinema, in its early days a 'plebeian spectacle', had been characterised by 'magic, extraordinary adventures, sudden reversals, the sacrificial death of the hero, violent emotions'. In contrast, 'Realism, psychologism, the "happy end" and humour reveal precisely the bourgeois transformation of this imagination'.[25] This movement in a more middle-class direction was certainly an overt and fully conscious one among Australia's cinema-owning elite in the 1920s, but *The Sentimental Bloke* was made before 1920 — and, as we shall see, that elite had a very different idea of what the middle-class wanted to Longford.

In this context, it is clear that Longford was a very early innovator within the global movement to 'realism'; and it was crucial also that, through his relationship with Lottie Lyell, he tried in *The Sentimental Bloke*, to extend psychological density to female roles. That extension was not part of the movement to 'realism' elsewhere.

However this proposal — that there was a development from the 'ideal'

(i)

(ii)

(iii)

National Film Archive. (i), (ii) Reproduced by permission of Jack Tauchert

(iv)

(v)

(vi)

National Film Archive. (iv) Reproduced by permission of Elsa Chauvel; and (vi) by permission of Jack Tauchert

The many faces of Arthur Tauchert: (i) *The Sentimental Bloke,* 1919; (ii) *The Digger Earl,* 1924; (iii) *Joe,* 1924; (iv) *The Moth of Moonbi,* 1925; (v) *For the Term of His Natural Life,* 1927; (vi) *The Adorable Outcast,* 1928.

to the 'typical' (or 'everyday') hero is confusing, in so far as it suggests that the concept of the 'typical' was in operation only at the end of the silent period; whereas it was in fact being invoked throughout, but with different ingredients. Further, as I argued earlier, in Longford's case the *particular* type has a specifically *historical* location — a somewhat sentimental inflection of very real late nineteenth century attitudes to the bush. Some theorists have, in fact, tried to historicise the very general ideal-to-typical thesis by considering stars as 'talismanic' or 'charismatic' figures in specific historical circumstances. W.R. Brown, for example, locates the popularity of Will Rogers in Hollywood within the crisis of American change from 'sturdy yeoman' values to those of urbanisation and a colossal market economy.[26] In the face of the corruption, greed and crime which that economy seemed to be generating in the 1920s and 1930s, Rogers re-affirmed the consensual 'American' values of individual dignity, democracy, hard work and belief in material progress.

There is a clear similarity here with the opposition of city and bush in Australia; and Longford did incorporate something of those affirmations in his films, especially *The Sentimental Bloke* and *Ginger Mick*. But to collapse Longford *into* such a unitary thematic opposition would be simplistic, because there were more important differences. To look at this theoretically we need to make distinctions between, on the one hand, stars-as-heroes whose charismatic role was to *displace* social contradictions (as, for example, conventional Australian films which displaced class contradictions onto city villainy *vis-à-vis* country purity), and on the the other hand those heroes who, in some way or another, *embody* contradictions, and place them before us on the screen. As Richard Dyer points out,

> In exceptional cases . . . certain stars, far from managing contradictions, either expose them or embody an alternative or oppositional ideological position . . . One can think of it simply as a clash of codes, quite possibly fortuitous, in which the very clash or else the intensity with which the alternative/oppositional code is realised result in 'subversion' (or, at any rate, make reading them 'subversively' possible or legitimate).[27]

I have already argued that the total narrative structure of *The Sentimental Bloke* subverts the conventional hero, replacing him with composite heroes located ambivalently between epic pioneering strength and socially stratified, institutional weakness. But there is another important element. One of the major ways in which displacement works through 'stars' is that evils (like lack of money, if you are working-class) are defeated by good luck and charity, or side-tracked by some active leisure-time involvement, where there might be a chance for the oppressed class to compete and win. In Australia this was especially the case with 'athletic' stars like Snowy Baker, who systematically augmented the conventional 'bush' displacement with a sporting one, and Annette Kellerman, who went to Hollywood in 1916 to combine swimming prowess with voyeuristic fantasy, in nude and near-nude spectaculars. In either case the place of *work* both in the production process and in the creation of change is submerged.

In his bush stories, however, Longford crucially emphasises labour. Fortune is the result of work. Further, the individuating function of stars, drawing, as Dyer argues, the audience's attention away from collective experience, does not have that effect in Longford. The importance of Dennis's verses in the film is in tying 'types' to the culture of a working-class collectivity, rather than the more conventional use of the 'type' as simply a narrative function (good, evil etc.) to drive the story along. The fact that Dennis' argot may not be representative of the working-class of the time or that the conception is sentimentalised, does not alter the fact that social process and change is anchored not, as in the Baker films, in individual capacity and motivation, but in Australian social-structural qualities.

What then are the contradictions that Longford's heroes embody? A major socio-economic change in the period was in the consolidation of a monopoly control in the cinema. This made a mockery of those bush-pioneering values which, in *Picture Show*, had so comfortably fitted with the ideology of individualistic capitalism. If we look for a classifying moment in a lengthy process, the sudden rush in September 1930 of many 'independent' exhibitors — all steeped (so the trade press related throughout the twenties) in the pioneering years of picture exhibition — to sell their holdings to Fox was symptomatic. Longford's view of this development was a romantic nostalgia for an earlier, 'freer' period of capitalist endeavour when, sure of their home market, cinema entrepreneurs could still make fortunes with their films. Locked emotionally and ideologically into that earlier form of capitalism, Longford could never feel that the system itself was wrong. His conception was of the individual pioneer, up against the crushing monopolies as David to Goliath, and that opposition, between small, individual, independent, human qualities and huge, impersonal forces is deeply imprinted in the structure of *The Sentimental Bloke*.

From reviews, *Ginger Mick* (made in 1920, with no print surviving) seems to have been even more clearly structured in this way; the film moving via flashbacks and dissolves from the simple human squabbles of Doreen and Bill with their hopes in their growing son to the implacable death-dealing of the Great War, which reaches out and plucks the no-good Ginger Mick from his close Woolloomooloo urban network into the universal, classless fraternity of the men who enlisted to die. Thus was a pioneering heroism located in precisely that working-class network — as reviews noted, among the film's most striking titles were Dennis's lines:

> I dunno wot 'is ratin' was in this 'ere soshul plan,
> I only knows inside o' me, I intrajuice a man.

From the available descriptions of the film, it would appear that its finest moments were located in the stark contrasts, not just between the simple home routine and the glamour and collision of war, but in what this indicated of the gap between the real potential of the Ginger Micks, 'rough in speech, rough in manner', and the stulifying and deadening systems which they found it impossible to escape, whether the Australian class system or profiteer's wars. It was out of this impasse that Longford, himself a bushman and for many years a sailor, and deeply sentimental about pioneering, desperately forged those resolutions which critics then and now have called his 'human' touch: small relationships in open spaces valued at the expense of impersonal forces, and sentiment, the heart, drawn on in the place of analysis.

I believe that was why a reviewer could say of *Ginger Mick*,

> The receipt of the news of Ginger Mick's death by his cobber and his sweetheart is one of the finest pieces of acting in the film. It touches the delicate chords of human sympathy without in any way harrowing the onlooker.[28]

And that is why the critics and the trade spoke of Longford's *On Our Selection* and *Rudd's New Selection* in terms of their refusal to caricature selectors as Beaumont Smith did with his *Hayseeds* series. Broad farce there certainly was; but still the most powerful sequences of *On Our Selection*, and the most striking visually, are those evoking contrasts between the great implacable forces of nature and fate — the bush fire destroying the boundary rails — and communal vigour at the small, domestic level, in the shots of the family at work, clearing the ground, harvesting, and separating the corn.

In the end the Longford silent films are sentimental rather than harrowing because they emphasise the small, private human hopes and triumphs: in *Ginger Mick*, Bill's quietly hopeful vigil over his son after he hears of Mick's death; in *The Dinkum Bloke*, (1923: film lost) , the working-class father's self-sacrificial denial of his daughter so that she may marry into the upper-class. But however sentimental and consensual the resolutions, the contradictions are there clearly before us. Longford's juxtaposition of pioneering individualism and colossal impersonalities was a mark of the time, moving into the period of monopoly capitalism; but it was not a mere reflection of it. Societal forces were seldom noted by Australian film-makers in their specificity, let alone understood. But they were *experienced*, and these experiences were conceptualised to a greater or lesser degree.

The fate of Arthur Tauchert as actor, for instance, was that of a man located within the needs of a popular cultural system vastly expanding its capitalisation. The step from a minor vaudeville theatre playing black-face to a part in the most expensive Australian film ever made, *For The Term Of His Natural Life*, was in some ways a considerable one. Tauchert certainly thought so, and rated Norman Dawn as the best director he had worked under. Yet, Tauchert in his one-dimensional part as Warder Troke in Dawn's film was as much trapped in the fragmenting demands of the commercial institution as he had been, years earlier, in formula parts at the Golden Gate Theatre. Only the directorial perception of Raymond Longford gave the actor the chance to incorporate these contradictions *within* a part, rather than be repressed by them.

If Tauchert was unperceptive about these experiences, Longford was not. He interpreted his own role in the industry as that of a pioneer constantly victimised by monopoly forces, with agents whose motives he could hardly understand. However, his life, unlike his films, had no sentimental ending.

Longford's achievement lay in his presentation, via innovations in narrative and acting modes, of the experience of profound changes in Australian social and economic life. The vision that his films produced was always one of contradiction, tempered by the poignancy of an epic reward often beyond the graves of individual men and women. For *Picture Show*, in contrast, there were no such contradictions. Longford was assimilated as easily in its pantheon of uncomplicated pioneering endeavour as Lottie Lyell was by its fetishised notions of stardom. Typically, *Picture Show* reduced the problem of making *The Sentimental Bloke* to questions of individual striving and creativity. We hear in its early report how Longford spent months searching for artists who 'act the living part in the natural way' before faithfully re-creating Dennis' poem with 'a team as great in their particular sphere of acting as any teams D.W. Griffith ever assembled'.[29] But we hear nothing of Longford hawking his idea around to get finance and distribution. We hear of the assured future of a new star and the success of Australia's best film: 'Beaumont Smith has signed Mr. Tauchert up on a contract that will enable him to devote all his time to the movies

(ii)

Picture Show 1 August 1920 pp.44,45

(i) and (ii) Communal vigor in the family: *On Our Selection.* (iii) Films directed to the family audience: *Rudd's New Selection.*

These are cold nights, my brothers, and something better than just ordinary bread and butter features are needed to drag folk from cosy firesides.

Produced by RAYMOND LONGFORD for Southern Cross Picture Productions, Ltd.

Nobody will wi.lingly miss

Rudd's New Selection

Laughs rub against laughs and keep your audiences warm. It's the sort of picture the kiddies insist on seeing, the kind mum likes to smile happily over, that dad leaves his paper and his carpet slippers for, that big sister selects as the one her best boy should reserve seats for.

World's Exhibiting Rights Controlled by E. J. & DAN CARROLL, the Banking House, 228 Pitt Street, Sydney; also at Melbourne, Brisbane, Wellington (N.Z.) and London.

in the future. The result should be the development of an Australian character that will be as popular as the Western roles of Bill Hart, and as true to type as the Italian impersonations of George Beban'.[30] But we hear nothing of the differences of orientation between Smith and Longford, and the economic location of those differences which were to mean that Tauchert, far from being a super-star in the American sense, *or* a truly 'Australian character', was never, outside Longford's handling, to draw similar critical praise again.

A Time of New Beginning

Beaumont Smith was in fact working on his film *Desert Gold* at about the same time Longford was filming *The Sentimental Bloke*. For *Picture Show* this was a time of new beginnings, and innovation was in the air.

> There used to be a recipe that never failed when applied to Australian dramas. This was: Take two bushrangers, ten policemen and twenty aborigines, mix well, and serve quickly in three or four reels. Then the police stepped in and cut out the bushrangers and the other two ingredients were not strong enough to stand up by themselves. Mr. Beaumont Smith has now struck an entirely new mixture for his drama, *Desert Gold*.[31]

What that mixture was, however, *Picture Show* does not make clear, except that it involved the 'realism' of filming at actual race meetings, the 'skill in direction' of filming an actress with a broken arm as though she has not got a broken arm, and the 'thrills' of a fight to the death on the edge of Echo Point, Katoomba. It is tempting to think that this is the particular piece of Smith melodrama Longford was sending up in his additional cliff-edge fight sequence in *The Sentimental Bloke*. In any case *Picture Show*'s caption for the Smith sequence, 'and yet they say there are no risks in movies nowadays', and their hopes for this producer make it appear that falling off Echo Point was the only sort of risk in making movies and that the penetration of the international market rested on initiative and creativity alone:

> Australian production will only get on its feet when a few other thorough producers come into the game and turn out pictures of equal merit to *Desert Gold* which has a better chance of getting a hearing overseas than most other locally manufactured dramas.

Just two weeks later another of these 'thorough producers' leapt into the pages of *Picture Show*. On 24 May 1919 only one month after beginning

(ii)

Now Releasing:
"The Sentimental Bloke."
"Ginger Mick."
"The Lure of the Bush."
"The Man From Kangaroo."
"The Shadow of Lightning Ridge."

E.J.Carroll's Intentions

TO PRODUCE STANDARD PHOTO-PLAYS MADE IN AUSTRALIA FOR THE WORLD'S MARKETS.

TO OPEN THE DOORS OF OPPORTUNITY TO AUSTRALIAN TALENT AND AUSTRALIAN BRAINS.

TO SEND **FILM FOOTAGE** OUT OF AUSTRALIA AS AGAINST THE FOREIGN **FILM MILEAGE** THAT NOW COMES IN.

TO AUSTRALIANIZE MOTION PICTURES AS AGAINST THE AVOWED AMERICANISATION OF THE INDUSTRY

TO MAKE AUSTRALIA REALISE THAT WE, TOO, HAVE SUFFICIENT ROMANCE IN THIS COUNTRY TO ENTERTAIN OURSELVES AND THE WORLD.

Our productions will be so strong in dramatic appeal that every good Australian will want to see them on their merits alone. It will not even be necessary to appeal to your Australian sentiment.

The manager of your best local theatre will screen our pictures.

Let him know you want to see them.

E. J. CARROLL,
BANKING HOUSE,
228 PITT STREET, SYDNEY.
BRANCHES ALL CAPITAL CITIES.
Also Representatives London and New York.

Just Completed:
"On Our Selection."
In Preparation:
New Snowy Baker Film.

(i)

Picture Show (i) 1 July 1920, p.48; (ii) 10 May 1919, p.13

Picture Show's notions of the risks of movie-making: (i) 'Dirty Work in the Blue Mountains. This scene was taken right on the edge of Echo Point. There's a clear drop of a few thousand feet if he pushes too hard, and yet they say there are no risks in movies nowadays.' (ii) Hopes for a world market.

publication, and with Longford and Smith already in its bag, *Picture Show* presented a pioneer closely moulded on the values of its April 26 editorial.

> 'Motion-Picture Australia is looking for a man! He must be strong. He must be a fighter. He must have imagination. His business ability must be sound, and, withal, he must have Australia always uppermost in his heart and emblazoned upon his coat of arms. That man is to be the champion of our big dreams of a picture producing land of the wattle — a leader with a sincere personality and steadfast purpose. To such a man as this, one who will not become drunk with the intoxication of success, nor too blinded by the greed of gain, a whole nation of picture enthusiasts will give a warm and whole-hearted support. There will be hard knocks to take, dark and depressing days to pass through, for the goal is not worth having that comes like manna in the morning dew; but Australia is looking for the man.

This remarkable piece of journalism had the title 'Will "Snowy" "Get There"?'. *Picture Show* answered its own question with a resounding 'yes, we are sure he will' because Snowy Baker had a *plan*, as well as the virility of an Olympic athlete. First he would work hard, then aim at the international market, then undertake regular production of 'wholesome and clean' *Australian* films, for which he would import American leads and directors. Finally he would see 'Made in Australia' flashed on the screens of the world. *Picture Show* was not abashed that the Australian themes it wanted so much would come from an American scenarist, Bess Meredyth, because the original story was to be written by an Australian — Mrs Baker. And still unabashed, it reported that under Meredyth's hand, of the original story 'nine times out of ten it is the name alone that reaches the picture-goer'. There were, after all, other things for the magazine to eulogise: that through his partnership with E.J. Carroll, Baker had not only secured the help of 'one of the wisest motion picture men in Australia with a supreme confidence in the ultimate success of the local movie', but also an assured exhibition through Carroll's big Queensland circuit; that in addition Henry Gee and Edwin Geach of Australasian Films, and Alec Lorrimore, managing director of Paramount had 'agreed to support and assist this undertaking in every possible way'; and that Carroll was about to arrange distribution in the United States, England, France, South America, South Africa and the Far East.

Soon it appeared that Australasian Films, with the entire first release chain of Union Theatres and their associated exhibitors behind them, were to go into production themselves. *Picture Show* announced that Baker's company would produce six films a year and Australasian Films another six; the public would benefit from increased competition and, best of all in this idyllic consensualist world, American producers, noting that the two Australian companies had finalised distribution arrangements in the United States, would themselves be attracted to Australia and a share of the cake. 'Within two years', said *Picture Show* hopefully,

> it is more than likely that we will have half-a-dozen different producing companies permanently established here . . . The whole thing constitutes the gladdest news *Picture Show* has been able to convey to its readers since its inception'.[32]

By October, with Longford at work on *Ginger Mick*, the Australian premiere of *The Sentimental Bloke* set for Sydney on October 18, with Beau Smith's *Barry Butts In* ready for release, D.B. O'Connor's *The Face at the Window* in production, Fred Ward filling the Australasian Films' studio with extra girls for *Why Mabel Learned to Jazz*, and the Baker operation efficiently on location in Kangaroo Valley, a *Picture Show* editorial could complacently argue: 'We are not a little proud of what we have accomplished in Australia. We can fairly claim to have played some part in bringing about the present activity in local production'.[33]

Its cup was running over. Was not Longford's *The Sentimental Bloke* 'the best picture we have yet produced'? And was not Beau Smith, about to leave temporarily for America, 'Standing alone as a producer of Australian successes' with 'many cool thousands' profit from his *Hayseeds*-comedies, his *Desert Gold* and *Satan in Sydney*? Had not E.J. Carroll sufficient faith in local production to offer Steele Rudd the unheard of sum of £500 for a scenario? Was not Fred Ward achieving the heights of technical sophistication by putting through 'eight hundred feet of film in one day last week, and every foot of it was used'? And, best of all, there were the Americans, Lucas and Meredyth, in Kangaroo Valley filming with three cameras simultaneously; while in Sydney, Lucas and *Picture Show* editor Reg Long were teaching aspiring screen artists the latest American methods of acting. By November Franklyn Barrett was planning *The Breaking of the Drought*, and Thomas H. Ince was thundering portentously from Los Angeles to *Picture Show* readers that he intended to produce a great Australian epic 'with no shock to realism' in the Californian landscape.[34] Beaumont Smith was planning to go to Hollywood to do the same, while at home abundance was the word. *Picture Show* produced a bevy of photographs: 'Australian girls who some day may be stars'; and on the facing page E.J. Carroll advertised his ambitious schedule of producing, one a month, two more Baker films and three Longford films between November and March.

"Snowy" Baker gives an account of himself

We are in the throes of producing the greatest Motion Picture that has yet been credited to Australian brains and effort. I have jumped into this page to tell you about it. Can't stay long, as I am wanted back at Kangaroo Valley, where Mr. Wilfred Lucas is waiting to "shoot up" some more scenes.

Mr. Lucas says I am a better Stunt Actor than anyone living. He ought to know. Anyhow, he has had me leaping from crag to crag, diving hundreds of feet into roaring chasms, saving heroines—by the hundred it seems to me—fighting for my life—and these toughs Wilfred picks out are the real thing. They come at me with murder in their eyes. I have got to beat 'em up. I do! Because I know that the crank of the camera is relentlessly grinding on and on, and every punch I "get home" will be recorded on the screen for you.

And, boys! You ought to see Brownie Vernon. She is the sweetest little screen actress. As a heroine she is well worth fighting for. You will understand when you see her. This is going to be a great big winner—this first picture of ours. Mr. E. J. Carroll certainly does things right. For further particulars, get in touch with your local Theatre Manager, or

E. J. CARROLL,
BANKING HOUSE, PITT STREET, SYDNEY,

controlling world rights for Raymond Longford's production for Southern Cross Feature Films, Ltd., "The Sentimental Bloke."

Productions in preparation and for early release:—

November—A. Reg. L. Baker film, produced by Wilfred Lucas from a scenario by Bess Meredith.
December—"The Moods of Ginger Mick," by C. J. Dennis, produced by Raymond Longford.
January—"On Our Selection," by Steel Rudd.
February—A. Reg. L. Baker film.
March—"On Our New Selection," by Steel Rudd.

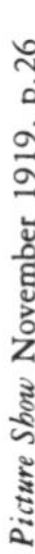

Australian abundance — of films and stars.

AUSTRALIAN GIRLS
Who Some Day
MAY BE STARS.

PORTRAITS BY JOHN W. WALKER, 99 CASTLEREAGH STREET, SYDNEY.

Picture Show November 1919, p.27

Picture Show, on location with *The Man From Kangaroo*, responded with populist jubilation:

> Australians are too modest, yet we have more to be proud of than nations of braggarts . . . Rather than exaggerate, we have a tendency to fail in doing ourselves common justice. Mr Lucas thinks so . . . Mr Baker thinks so too. Mr E.J. Carroll, having an undying faith in his native country, Australia, also thinks so, and is prepared to back his opinion with his money . . . And these pioneers — pioneers in the sense that they are the first to exploit Australian motion picture possibilities on a huge scale — are undoubtedly the "chosen people" for the job. Messrs. Carroll and Baker are not overawed by the deeds of the great corporations in other countries. They say, "We can do as well here. Australia shall be a great motion picture centre".[35]

In amongst the sentiment, there were some serious economic facts: a huge administrative organisation will be needed 'so that these great productions, when completed, can be handled in every part of the world'; the Americans have huge advantages in finances, legions of players, 'thousands of cinemas craving a supply of screen stories compared with the hundreds here'. But what were mere economic disadvantages before a 'mentality actuated by an ideal'?

> For a compelling purpose is a greater force than steam or electric power. It removes mountains — if they are in the way. Further, such purposeful personalties have the vibrant courage of conviction. What they undertake they carry out . . . Patriotic enterprise such as activates the promoters of this new Australian industry will find echo in the heart of every true Australian.

But patriotism was not all:

> The creation of the real Australian picture will carry a message to Europe and America that will bring back a reward of commercial and national respect, and we shall reap materially as well as socially the seed of dignity and self-reliance we have sown.

Just occasionally others brought a different emphasis — of doubt — into *Picture Show*'s pages. Pioneer producer Alfred Rolfe pointed out in August 1919 that it was not so much initiative as hard cash that was needed; and further, that though Australian films appealed to Australians, 'for many reasons which I will not go into, they have a poor chance of reaching the public'.[36] One of *Picture Show*'s readers was more blunt. Les Williams wrote on May 24 that if *Picture Show* honestly wanted to promote local production it was going to need a lot of help.

> You're up against a solid proposition, both from film importers and the film-eating public. The first because the huge vested interests on the other side, will naturally do anything possible to push the local industry out to serve their own trade . . . and the public, because . . . they've had the perfections of the foreign article drummed into them for over a century (not pictures only, but everything else) until the mistaken idea has taken root: 'Anything Australian can't be any good because it *is* Australian'.[37]

Picture Show did not agree, and was never to print an argument like Williams's again. Its response was that Australasian Films Ltd was not against local production, that the problems lay rather with 'utter lack of business knowledge' on the part of producers and the 'spasmodic and inconsistent production that is going on'.

> 'We believe firmly that the whole trouble is with our own people, and lies in the fact that Australians have not yet set out to support wholeheartedly their own Australian interests . . . It is ourselves who are really responsible for the film outlook at the present time. The opening is there, and it remains for us to make the best possible use of it.

There were half-truths in this position: spasmodic production *was* a crippling feature of the Australian industry; and lack of Australian investment *was* the most important reason for that. But the problems were always phrased in populist terms, in that: (i) the Australian people, not the development of Australian capitalism, were blamed for the failures of local production; (ii) individual hard work and small-scale communal enterprise (rather than anti-monopoly legislation) was thought to be all that was necessary to attract that support; and (iii) when anybody was blamed other than the producers themselves, *Picture Show* tried to rally public support against narrowly specified targets like 'profiteers', by which it meant not capitalists but the Government which was imposing 'unjust' taxes on the cinema industry.

Picture Show's populist position was not surprising given its economic basis in a small independent company, Cartoon Filmads, which produced animated cartoon advertisements for 'One hundred and ninety-two cinemas from Cooktown to the South Australian border'. These were drawn by *Picture Show* editor Harry Julius who also did caricatures for the *Bulletin*, *Steel Rudd's Magazine* and *The Worker*, and who as 'the only bioscopic cartoonist in Australia', was regarded by the press as a 'pioneer in a new arena of film art' which, because of its propagandist value, one day 'may revolutionise the world'.[38] With an Australian film 'pioneer' on its editorial board, and the company's attempts to capture the local market in film advertising *and* film magazines for Australian productions, *Picture Show*'s pioneering nationalist populism was to be expected. At the same time, though, these were all *support* features of the film trade which knew it must continue to rely, for its own survival, on Hollywood features for the foreseeable future. When a correspondent urged in May 1919 that they should not review American films at all, *Picture Show* replied that 'at the present time there is no Australian industry — that is to say . . . large enough to support its own paper'.[39] To try to shut out the Americans would be impossible, and even if achieved would lead to the 'annihilation' of Australian film. Ignoring its own perception that the triumph of *The Sentimental Bloke* lay in its unique innovation of blending film and Australian verse, the magazine argued that the United States was the only source of inspiration and learning for the Australian industry.

Everything seemed so good for local production in *Picture Show*'s view that within the mythology of laissez-faire capitalism, the early signs of a major American invasion could be treated with generosity. In December 1919 the *Picture Show* editor wrote,

> Right from the start we have been staunch advocates of local production; but we have also encouraged the overseas concerns which bring capital to Australia, and give employment to Australians — and that from start to finish will be the policy of this paper.[40]

Under the heading 'The Overseas Invasion' he continued:

> The arrival of three representatives of Selznick Pictures to open a branch office in Australia may be taken as the start of an influx of overseas concerns to conduct their own business here instead of selling their film to an exchange as has been done in the past. This means the introduction of new capital to the Commonwealth, and will not necessarily entail the squeezing-out of the already-established exchanges. The growth of the business during the next few years will allow room for all, and the development of our own Australian productions will add to the prosperity of the industry as a whole.

This idyllic future was not to be. *Picture Show* found that it could not be a staunch advocate of large-scale local production and at the same time get the support of these overseas concerns; that there was not, in fact, 'room for all'. Like local production, *Picture Show* itself was to collapse before larger forces with a stronger American orientation. The course of Australian film-making from the peak of euphoria in 1919 through its decline to the nadir of 1929 was complicated; but it formed a broad current in which there is space here to look only at the directors who formed the major eddies. Each director suffered a different fortune, according to his economic situation and his character and ambitions. But there were also traceable continuities: some were already apparent by 1919. The naive optimism of that year would vanish, but the trade's open-handed attitude to Hollywood, and the general assertion that Australian production needed only initiative and enterprise, hardly began to change until the early thirities. What was changing was the economy: from classical to monopoly capitalism, as large Australian corporations gobbled up smaller ones and then were taken over in turn by larger American ones. With it, the beliefs and values of those strongly involved in the industry moved away from the naive populism of *Picture Show*. But the ideological expression of that interest — the message repeated by the trade papers and received by the audience — varied little from year to year.

The Picture Show Screen Club

For the benefit of new readers we here reprint the objects of the Screen Club:—

1. To help make the Motion Picture Industry in Australia a self-supporting industry in every branch and an organised one in every respect. One able to hold its own with those of the other countries of the world and that will give Australian talent full scope for expansion.
2. To help create an enthusiastic film atmosphere in our own country and to take active steps in pushing Australian interests and to give support to worthy Australian efforts.
3. To form a link between all the different threads of the screen art, and give encouragement to those seeking an outlet for real and earnest effort.
4. To create and keep clean an atmosphere around the work that is being done in this country and to educate at every opportunity appreciation of clean drama.

The Preparation of the "Screen Club" Programme.

Owing to the influenza we have been unable to complete our programme for "The Screen Club."

Many of the producers have taken the opportunity of getting away into the country for the filming of exteriors, etc., but otherwise our arrangements are going on successfully. Our programme will consist of getting together all the master minds in the different sections of production for the purpose of creating a central body. This will be detailed more fully at a later date.

Reviewing the Field for Your Ambition.

In the first place it is necessar- that every member of "The S- Club" should get an absol- rect viewpoint of the fi- as it exists at the - this country. - you will go - wrong wa- dition- if y- if no- tralia, - time wr- a setting - know that - racing scen- you will be- writing one o- is just the n- closely the con-

Getting the "Ma- Idea

Some day you hope star, a scenario writer man; you have not suffi- to go to Los Angeles, and you would probably meet fate of hundreds of others h- self, who have spent their al- to get into the movies by tak- trip to the other side of the w- There are a thousand and one - sons why many of them can nev- get a chance to play a part, muc- less star in America, and too many prove this only after they have spent their all in some ill-fated trip to America.

DO YOU KNOW THAT THE NUMBER OF STRANDED AUSTRALIANS SEEKING EMPLOYMENT AFTER SPENDING THEIR ALL ON A TRIP TO LOS ANGELES WAS SO GREAT, THAT A SPECIAL DEPARTMENT HAD TO BE CREATED THERE TO KEEP -HIPPING THEM BACK TO -RALIA WHEN THEY - ENNILESS!

-our aim should be to - proper viewpoint of - and work along -our ambitions here - by giving your - to Australian -rn all you can -s who are -on of film. -YOU MAY IN THE FIGHT- these -stand- by -iv- -it - -me -e first -owed out by -Screen Club" MADE IN AUSTRA- -RODUCTIONS ALWAYS - WHOLE-HEARTEDLY.

(To be Continued Next Week.)

Opportunities for all

Picture Show 10 May 1919, pp.32,33

PART TWO

Producers and Constraints of Production

'Steeped in Americanism . . .' Cowboy with kangaroo motif: Snowy Baker in *The Shadow of Lightning Ridge*

Picture Show 1 March 1920, p.32

2

The American Invasion: First Wave

Snowy Baker, Bess Meredyth and Wilfred Lucas, Lawson Harris, Yvonne Pavis, Harry Southwell

TEN LESSONS—£3/3/-.
Full particulars on Application.

MUNICIPAL BUILDINGS,
82A OXFORD STREET
(Corner Crown St.), SYDNEY.

PICTURE ACTING REG. L. BAKER FORMS A SPECIAL CLASS

So many people are ambitious to take up Picture Work that after repeated requests I have formed a special class in connection with this work. This will include the Woolley Grecian Body Culture, Deportment, and Facial Expression as applied to film-acting—which will all be valuable steps in the right direction. There will also be special instruction in photo-play "make-up."

At each class a short helpful lecture will be delivered, imparting the valuable knowledge gained during my recent visit to the leading Studios in U.S.A., where I spent months working with world-famous Film Stars under well-known producers, during which time I acquired a very comprehensive knowledge of Motion Picture Work in all its branches, which, combined with my experience in locally-made pictures, places me in a position to control every phase of the work.

My own picture, "The Lure of the Bush," was taken in its American version under the direction of the famous Walter Edwards and Crawford Ivers. I also worked with

ALLAN DWAN, CHARLIE CHAPLIN, WILLIAM S. HART,
SESSUE HAYAKAWA, CONSTANCE TALMADGE,
and other celebrated Film Artists.

MY GUARANTEE.

I have such confidence in my Picture Class that I guarantee if, at the end of a month's trial, you are not perfectly satisfied that my system is all I claim for it, to refund, without question, the entire amount paid by you.

In conjunction with Mr. E. J. Carroll, I have formed a Film Corporation, and intend to extensively develop the picture business in Australia, which will open up opportunities for those who are ambitious to win fame on the screen. The first of a series of pictures will begin in September.

Pupils are requested to specially note that an actual film test will be taken, and both the negative and positive of the film will become their property. I do not guarantee any pupil a position in these pictures, but if opportunity offers will endeavour to use their services.

CLASSES ARE NOW IN OPERATION. NEXT CLASS MEETS THURSDAY, 2.30 P.M.

Private and Individual Instruction, and small parties taken by arrangement. Those desiring to join are asked to make early application.

REG. L. ("Snowy") BAKER
Natural Health and Physical Culture Expert.

PAGE FIFTEEN

Picture Show 9 September 1919, p.15

No other production venture of the 1920s more carefully followed its own blueprint for success than that of Snowy Baker for the entrepreneurs E.J. and Dan Carroll. Baker worked methodically through the Australian production needs he had first announced in *Picture Show* in May 1919. The problem of what sort of films would appeal to the international market was a major question in the trade in the 1920s and was too often presented as a simple opposition: local 'bush' themes versus 'universal' themes such as the 'love triangles' supposedly typical of 'society' dramas. Baker saw as clearly as anyone that this was not necessarily an either-or proposition. Why was it not possible to present issues of universal appeal, such as 'open air, free life and nature in all its beauty' with an Australian *inflection*, 'depicting our station and bush life, introducing plenty of Australian scenery, horses and cattle'?[1]

Once the question of what kind of film had been resolved, Baker's next problem was how to achieve the required international standard. He recognised that the critical areas of inadequacy in his own films, *The Enemy Within* and *The Lure of the Bush*, were in the correct preparation of the scenarios and the directing of the films. In order to remedy these problems he went to the United States to import, in Wilfred Lucas and Bess Meredyth, 'the best director and continuity writer possible'. Lucas, like many later American imports, was probably already finding the pace of competition in America too hot and, attracted by the offer of £500 a week to direct for Baker, had announced his wish to 'stay here, work for success and grow up with the motion picture industry in Australia'[2] as he had done in America.

The next stage in Baker's design was the choice of stars. The success of Enid Bennett, Sylvia Bremer, Louise Lovely, House Peters and many others in Hollywood proved that Australia had a wealth of acting talent lying dormant. All he felt was necessary now was proper direction and the example of one good star imported from America.

With typical efficiency, Baker got both schemes under way immediately. Brownie Vernon came from America with Lucas and Meredyth to play female lead in the new venture. By 4 September 1919, when Lucas and company docked in Sydney, Baker had already opened his acting school and given his first lecture, in which he impressed on the students 'the necessity for absolute seriousness'. He spoke of picture acting as 'the new art', and the motion picture industry as 'one of Australia's future leading industrial achievements'.

As Baker himself, with his international athletic, gymnastic and equestrian background, was to play male lead, inevitably the films were to become vehicles for his stunts. But one should not write the films off too quickly for that reason. It is easy to dismiss the highly limited actor of the boyish grin and the superman stunts, but in fact Baker the producer was here sensibly placing in the Australian context a formula already successfully applied by Tom Mix in America, and adapting it, as he said he would, to the 'Australian romance' of which he himself was undoubtedly a part. It would be wrong to think of these as naive Australian productions. They were the result of careful business thinking, and would not have attracted the support of E.J. Carroll, who was widely regarded as one of the shrewdest entrepeneurs in the game, had they not been.

Another aspect of Baker's business thinking, and the final part of his plan, was to avoid being tied down to elaborately equipped studios in the early stages. Unlike Arthur Shirley, whose commitment to studio costs caused him difficulties from the start, Baker argued that:

> the many difficulties a studio would entail can be passed over and the same results secured in other effective work. In America they specialise in creating wonderful interiors. Why shouldn't Australia specialise in presenting equally wonderful exteriors that are so plentiful in this beautiful land?'[4]

With each stage of his plan now under way, Baker set off for Kangaroo Valley and Gunnedah to produce the first of the films in fulfilment of his hopes 'to see the words "Made in Australia" flashed on every screen where the motion picture is shown'.

It was at Gunnedah that Baker first learned that films shot entirely on location were not necessarily cheaper than those made in studios. The drought forced the company much further into the bush than was intended, and the shortage of grass meant transporting fodder for 150 horses wherever they went, adding the significant sum of £225 to their bill. Despite this, the Americans pronounced themselves well satisfied with the locations. Bob Dorreir, a cameraman with eleven years' experience with major Hollywood studios, including work on important films of William Hart and Charlie Chaplin, was, not surprisingly, impressed with the light, atmospheric conditions and locations: 'your country is just unique in its advantages. Why, within half an hour of the city we have seen locations that we would have to travel for days to find in my country.'[5] Lucas, too, appreciated Kangaroo Valley's proximity to Sydney as it enabled him to send his unsettled £1-a-day six-year-old child lead back to visit his mother in Woolloomooloo without much break in production. Besides, the occasion offered a chance for publicity, with the child carrying 'two huge loaves of bread' from the Americans to a Sydney working-class home suffering from a 'raging' bread strike.

The selection of six-year-old Jimmy after two weeks spent searching in 'grimy streets and smelly localities' provides an insight into the problems faced by producers who wanted to make 'Australian' films which still adhered to the dominant Hollywood notion of 'types'. In an industry with a defined notion of what each character part should be, and directories indexing the wealth of acting talent according to facial features, mannerisms and other characteristics deemed appropriate to these stereotypes, 'typing' was a major aspect of Hollywood's time-saving, cost-saving shorthand. Thus: 'A vamp is a woman conscious of her charms and piquant appeal and capable of accentuating these charms to the point of fascinating a man and completely

(i) (ii) (iii)

(i) *Exhibitor* 16 September 1925, p.5; (ii) *Photoplayer* 13 October 1923, p.37; (iii) still from *Camille*

'A woman conscious of her charms and piquant appeal': Hollywood vamps (i) Greta Nissen, (ii) Nita Naldi, and (iii) Nazimova subjugating him to her slightest caprice'.[6] Theda Bara, Greta Nissen and Nita Naldi were held to combine the necessary 'see-saw of the emotions' from 'veneer of civilisation' and sophistication to 'primitive instincts' of the bloodsucking animal which were the 'essence' of the part. But although a trade critic said *The Man From Kangaroo* would succeed where earlier Australian films failed because it captured 'the outback people' as authentic 'types', it was not clear to anyone what that really meant. There was Baker's athleticism, but Annette Kellerman had already taken that supposedly Australian quality to America to star for Herbert Brenon in Hollywood spectaculars that were said to rival Griffith's.

The whole question was further complicated by the association of the 'type' with the trend in acting conventions. Wilfred Lucas told the students at Baker's acting school: 'Learn not to act . . . Perfect naturalness is one of the absolute essentials for the picture artist, and extravagant gesture has no place on the screen.'[7] This new 'realism', which Lucas had learnt from Griffith, was, of course, no less conventional than the earlier elaborated style, and tended to be a realism of surfaces only, since the impersonality of characterisation which it engendered made it very difficult to portray subjective states. The result among less accomplished actors, like Snowy Baker in his attempts at 'restraint', was a woodenness of expression and fixity of stare that is sometimes disconcerting.

The 'type'

The link between naturalism and 'typing' was the belief that a long enough search of the highways and byways would reveal a *real* type, like the tramp who was cast as Cranky Jack in *On Our Selection* or Jimmy in *The Man From Kangaroo*. On the European scene Eisenstein was soon to use a theory of 'typage' also based on recognisable facial characteristics, but this was part of a very un-naturalistic principle by which he sought to shock audiences into a new ideological awareness through the collision of diverse but instantly recognisable images. The Baker–Lucas notion on the other hand was that the most authentic naturalism could only be achieved by the man who played himself. Like Lucas, Eisenstein often spent months looking for the right person. But the contrast between Eisenstein's theory and the Australian concept of 'types' is clear in his choice of a man he found shovelling coal to play the doctor in *Battleship Potemkin*, whereas the Australian trade press complimented the McDonagh sisters by noting that 'a particularly convincing doctor' in *Those Who Love* had been played by an actual doctor who merely had to 'be natural and not to act'.[8]

The 'craze for types' dominated American cinema and theatre throughout this period. Elsa Chauvel, for instance, was still complaining of this 'bugaboo' in 1929.[9] In contrast, even the local trade press occasionally noticed that Australia's real strength lay in its reservoir of supporting stage actors who could 'ably enact any part'. In 1921 *Everyones*, which was at that time still more committed to the stage than the cinema, argued that producers should first see whether some of these stage actors could fill their needs, before going out to get one 'who looks the part, but may not be equal to the interpretation'.[10]

But Baker was too committed to his blueprint for Australian production to agree. He felt that 'a great deal of the success of pictures manufactured in America was due to the facility with which the producers were able to obtain the various types needed.' In the absence of America's quantity of types, Baker argued that his search was for quality of types, in which he felt Australia was particularly rich: 'I claim that I am a certain type — the athletic type, and where in the world would you get a better type than my old friend Arthur Tauchert?'[11]

However, a number of factors worked against Baker's attempt to locate 'Australian-ness' in his concept of typicality. First of all there was no philosophical theory of typicality in Western culture such as existed in the socialist world, whether from practitioners like Eisenstein or theorists like Lukàcs, who placed the type in an historical and social context. The Hollywood notion of 'type' was purely descriptive in its intention. Hence no contradiction was noticed in choosing Jimmy, an urban working-class child, to portray a country-town kid: it was enough that he was a 'fighter'.

Secondly, there was the problem of the interpretation of Australian 'types' by American stars. The trade press put on a bold front over the 'surprising performance' of Wilfred Lucas as a cattle duffer. 'One might reasonably expect', *Picture Show* told its readers, 'that a man who has spent his entire life in America would have difficulty in really getting into the ways, habits and appearance of the bushman, but Lucas has accomplished it, and thus makes an unique addition to his already long list of character roles.'[12] But the last point was the giveaway. Lucas was simply drawing on the American repertoire of static types such as 'Wilfred the wowser' and 'Wilfred the ne'er-do-well' for which he was noted, and this was bound to work against Baker's *national* concept of types. Raymond Longford complained that when he protested to Lucas about Americanising Australian films, Lucas replied that:

The Great Australian Kid.

"Jimmy," the six-year-old kid in Snowy Baker's "The Man from Kangaroo," doesn't want to be a star if he can't take his "mudder" on location.

Picture Show 1 December 1919, p.59

Type casting: Jimmy in *The Man from Kangaroo*

Picture Show (i), (ii) 13 September 1919, p.9; (iii) 1 December 1919, p.50

Wilfred Lucas playing 'types': (i) the wowser and (ii) the ne'er-do-well; and (iii) his 'surprising performance' as an 'Australian type' — a cattle duffer in *The Man from Kangaroo*

> he did not want to worry about maintaining the Australian setting . . . 'If I want to get one of your Aboriginals or natives in a picture, I am going to get him; and if I care to stick a few feathers on him, that is my business. I am looking after my home market, and am not worrying about the Australian end of it'.[13]

The third problem was the importation of Hollywood genres, like the Western. Robert Sklar has noted that what characterised the early postwar films of Mix, Fairbanks, Rio Jim and others were bronzed, strong men controlling complicated plot lines 'ending in the robbing of banks, in violent deaths, in discoveries of gold mines . . . Americans had physical genius; they held the secret of action',[14] and the world, including Snowy Baker, went to American movies to experience that secret. These outdoor qualities particularly suited an Australian cinema already steeped in bushranging themes. But Baker's adaptation of the Hollywood formula to suit his own skills, together with the already Hollywood-dominated trade attitude to women stars, overlaid the Australian context with the 'bronzed-active-male rescues passive-pretty-female' scenario so familiar in Hollywood. Typically, publicity for the film emphasised the broken fingers and noses associated with Baker's stunts while Brownie Vernon's publicity was either about bush romances or about her 'eyes so deliciously brown' and sun-gold 'prettiest fair hair'.[15]

Fourthly, there was the fact that melodramatic acting conventions were still strong in 1919. This was partly because the lack of continuous cinema production in Australia had prevented the building up of stock companies which would have eased the need to draw on the stage for film actors. It was also partly because 'the type', lacking a socio-historical identity, could most easily be placed cinematically by iconography and gestural style. The cigarette, for instance, was generally associated with the male rotter and seducer, as was the sly, sideways eye movement. *Picture Show* Screen Club gave this old and traditional theatrical advice to new and aspiring movie actors in 1919:

> The eyes raised upwards signifies prayer, supplication. The eyes downward, modesty, shame . . . Hatred — head turned slightly from object, eyes fixed on it, etc.[16]

Snowy Baker used these codes to illustrate 'two of the fundamental emotions in facial expression' in his first acting-school class. This is not to say that an accomplished actor or actress could not incorporate these gestural codes in constructing a naturalistic Australian 'type'. Lottie Lyell

 (i)

S The Picture Show Screen Club S

In continuing the article of last week on make-up, we shall go on dealing with the eyes.

Last week we dealt briefly with the essentials of groundwork and the things to be borne in mind, and we now repeat again that the make-up for picture acting is totally different to that used on the stage.

Here are a few hints on the value of the eyes:—

The eye naturally opened and looking straight forward signifies calmness, confidence.

The eye raised upwards signifies prayer, supplication.

The eye downward, modesty, shame.

The eye vacant, abstraction, forgetfulness, oblivion.

The eye staring, fear, fright, horror.

Reflection—in deep thought—the eyes are fixed on vacancy, or move listlessly from object to object.

Hatred—head slightly turned from object, eyes fixed on it.

Wonder—eyes wide open.

Melancholy and sorrow—eyes wide open with abstracted gaze.

The attitude of the head must be carefully observed before you can determine the signification of the eyes. For instance, the head drawn back and the eye direct will give the effect of harshness toward the person or object you are looking at.

The auditor unconsciously concentrates on the eyes. They are the messengers with which the artist sends his innermost thoughts and feelings to the spectators. In the eye, gesture has its birth. Like the lightning flash that springs from the clouds and illuminates the earth, so thought radiates from the eye and reflects the soul within. With the eye one can speak intelligently in all languages to all people.

PAGE

(ii)

(i) *Picture Show* 7 June 1919, p.32; (ii) *Everyones* 1 April 1925, p.27

The eyes and gestural style: (ii) 'Hatred — head slightly turned from object, eyes fixed on it', Pola Negri in *Queen of the Hearts of Men;* (iii) 'The eye downward, modesty', Lottie Lyell in *The Sentimental Bloke.*
(iv) The Hollywood secret of action: bronzed strong men rescuing passive, pretty females: Snowy Baker and Brownie Vernon in *The Shadow of Lightning Ridge*

(iii)

(iv)

(iii) National Film Archive; (iv) *Picture Show* 1 April 1920, p.42

made consistent use of the melodramatic conventions of expression without in any sense stereotyping the Australian characterisation she was establishing in *The Sentimental Bloke*. But more often, as for example in the casting and acting of a typical Australian 'heavy', Charles Villiers in *The Man From Kangaroo*, a contradiction was set up between the naturalistic demands of the director and the melodramatic conventions of the actors — and this problem added to the one of 'restrained' style mentioned earlier.

None of these problems were features of the production of *The Man From Kangaroo* that the trade press noticed. What it preferred to see was the 'new' and 'modern' features: there was the major importance of a woman co-director on the set and Bess Meredyth, it was noted, worked in 'constant association and collaboration' with husband Lucas and had an 'unusual tendency to improvise on the script' during production. Then there was the fact that *three* cameras simultaneously shot each scene from a variety of angles and 'for the first time reflectors have been properly used in Australia'.[17]

Certainly, the lighting of *The Man From Kangaroo*, with the vivid contrasts of the opening sequence of a swaggie in arid desert followed by a lush tree-lined countryside, with well-handled 'moonlit' shots of Baker and Vernon sitting on a big garden wall, and with the occasional dramatic contrast conveyed by light and shadow as when Lucas bursts into Baker's 'church', is vastly superior to the lighting in Baker's only surviving earlier film, *The Enemy Within*. And, to be fair to Lucas and Meredyth, the acting is more restrained as well, including Baker, who otherwise plays his usual swashbuckling hero, and perhaps even Villiers, who the trade press felt had 'never been so smooth and finished as in this picture'.[18]

Released as *The Better Man* in 1922, after the later Baker films in the United States, *The Man From Kangaroo* won more praise from American magazines than from many an Australian one for its continuous action, stunts and 'fine display of the open country punctuated by clear photography'.[19] The American magazine *Motion Picture News* argued that:

> *The Better Man* may be called a Western because it contains the vital qualities which have characterised this brand of production . . . but . . . it is a picture which is far above the average of the ordinary Western. Baker will not need to take a back seat from any American star.

In contrast, the *Sydney Mail* complained about the Americanisation of a film which was advertised as purely Australian:

> Apart from the fact that the scenes have been taken on Australian soil and that the leading man, 'Snowy' Baker, is an Australian, there is nothing

> in it that is not steeped in Americanism. Director, authoress, leading lady, cameraman, supporting cast . . . all are imported from the U.S.A.[20]

The point, of course , of importing the Americans was to gain access to the American market and, judging by *Motion Picture News*, Baker had hit that market with exactly what it wanted:

> Snowy Baker made such a favourable impression with his two previous releases . . . that the picturegoing public is certain to look forward to any document that features him. This versatile artist from the Antipodes is so gifted in horsemanship and gunplay, he is so capable an athlete, that the most ordinary story imaginable would appear exceptional with him lending his personality for expression.[21]

But that review was still in the future. *The Man From Kangaroo* was released by Union Theatres in Sydney in January 1920 and the Lucas–Baker–Meredyth team went quickly into production of their next film, hoping for release in April of the same year. In *The Shadow of Lightning Ridge*, Baker compromised to some extent on his original plans. Clearly believing the earlier film *had* typified bush life, *The Shadow* was advertised as, 'undoubtedly the greatest picture of *general* interest yet produced in Australia. It is NOT intended to be typical of Australian life'. *Picture Show* noted that like *For the Term of His Natural Life*, the story derived its strength from spanning more than one continent. Although Baker played an Australian bushranger, Meredyth's script employed the flashback to present his daring exploits in a number of countries before he comes to Australia. Insured for £500,000, Baker was put through a series of amazing stunts: these included leaping from a galloping horse on to a moving train; fighting with a guard in the horse box, underneath the frightened animals' hooves; riding his own horse Boomerang along a narrow fifty-foot log above an abyss while his police companions crawl across on hands and knees; and, in a final piece of daring, jumping Boomerang from thirty feet up a mountain through the roof of a remote hut to save Brownie Vernon as heroine from the real villain.

Much inspired by this 'realism', the trade press stressed the importance of horses in the film which reveals another significant detail about 'bush' productions. It was not just a pool of acting 'types' that was lacking in Australia, but of trained horses too.
As *Picture Show* pointed out, whereas in the United States

> they make a special business of training horses for picture show work . . . The horses for the local film productions have to be purchased outright. Well-bred horses are essential, and it is difficult to find any owners of good animals who are willing to hire them out for pictorial purposes.[22]

A thrilling drama of the great outback, bringing the life, the glamour, the color, the adventure of the Wonderful West glittering to the screen.

Thunderbolt's break for safety is nothing to the stunt performed by Snowy Baker and Brownie Vernon who leap 80 feet from the top of a coach into a flooded river in this great Australian-production----!

E. J. Carroll's forthcoming pictures are:

(*a*) "*The Story of Ginger Mick*"

By C. J. Dennis. A sequel to "The Sentimental Bloke"

(*b*) "*The Shadow of Lightning Ridge*"

(*c*) "*On Our Selection*"

By Steele Rudd

'The Baker punch: trick riding, fist fighting, bronco busting and other stunts come before the eye'. *Motion Picture News*

SPECIAL RETURN SEASON

Kangaroo Valley

Saturday, May 29th

E. J. Carroll presents

The Man From Kangaroo

A real Australian Picture at last—featuring the champion stunt actor

National Film Archive

(i)

National Film Archive

The most prolific and successful title artists in Australian silent cinema were Syd Nicholls (cartoon creator of Fatty Finn, subject of *The Kid Stakes*) and Will Cathcart. Within two years they had designed together the titles for *The Man from Kangaroo, On Our Selection, The Shadow of Lightning Ridge, Robbery Under Arms, The Jackeroo of Coolabong, The Man from Snowy River, Silks and Saddles, The Betrayer, The Gentleman Bushranger, The Blue Mountain Mystery, Circumstance* and *Rudd's New Selection*. Examples of titles from (i) and (ii) *The Shadow of Lightning Ridge* and (iii) *Ginger Mick*.

(ii)

(iii)

National Film Archive

(ii)

(i)

(i) National Film Archive; (ii) *Exhibitor* 17 March 1926, p.2

Vamps Australian (Vera James) and American (Pola Negri, inset)

Vamps American . . .
Gloria Swanson

(i)

(ii)

Picture Show (i) 1 November 1919, p.1; (ii) 1 January 1921 p.8

and Australian . . .
Berenice Vere

Baker had to buy thirty valuable blood horses for the film, as well as employ a retinue of grooms and stable attendants, which added considerably to the cost of production.

On the other hand, Lucas confirmed his opinion that production costs could be cut considerably in Australia by the availability of a great variety of scenery close to Sydney, a matter of some importance with a large production staff and animals to transport. Some of Baker's other predictions also seemed to be coming true: for instance, in the discovery of local stars. Berenice Vere played the part of the dubious Portuguese Annie in *The Shadow* and clearly outacted Brownie Vernon, whom *Picture Show* found 'sulky' and disappointingly passive, whereas Vere, in her small part, was pleasing and 'with the dark eyes and suggestion of fire gives a wonderful impression of the woman from Southern Europe'. This was, of course, a key ingredient of the Hollywood-style vamp. Still under twenty, and with little acting experience, Vere was pronounced by Lucas to be his most exciting find ever. *Picture Show* predicted a star future for her, and did its own bit to turn wish into reality by giving her 'star' presentation in its New Year issue for 1921, including an interview with the appalling 'Ambrose Adagio'. During the four years of *Picture Show*'s existence, Adagio conducted a series of interviews with stars which are notable for telling us much more about his conceit than anything about the actresses interviewed: of Brownie Vernon we learn only of 'the laughter in her eyes, and the sunlight in her hair', and of Vere 'dark eyes and hair . . . a vivid, mobile face; a figure slight, but not of that barbarous leanness which my soul detests'.[23]

The interesting thing about this kind of publicity, however, is what it reveals of trade preconceptions of 'good acting' and 'stardom'. Adagio in this interview muses on what 'type' Vere will most happily act, given her professed dislike for the dubious women she played in the Baker productions.

> 'Not the sweet ingenue, surely — the sugary, curly flapper who makes a man want to spank her!' Vere answered in kind: 'The Nazimova type of role . . . I don't want villainy, and I don't want silly innocence. I want to impersonate characters with fire and dash to them, but with sympathy as well'.[24]

It took Longford to draw Vere out of the preconceptions she and the trade had about the earthy and tempestuous 'southern european' type. Then she followed her heroine Nazimova to Hollywood and signed with Universal.

(i)

(ii)

Picture Show (i) 1 August 1920, p.15; (ii) 1 July 1920, p.36

'Stirring melodrama': Snowy Baker in action during the shooting of *The Jackeroo of Coolabong* at Mulgoa.
(ii) Palmerston: the open-air stage under construction

On its opening in May, *Picture Show* called *Shadow* 'stirring melodrama' and 'a fine achievement in almost every way'.[25] At this point things looked good for the production company, even though the 'extensive rather than intensive' scenario of *Shadow*, with 'action scattered from Pole to Pole' was precisely the kind of thing that Hollywood studios were rejecting as rankly 'amateur'.[26] Much of Baker's blueprint had been followed with apparent success. All the stages of the 'infancy' period he had predicted a year before had apparently been accomplished and it was now time to acquire the 'elaborately equipped studios' which had been intentionally delayed until production was well established.

Carroll-Baker Picture Production

The original Carroll–Baker partnership was more ambitiously re-founded as Carroll–Baker Picture Productions with a capital of £25,000. The subscribers were 'E.J. and Dan Carroll, Reg. L. Baker and the Southern Cross Feature Film Co. Ltd. of Adelaide'. In April 1921, *Picture Show* announced that the big deficiency in Australian production, which had otherwise 'been going ahead at a wonderful rate', was to be made up:

> There has been no big photoplay studio erected in this country. The scenes have been shot wherever the facilities of the moment were best, and much delay has been experienced owing to unsuitable weather and other disadvantages.

But now the Carroll–Baker organisation had

> acquired the magnificent mansion of twenty-eight rooms, known as 'Palmerston', situated at Waverley. The house stands in five acres of ground, ideally suited to the purpose of picture-making. There are picturesque gardens, containing artificial lakes, rustic bridges, a natural fernery and stately timber. Anything from a bush scene to a South Sea Island setting can be taken right on the spot. A fine open-air stage is also being erected.[27]

Each room was to be fitted with modern lighting apparatus, some of which Lucas would bring back from America, but

> fully ninety per cent of which would be manufactured in Sydney . . . The establishment of this studio will be a big thing for the film industry, and for Australia generally. It will use much material and employ many people, and will be equal to anything of its kind in any part of the world.

On his return in June from visiting the huge new Hollywood studios, Lucas was less sanguine but did pronounce Palmerston to be 'the most compact studio in the world', and announced his intention of making, in addition to further Baker films, others of 'Australian interest only', which would add up to eight films a year for the Carrolls. He also planned to make films independently in order to retain some of the 'thousands of pounds of Australian money' going to the United States in film rental. Throwing down the gauntlet to local investors he said, ' I think it is up to all you Australians to see that some of that wealth is kept in your own land'. For himself, he would ensure that his films would present Australians 'in their true light — as people with a little dignity rather than as a half-savage bush folk'. He hoped that Bert Glennon, who had returned with him from America as co-producer, would shortly be directing him in a sympathetic role in a series of films which, like the Baker films, would 'show Australia form every aspect'.[28]

The Jackaroo of Coolabong was completed in a little over four weeks, close to a record speed according to Dan Carroll:

> There's proof that plans were well laid before they started the actual production. All locations had been selected in advance, and all details of working arranged, so that only two days have been lost since filming commenced. And even that loss was due to wet weather.[29]

Once again Baker's part was mainly a matter of stunts. 'But', *Picture Show* added, 'Snowy Baker, the actor, is improving. His smile may be rather frequent, but it happens to be a pleasant one, and gives the picture a certain cheerfulness'.[30] Baker had again played the role of a genteel 'new chum' coming out to his country property in Australia incognito, to subsequently impress his station hands with physical skills that his appearance and accent belie, and finally to rescue the station manager's daughter from city vice and corruption. The trade press was again impressed with 'a dark-eyed girl with a gift of expression; a young actress who promises to go far'. On this occasion it was not Berenice Vere, whose part as the city vamp gave her 'little chance to show what she can do', but Kathleen Key, who had recently been brought back from America by Lucas to make her one Australian appearance as a pure country maiden oppressed by city thieves led by Arthur Tauchert.

Apart from the acting and 'conspicuously good' photography, the trade press was, as usual, impressed with Lucas's 'realism'. A real cabbage-tree hat had been acquired after an 'Australia-wide' search and was to be used in yet another Bess Meredyth flashback to incorporate pioneer days. 'A kangaroo hunt, complete in every detail' was shot after extensive planning and preparation of miles of road for the car-borne cameras. 'The achievement,' claimed *Picture Show*, 'ranks high in Australian photoplay-making

"Bai Jove! Perfectly Topping!"

"Course, ya' know, you priceless old bean, 'twas a little wuff t' start with on that bally old station—but I conquered 'em! Why I handed out a positively ripping hiding to half a dozen or so. Oh, I had a delaitful time for a while, and I gave those perfectly charmin' blighters something to show their maters!"

"The Jackeroo of Coolabong"

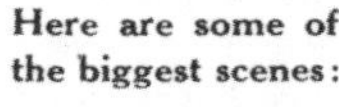

Here are some of the biggest scenes:

A whirlwind kangaroo drive right up into the camera lenses, with dozens of 'roos and hundreds of stockmen in full flight.

A death encounter with wild aboriginals and their amazing Devil Dance.

A 60ft. dive into the harbour — a fight for liberty in Sydney's underworld.

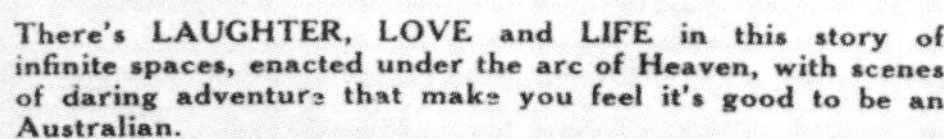

There's LAUGHTER, LOVE and LIFE in this story of infinite spaces, enacted under the arc of Heaven, with scenes of daring adventure that make you feel it's good to be an Australian.

AND IT'S LABELLED "MADE IN AUSTRALIA."

Presented with an All-Star Cast, including Snowy Baker, Kathleen Key, Bernice Vere, Arthur Tauchert and Arthur Greenaway.

Written and Directed by BESS MEREDYTH and WILFRED LUCAS.

World's Exhibiting Rights Controlled by

E. J. CARROLL, The Banking House, SYDNEY

And at MELBOURNE, BRISBANE and WELLINGTON, N.Z.

Picture Show 1 November 1920, p.44

effort'. It also cost the life of a young Narrabri woman who fell from her horse during the kangaroo chase, *Everyones* commenting rather disappointedly that, 'the cameraman did not, as stated in an evening paper catch the full details of the incident', since in his shock he forgot to turn the camera.[31] The costs of this spectacular cameo were offset by the use of Palmerston and the scenic resources of its gardens.

Once again the Lucas–Baker–Meredyth team had tried to play both ends against the middle in terms of local and international appeal. *Picture Show* said that 'in the parts dealing with the bush, *The Jackaroo of Coolabong* has the really Australian flavour which all Australians must love. The city events are not stamped with any nationality in particular, and the picture therefore has something more than a domestic value. It should appeal elsewhere as well as here.'[32]

The attempt failed. The film was released by Union Theatres in Sydney in October under the banner: 'Kangaroo hunts! High dives! Wild blacks! and a bit of Sydney's underworld'. But long before that, on 11 August, *Everyones* coolly announced the shock information that, 'Wilfred Lucas, who produced the *Lightning Ridge* picture for E.J. Carroll, returns to America very soon. Snowy Baker goes also'. Three weeks later *Picture Show* announced the end of their Baker dream with the news that the Carrolls had terminated the engagement of Lucas, Meredyth and their staff, and would keep the Palmerston studio going with Raymond Longford in charge. Stoically, the magazine remarked, 'Of course, this latest move is something of a setback to the film producing business here. Still, the Carroll firm has done its best to give the industry a firm footing, and will do more, but in another way. The experiment of using Americans with moving picture knowledge may not have succeeded, but the company will still make entirely Australian films.'[33]

What went wrong so suddenly? It was only a few days before the termination of their contracts that Dan Carroll had enthusiastically announced the highly successful work of Lucas and Baker on *Jackaroo*, that E.J. Carroll had telegraphed from England with news of the successful exploitation of the films in Britain and South Africa, and that copies of the two earlier films had been received in the United States.

Since all three films were in fact sold in America, a 100 per cent record not matched by any other Australian producer, presumably the reception there, which Dan Carroll was waiting for news of, cannot have been the cause of the sudden change of policy. *Picture Show* explained that:

> the Australian firm found American methods of production too expensive, considering the results. A local picture would have to be superlative to be acceptable anywhere else, and at present there isn't enough capital in the film business here to allow makers to compete with the American companies, to whom a £50,000 expenditure for one picture is not remarkable.[34]

Picture Show's editorial for the same issue criticised the 'unwarranted extravagance' of a system in which 'the man with anything at all to sell which the studio wants, gains his share of the goldmine by charging an exorbitant price', and the 'producer . . . seldom having to use his own money, troubles little over economy, and the bills reach formidable size'.

In her film compilation, *The Passionate Industry*, Joan Long argues that money *was* made on the films in the United States, but that the American company handling them cheated the Carrolls out of a small fortune — a fact not discovered until much later, when it was too late. Yet the Carroll's decision seems to have been made when the films had only just reached America, and certainly before there was time for real negotiations to have taken place.

At the 1927 Royal Commission Longford spoke of pressure on the Carrolls, as Queensland exhibitors, from distributors who felt threatened by Australian production, and the director Vaughan Marshall related the rumour that Snowy Baker was 'taken over' by American interests because he was producing Australian films. Conspiracy theorists might make something of the return of E.J. Carroll to Australia with the man who Longford said had done most to suppress Australian production, Harry Musgrove. Musgrove, who had been general manager of Australasian Films and Union Theatres until he resigned in 1920, returned from America with news of two 'big new projects'. One was a plan for a new Carroll–Musgrove theatre 'to equal anything in New York'. Regarding the second, Musgrove announced that he would set up as a distributor, opening an exchange for First National, which he did as an independent until Head Office squeezed him out. During his time with First National, Musgrove acquired a lease over the Tivoli Theatre chain, which he intended 'to make . . . first release houses for First National productions'. *Picture Show* reported in 1921 that 'the theatres will open under the control of First National Exhibitors on 26 March', and *Everyones*, referring to the Sydney Tivoli as 'a First National Theatre', added, 'First National considers itself fortunate in securing a string of metropolitan theatres throughout Australia which will enable it quite early in the piece to carry out its ambitious programme'.[35] In other words, it appears to be the case that First National executives, who at that time were dreaming of an enormous merger in the United States between production, exhibition and distribution facilities, were close to that position common in England, but virtually unknown in Australia, whereby their exhibition outlets would be directly under their own control. Musgrove, as their representative in Australia, with an interest in two Australian exhibiting chains, may have had the influence, had he so wished, to persuade the Carrolls to halt what was regarded as the more competitive part of their production enterprise, leaving Longford to work only for the local market.

But that is speculation. A less conspiratorial view might be that the Carrolls, thinking they were about to launch into a major building project with Musgrove, decided to cut back on their expensive American experts. The independent exhibitor W.J. Howe was later to say that the Lucas films failed at the Australian box office, and the Carrolls said they lost £25,000 on the venture.

On the other hand there may have been a positive pull from America. It was just at this time that the larger Hollywood production companies were beginning to move away from the single-star policy and towards attracting new production staff and actors in order to cut costs. Interestingly enough, First National was foremost among those companies which were 'leaving no stone unturned in their efforts to uncover new talent'.[36] Perhaps, via the First National–Musgrove–Carroll–Lucas link, one of those stones was an Australian one. Or perhaps the Lucas team, with very recent information on Hollywood, simply followed their earlier policy of looking for greener pastures. If this was their dream, little came of it except for Bess Meredyth, who became one of the highest paid scenarists in Hollywood, with major successes like *Ben Hur* and *The Hunchback of Notre Dame*, and Bert Glennon, who became head cameraman at the Lassky Studios and later a director at F.B.O. Little of consequence came of a much-heralded contract between Baker and the Selig studios, where he was presumably hoping to repeat the success enjoyed by Tom Mix. Baker did little feature film work before or after the three films completed for Goldstone Productions in 1923.[37]

Whatever the causes, the reaction to the failure of the Baker project exemplified the twists and turns the trade made to justify what had already happened. *Picture Show*, in a more chastened mood than a year earlier, had this to say:

> It seems that at present the only safe methods for making Australian films are those employed by Raymond Longford for Carroll's, and by Beaumont Smith, who works independently. Their idea is to produce pictures with a strong appeal to Australians rather than a vague general appeal. Their

> mode of working is economical, and even if their productions don't take the world by storm, the success of those films is assured here, and the financial returns more than cover the original outlay.[38]

However, the future for Longford and Smith was by no means assured, nor was the American invasion anything like over.

Lawson Harris and Yvonne Pavis

In 1922 another American producer–scenarist–actress team began Australian production. Lawson Harris had spent some years with various Hollywood studios before coming to Australia with Arthur Shirley as production manager for *The Throwback*. The task of selecting his cast for the film made him realise the expensive problem producers had in Australia, coaching totally inexperienced actors and actresses. Nearly all the applicants for parts were

> absolutely raw material. They knew nothing whatever about make-up, less than nothing about acting. We had to set out and teach them from the very beginning. In America the artists have the rough corners knocked off, as 'extras', long before they are given parts. In Australia, production is so limited that there is little opportunity for that sort of thing.[39]

In response to this problem Harris had set up a screen acting academy in May 1921 with Vera Ramée.[40] The idea was to run it as a school which coached in camera make-up, deportment and screen acting and also to be a bureau similar to the American employment exchanges from which Australian producers could select the 'types' they needed. Harris's businesslike vigour, combined with his recognition of the need to learn from American methods, reminded the trade of Snowy Baker and marked him for special support from the beginning.

A number of bogus acting schools had already been started which promised aspirants screen careers but simply took their money. The trade press was to use the example of these schools as an excuse throughout the 1920s to oppose the idea of Australian quota legislation. It argued that the 'artificial' stimulus to production of such legislation would encourage more fly-by-night companies, seducing more investors into losing their money and it was this kind of thing, rather than anything systematically wrong with the industry—such as block-booking, which scared off local capital. *Picture Show*, however, distinguished Harris's venture from these others, and so began a trade support for Lawson Harris which continued through all his productions.

In February 1922, Harris expanded his ambitions into film production. He brought to Australia Yvonne Pavis who had eleven years experience as a leading actress, assistant director and scenario editor with a number of studios in Hollywood, including Triangle, Universal and Fox. A new company, the Yvonne Pavis Productions Syndicate was formed, backed by a number of respectable Sydney businessmen. This was a time when some American exhibitors were forecasting an input of non-American films to offset the decline in cinema attendances in the United States and pull the American producer 'out of the fatal rut he has got into'.[41] The Harris-Pavis films are interesting in that they were all made on low budgets during a period of slump, and yet, because of the rumoured openings in the United States, were all aimed at an international market.

Under these uncertain conditions, production plans at the beginning were necessarily tentative, and the producers made their first film, *Circumstance*, 'more in the nature of seeing what could be done in this country without having to go to undue expense to find out'.[42] Shot quickly and cheaply in Sydney, it was a 'drama — not of the bush, or its outlaws', which would have required expensive location work, 'but of society' with Pavis playing 'one its outcasts who lives to prove that even the worst of her sex — may love'.

This production proved such 'a happy augury for future efforts' that, immediately *Circumstance* was edited, the small company went straight into its first location shooting fifty miles from Mudgee. This was an ambitious undertaking, considering that the most established Australian producer, Beaumont Smith, very seldom selected his locations beyond the foot of the Blue Mountains. The trade responded favourably to Harris's 'spirit and ambition'. *Picture Show*, noting that *Circumstance* had been snapped up for first release by the Haymarket theatre, said it was 'good drama, well acted', and showed careful production which 'speaks volumes for the good work of this team and promises well for future films which they intend turning out here'.[43] *Everyones'* response was remarkable, since it accorded this unknown American director, whose first film had not even been released, the privilege of its leading article on 24 May 1922, and, even more unusual for an Australian film, Yvonne Pavis in *Circumstance* was featured on the front cover the following week.

The interview with Harris stressed the support he had obtained from local investors, and his opinion that with the excellent light and scenery, adaptable technicians, the good fortune to have a world-class cinematographer in Arthur Higgins, the consistent acting of his small cast, and above all with the all-round skills in acting, writing and continuity of s.w. ... VARIETY AND SHOW WORLD

Producer of Austral Super Films

Mr. LAWSON HARRIS.

LY recent
hores is Mr.
an astute
nection with
charming
from the
been res-
fances," a
ve its Aus-
Haymarket
reek.
engaging
ith a very
he film in-
s, has had
in the Los
elsewhere,
as brought
purpose of
a worth-

Mr. Har-
known as
of which
and pro-
el of the
des some
ness men,
nthusiastic
film pro-
every be-
industry.
l, tempor-
Sydney,
e business
e will be
y.
thusiastic
arris, and
of motion
stralia, is
that with
and most
ountry of-
s for the
now op-
ctures of
ecessarily
lian sub-

r. Harris

ed at the
Our in-
e to be-
ll follow,

fine manner—and you will bear me out after witnessing the picture. They are all secured in this country, with the exception of Miss Pavis, who plays lead.

"Miss Pavis, by the way, was brought out from America to fea-

In further course of conversation, it was gleaned that Mr. Harris was already busy on the second of a number of local productions. The story is entirely different in character to 'Circumstances,'

M
offe
urba
ord
have
trali
abro
sure
co-o
hibit
sam
C
view
very
sista
class
out
are
polic
who
powe
tion
Pr
not,
the s
the
biliti
with
posal
Mr.
that
how
tures

IF
W

Everyones 24 May 1922, p.3

Unusually prominent publicity: part of an *Everyones* leading article on Lawson Harris and a cover for Yvonne Pavis the following week.

HOYT'S DE LUXE, GEORGE ST.——Sydney's Leading Cinema House.

EVERYONES

With Which is Incorporated VARIETY and the Australian Show World

Vol 3 No. 117 SYDNEY, MAY 31, 1922 Price Threepence

(Registered at the General Post Office, Sydney, for Transmission by Post as a Newspaper.)

YVONNE PAVIS

Featured in

"CIRCUMSTANCE"

Opening at the Haymarket, Sydney, Next Saturday, JUNE 3rd.

Everyones 31 May 1922, cover

Pavis, he had solved Australian production problems and made 'worthwhile pictures at a moderate outlay'. *Everyones* pointed to optimism and harmony in every direction. Harris and Pavis would 'offer exceptional facilities to suburban and country showmen' and would gain 'the hearty cooperation of any number of exhibitors' in return. Goodwill towards Harris seemed universal, and, contrary to the recent experiences of Franklyn Barrett and Harry Southwell, extended to the police and officialdom. Harris thanked them for doing 'everything in their power to make the initial production an artistic success'.

This honeymoon image of love and consensus was built up further in the trade press the following month. Reports were released that exhibitors were rushing to this Australian film 'just as in the good old days', following its triumphant premiere at the Haymarket where Pavis found herself 'bowing to the most consistent thunder of applause' she had ever received. At the same time, the stall for Pavis–Harris Austral Super Films at the Kinema Trades Exhibition was 'patronised more than any other in the exhibition'. Australia's showmen were said to be laying out the welcome mat in a big way for the new American film-makers, while in return Pavis and Harris were promising to do their utmost 'to make Australia the film-producing centre of the future'.[44]

Compliments flowed — Pavis praised Harris who, she said, 'has the knack of getting everybody to work their darndest without seeming to care whether they do or not'; she praised sales manager Cecil Hargraves for 'keen judgement' and the ability to place *Circumstance* 'in the State's finest theatres', and applauded Arthur Higgins for his fine camerawork. Harris described Pavis's all-round competence as essential to the success of the production company: *Everyones* described in detail the 'amazingly busy' daily timetable of this 'streak of chain-lightning' star, who divided her time between Haymarket stage appearances, film-making and her stall at the Kinema Trades Exhibition. *Picture Show*, beneath production details of her next film, added, 'Woman, made from the rib of Adam, is yet the backbone of the motion picture industry'.

The peak of this optimism was reached during the shooting of their second film, *A Daughter of Australia*. Pavis, who had again written the scenario and continuity with Harris, said she hoped to become a permanent resident of Australia and 'turn out many pictures which will please the Australian public and picture lovers in other parts of the world too'.[45] The trade press released photographs of the company showing 'typical' incidents such as sheep dipping 'to interest picturegoers in other countries besides Australia'. Harris argued that the country section of the film would

(i)

BOOK THIS RECORD-BREAKER!

The first Australian picture to be screened at the Haymarket Theatre, Sydney. Now playing in the best theatres in the State—and leaving a line of broken records in its wake.

GET YOUR DATE RIGHT NOW!

He Stared Down Into the Beautiful Face of the Strange Girl-Creature, an inert heap in his powerful Arms—and—wondered!

Just imagine his position. A reckless man-about-town suddenly in possession of a beautiful girl whom he had never seen before.

Just imagine her's. A destitute outcast fighting bravely to live in happiness—and held down by society's barrier—and the scornful glances of such men as he.

MISS YVONNE PAVIS

IN

"CIRCUMSTANCE"

A drama—not of the bush—or its outlaws—but of society and one of its outcasts who lives to prove that even the worst of her sex—may love.

"There's so much good in the worst of us,
And so much bad in the best of us,

THE BEST AUSTRALIAN PICTURE YET.

FILM MAKING IN THE BUSH

(ii)

(i) *Everyones* 26 July 1923, p. 20; (ii) *Picture Show*, July 1922, p.41

Yvonne Pavis in *Circumstance*
(ii) Life on an Australian 'ranch': shooting *A Daughter of Australia* near Mudgee

not, 'as in the past, be neglected, but will therefore be more appreciated by overseas audiences, who have no idea what life on an Australian 'ranch' means'.[46] *Everyones* advised exhibitors that the films were a good investment, and that *A Daughter of Australia*, which was almost finished a month after first production, was going to be 'something special'.

Meanwhile it was announced that all Austral Super Films, which until then had been under the name of Yvonne Pavis Productions, would henceforth be called Lawson Harris Productions. This would 'give the pictures the hallmark of quality'. Despite this implied slight, the trade press still deferred to Pavis who was thought to have brains as well as being a 'dainty little woman'. Ambrose Adagio of *Picture Show* went to interview her and report, in his usual manner, that her eyes were 'brown and sparkling with life and enthusiasm'. To his surprise, however, he found no 'ornamental cushions and heavy perfumes', but a star 'dressed in trim business clothes' sitting behind a 'desk covered with papers that obviously weren't just camouflage'. Pavis told him she supervised much of the business side of the productions.

> It gave me a new respect for a girl I had admired on the screen. However much the feminists may stand up and assail me, I must say that in the limits of my experience brains and beauty have so seldom gone together.[47]

This combination of 'brains and beauty' was presumably deemed sufficient qualification for an American star who had been in Australia only a few months to play the country's most representative heroine in *A Daughter of Australia* — the independent bush woman. Pavis was billed in the film as 'a daring Australian girlie who preferred to stay on her own land and 'do big things', rather than laze away her life in luxury'. Harris said he was making 'credible stories that audiences here want'. But despite the emphasis both by Harris and in the trade press that the significance of his productions lay in cheap programme pictures produced quickly and with low overheads, *A Daughter of Australia* was *advertised* as a 'gigantic photoplay, gorgeously mounted, lavishly produced', and 'the picture with the most elaborate settings and scenic effects ever used in an Australian production'.

As with the second Baker–Lucas production, there was an attempt to appeal to an international market with extensive locations: 'a thrilling drama of the bush and its wonders — of society and its glamour — of England and its life — and of love and its joys and sorrows'. *Everyones* announced that the 'typical' country scenes should make a special appeal to city dwellers, whilst it will be of extraordinary interest to overseas audiences'.[48] The characters were, supposedly, equally cosmopolitan, with Lawson Harris playing an upper-class English fugitive from justice who comes to Australia where he finds that brains and brawn rather than refined blood are what is required to win his true Australian country girl, since she scorns upper-class city luxuries. Dorothy Hawtree, a young Australian beauty contest winner, played a French maid in the film, and Gilbert Emery followed up his *Ginger Mick* role as the young Englishman's tough outback mate.

By October, after a four-week run at the Apollo Theatre, *A Daughter of Australia* was being billed as 'the first Australian production to be given a long run in a first release Sydney theatre'. The third film, *Sunshine Sally*, was almost complete and the honeymoon with the trade continued. *Picture Show* declared that 'Mr Harris and Miss Pavis are working along the only lines where success is possible in Australian production. They are using stories with everyday Australian appeal, and are not burdening themselves with heavy overhead expenses'.[49]

Sunshine Sally

The story of *Sunshine Sally*, originally entitled 'Winnie from Woolloomooloo', had been writen by the Australian stage actor, John Cosgrove some time before, and had nearly been made into a film by Beaumont Smith in May, 1921. Cosgrove clearly had himself in mind when writing the story for both this film and *Silks and Saddles* (produced in 1921 by Jack Wells), since in each he played a major role as a comic, heart-of-gold fat man who loves the young heroine, but on losing her finds decent solace in something else — food in *Silks and Saddles*, drink in *Sunshine Sally*.

Pavis, like Lottie Lyell, was by now becoming more interested in production than in acting and was hoping to head her own company in the new year. She was acutely aware of production difficulties on modest budgets. Since the players were not on contracts, Cosgrove had to be borrowed from the theatre where he was playing evening performances in *Cairo* before coming to the film studio. This meant late night shooting under very inadequate lighting, an experience which determined Pavis to go to America to obtain a modern studio set-up as soon as possible.

Pavis argued that *Sunshine Sally*, 'a story of both slum and society life', would be entirely different from the earlier films and would rely heavily on Australian slang. 'We don't want any of our productions to be alike'.[50] In fact, the Harris–Pavis productions all operated on a single picaresque theme in which the apparent social breach between hero and heroine is eventually resolved when the less adequate of the pair is found to have

National Film Archive

(iii)

National Film Archive

Frame enlargements from *Sunshine Sally:* (i) and (ii) Architectural balance, Woolloomooloo as scenic location; (iii) Yvonne Pavis in her preferred gamine role had the right social qualities all along. But this happens only after a variety of adventures and settings which illuminate different social worlds and prove in the protagonists a worth beyond their breeding. The stories tended to be regarded at the time as 'not particularly strong or very original' but 'pleasing', and Higgins' photography was always noted. We can see from their one surviving film, *Sunshine Sally*, that the blend of Arthur Higgins' camerawork and the architectural training of Lawson Harris as director created an outstanding scenic location — a *picture* rather than an interpretation of Woolloomooloo — for Yvonne Pavis to insert the 'gamine' role she clearly favoured.

In January 1923 Pavis left for America with her films which, in *Everyones'* hopeful opinion, should 'still further enhance the prospects of this country in the eyes of picture producers and capitalists who may have designs on Australia'.[51] On January 24 *Everyones* also announced that Austral Super Films, having recently been re-capitalised with backing from several new influential Sydney businessmen, were

> so pleased with the success of the pictures that they decided to go into film production on a large scale. They are opening their own studios here, and are sending Mr Harris to the United States in order to purchase camera lights and other accessories.

Before leaving, Harris bought a scenario for a ten-reeler called *Yellow* from Hal Carleton, who was then advertising manager for the Haymarket Theatres, and it was announced that the next film would be 'a South Seas picture', to be made at Melville Island (off Darwin) which belonged to one of the directors of the company.[52] It was also announced that Arthur Higgins had been permanently retained for future Lawson Harris Productions.

At the end of January, *Everyones* was arguing that 'those who know the business' were expecting to see Lawson Harris 'one day accepted as the pioneer of movie picture-making in Australia', adding that it was to be hoped that Pavis and Harris 'will not be persuaded to stop in America, for Australia can ill-afford to spare men and women who have the knowledge and experience of the motion picture industry like these'.[53] At the beginning of February, *Picture Show* was also impressed by the huge expansion plans announced for Austral Super Films:

> It has always been the opinion of *Picture Show* that Yvonne Pavis and Lawson Harris were working along the right lines in the films they have made here . . . "I do not claim that our pictures have been world-beaters, by any means", Mr Harris told *Picture Show*. "Our capital was limited, and we knew that

> the films would have to be produced economically or not at all . . . Since these have been successful, we are now being given the opportunity to produce bigger things. We shall have more to spend upon each picture, and will have a better chance of making first-rate stuff'.[54]

Once again things looked good for an Australian production company headed by Americans. Austral Super Films had more money, a new studio planned, the latest equipment, and an extraordinarily friendly trade. *Sunshine Sally* was going the rounds of Sydney and Melbourne advertised by J.C. Williamson Theatres as 'An Australian picture we genuinely recommend', and was described by *Everyones* as 'photographically one of the best advertisements that Australia has yet secured on the screen'.[55]

But Pavis and Harris did not return to Australia, and Austral Super Films was forgotten. The Longford theory was that whenever Australian producers began to make big production plans, the industry closed in and squeezed them out — and it is a piquant fact of these years that, apart from Longford, Baker, Lucas and Meredyth, Pavis and Harris, Arthur Shirley and Beaumont Smith all ended their Australian film-making immediately after announcing plans for expanding production. But there is absolutely no evidence in the Harris–Pavis case to support Longford's rather simplistic theory, and not much in any of the others. Another explanation could be derived from a tiny news item that appeared in *Everyones* in 1925, announcing a divorce granted to Pavis against Harris in the Supreme Court. The story stated that Pavis had married Harris three years before. However:

> Twenty days later Harris is alleged to have told the bride that she hindered him in his work — and then he deserted her . . . It was brought out that on their honeymoon trip the wife admitted to Harris that she was eight years older than he. His love is alleged to have cooled and all she got from him, so her testimony went, was 'cigarette money' and a few trips to the picture shows.[56]

Harris was certainly an unpredictably fiery character: in August 1922, he had been taken to court by Arthur Shirley for sending through the post a letter threatening to give the latter 'the thrashing you deserve' for 'molesting me in the public streets of this town'; and his male chauvinism in relation to Pavis had been indicated at about the same time in the change of title of the production company. So Pavis's story could have been true — and she did win her case. They were in fact married in America and separated at the beginning of 1923. That would account for the end of their business relationship, but does not explain why the ambitious Harris did not go on with production plans in Australia with a new star.

The core of the explanation is probably neither a matter of monopoly conspiracies nor of private personality feuds. At the Royal Commission of 1927, their business manager, Cecil Hargraves, said that of the three films 'the first made a profit, the second made neither profit nor loss, and the third made a slight profit, but the overhead expenses and the time wasted waiting for release settled the production'.[57] Hargraves did not accuse Union Theatres of strangling the company as Longford did for his own failures. He argued that exhibitors were more than willing to screen the films, but often at low prices and only after a long wait because of fully-booked programmes.[58] Meanwhile, overheads mounted up.

Against Hargraves's position is the trade argument that, without studios, a permanent company and regular studio staff, overheads were low, and that in fact none of the first release dates were especially delayed. However, it is the case that for *Sunshine Sally*, which ran in Sydney in December, and in Melbourne in February, state rights were still for sale five months after the completion of the film. The independent distributor, John McGeorge, said that only one of the films was ever released in Queensland, that *Sunshine Sally* only got two screenings in Tasmania, and

> was released by Paramount in Melbourne, but only at the daytime sessions, and got very little hirings in the country. It obtained that release in Melbourne because, so I understand, the sales manager used the big stick on Mr Thring, and said that if he did not show it after having put on some German pictures he would expose him in *Smith's Weekly*.

Although it was good box office and gained spontaneous applause ('something unknown in that theatre'), the Exchange manager called *Sunshine Sally* 'the worst of the lot'. 'That', said McGeorge, 'is their method of killing Australian pictures'.[59]

McGeorge also said that he had offered *A Daughter of Australia* to Paramount, Australasian Films and the Birch, Carroll and Coyle circuit in Queensland, but in each case was told that they were fully booked up. The 'manager for the Haymarket Theatre declared that those pictures were up to standard, but because of the treatment they received, the company went out of existence'. However, at least some of these efforts by McGeorge were made long after the company had folded. The issues at the time may have been broader. It is more than likely that the £25,000 in £1 shares that the new company floated was not adequately subscribed, and the amount in any case not sufficient for the ambitious future production plans of the company. This was a time of acute slump in the cinema industry. Beaumont Smith's report from England in January 1923 made it clear that there was little hope of selling the films there, nor were they sold in America, despite Pavis's confidence. As to the situation in Australasia, the New Zealand entrepreneur, Henry Hayward, was given the lead article in *Everyones* in February 1923 to say 'at the present time, there is something radically wrong with the movies'. The main cause of the slump, he argued, was the overproduction of films. Following the self-interested lead of American exhibitors, he wanted to get rid of the double feature, which he admitted would make things cheaper for the exhibitor, but would also end the system which 'brings the dudest duds into our programmes as supports' and 'destroys the appetite of the public for pictures'.

Without a double feature programme, Australian films, which found it difficult enough to get bookings, would have had no chance at all. The films produced by Austral Super had always been sold as *support* features. So this prominent article by a major exhibitor in the leading trade journal, just at the moment that the company was bent on considerable expansion, can have done Austral Super Films no good at all in their search for potential investors.

There is another way to look at the rise and fall of the Pavis–Harris enterprise. These were years of mounting pressure in Australia against the power of the American and Australian combines, which were said to be strangling Australian production. The unusual publicity given to Harris and Pavis in *Everyones* in May 1922 needs to be set against otherwise almost total silence, broken only by small notes (in the very same issue of the journal) which spoke of the desperate struggles of Longford to continue production and the final failure of Franklyn Barrett. Harris and Pavis were by no means the last producers who, whatever the quality of their work, were used by the trade to draw attention away from issues that it did not particularly want to see or speak about. It is certainly not a coincidence that the first line of the review of *Sunshine Sally* should place the film in the context of Australian quotas which 'sooner or later' were 'inevitable'. Nor was it a coincidence that an article in *Picture Show* in January 1923 (when their film-making career was in effect over) should, with an explicit reference to the success of Austral Super Films, once again use the old issue of fake film companies ruining the image of Australian films to sidetrack attention away from exhibitors and distributors who were hostile to local production.

This was arguably a period when the trade was backing cheap local films (such as Beaumont Smith's) which could be absorbed as supports without too much threat to the status quo, even if the feared Australian quota should materialise. *Picture Show* had consistently repeated the remarks it made after the failure of Snowy Baker for Lawson Harris — the need it saw was for cheap films which could cover their production costs locally. About *this* kind of film the trade could afford to be exuberant. And stripped of all this fanfare perhaps the failure of such very cheap and quickly produced films is less surprising.

Harry Southwell

In contrast, one of the directors *least* favoured by the trade was Harry Southwell, a Welshman who had come to Australia in the optimistic year of 1919 after five years in Hollywood making the O'Henry films for Vitagraph. His unpopularity with the Australian (but not English) trade took two forms: he was either ignored, or he was given unfavourable production coverage at a time when trade papers seldom criticised.

Picture Show, for example, said of *The Kelly Gang* in 1920:

> It is rather a pity that Mr Southwell chose the exploits of notorious bushrangers as the subject of his first Australian film. A criminal record can only have a limited appeal as entertainment . . . The producer's experience and ability would have been better seen through a different medium.[60]

Southwell's next release was in fact different: a society film — but the trade press was even more hostile. Whereas *The Kelly Gang* had at least been praised for its good acting and make-up, *The Hordern Mystery* was described as a weak film 'lamentably reminiscent of the poor acting and jumbled plots of pictures in days long gone by'.[61] As Southwell's career as a silent film-maker in Australia continued, constant trade criticism became customary — of his films, of his backers, even of where he shot and which cameramen were used.

To start with, and for a very short time, things had been different. The Hollywood aura was sufficient to gain Southwell the only reasonably extensive coverage he was ever to get in the trade press, running to two pages of *Picture Show* for *The Kelly Gang*. At this point, for the only time, there was optimism in the trade about Southwell who was hoping to produce four films a year in New South Wales, using local actors and a studio measuring 200' by 250' which he intended to build near Lane Cove in Sydney in order to have access to water. *Picture Show* was impressed with these grand plans, and by his criticism of fraudulent picture schools. Southwell said that he had encountered trouble on location with actors who had 'taken lessons in the least reputable of photoplay schools' and who had to be retrained. In view of criticism of old-fashioned and mannered acting in his films, it is ironic that Southwell complained that the men and women who came to him for parts overacted and that he then chose those 'with little knowledge of acting — not those who are *slave* to acting . . . whose every gesture is studied and theatrical and . . . hopeless for the camera'.[62] His other principle of selection was to find 'the best types', and this again led him on occasion to reject experienced players for those who were less well-known but who looked the part. This was how a Hollywood producer was *expected* to talk — adhering to American methods, criticising the primitiveness of the local production industry — and the trade press liked him for it.

Southwell's plans were ambitious and patriotic. Commenting on the fact that Australians knew more about America than their own land as a result of the flooding of their screens with Hollywood movies, he said he would make films which were authentically Australian in script, theme and location as

> a link in the chain of national propaganda. Wherever the scenes are supposed to be laid there will the Southwell players and cameramen actually be . . . We intend to depict Australian life as it was, and as it is, according to the particular story filmed.

But Australian life 'as it is' did not appeal to the people who had most power to be articulate either within the film industry or outside it. In October 1922, the New South Wales Chief Secretary reported in the Legislative Assembly that he had decided to ban *The Kelly Gang* which was 'particularly objectionable at the present time when the police force was put to its utmost endeavours to deal with crime that was unusually prevalent. He would not permit the police to be held up to ridicule'.[63] The trade press was not surprised or angry, but expressed sympathy for 'this most considerate actor-manager' as he had just completed a new and more expensive version, *When The Kellys Were Out*, and it seemed that Southwell's company would be, after all, one of those which lost investors all their money.

However, Southwell eliminated some sequences, added others which emphasised the courage of the conscientious troopers, and incorporated such inter-titles as: 'The inevitable fate of all those who wantonly rebel against the righteous and mighty forces of law and order' to accompany the capture and death of Kelly. Today it seems like a parody, but it was probably seriously intended. Even this, however, did not hide the earlier emphasis of the film, which was on the 'consummate daring' of the Kelly Gang — the tricking of the police by Kelly's sister, their superiority over the Jerilderie police, both in fooling them so easily and in their considerate behaviour ('lock 'em up — but be decent'), in contrast to which the police appeared rough. Despite the fact that the film passed the censorship outside N.S.W. and began its long career in suburban and country theatres, the trade was most concerned when it was announced that it was going to be released in England in 1924. Southwell was by then in London, having failed in his ambitious Australian venture, and *Everyones* remarked,

> It is to be hoped, for the sake of the Australian industry, that the English people will not take his production as an example of the standard of art so far as it applies to the movies in Australia.[64]

This was quite remarkably different from what the journal had said when Yvonne Pavis had taken her films to America to sell, and, ironically, whereas the Pavis films made no impact, Southwell's was a success. The English trade press gave the film excellent reviews, praising the scenario and continuity which 'very wisely refrained from introducing any extraneous love matter or sob stuff', and called the photography and acting 'excellent'. 'They are perfect types, unhampered by make-up or anything artificial.'

Southwell's film was handled in England by the Australian producer and entrepreneur, A.C.Tinsdale who intended to release £40,000 worth of Australian films throughout Britain. Despite disagreements with the producers, Tinsdale's extensive newspaper publicity about the film and the Kelly legend augmented the initial success of *When the Kellys Were Out*, with the result that Southwell found it much easier to raise money in England than Australia for film-making. In 1924 he made a joint English–Belgian (Australian Famous Players) production, *David*, on location in Palestine.[65] This film also gained the support of the British trade press, *Kinematograph Weekly* answering *Everyones* fears by saying that, 'from a producing point of view . . . Australia appears to be coming forward and entering the business earnestly'.[66] Another British–Belgian co-production, *The Bells*, followed in 1925, based on the play Henry Irving made famous. Southwell followed his Australian policy of shooting the scenes in the locations of the original story, and was again praised by the British trade press for a film that 'will rank high among the super productions of the year'.[67]

Three successful films in Britain gave Southwell both the confidence that he could now produce Australian films for the British market *and* the backing of a major British distribution company, W&F.[68] At this time W&F were having trouble getting production advances against the returns of previous films which had been heavily delayed because of block booking. As a result they were doing a number of deals with German firms whereby W&F distributed films made with foreign money by such notable producers as Hitchcock and Balcon. It was essentially just such a deal which W&F made with Southwell, who had to raise production costs in Australia, while the British distributors handled the costs of the trade screening and of subsequent advertising. W&F had also supplied the production unit for Balcon and Hitchcock in Germany, but for Southwell they proposed an attractive alternative: a deposit of £3,000 against each production within seven days of arrival in London, and an equal division of the profits.

This would, of course, have mitigated the worst effect of block-booking — the slow return of money — and would have given Southwell the chance of maintaining continuous production. With W&F soon to be swallowed up by Gaumont, and Gaumont in turn by Fox after the British quota came in, there is no doubt that Southwell's Australian films would have gained regular British screenings, if only as quota films.

Southwell arrived back in Australia in February 1926 with a contract to supply W&F with up to six films, 'Australian in history, sentiment, scenery and type' within two years, and optimistically talked of starting 'a steady flow of Western Australian productions overseas'. The Australian trade press immediately criticised this location, since all the adequate studio facilities were in the Eastern states. Perhaps there was a link with A.C. Tinsdale who had established a small studio in Perth some years before. Southwell himself said he chose Western Australia because the light and clarity of air was superior there; and probably his proposed series of films on themes written around forestry, mining and pearling would not have required much studio work. Whatever the reason, a production company, Anglo–Australian Films Ltd was set up on local capital, and Lacey Percival and Cliff Thomas, cameramen with considerable Australian and Hollywood experience between them, joined Southwell. Production was begun on *Greater Love Hath No Man* in July 1926 with a local Perth cast. As *Down Under* it was reported to be near completion in November and little more was heard of it until January 1927 when a debate began in the Perth papers over the merits of Southwell's film.

The editor of *Film Weekly* took the opportunity to carp. He grudgingly reserved his opinion until he had actually seen the film, remarking that 'as a purely West Australian production, it is a pity that local cameramen were passed over in favour of others from the Eastern states'.[69] Earlier, of course, the criticism had been that Southwell had passed over the facilities of the East for those of West Australia!

Westralia Film Productions

Down Under was not well received in Australia, and had its first English screening some months before it opened in Perth. No money was forthcoming for further production and the deal with W&F lapsed. Two years later, among the rash of companies that hoped to cash in on the proposed Australian quota, Southwell issued a prospectus for Westralia Film Productions with a capital of £10,000 in ten shilling shares, 1,000 of which were issued to the 'preliminary syndicate', 10,000 'held in reserve for future issue' and 9,000 offered to the public. From this very limited sum of money, Southwell hoped to produce *Modern Chariots*, based on the forthcoming trotting championships. Though there had already been a number of horse-race films, the most recent of which had been Arthur Higgins's 'quota' film, *Odds On,* there had been little on trotting. The idea was one of sufficient novelty-within-convention to have normally appealed to the trade. With Southwell behind the idea it did not. *Everyones* wished the venture well, but said it would have to be a lot better than *Down Under,* that Southwell could not successfully be 'producer . . . actor, story writer, scenario writer, and several other things at the same time', and was dubious about a 'directorate that consisted of a trotting-horse owner and driver, a butcher and a doctor who knew nothing about film production'.[70] Why this directorate should have been any less able to finance adequate film production than the usual businessmen, accountants, squatters and Jockey Club stewards, the journal did not say. *Film Weekly* said that the intention to set up a booming industry in Western Australia was nice, the climate was fine, but that was all the company had going for it since the last weak effort 'made with local talent under Mr Southwell's direction, seems to have disappeared into the unknown'.[71] And that, indeed, was also the fate of *Modern Chariots* and Westralia Film Productions.

The Australian trade's hostility to Southwell is not easy to explain, given the normal reaction to Hollywood directors. Certainly the acting was often stagey, and the scenario and continuity for all the Kelly Gang films he made (including the sound version) were unimaginatively repetitive. Yet he was certainly far more skilful stylistically than other producers of cheap Australian films — for example George Palmer, whom *Film Weekly* constantly encouraged. In both the silent Kelly Gang films, despite a lot of indifferent work, there are good contrasts in light, shade and texture, and some interesting set-ups and framing. The first Kelly film also contains the one really innovative sequence in any of Southwell's surviving work. In it, the final terror and death of Sherrit is conveyed by vivid chiarascuro,

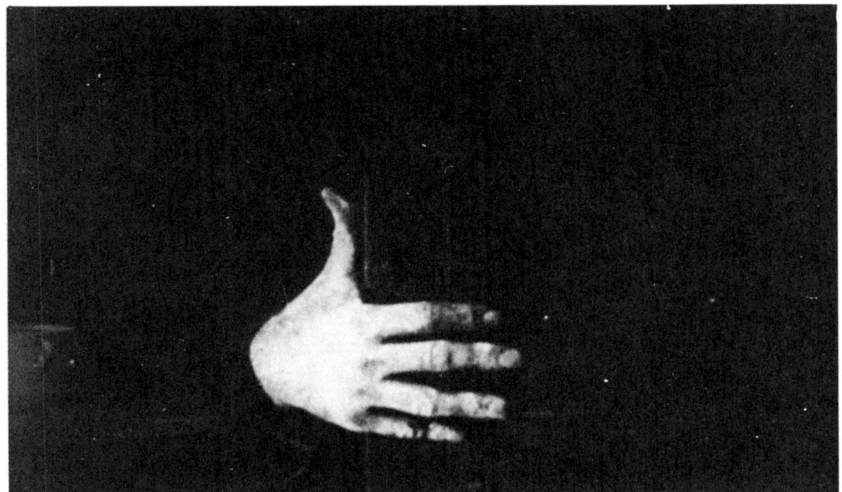

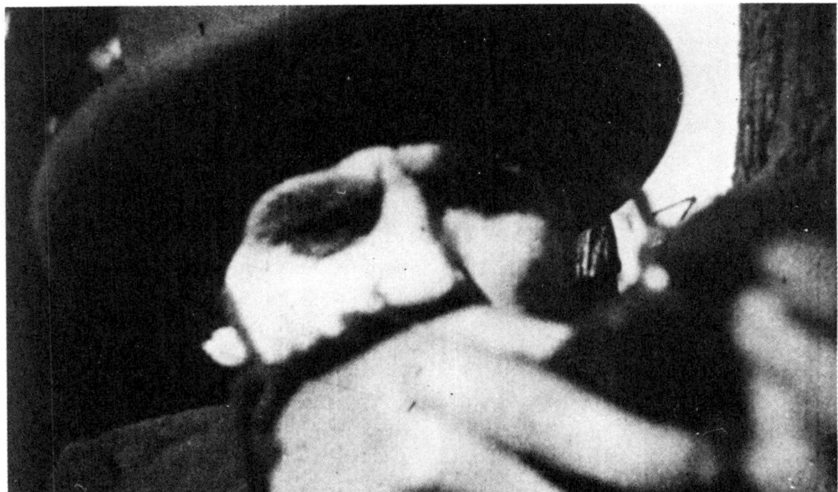

National Film Archive

The death of Sherrit: frame enlargements from *The Kelly Gang* the victim's hand lingering terrified on the door he has just passed through, and by the rapid intercutting of the frightened man's face with extreme close-ups of the gang's rifle barrels and of Ned's eyes and hat-brim over his rifle hand. Southwell's repeated motif, used in all his films — the wretched being who has betrayed his family and is 'tortured between remorse and lust for gold' — might also have been expected to appeal to the conservative values of a trade press which criticised him for undermining the best traditions.

Southwell's dabbling with small 'mushroom' production companies certainly displeased the trade press, which made no secret of its preference for big organisations such as Australasian Films rather than for those 'public companies floated for production purposes'. But the trade press carped even when Southwell had the apparently sound backing of the weighty W&F. The real reason for the hostility lay in the fact that an American-trained producer, who was *expected* to castigate the primitive quality of local production, should turn to what was regarded as the most primitive aspect of local matter and make it his special theme.

Ironically, it was Southwell's identification with the most Australian of themes — bushranging — which gained him opprobium. In November 1923 when Southwell's second Kelly film was booking in country districts, Paramount's house journal, *The Exhibitor*, quoted with approval an appeal by the editor of the Geelong *Advertiser* for an epic film which would do for this country what *The Covered Wagon* had done for the United States.

> 'One thinks . . . of a great screen epic built up round the days of the goldfields, with not too much about the Eureka stockade, and with no portrayal of bushrangers, save as the scoundrels they were.

It was to be fervently hoped, the editorial continued, that films of bushrangers, urban 'push' land and selectors would never 'be sent abroad to be taken as typical of this country's dramatic conception'. What *should* be shown was the epic of the pioneers who, before the days of government aid, were 'self-reliant', and began 'their advance into an unknown continent to lay the foundations of this country as a home for white people . . . only two generations ago'.[72]

The conservative nature of the editorial needs no special emphasis. What *does* require comment is the fact that this kind of opinion was widely held at the time. It was not only conservative newspaper editors or imperialist politicians like Senator Guthrie who were worried about Australia's image abroad in this context, but also film-makers such as Raymond Longford[73] and the editors of powerful film trade journals. *Everyones* criticised the 'earlier screen atrocities of this country' which 'dealt largely with the daring exploits of bushrangers and belittled that much admired body, the Police Force'. Now, Southwell was returning to the days of these film 'atrocities', and *Everyones* criticised him specifically as one of 'those who are seeking to make capital out of the drab and sordid days of Australia'.[74]

Everyones made its broadly economic reason for this hostilility to films of convicts and bushrangers clear. It believed that even though no other country 'has gone ahead in such a brief time as Australia', the Southwell films were threatening immigration and investment by presenting an unfavourably rough image of Australia.

But there was another economic reason, much closer to the film trade, and no doubt more important. In October 1923, the same month as the Geelong *Advertiser* editorial, W.A. Gibson of Australasian Films pointed out that crude bushranging stories kept the decent class of patron away from the cinemas. 'While films of this description may appeal to certain audiences, they would not meet with a favourable reception in the better-class picture theatre. By this I mean that among the more cultured section of the community the presentation of such films will be resented'.[75] When Gibson argued that 'In my early experience any old hall was considered good enough for pictures' whereas 'today the public expects, and rightly, the same comfort in a picture theatre as is provided in . . . the ordinary theatre',[76] he was in fact referring to two different publics. By the mid 1920s, the Australian cinema circuits with their lavish theatre-building programmes, more tasteful' advertising[77] and more 'respectable' films were looking to the affluent middle class to buy their more expensive seats.

Like *Everyones,* Gibson boasted of the huge and rapid strides in Australian civilised development, but he brought the argument home to the pocket of the trade itself. Southwell belonged, in the trade estimation, to an era which should have been superseded — the period of cinema pioneers when Gibson himself had been involved with the first bushranging film. In contrast, now was the time of cinema tsars, with Gibson and Doyle the powerful and wealthy heads of Australasian Films and Union Theatres Ltd. It was quite acceptable for visitors from Hollywood to consign current Australian *production* to the crudities of those not so far off days; but it was less than acceptable to devalue the pretensions and aspirations of the current leaders of exhibition and distribution. Southwell's mistake was to confuse the days of Gibson the film pioneer with the current reality of Gibson the cinema mogul.

(i)

(ii)

Picture Show 1 May 1920, pp.57,58

Attracting the 'discriminating patrons': A 1920 design for building a new Union Picture Theatre 'on a magnificent scale': 'Comfortable divans and writing tables . . . refreshment tables served by hidden soda fountains. Window boxes filled with flowering plants and a running fountain with tiny lily pond . . . private boxes fitted with telephones, bells for attention, radiators and foot-warmers for the cold nights and iced water and fans during the summer. All the seats . . . made on the same principle as the seats of the highest-priced motor cars . . . the big sign outside will rival even the pretentious ones of Broadway.'

Pointing the Way to Pictorial Perfection!

¶ She follows the symbol because she knows what it stands for—quality, plus perfect presentation, and environment.

¶ The girl who points the way to the ultimate in motion-picture projection is typical of the vast and ever-growing army of discriminating patrons

¶ This film epicurean knows from experience that the UNION THEATRE SIGN symbolises all that is honest and worth while in the realm of the magic shadow shapes.

¶ You're going to learn, too, because there'll be a UNION THEATRE everywhere!

UNION THEATRES ALL-AUSTRALIAN CIRCUIT:

Sydney, Melbourne, Brisbane, Adelaide, Perth, Tasmania, and throughout the Commonwealth, India, Java, Singapore, Japan and China.

Managing Directors: EDWIN GEACH, W. A. GIBSON, STUART F. DOYLE.

Union Theatres advertisement

Picture Show 1 January 1921, p.50

(i)

Page Twelve. EVERYONES. December 10, 1930.

Please, Mr. Policeman, May I Make a Movie?

For "Everyones" by Franklyn Barrett.

One of the pioneers of Australian film production, Franklyn Barrett, in this special story for "Everyones," tells the official obstacles that were put in the path of early film-makers. And even now these have not been removed.

Franklyn Barrett

Although the sentiment of all Governments will be behind any revival in Australian production, so far there has been no relaxation of regulations that hampered past efforts. How soon can producers expect official support?

AS one of the pioneers of picture production in Australia, I am greatly interested in the proposed production schemes of F. W. Thring. I sincerely hope that he will be successful and that Australian talkies will take their place on the screens of the world.

That there is such a place is proved in the words of Mr. Chas. Urban uttered some years ago in London.

I DID contributory work for the Chas. Urban Trading Co., in those days; and, in saying good-bye to me, he concluded with: "Why don't you make pictures in Australia? It is a land teeming with romance. The South Sea bubble is English history. Send us your pictures. We

was that disaster did not crush the Australian squatter: that Australia quickly reacted when

sequence of opium smuggling. Edwin Geach arranged that I meet the Inspector of Water Police with the idea of getting some authentic incidents that could be incorporated in the picture. I spent a very interesting and profitable hour listening to the many ruses and tricks that had been discovered by the guardians of our waterfront.

Plain Clothes Only.

Mr. Inspector closed the interview with: "I hope, Mr Barrett, that you are not contemplating asking for the co-operation of the Water Police, for we cannot help you in any way."

I assured him that we should use actors right throughout the picture. His final words were: "I must warn you that you must confine your work to plainclothes officers, for we do not allow police uniforms to be used either on the stage or in pictures."

(ii)

Mocking the weary wayfarer
with its empty promises
came the elusive Mirage.

His many years of work within the cinema trade seem to have given Barrett greater access to the mouthpieces of the trade than other directors — though only after his film-making career was safely over. Note that though Barrett's articles usually carried an anti-American-monopoly sting in the tail, the overt presentation attacked the trade's enemy — officialdom.
(ii) Natural mirages as metaphor for the spiritual drought of the city

(i) *Everyones* 10 December 1930, p. 12; (ii) National Film Archive

3

The Scent of Gum Leaves and Wattle: Franklyn Barrett

As an innovator on the broader front of cinema, Franklyn Barrett has a greater claim to pioneering status than Raymond Longford. He was the oldest Australian producer of the 1920s, and had behind him experience in the cinema business as theatre musician and conductor, dark-room assistant, cameraman, exhibitor, buyer, projectionist, director and producer. His career had begun in 1898 with the Warwick Trading Company; with them he had helped produce the second only public exhibition of films in London. Later, he had toured the whole of New Zealand with two programmes of films as a travelling exhibitor, had made 'scenics' for the Pathé company throughout Australia, New Zealand and the Pacific Islands, and for a while worked in outback Australia as projectionist for John Lemmone's 'circus', travelling on top of a four-in-hand coach with his projector and gas bag strapped on behind. Other early associates were the Pugliese family, who had added films to their waxworks show and Robert Thorne Haines, who had invented an early version of the 'talkie' as well as a 'kinemacolour' process.[1] As a cameraman one of the innovations of which Barrett was most proud was his work on the Melbourne Cup, which he filmed each year for over twenty years. In 1912 he became the first to film the whole race for the West's studio, by using a long-focus lens.

Towards the end of The Great War, Barrett introduced Snowy Baker to the screen in *The Enemy Within* and *The Lure of the Bush*. The latter film sufficiently impressed Bland Holt with Barrett's attention to detail, and ability to capture the Australian bush on film, as no one else had done, for the theatre manager to break his long standing rule of not selling the film rights to his successful stage version of *The Breaking of the Drought*. Barrett was joined by Jack North, a journalist who had won the Bulletin prize for his 'Lure of the Bush' scenario, and John Faulkner, the English actor and 'heavy' star of several Australian productions. Like Faulkner, several Sydney businessmen, prompted by C.F. Pugliese, were sufficiently encouraged by the very recent success of Longford's *The Sentimental Bloke* to sink money into the new syndicate, which was known as Golden Wattle Films. Faulkner declared the usual platitudes of the period about Australia having 'all the essentials necessary for success: scenery, light, surroundings, talent and ability'. But he also, like *Picture Show*, hoped that the tie-up of the Anzac tradition with pioneering Australian production would ensure success:

> Here in Australia we have a distinct type of manhood. That fact has already been proved to the world during the war. We have also a distinct Australian atmosphere peculiar to the country, which is capable of being transferred to the screen. Take, for instance, Franklyn Barrett's photography in *The Lure of the Bush*. He gets there; it is Australia; one can almost smell the gums and the wattleblossom . . .Even the peculiar colouring of the soil is there.[2]

Barrett has always been acknowledged as a brilliant bush photographer, but until recently he has received scant recognition as probably Australia's most significant silent film-maker after Longford. He was also, bar none and including Longford, the most clear-sighted of all Australian producers concerning the systematic nature of the economic forces exploiting them.

As a film-maker Barrett is particularly interesting for his two surviving 'bush' films, *The Breaking of the Drought* and *A Girl of the Bush*, not simply for the quality of the photography, but also for the attitude to film conventions that it engendered. Bland Holt's play had already attempted with its sensational bush fire a blending of naturalism and melodrama. Barrett, who always chose his own locations, added considerably to the naturalism by seeking out fearful drought conditions at Narrabri in New South Wales. Before filming started, he wrote an article for *Picture Show*, 'The Real Breaking of the Drought', which made his 'realist' intentions as a film-maker quite clear. He had seen starving sheep feeding on the young leaves of scrub, the bush tracks a foot under billowing sand, the feed cart scattering corn on the sun-baked earth for the desperate animals, and the carcasses everywhere: 'the eyes . . . picked out by the ever present crow which does its cruel work while the victims are yet alive, but too weak to guard themselves'.[3] These, almost to the detail, were the images he put into his film. As *Picture Show* pointed out at the time, Barrett captured the drought poignantly and graphically: 'the opening views of the regions that suffered from the rain shortage are remarkable. Here are great stretches of dusty earth instead of green paddocks; baked clay riverbeds instead of flowing streams. Sheep that are living skeletons rush the trees that are

(i), (ii) *Picture Show* 1 April 1920, p.27

Chiaroscuro and melodrama: John Faulkner and Marie La Varre in *The Breaking of the Drought*

National Film Archive

Marie La Varre: frame enlargement from *The Breaking of the Drought* the only Australian feature film to be refused export permission under the provision. Fortunately for Barrett the state censorship authority passed the film for local viewing, despite federal pressure not to do so.

Regulations of this kind are, of course, all too frequent in the history of cinema, and all too easily criticised. What has to be remembered is the social and economic philosophy of the period which brought about the regulation. The debate which raged during the 1920s about fostering British Imperial sentiment was firmly premised on the profound Australian fear of the 'vacuum' of the outback, protected only by the British navy from invasion by yellow hordes spilling down from Asia. The conventionally easy and often facile association of the bush and Anzac legends helped motivate one solution to fill the vacuum: the scheme of placing returned soldiers on the land was begun. But this alone could never be enough. Private and public bodies (including *Picture Show*) supported schemes to make the parched inner lands blossom, mainly by the large-scale importation of British migrants. The most forceful exponent of these schemes was the former New South Wales Premier and current Nationalist leader in the Legislative Assembly, Sir Joseph Carruthers. By the early 1920s he had elicited the help of the cinema trade in his propaganda work. As the subject of a lead article in *Everyones* he spoke of his fear of the world's eyes resting

> on the inherent weakness arising from our sparse settlement of a vast continent within a few day's sail of the most crowded population of the East . . . I adopted the slogan of 'A Million Farms For A Million Farmers'. That slogan stands for the filling up of our empty spaces with men of the British breed, so as to have a really white Australia — safe for all time against all danger of foreign invasion or conquest . . . To my mind the picture theatre presented exactly the form of appeal that would teach the people. My good friend, William Howe, was an enthusiastic supporter of the 'Million Farms' slogan, and when I discussed the matter with him, I found exactly the lieutenant I needed. Together we planned a campaign, plotted the class of films we required, and got to work to secure them, and then prepared slides, and the text to illuminate and convey to the audience exactly what the slogan and the policy meant . . . Mr S. Doyle presented me with a fine film specially prepared by him, showing Australia in its virgin state, in its rising tide of prosperity and dramatising what a foreign invasion meant to our cities and to our countryside.[12]

Carruthers' connection with Longford's two *bêtes noires*, W.J. Howe and Stuart Doyle is interesting, but not surprising given the common meeting point of their beliefs in 'what a great country Australia really is, what can be done with its lands, and how it can be transformed from a wilderness into smiling farms, and prosperous homes'.[13] But it does indicate the potent forces, both within the cinema trade and outside it, which Barrett was offending with a film that was deemed to threaten prospective immigration by emphasising the harsh conditions of the interior. Longford, who had earlier made a film about the invasion of Australia by Asian forces (which had been shot and written by Barrett!), was himself not impressed, and later went on to produce propaganda films for the Commonwealth government to attract British immigrants.

Nobody seems to have noticed Barrett's use of the drought as a metaphor for that traditional Australian belief in the *spiritual* drought of the cities, nor the irony of a city official returning to the metropolis intent upon blighting this film about country strength and purity. The banning of the export of the film was a big blow to the hopes of the Golden Wattle Company, considering the great British success of *The Sentimental Bloke*. And it was a special blow to Barrett who had always intended his films for an iternational market, using the novelty of 'virgin Australian material in our sheep and cattle stations, our coal fields, goldfields, and canefields, and in our bush life generally'.[14]

Fortunately for Barrett, Doyle and Union Theatres clearly did not consider drought films as big an insult to Australian civilisation as bushranging ones, since they gave *The Breaking of the Drought* a Sydney release. It was sufficiently successful for Barrett to immediately plan his next film, *A Girl of the Bush*, as 'the first of Barrett's Australian Productions'. As usual, Barrett chose the locations at Bathurst, Warren and Cowra himself, and this time received a lot of support from local officials, through the intervention of his good friend Charlie Jones, secretary of the Federated Picture Showmen's Association. Barrett spoke highly of the help he received from the deputy town clerk at Bathurst and from local squatters who lent their properties and facilities during the busy shearing time. The trade press noted with satisfaction that the 'shearers themselves play the small parts in these scenes, as the local residents do in others, thus ensuring correct types'.[15]

As leading lady Barrett chose Vera James, who was later to have a minor Hollywood career. Although advertised by Barrett as perfect for the station-running heroine of the film because she was 'a good horsewoman and swimmer', James later said that far from being the classical country type, she could neither ride nor swim, took her first riding lessons in a city suit, turbanned hat with a quill and very high heeled shoes, and that her only screen parts had been in 'society' roles for P.J. Ramster. The male lead,

Jack Martin was supposedly also a great horseman, while most of the rest of the cast were veterans of the stage, including Stella Southern who had already starred in Beaumont Smith's *The Man From Snowy River*.

Girl of the Bush was completed within two months but had to wait for four months before being released by Union Theatres in April 1921. In fact, it opened earlier in New Zealand, where Vera James' father had the film rights, and in Brisbane. In both places it was said to have 'broken screen attendance records'. The trade press was reasonably impressed, though less with the plot than with the 'lifelike' features which made it 'a faithful picture of bush life without burlesque'. 'When you are seeing a mob of cattle being mustered into the yards by a gang of yelling horsemen, you are not watching something which is merely acted. The scene is a real one out West, and Barrett saw to it that he and his camera were on hand at the right time'. Despite her 'city' affiliations, Vera James clearly passed *Picture Show*'s test of the correct 'type': 'a living, human creature, who is expert at branding, at mustering, at doing a thousand other station jobs . . . She is Fairbanksian in her athletic skill, and her personality simply radiates good-fellowship from the screen. If we are to possess screen stars here in the future, Miss James should be close to the top.'[16]

This eulogy displayed a confusion of conventions and types, American and Australian, which Barrett clearly shared. During the shooting of *The Breaking of the Drought*, Barrett had re-affirmed his attitude to Australian production. 'What's the use of making an Australian production if it has nothing to show that it is one? . . . If it is not possible to make interesting motion stories of our own land, then we'll give up the ghost'.[17] Despite this, his next film was to be based in Sydney, and despite his opinion that Australian films should not try to compete with the sumptuous sets and huge casts of Hollywood, he announced that this film would 'call for the employment of hundreds of supers and the expenditure of more money than has ever been given to the production of a single picture here'.[18]

As it turned out Barrett seems to have dropped the ambitious winter sports sequences planned for Kosciusko, and most of the film was shot in the cramped sets at the Rushcutters Bay studio. Casting became a problem: Stella Southern, saying there was not sufficient employment in film acting, announced her return to the stage; and Wendy Osborne withdrew from the film 'because the story offended her moral senses'. In her place Barrett began the career to notoriety of Lotus Thompson.

In what the trade press called 'probably the first sociological drama ever made in this country',[19] Barrett was in fact breaking new ground, since a major character in the film called for an Act of Parliament to allow the birth of an illegitimate child to constitute a common law marriage between the parents, and to allow the child to legally take the name of its father and be his heir. These progressive sentiments proved too advanced for police censorship, which held the film up for several months. However, *Know Thy Child* received the State Governor's approval in September and was released to good reviews in October 1921. *Picture Show* commented: 'Here is the drama of an unmarried mother and the man who does not know his own child when he meets her later in life. The story is told well and its strength compensates for occasional crudeness in scenery and photography'[20], a reversal of its opinion about his bush films which were praised for their camerawork rather than story or continuity. *Everyones* praised Barrett's continuity, handling of actors, exceptional care for detail, and control of a 'somewhat melodramatic' narrative which, it noted, had already been made into films in other countries. However, 'the Barrett film will come out favourably with the best that has been done here, and will also give overseas producers a very definite idea that there are other subjects, besides Australian, that they will have to fight from this time onwards'.[21] *Know Thy Child*, with its unusual social comment and as a radical departure from everything Barrett both earlier and later said he wanted to make, represents one of the enigmas of the Australian silent period. Since no prints are known to exist, it is also one of the more serious losses. It seems to have been popular with exhibitors, running in the suburbs into the first months of 1922 and gaining release in most Australian states.

Barrett met censorship problems whether he made films about the bush or the city, and he seems to have decided to play safe with his next film, *A Rough Passage*, by choosing a sporting theme. But apart from noting that the cast contained Gilbert Emery, Stella Southern, Elsa Granger and the well-known English screen actor, Hayford Hobbs (who also co-produced), the trade press had nothing to say about *A Rough Passage*, which was to be Barrett's last film. It had minimal release after opening in Sydney in July 1922. Long before that, in May 1922, *Everyones* announced that Barrett had vacated his offices in Pitt Street, unable to afford the overheads. The journal was sympathetic, but pointed out that his mistake was in trying to do too much in the production of his films. It is true that Barrett did a great deal, normally choosing locations, adapting the working scenario, superintending the interior sets, choosing the properties and doing all the camera work, in addition to the basic production work and much of the directing. But he worked in this way only because he did not have the money to do it any other way. As he pointed out in relation to one of his many tasks, 'An Australian with a knowledge of Australia (as separate

National Film Archive

'First sociological drama': *Know Thy Child*

from knowledge of one State only, or perhaps one city), who knows what is wanted and where to look for it, can save his salary ten times over on transport and location'.[22] *Everyones* admitted that in terms of access to capital 'the lot of the Australian producer is a very unenviable one', but argued, as the trade press always did, that the answer was to produce films of a quality equal to the overseas standard. 'Australian pictures have lost a good deal of their sentimental value. Those subjects considered typically local and worthwhile have been utilised, until now the producer has to look for material that will be of general appeal'.[23] It is possible that Barrett's sudden change of direction after *Girl of the Bush* was an attempt to look for material of 'general appeal'. But, for all its paternalistic wisdom, the trade press knew no better than anyone else what that 'general appeal' should comprise, and Barrett was quite aware that what had been 'lost' was not local sentiment but the Australian market.

Barrett's experience in the 1920s as an exhibitor in Canberra, his time with United Artists, Australasian Films, Paramount, and later Hoyts, after he stopped film-making, together with his early pioneering experience, brought him much closer to the trade than other producers like Longford; certainly closer than the parliamentarians and pressure groups who fulminated against the 'American combine' that was stifling Australian production. Barrett's time on the road for Paramount taught him that there was (as the American distributors always claimed) intense competition between individual companies. As a result he could honestly say to the Royal Commission that 'there is really no combine in Australia.' But there was something else.

Producers' Advocate

One of the lesser-known features of Franklyn Barrett's career is the calm and steady pressure he exerted through the 1920s on behalf of Australian producers by pointing out again and again the *systematic* nature of American exploitation. Sometimes he raised the issue at producers' deputations to State and Federal ministers, but generally he took a less flamboyant line than Longford or Shirley and made his protests shrewdly through the trade papers themselves. In return they gave Barrett much more space to make his replies than to the others. One has only to see the trade papers' distortion of producers' arguments at deputations to realise what an advantage this direct access to the trade was to Barrett.

The American distributors' case, which Barrett opposed, had some variations according to the exact position within the industry of whoever

Exhibitor 24 March 1926, p.11

The Barrett camerawork the trade did want: In 1926 Franklyn Barrett as Paramount Exploiteer takes photographs of Queensland cinemas and arranges a procession of 'Red Indian Motor Cycle Riders' to promote *The Vanishing Race.*

was putting forward the argument, but essentially it was based on two principles:

1. We live in an open market system which depends on the free forces of supply and demand. In this situation of the 'survival of the fittest', the best films find a market. The United States produces the best films and so dominates the market. Any other country could do the same, provided that it is prepared to compete with the United States, particularly in spending money on production and on distribution facilities. The argument of Australian producers that their films cannot get a screening because of an American combine which unfairly controls the market is (a) maliciously incorrect because there is an intensely open market in which the American companies compete with each other and have no financial interests in, or shareholder control of, the large Australian theatre circuits; and is (b) merely the gripe of incompetents who want to float mushroom companies to create inferior productions, thereby fleecing the public both as investors and as tax payers contributing to any government subsidy to local production. Any government 'interference' which tried to protect the local production industry with quotas and other means would simply give more leverage to these mediocre producers to lure further money from gullible investors in third rate ventures; and would have the additional disadvantage of bankrupting local exhibitors who would be forced to screen films that the public would not pay to see.

2. We live in a huge country where, because of difficulties of communication, exhibitors demand long-term contracts to secure their investment in theatres. Their need is for an assured continuity of supply in a situation where they are unable or unwilling to come to the city exchanges to choose for themselves. Hence there has arisen in Australia the system of block booking (of a complete supply of films for up to twelve months ahead) and blind booking (of films they have not seen, and in many cases have not even been made). Far from being invidious, this is good business practice, and exhibitors can rely on the reputation of distributors and on whatever advance publicity they are able to give. If they do not like it, they can always, in an open market, go elsewhere; and therefore any distributor who does not regularly deliver 'the goods' will not survive. The system of block and blind booking is not to ensure adequate production finance for the future films of American production companies. Indeed the system is not in the interests of American companies at all, but rather benefits the Australian exhibitors. Evidence of this fact is that whenever the distributors try to end or modify the system, as Paramount did in the

mid-1920s, it has to be re-instated because of the exhibitors' pressure. The arguments of Australian producers that block and blind booking prevents the screening of their films is just an excuse to hide their own incompetence. Few exhibitors book up 100 per cent, there is always room for 'floaters', and country showmen tend not to screen every evening, so that Australian producers only have to pursuade them to open on another night, which they would willingly do if the film was good enough. Even when exhibitors *say* they are unable to take an Australian film because they are fully booked up, this is only an excuse to prevent having to tell the producer how bad his film is.

These were the arguments,endlessly repeated, that Franklyn Barrett and other Australian producers had to face. His answer usually began with an economic explanation of the historical evolution of the block-booking system that was rather more accurate than the geographical determinism of the Americans' argument.

> In pre-war days each exchange, all Australian-owned, had its buyer in London selecting only those pictures suitable for Australia and only in sufficient quantities to cover the needs of their exhibitor-customers. There was no such thing as a contract. Exhibitors booked their programmes where they liked. Under these conditions an Australian picture was welcome and received a lot of support. At a cost of £1,000, an Australian picture could show a profit in its own market . . . After the Great War started the American houses became dissatisfied with the Australian returns and gradually established their own branches here. Equally gradually the Australian-owned exchanges were compelled to drop out. Under the original scheme the buyers rejected about 60 per cent of the market offerings as unsuitable for Australia. Under the new scheme the contract system was introduced, and each American branch imported the full 100 per cent output of the head office, resolutely denying that any of their pictures could possibly be unsuitable for anywhere. The contract system forced upon the exhibitor the 60 per cent of rejects that would never have come to Australia under the old system. The audiences soon demonstrated that the old buyer was right, so to cover himself the exhibitor had to enter into still another contract in order that, by having two programmes booked for one night, he might be able to get one good programme for his patrons . . . From this period onward Australian pictures even at £1,000 began to be an unprofitable speculation. Attempts were made to improve the Australian film by spending lots of money on them with the hope of sales abroad making up the difference. Unfortunately the same contract system has been introduced almost everywhere and our little pictures cannot even push in.[24]

(i)

(i) *Everyones'* report of the 1925 Australian Picture Producers' request for a quota is overshadowed by proprietor-editor Archer Whitford's own scheme for advancing Australia by way of the cinema screen: the 'so-called American propaganda and Hollywood *kultur* said to be degrading our youths into star-spangled banner advocates' would be offset by displaying the Australian flag on the screen at the end of every performance.
(ii) Ironically, but presumably unintentionally, the trade displays itself as a bunch of puppets in the hands of American distribution in this Australian Exhibitors' presentation to Stan Crick, Australasian manager of Fox Film Corporation prior to his departure for America.

Everyones (i) 11 February 1925, p.77; (ii) 9 April 1924, p.7

Because of the huge home market in which they were able to recover their production costs, American films could be 'dumped' in Australia at prices lower than local producers could afford. So, as Barrett well knew, Australian films suffered two disadvantages in the eyes of the local exhibitor. They tended to be more expensive, and to put them on he normally had to take an American one off while still having to pay hire charges on it. Often the Australian producer would have to 'carry on his back' the cost of the replaced American film before the exhibitor would consent to screening his film.

Further, the dependence on the goodwill of the exhibitor illustrated the *ad hoc* nature of the business Australian producers had to conduct compared with the *systematic* advantages of American films. All the argument which distributors put forward about exhibitors keeping free nights and so on was equally *ad hoc,* leaving openings for Australian productions only in the interstices of the exhibition system, and depending either on individual exhibitors being in the right frame of mind or on a film's superior qualities, such as those of *The Sentimental Bloke*. In contrast, *all* American films, bad and good, were released because of the contract system. Barrett's estimation that 60 per cent of all U.S. films would not sell but for the block-booking system may have been much too high, but the fact is that even exhibitors who were hostile to the Australian producers' arguments often admitted to the Royal Commission that 15 to 20 per cent of American films were useless. Many of these were 'quickies', shot with a borrowed star in a few days for very little money — and yet they were guaranteed a release.

The argument that exhibitors did leave room for 'floaters' and 'specials' also missed the point since, firstly, many exhibitors did not, and Australian films needed the *whole* market to have a chance of a profit; secondly, in the case of those that did, this was to force Australian releases to compete with American super-productions, since it was these that distributors tended to release as 'floaters' and 'specials' outside the block-booking contract — and there were more and more of these 'floating' around to fill whatever spaces were left open. Under this system, a £10,000 Australian feature would have to compete with American films which had cost hundreds of thousands of dollars. Few *American* standard programme features could have withstood this kind of competition. As Frank Thring was to say later:

> Every producing company must expect to make a proportion of films that will not prove outstandingly popular with the public. Yet Australian producing companies are expected to make only box-office attractions. Anything else will be given such low terms that it will be impossible to get

> back half the cost of production. American producers, on the other hand, are guaranteed satisfactory returns for the whole of their product, with special terms for outstanding box-office attractions. It is obviously impossible for the home-made product to compete with that of America, even in its home market, unless legislation is introduced that will overcome these disabilities.[25]

With his years of experience as a senior executive of both Hoyts and Union Theatres, Thring knew exactly what he was talking about. But he had never spoken out in the 1920s, and only said it when he did, in 1933, because he was now producing Australian films himself after being shaken out of Hoyts by the Fox takeover. Barrett *had* been saying these things for years. The main aim of the producers' deputations during the 1920s was for government legislation to secure a reasonable proportion of the home market via a quota system. Barrett could do nothing about the overseas market which was equally dominated by block-booking, and was forced to speculate as to what kinds of film would be most likely to sell abroad. As discussed earlier his initial hopes of gaining a market abroad through the novelty value of presenting Australia 'like it was' ran into quite different opposition and had to be abandoned.

While Longford was helplessly embroiling the Royal Commission in his conspiracy theory, Barrett was pointing out to it the real issues that faced most Australian producers:

> The difficulty with which the Australian producer is faced is not so much the making of a picture as the handling of it. Distributing houses can very well afford to send out representatives to make contracts for 52 weeks, but, as an Australian picture represents only a portion of a programme, the overhead charge in connection with its distribution must necessarily be high. It would be better, I think, to enact a law providing that distributing houses should put out 5 per cent of Australian pictures; provided, of course, that they were up to standard.

The concern by both Barrett and Longford for *quality* control by a government-appointed board was at once a measure of their own confidence in their film-making abilities, an answer to opponents who said that proposed quotas were no more than smoke screens for incompetents, *and* an indication of their anxiety not to alienate their direct paymasters. Raymond Longford's son, Victor, stressed at the Royal Commission how anxious his father was 'to conciliate the distributing authorities', and the scheme Longford proposed at the Commission certainly went out of its way to appeal to them. His proposal was unique in suggesting that rather than

(ii)

Everyones (i) 13 December 1933, p.11; (ii) 12 December 1934, pp.18,19

(i)Syd Nicholls' cartoon supporting Frank Thring's assertion that American companies were thwarting or fooling Australian preference legislation and retaining a stranglehold on the local industry
(ii) *Everyones'* cartoon attacking the idea of Australian quota legislation as opening the way to 'mushroom companies fleecing the public'

forcing distributors into a quota, a more permissive scheme might work better. The American companies, he argued, should be given back the many thousands of dollars they paid the government each year on import tariffs and required to pay out only a portion of this to subsidise Australian production. Barrett was equally keen to conciliate, but his feelings were far more in favour of the exhibitors. He had, after all, been an exhibitor, and would be again. He knew that many of them lived a precarious existence, as trapped in the Hollywood-dominated system as he was, and therefore opposed all solutions which would increase their costs.

Franklyn Barrett was a modest man and, unlike Longford, was not prepared to make global comments on 'the operation of all economic laws'. He refused each attempt by the Royal Commission to lead him into broader theory with the repeated remark: 'I cannot speak about industries in general. I am a picture man'. But the years of experience as a 'picture man' gave Barrett a shrewdness in debate often lacking in his colleagues. Two examples will make the point. In 1925 a producers' deputation requesting an Australian quota from the Minister of Customs, Pratten, was abused in every quarter of the cinema trade. The trade press accused it of 'superfluous hot air' and both the Motion Picture Distributors' Association and W.J. Howe, for the exhibitors, chastised the deputation for trying to force inferior pictures on cinemas. Barrett's reply was typical of him in spotlighting the consensus-making manipulation his opponents were involved in. 'No suggestion was made by the deputation that theatre owners should be compelled to show 15 per cent of British and Australian pictures on their programmes. Referring to the representative of the M.P.D.A. he said:

> That is Mr Connell's own interpretation, specially broadcast to antagonise the exhibitors. The references to the exhibitor buying 'the class of pictures his experience and his invested capital demands' is also calculated at once to flatter, by the word 'experience', and to antagonise, by the mention of 'invested capital'. I note that Mr W.J. Howe, president of the Federated Picture Showmen's Association, has risen to Mr Connell's bait. The Australian producers hasten to assure Mr Howe, they are just as anxious as he is that unskilled producers shall not be allowed to make pictures for the sake of the subsidy . . . If the exhibitor would turn his ears away from the foreign importers' reiteration that his films are 'the world's best pictures', and listen to the comments of numerous disgusted patrons, tired of the continual hackneyed American themes, he would conclude that his 'invested capital' is in no wise endangered by introducing a little British sentiment, preferably of the Australian variety'.[26]

A month later, an exhibitor representing a West Australian showmen's association returned to the attack by supporting the 'reasonable and lenient' attitude of distributors when unexpected films cropped up. 'In many cases I have been permitted to pick up the discarded programme at my own convenience, and in some cases have been allowed to pass it altogether, and have not been charged'.[27] Barrett replied: 'Mr Appleby discloses the weakness of his association when he states that he has been 'permitted to pick up the discarded programme . . . and . . . been allowed to pass it altogether . . .' The use of the words 'permitted' and 'allowed' proves our claim that the exhibitor has very little choice in the programmes screened at his theatre, and that the foreign distributor controls the industry'.[28] As Barrett was well aware, no combine *needed* to exist, in the strict sense of the term, for that control to continue. All that was required was the relatively automatic working of an economic system (which today we would call media imperialism). On the one hand, as long as potential investors knew that Australian films could not obtain adequate screenings they would hold on to their money and there could be no hope of the *continuous* production needed to challenge the American control. On the other hand there was the MPDA, which the distributors were correct in insisting was not a combine but was, by their own admission, a 'trade protective' organisation designed to protect them against adverse legislation. The Association's task was to watch over the 'open market' system and keep it in its 'natural' state whenever threatened by 'artificial' government regulation.

4

'The Subject of Attack': Raymond Longford

It is worthwhile tracing the outlines of Raymond Longford's career as *he* interpreted it, as much to gain an understanding of the world view of the director who made Australia's greatest films as to find out what actually happened, since most of Longford's accusations remain uncorroborated, and a few of them are clearly inaccurate.

Longford's statement to the Royal Commission on 16 June 1927, begins as follows:

> The evidence I am about to give is the result of seventeen years' experience in the writing, directing and production of local pictures, and since I have been, and still am, the only outstanding figure in the industry, I, mainly, have been made during that period the subject of attack by Australasian Films, hereinafter termed 'the combine'; and I solemly state that had it not been for the activities of that firm to crush it in infancy, the local picture industry would now be ten years at least advanced to the height now attained by the Americans. Since the monopolistic activities have been exercised by Australasian Films from the earliest inception of the industry, and since they have in the main been directed against me personally, I must beg the patience of the commission while I retrace the history of the industry in this country.

Having established this opposition between the individual creative genius and the monopolistic juggernaut at the beginning, Longford went on with his history. He had been a stage actor and producer at a time when the only local films, *The Kelly Gang* and *Robbery Under Arms* were 'horribly crude, even for the time'. Cozens Spencer, 'one of the greatest showmen the country has produced', booked Longford to act in much superior productions of well-known stage plays, *Captain Midnight*, *Captain Starlight* (*Robbery Under Arms*) and *Rufus Dawes* (*For the Term of His Natural Life*). These were sufficiently successful for Spencer to engage Longford ('in conjunction with my partner, the late Lottie Lyell',) to produce further films. Longford then produced 'the first domestic dramatic picture using interior scenes done in Australia', *The Fatal Wedding*. The film cost £600 and netted over £16,000 in Australia and England: 'I state these figures to prove . . . that the statements made by the exhibiting interests as to the financial failure of local pictures is mere calumny'. He then produced *Margaret Catchpole*, starring Lottie Lyell, and *Sweet Nell of Old Drury*, starring Nellie Stewart, which were such a success that Spencer was able to spend the large sum, at the time, of £10,000 to build a studio at Rushcutters Bay in 1912.

The first threat to local production came after he had made several more films. While Spencer was away in America, the proposal to set up 'the combine, or Australasian Films' was mooted for the first time, and by the time he returned in 1913 the combination of Spencer's Pictures, J.D. Williams and Pathé Frères as Australasian Films Ltd was a *fait accompli*. 'American interests predominated' and Spencer was outvoted on the question of the importance of local production. Longford was sacked.

Longford then produced for Frazer Films and other private syndicates, but was refused both the studio facilities at Rushcutters Bay, now controlled by (but not used by) Australasian Films *and* first-release facilities. This crippled his highly praised *The Silence of Dean Maitland*, because the 'great necessity of a picture is a theatre in which to give it a premiere, which is really an indication of its value elsewhere'. When the independent entrepreneurs, Dix and Baker,[1] gave *Dean Maitland* a premiere, 'the combine' threatened Baker with cutting off his supply of films and forced other independent showmen 'to sign an agreement whereby they were stopped from showing any film obtained from any source other than the combine'.

Longford took the matter to the Supreme Court of New South Wales and the High Court, alleging restraint of trade, but lost the case. He then tried to get the support of the press, but 'they invariably stated they would jeopardise their advertising contracts by attacking the combine'.[2]

Later, in attempting to make a film for the actor, Allen Doone, Longford was told by Harry Musgrove, then managing director of Australasian Films, that Doone could use the Rushcutters Bay studios but he could not. Longford was forced to leave Australia and made *A Maori Maid's Love* in New Zealand, but 'failed to secure a release owing to the opposition of the Hayward–Fuller organisation . . . whose interests were allied to those of the combine'. At Longford's instigation, Stanley Crick and John C. Jones, who later became chief Australian executives for Fox and First National respectively, but were then independent distributors, formed a syndicate with J.D. Williams and Longford produced 'the first historical picture done in Australia', *The Mutiny of the Bounty*. The film was refused a release by the combine through its Union Theatres circuit, but given

Everyones (i) 12 August 1925, p.6; (ii) 21 October 1935, p.3; (iii) 12 August 1925, p.5

(i) Harry G. Musgrove; (ii) Raymond Longford and (iii) Hon. H. D. McIntosh, MLC a premiere by Hoyts. Longford was then financed by Humbert Pugliese, who had been the only Sydney exhibitor to show *A Maori Maid's Love*, to make *The Church and the Woman* which was also refused release by the combine. Next, he made *The Woman Suffers* for the Southern Cross Feature Film Company which was 'the first local done in South Australia'. It was released by the combine, but was recalled by the censor because of public complaints from persons unknown. Longford clearly suspected further underhand dealings on the part of the combine; and Musgrove had told him that 'as I had cost them a deal of money in securing the duty on American films, I could not expect any consideration from them'. Longford now made *The Sentimental Bloke* for Southern Cross, and again was refused a release by the combine. E.J. Carroll, however, liked it and handled it in Australia and abroad.

The Sentimental Bloke

At this climactic point in Longford's career (which also marks the starting point of this book) it is necessary to leave Longford's interpretation for a while and trace his career until the next major crisis, before returning to his evidence — but noting in doing so the consistently Manichean division Longford makes between the great creative individual (repeatedly creating 'the first . . .') and the crushing impersonality of the monopoly.

Some of the financial problems faced by Australian producers are revealed independently of Longford's evidence by W.J. Howe, head of the New South Wales Showmen's Federation, and a major independent exhibitor at Bondi. He told the Royal Commission that when he screened *The Sentimental Bloke* he retained, *after* deducting working expenses, 50 percent of the takings, which for three nights amounted to £85. The producers would have received whatever was left out of the other £85 only after the distributors had taken their cut. Even worse was the deal with Hoyts City Theatre where, after a week of screening the film three times a day, the producers got only £30![3]

The Sentimental Bloke was a major success both in Australia and England. *Picture Show* said: 'There is a uniqueness about the picture which adds to its attractiveness, due to the fact that the artists act the living part in the natural way.[4] C.J. Dennis said the film left him 'almost believing in miracles. I would have thought it impossible to do what has been done, and the difficulties which I thought would arise have all been admirably swept away'.[5] In Britain, among the numerous favourable reviews were the *Glasgow Citizen's* 'the finest new film of the year', *Bioscope*'s 'one of

(i)

(ii)

(i), (ii) National Film Archive, reproduced by permission of Jack Tauchert

(iv)

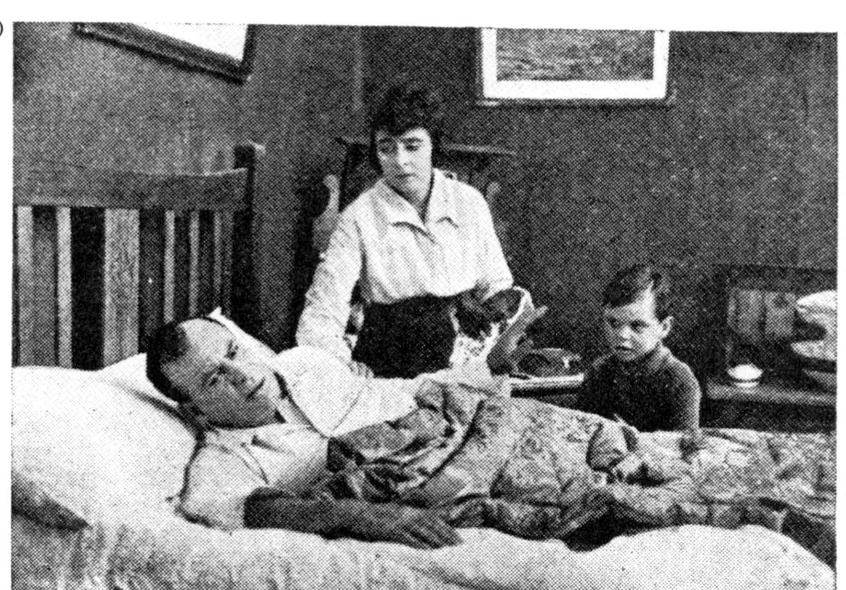

(iii) National Film Archive, reproduced by permission of Jack Tauchert; (iv) *Picture Show* 1 February 1920 p.51

(v)

National Film Archive

Trade criticism of Longford, 'no beauty comparable to the Americans': (i) Arthur Tauchert and Lottie Lyell in *The Sentimental Bloke;* (ii), (iii) and (iv) 'crude scenes "on our selection" to studies of "push" land . . . vulgar without being funny', — hayseeds in *Rudd's New Selection*, larrikins in *The Sentimental Bloke* and the Bloke receiving a 'dinkum, red hot poultice' in *Ginger Mick*
(v) Trade praise for Longford: '*Ginger Mick:* Arthur Tauchert is the same inimitable "Bloke" and Lottie Lyell impersonates Doreen with the same freedom and national realism as in the previous film.' *Picture Show*

the most successful pictures yet made by any producer', and *Kine Weekly*'s 'practically a faultless production'.

However, not everybody approved. The editorial of the *Geelong Advertiser* complained of Longford's films in general when it spoke in 1923 of 'crude scenes "on our selections" to studies of "push" land' which 'have merely succeeded in being vulgar without being funny'. The editor of *Everyones*, Gayne Dexter, used this and other Longford films to explain to the Royal Commission that Australian films could never succeed because a nation of Taucherts and Lyells had no beauty comparable to the Americans.

The real reason for the failure of *The Sentimental Bloke* in America may have been the simple one given in the trade press at the time. Longford cited some comments from the *Oakland Inquirer* of 20 December 1919 which, though very impressed with the film, said that 'some of the slang words are too hard for a movie audience. They require thinking out, and I have yet to learn that a typical movie audience pays its money to think.[6] The paper suggested translating the Australian slang into American slang 'without destroying the racy flavour of this Australian classic'. In order to meet this problem Wilfred Lucas cut the film before he left Australia and Beaumont Smith 'Americanised' the titles, further shortening it to about three-quarters its original length. However, the film made little impact, not surviving First National's public tests, and after that being withdrawn from their schedules. Gayne Dexter denied that the Lucas–Smith alterations had either destroyed the sentiment and rhythm of the original or that the American audience had not understood the slang. He put the failure down to 'inferior production qualities'. And, of course, to the ugliness of its stars.

Nevertheless, in Australia *The Sentimental Bloke* was from the outset generally regarded as a classic. The follow-up, *Ginger Mick*, turned out not to be so successful. One Melbourne critic thought it better than *The Sentimental Bloke*, but another reviewer shrewdly remarked that it suffered from C.J. Dennis's 'Ginger Mick' verses being much inferior to his earlier ones. There were also comments that the length of the verse destroyed the continuity and *Picture Show* said that the film would benefit by being cut considerably before the English trade screening. The film was successfully released in Britain, the *Times* praising it for being 'so absolutely natural'. Having complained recently of films with 'decidedly dago' characters 'doing improbable things in . . purely foreign or cosmopolitan places', the *Times* now praised *Ginger Mick* and *The Sentimental Bloke* for 'a real Imperial service in that they have given us films of real persons doing real things, and making the whole thing attractive to an extent to which few of the dago type of picture have ever aspired'.[7]

The Carroll Partnership

In contracting Longford to make *On Our Selection* and *Rudd's New Selection*, the Carrolls were shrewdly testing out the sales potential, both locally and on an international market, of two very different kinds of product. With the Baker–Lucas–Meredyth combination they were blending American scripts with 'unusual' Australian locations, adding a dash of cosmopolitanism and a deluge of physicality and aiming decidedly at the American market. With the Longford films they were depending heavily on local sales and proven box office, both in paying Steele Rudd the sum unheard of in Australia of £500 and in engaging Longford, whose *Sentimental Bloke* had broken all Australian box office records.

A lot of emphasis was placed on the 'true' Australian quality of these productions. Dan Carroll said that *On Our Selection* had taken the broad comedy from Rudd without burlesque: '*On Our Selection* is human, absolutely Australian'. *Picture Show* commented:

> 'There is no resort to buffoonery or exaggeration, no departure from the realms of possibility, in order to emphasise either the pathetic or the funny side of this most human narrative. Dad is just the Dad of hundreds of backblock selections throughout Australia — big-hearted, hard-working and irascible; and Mum is just the Mum that bakes the bread and mends the clothes, and darns the socks, and raises a brood of hardy, self-reliant young diggers whom the world has learned to know and respect.[8]

Longford's 'realism', it was said, depended on his own bush experience.

> He has lived with them, and understands the real difficulties that beset them in their early efforts to wrest a living from the soil . . . He has seen the horrors of a drought and understands the tremendous amount of work entailed in clearing and burning-off dense scrub and heavy timber in order to raise the crops. More important than all, he has the true Australian's love for his country, and consequently objects strongly to seeing the characters which are presented to the public as natural types, turned into ridicule. This has been done frequently on both the stage and the screen, with the result that those not actually acquainted with our bush pioneers go away with the impression that our backblocks are populated with a race of unsophisticated idiots.[9]

The sentiments behind these comments are certainly Longford's, and the current object of the criticism was probably Beaumont Smith.

On Our Selection was the first film Longford shot at the new Waverley studios, and he used the grounds extensively. He also bought some bush land, and the cast helped to clear it, Longford filming them as they did so. Since there was heavy drought, the costly decision was made to transport

(ii)

Bushfires: in Longford, the endless struggle of small communities against nature to save simple things — boundary rails and slab huts; in Beaumont Smith and Franklyn Barrett, melodramatic signs for the hero's bush manhood. (i) Longford's *On Our Selection;* (ii) Barrett's *The Breaking of the Drought* the whole company several hundred miles to Leeton to shoot the luxuriant harvest scenes. *Rudd's New Selection* had more location work, mainly in the Megalong Valley of the Blue Mountains. This was further afield than Beaumont Smith tended to take his cast, filming his location work at Mulgoa and Windsor; but Longford usually took several months in filming while Smith took only a few weeks.

Longford regarded *Rudd's New Selection* as 'far better' than *On Our Selection*, possibly because the affluent status of Rudd in the new film enabled him to satirise him: 'a friendly satire, mind you. It shows you the Rudds in their prosperous days, and has given the players and myself greater chances than *On Our Selection* did'.[10] Both films were taken by the combine, *On Our Selection* doing sufficiently well in the second half of 1920 for Union Theatres to give it a Boxing Day revival. *Rudd's New Selection*, which opened at the Strand and Lyric cinemas in Sydney in May 1921, drew immediate praise from the critics. They claimed that it did for the bush what *The Sentimental Bloke* had done for the city, and praised the high-quality photography and all-round acting. Tal Ordell as Dave drew special praise, and more than one critic called for a film based around Dave himself. Longford was praised for work that 'has reached a standard of efficiency which places him in the ranks of the first men on the other side of the water',[11] and *Picture Show*, implicitly making a contrast with Beaumont Smith, noted the value of Longford being able to work free of a time schedule: 'Instead of trying to make a photoplay in record time to save money he has turned out a film that will stand the test of time'.[12] Pre-dating trends on the other side of the Atlantic, it was remarked that Longford had produced 'a picture that goes as near to having an all-star cast as it is possible to get',[13] and at a time when the first major parliamentary attack on American control through block booking was under way, suburban and country showmen were apparently giving good prices and creating no difficulties about screening the films.

Encouraged by this success, the Carroll–Longford team launched into what was to be their last production, *The Blue Mountains Mystery*. The trade press announced early on that Longford was breaking new ground, since this was to be 'a drama dealing more with society life, and possessing an element of mystery'. Certain factors appear to have been important in deciding on the *Blue Mountains Mystery*. In the first place the company had been at Katoomba and Medlow Bath for the previous film, which meant that the locations had already been researched, saving time and money. Secondly, and crucially important to Australian production companies with limited budgets and no Hollywood-type warehouses full of appropriate

(i)

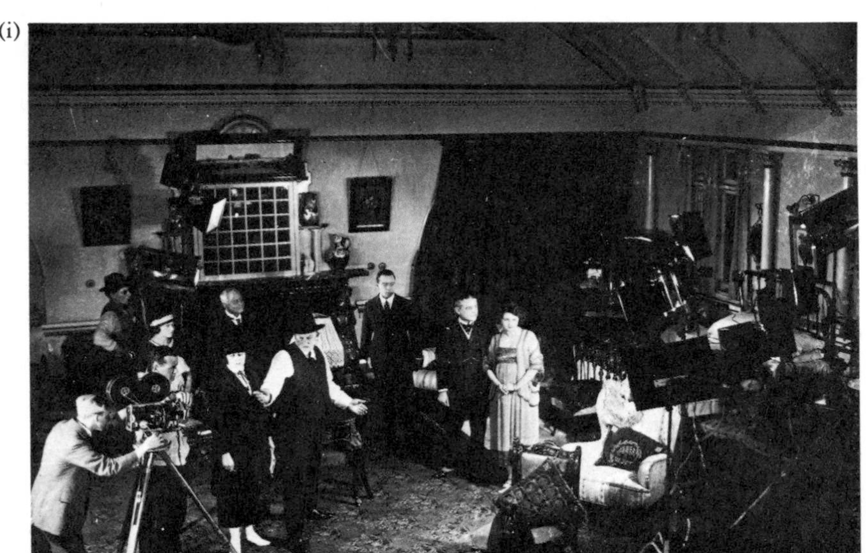

(ii)

(i) National Film Archive; (ii) *Sea, Land and Air* 1 March 1921, p.764

(i) Ready-built society sets: Raymond Longford and Lottie Lyell directing *The Blue Mountains Mystery;* (ii) Longford directing old stage stalwarts, J. P. O'Neill, Ada Clive, Tal Ordell, Lottie Lyell and returned servicemen newcomers E. R. Hearne and Dick Varley in *Rudd's New Selection* props, the 'society' sets were already built and waiting — at the rather grand Carrington Hotel, Katoomba and the Hydro-Majestic Hotel, Medlow Bath. Thirdly, a number of Americans, both as visitors to Australia and at home in the United States, had already expressed their admiration for the Blue Mountains scenery and talked of the drawing power it would give the film in the United States. Characteristically, one of them seemed more interested in taking the mountains home to America than the films. Finally, with the Lucas–Baker films a failure, the Carrolls were clearly making one more attempt on the American market, switching Longford from his 'mainly for Australia' production.

With this in mind, perhaps the Carrolls gave Longford slightly less freedom than usual with the casting, in so far as Dan Carroll insisted on using a Sydney society woman, Mrs Henry Hill Osborne, who had not acted before but who had two advantages. She was fashion director at Farmers, which would ease Dan Carroll's perennial worry about fashions in a 'society' film being out of date. She was also a woman of considerable interest and personality, with whom Longford himself seems to have got on well, probably because there were similarities between her views and Lottie Lyell's. Mrs Osborne had spent a number of years in isolation running a Queensland station, and consequently preferred 'girls who earn their own living . . . They are the ones with real interests . . . they gain poise and independence and strength of character'.[14] Ambrose Adagio could not understand why Lottie Lyell was so keen to direct the film: 'If I'd been a nice-looking girl used to having the camera tick off thousands of photos of me . . . a few steam cranes would have been necessary to pull me away from the set'.[15] Mrs Osborne had a more independent view of women:

> Lottie Lyell . . . appeals to me. I like brains in a woman, and she has them. Her work in this picture is more on the directing side than the acting. She assists Mr Longford, and the two of them have plenty of healthy argument when their ideas about a scene are different.

Lyell herself regarded *Blue Mountains Mystery* as a more demanding film than the others she had made with Longford, requiring two directors, which gave her the opportunity, as well as editing the film, to co-direct more fully than she had done before. Adagio, interviewing her on the set, was much relieved that this 'brainy woman' he had heard so much about did not pour out 'a lot of cold knowledge' about 'Socialism versus Individualism'. Struck out of his normal star-gazing paradigm of 'luminous eyes and sun-kissed hair' by Lyell's 'keen mind', Adagio felt that she was 'the sort of woman who will go far in the work she has chosen, and will be a big factor in Australian production generally'. Tragically, Lyell had only four years to live, and when she died the trade let her go with hardly a comment.

Apart from the choice of Mrs Osborne, Longford had complete control over casting and he exercised his usual care. Berenice Vere, who had long wanted a change from the exotic bad-girl type that Lucas had cast her in, was a youthful heroine for the first time. There had been some doubt about her versatility beforehand, but under Longford's direction she was said to have made a good showing. According to *Picture Show,* Longford similarly drew from John Faulkner, usually typecast as a 'heavy', 'the best performance of his screen career'. Faulkner had a double role to play, which was the focus of the murder mystery, and the reviewer remarked that he managed to convey the different inner states of mind of the two parts admirably. The film continued Longford's innovative all-star policy: *Picture Show* noted that 'no player was given special prominence' even though the cast was a mixture of experienced screen actors, inexperienced actors from the stage, and others with little or no experience at all: 'The work was pretty evenly divided . . . between a number of men and women, all of whom acted consistently and contrasted well with each other'.[16] The interior photography of Arthur Higgins was thought to be 'quite the finest yet seen in Australian pictures. Outlines are sharp and clear and some notably good work is seen in the casting of a man's silhouette on a blind, and in double exposures'. *Everyones* commented on the spectacular outside shots: 'Vast open spaces, imposing mountain heights, and a wonderful amount of fertile country is introduced in panoramic fashion'.[17] *Mise-en-scène* and costumes were also thought to be suitably 'lavish'. 'So often the "wealthy" players of a local film look as if they have walked out of a second-hand store and will walk back again when the picture is finished'.[18]
In *Everyones'* opinion:

> This is just the type of picture that will make effective propaganda for a land that is too little known, not only overseas, but amongst our own countrymen . . . it shows our own producers to be capable of the best in film production when given the opportunity.[19]

After opening in Sydney and Melbourne in late 1921, and successful country tours, the film was shown throughout the United States. It received favourable reviews which praised the mountain scenery above the plot. In November 1921 Dan Carroll supplied the lead article in *Everyones* in which he spoke very hopefully about the future. The three Baker–Lucas films had sold well in the United States and he was hoping to net £50,000

(i) Dan Carroll;

(ii) E. J. Carroll

(i) *Everyones* 2 November 1921, p.3; (ii) *Picture Show* 1 December 1920, p.67

from their State's rights exploitation by the Aywon company. *The Sentimental Bloke* had been wonderfully received in England and was, he hoped, just about to be released in the United States by First National. *Ginger Mick* had also been successfully marketed in Britain, and they hoped it would return about 70 per cent of *The Sentimental Bloke*'s earnings there. Only *On Our Selection* and *Rudd's New Selection* had not been marketed abroad because 'these films are so typical of the Australian character that audiences abroad cannot grip the meaning of their comedy'. They, of course, had made a profit in Australia alone. Carroll argued that the producers' main problem, apart from inexperience, was the need for continuity in order to keep down overheads while profits were coming in gradually; but 'we are now at the turning point where our income from local and foreign marketing exceeds our expenditure on production, and, as a result, we will from now on have a producing unit working regularly.' The next film would be

> a story written by Miss Lottie Lyell and Mr Raymond Longford for Arthur Tauchert . . . on the lines of *The Sentimental Bloke,* but entirely different in theme, and we are looking forward with great confidence to the result.

Noting that their success in local production derived from Longford's direction, Lyell's continuity, editing and wardrobe work, and Arthur Higgins's photography, Carroll added: 'We have splendid team work in our organisation, and there is complete harmony, because we are all after the one thing — success.'[20]

And yet, as in the case of Carroll's hopeful comments about the Lucas films earlier, there was to be a sudden reverse. In the same month of November, while he was already working with Lyell on the script of *The Dinkum Bloke*, Longford heard that the Carrolls were ceasing production and had suffered a £25,000 loss. His services were terminated, and by mid-December, before *The Blue Mountains Mystery* was even out of Sydney, Berenice Vere, the major Australian talent that the Carroll venture had discovered, was in America trying her fortunes there, and John Faulkner was announcing his plans to return to England. *Everyones* commented that

> Men who have been encouraged by the way their work has been received upon the screen, have, perforce, abandoned all hope, for the present at any rate, of getting anything like a continuity of engagements. They now realise that the field is far too small, and that capital is not sufficiently interested.[21]

The End of the Carroll Venture

In order to consider what went wrong we need to return to Longford's later account of the story of his relations with the Carrolls, given at the Royal Commission. His tale of personal persecution by 'the combine' looms large, beginning with Union Theatres' refusal to take *The Sentimental Bloke* and its successful handling by the Carrolls. *Ginger Mick* had also been handled by (and in fact subsidised by) the Carrolls, and after Lucas turned down *On Our Selection* they offered it and *Rudd's New Selection* to Longford.

> At this outburst of activity on the part of the Carrolls the combine grew interested. On several previous occasions, whenever attention to the local picture industry was aroused in the legislatures, it was their custom to draw attention by wide publicity to their activities in the field of production. About this time, and as an offset to the Carroll publicity, they advertised for an experienced producer . . . about 1918. I applied but my services were declined. Instead, Mr Ward, now editor of *Everyones*, was engaged who had had no experience in production. He actually set out in production at the combine's studio, but the results were never seen. The combine explained to their studio cameraman that it was only an answer to the Carroll publicity. Mr Lucas meanwhile returned to the United States of America.

Longford's account here is chronologically inaccurate, and, to put the best interpretation on it, hazy and ambiguous. He claimed this all happened 'about 1918' whereas, in fact, Fred Ward was appointed in September 1919, made one film (*Why Mabel Learned to Jazz*) and the production company was wound up in January 1920, before *On Our Selection* was produced, and long before *Rudd's New Selection* or Lucas's departure for America. The combine could not therefore have been interested as a result of 'this outburst of activity', as Longford implies. And the major attention to the local industry 'aroused in the legislatures' by the Member for Dalley, N.S.W., Mr Mahoney, was not until late in April 1920, also after the winding up of the combine's film project, so again it cannot have been motivated by it. Further, the reason for ceasing production may well have been the executive changeover at Australasian Films. Production ceased at exactly the time of the big shake-up when W.A. Gibson replaced Musgrove as general manager, and also at the time of the merger with J.C. Williamson. These, rather than Longford's 'conspiracy', could have been the reasons for production ceasing. Doyle, who nearly always saw eye-to-eye with Gibson, later said Ward's film was useless to them and so was shelved.

On the other hand, to be fair to Longford, and allowing him a degree of haziness with dates which was often displayed at the Royal Commission (including Dan Carroll's account of this period), Longford also said it was the Carroll *publicity* which evoked the combine's response, and it is the case that Australasian Films announced their production plans in the very same week that there was maximum publicity for the Carrolls, with the arrival of Lucas and Meredyth in Australia. Further, the reason for Australasian Films *ceasing* production could very well have been the executive changeover, without this in the least affecting the reason for *starting* production suggested by Longford, since Musgrove, whom he regarded as his arch enemy, was still then in control.

Longford then goes on to say that on the completion of *The Blue Mountains Mystery* he was notified that his services were no longer required.

> I interviewed Mr E.J. Carroll, who was then in hospital. He informed me that the outlook for local production was very dark. Their dealings, as owners of a chain of Queensland theatres (the Birch Carroll Circuit), with the combine were unsatisfactory. He depended on the combine for the supply of his film, and if they were opposed to local production it would be quite impossible for him to continue as they were the source of his supplies. This blow was a very serious one to the industry.

What evidence is there to support Longford's serious allegation of the combine's restraint of trade? Very little, but that is hardly surprising given the secretive nature of the supposed pressure. E.J. Carroll certainly was in hospital at precisely this time. More important than this trivial piece of circumstantial evidence, is an anxious and, on the face of it, rather bizarre postscript to Dan Carroll's highly exuberant article in *Everyones* mentioned earlier, where he strenuously denies that his firm had supported a film import duty on behalf of local production:

> We will swear it on oath at any time that we did not either before or after urge that the import of duty would help Australian production, not did we do anything to urge its impost or see that it was retained.

This presumably relates to Mahoney's attack on Australasian Films in Parliament earlier in the year as part of an American combine which was forcing local exhibitors 'to give Australasian Films Ltd a percentage of the proceeds from any local production before the firm would supply them with the rest of their programme'. Mahoney's solution was protection for the local production industry by a number of measures, including the impost of increased duty on imported films. Even so, Carroll's response does not make much sense, until we remember that the main reason that Longford gives for the combine's persecution of him, apart from Gibson's professional jealousy, was that he was responsible for the Fisher Government imposing a tariff which at the time cost Australasian Films a lot of money. Further, Mahoney had been inspired by a 'frustrated Australian producer'. The terms of his attack are idiosyncratically Longford's, and at a meeting of 'the leading Australian producers' in May 1921 (including Dan Carroll, Franklyn Barrett and a representative for Beaumont Smith) which assured the trade that they had no part in the attack, Longford was notably absent. Apparently the trade had not accepted Dan Carroll's disclaimer at that time, and in his November article he is obviously afraid of reaction of some kind. Perhaps it came from Australasian Films in the form Longford suggested, which killed the Carroll productions. The evidence is not clear enough, I think, for us to accept Longford's interpretation of the event as readily as most researchers have done up to now — particularly if we consider the trade's argument that there were at least ten different film exchanges that a pressured exhibitor could get his supply from (unless we also argue for collusion of distributors much earlier than the date of 1924, which is normally taken as the time of their formally getting together.) But Dan Carroll's obvious worry, the precise nature of that worry, and his immediate juxtaposition of it with comment on the need for the trade's goodwill, is certainly provocative.

Dan Carroll's own testimony to the Royal Commission, on the other hand, gives a totally different interpretation. Three things, he argued, brought an end to the Carroll's film production. The first was a lack of good stories. Bess Meredyth had reported after researching into Australian history and culture that Australians 'have no history or traditions suitable to stir patriotic emotions'. The only truly national subject was horse racing, which was of little use to the Carrolls since England was producing scores of turf pictures. They therefore tackled the 'only remaining possible environment, and that was stories around station and bush life'. After *The Man From Kangaroo* and *The Shadow of Lightning Ridge* were produced the second major disincentive emerged. Encouraged by the Carrolls' success, a 'flock of 'mushroom' producers — numerous small syndicates — rushed into film-making with minimal capitalisation and the results were so poor as to make Australian films 'the subject of ridicule amongst picture audiences'. This seriously affected the earning power of the Carroll's films of a considerably higher standard. Finally, a glut occurred in the overseas market due to many countries rushing into film production after the war, with the result that 'the earnings of our films, although they compared favourably with other products, were infinitesimal.'

Carroll is as vague as Longford in his dates, running together the reasons for dispensing with both Lucas and Longford, even though more than a year separated them. The increasing number of poor Australian films following in the wake of the Carroll's success (that is, at the very earliest, after the screening of *The Man From Kangaroo*) cannot have caused the ending of the Lucas contract, as he suggests, because by then only one new company was releasing films. Harry Southwell's much abused *Kelly Gang* had been released, but his *Hordern Mystery* did not reach exhibitors until after Lucas had left. Arthur Shirley had opened a studio, but had not released anything; and Franklyn Barrett's *Breaking of the Drought* which had first appeared in June was a considerably better film than *The Man From Kangaroo*.

However, by the time Longford was dismissed, several small companies had produced films, particularly: Brampton's *Robbery Under Arms*; Jack Wells's *Silks and Saddles*; P.J. Ramster's *Mated in the Wilds* and *Jasamine Freckel's Love Affair* (the latter completed in six days); Charles Villiers' *Possum Paddock*; John Cosgrove's *The Guyra Ghost Mystery*; and Tal Ordell's *Cows and Cuddles*.[22] And these were in addition to three Beaumont Smith films and a couple from Franklyn Barrett. There was also a slump in the international market, though this peaked later and one wonders whether the Carrolls, international entrepreneurs though they were, had really been affected by it by the time they sacked Longford. Carroll is nonetheless quite consistent in his evidence to the Royal Commission in his opposition to 'mushroom' companies, while genuinely seeking to stimulate local production. He is also consistent in his concern over poor stories and scripts. So his interpretation of Longford's dismissal, if not of Lucas's has to be taken seriously.

Longford–Lyell Productions

In 1925, *The Blue Mountains Mystery* was screened in England and favourably reviewed by *Bioscope* for Longford's direction which through 'restrained acting shows the force which a story gains in the telling'.[23] But by then another venture of Longford's had been tried and failed. On May 24 1922, *Everyones* noted the founding of the Longford–Lyell Australian Picture Productions Limited which hoped to secure £50,000 capital to make films. *Everyones* said that though Australian financiers were very cautious about investing in local films, 'from what this paper knows of

National Film Archive, reproduced by permission of Jack Tauchert

Longford's one society set: *The Dinkum Bloke*

the business, there is no time like the present', and added that the inclusion of W.J.Howe, president of the Federated Picture Showmen of New South Wales, 'should induce outside investors to realise that the proposition is a very favourable one'. In fact it was not a good moment to invest because it was just at this time that the slump in the industry in America was causing a closing of ranks among film workers and politicians against a supposed 'avalanche of cheap foreign pictures', produced on the much lower foreign salaries, which threatened to 'smash overnight' the 'fifth industry of the United States'.[24] So, ironically, there was a strong move afoot in the U.S.A. too to impose big tariffs on imported films.

Longford and Lyell were into production by August, using the scenario they had written for the next Carroll film, and announced that they intended to make four films in the first year, aimed at the overseas as well as the Australian market. They were unable to use Waverley[25] so they fell back on the out-dated Rushcutters Bay studios. The publicity spoke of a grand story, extending *The Sentimental Bloke* far beyond Woolloomooloo to both station and city society life. But despite this it is possible to detect financial stringency, as one reads of local people helping out with props and the construction of the single 'luxurious' society set.

In January 1923, however, came the news that John W. Hicks Jnr had agreed to release *The Dinkum Bloke* throughout Australia and New Zealand as a Paramount picture. This seemed an important breakthrough for the new company since, apart from the nationwide distribution, it meant the backing of a large publicity team. In fact the film was publicised like no other Longford film before or after. Full page advertisements emphasising the Australian-ness of this American publicity vehicle began appearing from mid-January. Juxtaposed with the Paramount peaks would be a large, central map of Australia, promoting 'Australia's Motion Picture Answer to the World. Conceived, made and acted by Australians for those countless thousands of Australians who are proud of the achievements of their own country'. For the first time for a Longford film, *Dinkum Bloke* advertisements twice made up the full front cover of *Everyones*, and, to balance the purely Australian emphasis, full page advertisements also began appearing linking the film with the latest from Rudolph Valentino, Pola Negri, Gloria Swanson, Bebe Daniels and Cecil B. de Mille. Even the campaign's single and double column blocks got bigger publicity than many another Longford film in its entirety.

But the fanfare of the big advertising campaign was also carefully balanced by the parochial and domesticated touch. It was to be a story taken

Everyones 9 May 1923, p.100

A balance of the international and the domesticated touch in part of the massive publicity for *The Dinkum Bloke*

FAMOUS LASKY FILM SERVICE LIMITED
PRESENTS A
LONGFORD - LYELL AUSTRALIAN
PRODUCTION

"The DINKUM BLOKE"

WITH

Arthur Tauchert

For Australians, by Australians, and with Australian materials.

There, indeed, is a wealth of appeal. But not alone is it, for there is to the picture a power of appeal which must rank it among the finest productions of this country.

A simple story of a man's sacrifice, charged with dramatic situations—yet withal remaining a sterling picture of a large and real slab of Australian life.

Played by a cast of favorites in an atmosphere dear to all. And directed by the man who made "The Sentimental Bloke."

The Players in the Cast—

ARTHUR TAUCHERT	LOTTIE LYELL
LOTUS THOMPSON	RENE SANDEMAN
CECIL B. SCOTT	JACK RAYMOND
DOROTHY DAYE	BERYL GOW

A Paramount Picture

Everyones 9 May 1923, p.52

Hoyt's de Luxe, George-st.——Sydney's Leading Cinema House

EVERYONES

WITH WHICH IS INCORPORATED AUSTRALIAN VARIETY AND SHOW WORLD.

Vol. 3 No. 163 SYDNEY, APRIL 18, 1923 Price Threepence

(Registered at the General Post Office, Sydney, for Transmission by Post as a Newspaper.)

THE SPIRIT OF AUSTRALIA

"The Dinkum Bloke"

A Paramount Picture

Everyones 18 April 1923, cover

Massive publicity for *The Dinkum Bloke: Everyones*' cover advertisement.

'amid scenes that are every day experience to most of us', adding 'an exquisite home touch to the picture, which makes it seem to belong to all who see it'. The cast was not, of course, one of Valentinos and Negris but local 'players who are rapidly coming to the front rank': Arthur Tauchert, Lottie Lyell, and Lotus Thompson. It was a carefully controlled publicity campaign which, from the first 'Dinkum Sign for the Dinkhum Bloke' advertisement to the lobby display presentation at Hoyts, Sydney, constantly combined the local Australian element with the American big time.

The Dinkum Bloke opened in Sydney on 2 June to good reviews. *Everyones* thought it close to, but better than, *The Sentimental Bloke*, and 'photographically . . . one of the best things yet turned out in this country'. By mid-June the film was touring country New South Wales, drawing good attendances at Dubbo despite the fact that its opening night in the open-air theatre coincided with storms that ended the drought. Publicity was still lavish, both in country papers and the Sydney trade papers which continued to give full page ads even during the country tour. The new Paramount house journal, *The Exhibitor*, remarked in October that a notable aspect of the tour was that the film was often being featured as the major attraction on the double bills, helped by personal appearances of Arthur Tauchert. In Fremantle there was a big publicity campaign which 'Played up the Australian angle big'. 'Dinkum Bloke' maps of Australia were given out to numerous shopkeepers for window displays, a 'Dinkum Bloke' essay competition was set up in the local schools, and 'The Dinkum Organ' was displayed in a store window, attracting a pavement crush second only to the crowds who queued at the 'House Full' signs at the cinema.

The film, according to British reviews, was well worth all the publicity, combining the familiar Longford hallmarks of extreme sentimentality and understated acting. *Film Renter* said that the 'conventional plot' (in which Tauchert is a navvy who fulfills his promise to his dying wife to work day and night to send their daughter to the best schools, only to have to give her up so that she can marry into a wealthy family) was presented with such 'kindly humour and sincerity of sentiment', with the 'remarkably natural acting of Arthur Tauchert', and such 'realistic Australian atmosphere' as to beat most of Hollywood's super productions.[26] This was clearly Longford at his sentimental best, with the moment when Tauchert 'unselfishly renounces' his last tie with his daughter, who herself is the last tie with his dead wife, rivalling the news of Ginger Mick's death as the tearful high spot of Australian silent cinema.

As always with Longford's career, it was not enough. Despite critical acclaim and, apparently, financial success, once again he met with failure.

Lotus Thompson left for America in February 1924 to become 'Lotus of the Limbs', and in June the Longford–Lyell company was liquidated.

The contrast of the pioneering publicity for *The Dinkum Bloke* with the quiet, sober, short paragraph announcing the liquidation was characteristic of the trade press, which always preferred 'House Full' signs to post-mortems. It is impossible, as so often with Longford, to clearly establish the real causes and contributing series of events. Any explanation must certainly begin by going beyond the question of personalities, which is where Longford's own explanation leaves it. As far as he was concerned, Hicks of Paramount was a real 'gentleman' and 'friend' who had his interests at heart, whereas W.J. Howe was yet another Australian turncoat who forced the company into receivership. An alternative explanation of Paramount's involvement in *The Dinkum Bloke* may be offered if we trace the concern of the American and Australian distributing companies during this period with mounting parliamentary hostility to their activities.

Distribution: Parliamentary Intervention

As early as 1921 the American distributors who had recently established themselves in Australia were beginning to be sufficiently worried for H.E. Ross-Soden, general manager of Fox films, to regularly sponsor a whole page advertisement article in *Everyones*.[27] These articles set the strategy which was by and large unbroken throughout the 1920s. The distributors, using the trade papers which usually supported them on the broader issues, claimed a spurious unity within the charmed circle of distributor, exhibitor and producer — provided the latter toed the line, otherwise he was consigned to the ranks of those *outside* the circle, which included wowsers, parliamentarians, R.S.S.L.A., Good Films League and other 'self-appointed' representatives of 'minority' forces working against the interest of the 'great public's' entertainment.

Soden on the one hand justified the large rental increases imposed on the exhibitors by characteristically deflecting attention outside the trade, arguing that because theatres charged far too much in comparison with cinemas, the latter could justifiably raise prices to pay for the best films in the world. 'Is it likely', he asked ingenuously, 'that any exchange would demand a rate from any exhibitor that he could not pay?', and *Everyones* obligingly enhanced his benign image with a lead article on Ross Soden under the title, 'The Friend of the Exhibitor'. On the other hand, Soden castigated the two major forces he judged to be outside the trade; the unions (which *included*, in his perspective, the musicians' and theatrical employees'

THE MOVING PICTURE WORLD

A PAGE FOR SHOWMEN.

Co-Operation——How Neccessary It Is!

By H. E. ROSS SODEN.

It is very gratifying to state that quite a number of replies have already been received from various exhibitors intimating that they are thoroughly in accord with the scheme for the forming of an Australian organisation. As another instance—and they are cropping up every day—as to why it is so necessary to have this Association, attention can be drawn to the demand of the musicians for an increase in wages. It is the intention of the Musicians' Union to claim seven pounds per week for any member of this Union playing at any Picture Show. It is unnecessary to emphasise the absurdity of this demand. It is somewhat surprising that it is made at this particular time, as there is a world-wide tendency to decrease the high cost of living; and consequently, should this—and it will—take place, it must necessarily force down the at present absurdly high rate of wages. And yet musicians are demanding an increase on their at present high rate!. This is where an Association is necessary, so that when the case comes before the Arbitration Court, whoever represents the Association, can voice the opinion of practically the whole of the exhibitors of Australia, instead of, as at present, being represented by two or three or perhaps more representatives who may somewhat differ in the aspect they take of the case and so possibly convey to the Judge that they are not quite unanimous on the point. We could secure the best legal representative in Australia, because we would have the money to do it. When the case referred to comes before the Arbitration Court, it will be fought perhaps by two Associations, namely, that of New South Wales and Victoria, and possibly Queensland. These Associations are not fully representative. They should be. But unfortunately there are too many exhibitors in Australia who allow their own petty personal quarrels to prevent them from supporting their local Association; this is very much to be regretted, but unfortunately it is only too true.. Now, if there was an Association which comprised the whole of the exhibitors of Australia, these petty differences, it is to be hoped, would sink into oblivion, and the larger issues would predominate in the minds of those exhibitors who are able to take a bread view and eliminate personal matters, and so materially assist the MOVING PICTURE BUSINESS.

That the claim of the musician is ridiculous every exhibitor in Australia will admit, and it is time that the Musicians' Union were shown how impossible it is to pay the high rate of wages which they demand.. It will only tend to the displacement of orchestras completely, as there is no exhibitor in Australia who will be able to maintain an orchestra of more than two or three, where at present he may have eight or nine; so consequently this demand of the musicians is going to cost a great deal of unemployment and will personally demonstrate how true it is that only the fittest survive.. The mediocre player—and there are many—will actually be forced t find other means whereby to earn his daily bread. . . . .

These demands for increases in wages are continually happening, and that is why a firm stand must be made and an Association formed immediately to fight against this ever-recurring demand. I feel sure that if an Association did exist at the present moment, the case would be placed in such a manner before the Judge that it would be perfectly clear to him that the demands made are excessive, and in all probability the matter would be definitely settled once and for all.

Every exhibitor must realise that the forming of this Association is a vital necessity. I have no axe to grind in bringing this matter continually under your notice. I am only actuated by an earnest and sincere desire to see the Trade united in one unanimous body which will be strong enough and broad enough to sink all past petty differences and have for its object the welfare and success of the MOTION PICTURE INDUSTRY.

A call for trade unity against a major foe: the unions

Everyones 16 March 1921, p.11

Everyone's-Variety

WITH WHICH IS INCORPORATED

USTRALIAN VARIETY AND SHOW WOR

l to the Moving Picture Industry, Vaudeville, Drama, Carnival, Circus and Kindred Ente

Published Every Wednesday, at 114 Castlereagh Street, Sydney, N.S.W.

801 MARTIN C. BRENNAN, Editor. HAROLD V. MARTIN, Manager.

THE FRIEND OF THE EXHIBITOR

iths now, picture
ghout Australasia
nall measure, con-
d of praise to the
nd emphatic ar-
y Mr. H. E. Ross-
ibuted, from week
e pages.

rybody knows, Mr.
e general manager
of the Fox Film
America, and, in-
e of the pioneers
picture industry in
applied to the dis-
it.

years ago, Mr.
one of the execu-
erican-Australasian
mpany, an organi-
its office in the
ng, Melbourne, for
which subsequently
iness owing to the
principal.

me attached to the
nd Films Ltd., and
this company for
which he became
ager for Crick and
ne time, looked as
become a mighty
d. With this com-
Soden remained till
with the Fox Film
ich he joined some
eing installed as its
ger.

he joined the Fox
ptional ability was
s new environment
nt opportunities,
rly availed him-

vance of the Fox
in the Southern
re than ordinary at-

H. E. ROSS-SODEN.

tion of general-manager of Australasia was offered Mr. Ross-Soden, he came across to the Sydney headquarters, but before leaving Melbourne was the recipient of many practical expressions of the esteem and regard in which he was held.

Organisation had always been this gentleman's principal endeav-

Although Mr. Ross-Soden has availed himself considerably of the press in advancing the best interests of picture exhibitors, it is with great reluctance that he can be persuaded to say anything in his own favour. However, the powers of observation are not altogether lost by the obdurate pressman in his search for information, and thus it is that we are able to give to our readers a pencil sketch, as it

this paper, an
considerable t
their compilati
his newspaper
man has occup
several import
film taxes and
extensive kno
tion has enab
place a most
comprehensive
before the Fe
liaments.

Despite the
connected wit
agement of s
Fox Film Co
throughout th
New Zealand,
ways makes
as much time
to all those w
of his advice
to the film b
byword among
courtesy of th
his staff in S

Apart fro
Ross-Soden en
other executiv
ject of picture
At the same
congenial comp
wit and spon
porary with hi

If the pictu
doubts about
opinions on
tax, let him ju
ter personally
manner, and t
one of the fine
torical effort

Just at pres
in conjunction
chief of the
busy preparing
furthering the

Everyones 27 July 1921, p.3

unions) and the government. He criticised the former for 'ridiculous' and 'continual' wage demands; the latter for threatening '*both sides* of the Picture Industry' (note the restriction to distributors and exhibitors only) with notions of raising the tariff on imported films and imposing an Australian quota on exhibitors.

In the former case his strategy was one of assumed consensus and reciprocity: 'Remember, the exchange cannot live without the exhibitor, and vice-versa', so 'live and let live',[28] 'adopt the spirit of give and take' — provided, of course, the exhibitors accepted the 'inevitable' increase in hire charges. In the latter case the enemy was clearly outside the 'consensus' and appropriately vilified: those whose 'sublime ignorance' led them to interfere in things they knew nothing about and which they should leave alone. Soden said 'it would be far better if Members of Parliament were to devote their brains (such as they have) and energies (which some possess)' to stopping exploitation of investors by mushroom companies rather than strangling 'a genuine business, which gives employment to a considerable number of people'.[29]

Against Australian producers and their 'wildcat' companies, against unions and against interfering governments Ross Soden constantly called for an association of exhibitors and distributors representing the whole (!) of the cinema trade to 'stand unitedly together' (ready to fight) 'an enemy who is likely to do anything that will be against the interests and welfare of the Moving Picture business'.[30] In the meantime, *Everyones* reported, Ross Soden and John Hicks of Paramount were joining forces in unilateral action to promote certain of the 'best interests of the picture industry'.

The parliamentary rumblings reached their first major articulation in mid-1921 with Mahoney's threatened bill to prevent the 'pernicious methods of an American combine with an Australian name, which is endeavouring to stifle Australian industry by refusing to supply any pictures to a theatre which is screening Australian production'.[31] Two champions sprang to the defence of the 'picture industry'. One was Ross Soden who declared Mahoney's ideas 'ridiculous . . . beyond the imagination' with the side-tracking argument which was to become familiar in the years to come: that there was no American money in Australasian Films Ltd. Soden spoke of 'some sinister influence at work' behind Mahoney and asked why a private feud between two certain people (Longford and Gibson?) should affect the whole industry. The other champion was W.J. Howe who, claiming the wisdom of twelve years in the picture industry compared with the ignorance of Mahoney's three months 'dabbling', argued that the only monopoly in the business was the government's tariff monopoly, that taxes and not distributors' rapacity led to the steep increase in hire charges, and that if politicians really wanted to 'butt in on a business that they know nothing about' they should get rid of the amusement tax which was a class tax because, once 'inevitably' passed on it hit the working class who made up a majority of the audience.

Two myths which, again, were to be central to the stand of the trade, were propagated: first, that the picture industry stood for the working class against a government, whether Nationalist or Labor, that would be better off taxing 'bridge parties, golf and polo'; second, that films were bought in the open market, and the ideal of the trade was pictures

> from every brain in the world that has a story big enough to tell the public. We want them from America, Rome, Sweden, London and Shanghai . . . We want the world's competition in production, not that of one country, or one section. Mr Mahoney wants 25 percent of Australian productions. Of course, that would not create a monopoly! Why, a child can see through it.[32]

Everyones obediently toed the line once again with a strategically timed lead article on Stuart Doyle and W.A. Gibson of Australasian Films Ltd under the heading: 'Buying in the Open Market' and, with editorial comment supporting the stance of Soden and Howe against mushroom companies and Australian quotas, reminding readers of how Soden had 'enlightened' Mahoney and Howe had shown the parliamentarian's knowledge to be 'very second hand'. Later, in the heat of battle, *Everyones* ran yet another lead article, this time on W.J. Howe entitled 'A Fighter Right Through', arguing that this former rugby star, film pioneer, boxing manager and manager of Fox films, this current hero 'alert in mind and body' deserved, like Ross Soden, the 'lasting gratitude of all picture showmen in this country' for putting 'the Picture Showmen's Association on the map of Australia' and fighting alongside the distributors against outside attack.[33] These were indeed crucial years for the Showmen's Federation of N.S.W. and its strength was forged in the heat of the American monopoly– Australian quota debate as Howe cried out for hard fighting from exhibitors to save themselves 'from unjust taxation, unreasonable and arbitrary unionism, foolish censorship'.[34]

The Showmen's Federation, under Howe, continued with the same policy throughout 1923 as renewed attacks on the combine came from within parliament, stimulated by W.W. Scott Fell MLA, and from outside, led by the Brisbane R.S.S.L.A. in deputations to the tariff board. In June, the month of release of *The Dinkum Bloke*, Howe took up the cudgels again

Everyone's-Variety

WITH WHICH IS INCORPORATED

AUSTRALIAN VARIETY AND SHOW WORLD

Devoted to the Moving Picture Industry, Vaudeville, Drama, Carnival, Circus and Kindred Entertainment

Published Every Wednesday, at 114 Castlereagh Street, Sydney, N.S.W.

Phone City 8801 | MARTIN C. BRENNAN, Editor. | HAROLD V. MARTIN, Manager. | P.O. Box 3208

(i)

BUYING ON THE OPEN MARKET.

Messrs. Stuart F. Doyle and W. A. Gibson, managing directors of Australasian Films Ltd., and Union Theatres Ltd., who returned to Sydney recently, after a most extensive and comprehensive tour abroad, were more than satisfied with the outcome of their trip.

"We had a wonderfully successful trip through England, the Continent and America," stated Mr. Doyle and Mr. Gibson on being interviewed by our representative. "Our first impression of England was how backward they are compared to Australia in the running of their picture theatres. No attempt was made to exploit a picture in any shape or form—it was simply put on for what it was worth; the public come or stay away in accordance with the drawing power of the picture. In our opinion, the average showman in Australia can show points to a lot of the exhibitors in England. However, as far ahead as we are of England and the Continent, with a few exceptions, American exhibitors are as far ahead of us in the method of presentation of their pictures.

"Our company has decided, after our investigations and our study of conditions throughout the world," stated Mr. Gibson, "to continue our policy of buying on the open market, and only buying good pictures. Indifferent or mediocre pictures we do not intend to purchase at all in future. To under-

MESSRS STUART F. DOYLE AND W. A. GIBSON.

ing pictures with his own money, and depending upon its earning capacity for his profit and, as the extravagant salaries to artists are to a very great extent eliminated, Associated Producers are in a position to put a greater amount of money into the actual production itself, which in the scheme of things throughout the world is really what is appreciated by the public. The personal drawing power of artists seems to be diminishing, with a few exceptions, but taking the general run of artists they are gradually dropping out so far as their retaining the big drawing power is concerned.

"One of the biggest pictures we purchased was 'Carnival'—an English production, by the Alliance corporation. This picture was shown at the Capitol Theatre and caused a sensation in America. To appreciate the value of this, it must be understood that English pictures are not very popular in America, and for 'Carnival' to achieve such a success it should be realised what a great picture it is. The whole of the scenes in this picture are set in Venice, and when shown in Australia it will create a tremendous amount of public interest.

"We went through the English and Continental market in detail and satisfied ourselves that there are certain lines of English and Continental films which would be successful in Australia. The principal studio at the present time that is

A Fighter Right Through

(ii)

recent controversy in the
ress regarding Australian
production has shown us
ere are at least two gentle-
epresentatives of the Ex-
and Exhibiting end of the
—who have the courage of
pinions, and who, in un-
d terms, have expressed
ves by a series of articles
st win for them the lasting
e of all picture showmen in
untry. The writers con-
are H. E. Ross-Soden and
owe respectively.

rs of this paper are very
ormed on Mr. Ross-Soden's
inasmuch as his weekly
tions to "Everyone's.
have done more to put this
al before the moving pic-
ople than anything else
d within its pages. Re-
tion of his ability, there-
quite unnecessary.

other gentleman who has
the cudgels so ably against
honey, M.H.R., is W. J.
Howe, a name to conjure
the Australian world of
ootball a decade ago. Ex-
y powerful in physique,
mind and body, "Bill"
as a tower of strength to
W. team of footballers, for
e played against New Zea-
d Queensland. After his
nt from active participa-
a member, he became one

W. J. HOWE.

fight. He toured Queensland for Mr. McIntosh, in conjunction with Mr. E. J. Carroll, with the fight pictures, and at that period it was a case of carrying your own electricity.

where he took up a Government position for some time, after which he returned to the boxing game, being appointed manager of the Olympia Stadium, Newtown. Dur-

subsequent developmen
what, a few years ago, w
paratively unknown bod

It may safely be said
Howe put the Picture S
Association on the map
lia. This was only acc
after a great deal of h
which was accompanied
tenacity of a determinat
of the cause. His work
dustrial courts has bee
recognised by all
throughout Australasia i
and so it is to this day.

When he joined up wi
Film forces, Mr. How
their offices in Brisbane,
there the N.S.W. Olympi
offered him his present
general manager of this
ganisation. Loving Sydn
only the place of his na
because he thinks there i
place on earth as good a
accepted the appointmen
his able management, the
has had a remarkable ru
cess, and the No. 1 Olym
tre is recognised as one
picture houses of Austra

For some years our
friend has occupied the p
vice-president of the
Picture Showmen's Assoc
his work amongst that au
has been greatly apprecia
exhibitors. In this con

Everyones (i) 17 August 1921, p.3; (ii) 14 September 1921, p.3

for the 'open market' against Scott Fell, and, for a moment squaring his interests as investor and exhibitor, argued for government intervention only in assisting Australian companies which made 'a first class picture, *The Dinkum Bloke* for example', and were not mere mushroom companies. *Everyones* again dutifully followed, combining an assault on Scott Fell with a plea for government help to local production. Worried by 'the utter lack of knowledge' of film production in the press, the journal argued in August, under the heading 'Film Industry Needs a Champion', that to combat the 'distorted figures' of 'those persons whose conception of the industry is almost a negligible quantity' the distributors must put aside money 'whereby the services of a good newspaperman may be secured'.[35]

Within a few weeks 'champions of the industry' emerged in two forms. At the beginning of October, Paramount launched the *Exhibitor*, which immediately attacked those members of parliament whose 'ignorance' threatened to put 90 per cent of the picture industry of Australia out of work. Articles by John W. Hicks, others of his staff and compliant exhibitors rehearsed the arguments Soden and Howe had been using for over a year — there was no monopoly, the Australian outlay to meet an Australian quota would be utterly prohibitive for a tiny population, American films succeeded because they had most money spent on them and therefore were best — and to these they added one or two of their own. Australian production was acceptable as long as it remained small, localised and (unstated) did not constitute a threat. As the *Exhibitor* pointed out, since Australia could never provide a market for all the films a quota would demand, she would have to immediately build a huge international market and (again unstated) compete with the United States. Meanwhile, Paramount argued, was it not doing everything needed for local production by distributing local films of merit, such as *The Dinkum Bloke*?

The other 'champion of the industry' at the beginning of October took the form of a counter-deputation to the Tariff Commission, which claimed that the exhibition trade was frequently run at a loss because American films in Australia 'that cost thousands of pounds to produce . . . have not earned half their costs in hirings', and that 'the picture exhibitor in Australia is free to screen whatever pictures he wishes to hire'.

As government interest increased, building up to the Royal Commission of 1927, so the distributors became increasingly well organised,[36] culminating in the announcement in November 1924 that:

> To protect the motion picture industry from the various attacks made upon it . . . representatives of the picture producers met and decided to join forces under the title of the Motion Picture Distributors of Australia

a fact which W.J. Howe in his Christmas message to the exhibitors of Australia greeted with considerable enthusiasm.

In the light of this history of strengthening organisation by the distributors, and in particular the consistent policy of Hicks at Paramount to waylay and side-track government intervention, it would be foolish to accept too readily Longford's separation of Hicks and Howe as the 'good' and the 'bad'. They were too close in their orientations and active political strategies for that to be possible. It is at the very least arguable that Paramount adopted *The Dinkum Bloke* in 1923, that First National distributed *Those Terrible Twins* in 1925 (produced by a naturalist with no feature making experience and which Jones of First National described as 'a terrible picture'), and that Australasian Films went into production of *Painted Daughters* in 1925, employing a man with Hollywood sub-directorial experience who happened to be in Australia at the time — all for the same reason: to deflect mounting criticism of the distributors and to either make a gesture towards, or else pre-empt threats of, an Australian quota.

If that was the case, there was little hope for Longford of any continuous support from the Paramount link-up, and his financial backing by W.J. Howe must also be seen to have been of dubious value. Longford himself said he thought allotting a hundred fully paid-up shares to Howe was 'a wise precaution'.[37] Despite nearly half of the £4,847 cost of *The Dinkum Bloke* going to Australasian Films for film, cameraman and studio, 'the combine refused to release the picture. Through Mr Howe's influence the picture was handled by Paramount Films for all markets except the English', receiving its premiere at Hoyts Theatre a full seven months after it was completed.

The account of what happened next varies according to whether one reads Longford's interpretation or Howe's. Howe, asserting that there was little or no delay in the release of the film, said that Paramount gave the producer 65 per cent and paid the cost of the publicity printing out of their 35 per cent. Returns of £3,990 for Australia and New Zealand and £2,000 for England were not sufficient to continue operations, and the company 'went into liquidation.[38] Longford, on the other hand, argued that Howe, who 'during the course of the proceedings of the company '. . . was unwilling to attach his name to any scheme to aid local production', was complicit in pressure to close down the company, and played a key role in the jockeying of Longford out of a decision-making position at the crucial moment.

Howe, it seems clear, showed a distinctly lukewarm approach to the Longford–Lyell company, and never advertised his name in its support, as he did for so many other causes at this time. But then, by Longford's own account, Howe was never really interested in the first place, and was brought in mainly for the company's use. On the matter of the release of *The Dinkum Bloke* the evidence seems only to give some weight to long-ford's account, since although there was an earlier trade screening, editing seems not to have been completed until the beginning of February, which would mean a gap before release of four months, in contrast to Longford's seven months and Howe's one.

What is certain is that as its first function the M.P.D.A. did irreparable harm to Longford's desperate search for more financial backing by stating publicly that *The Dinkum Bloke* had failed financially because 'the exhibitor would not book it', despite its being 'put out with all the resources of one of the biggest distributors, Paramount Films.'[39] At the Royal Commission Longford presented the auditor's letter, dated 6 November 1924, which made it clear that between 2 June and 27 September 511 exhibitors had paid rentals on the film bringing in £5,831 17s 6d, 'a record sum for an Australian production, and the booking of the picture still continues'. Although *Everyones* printed a short letter from Arthur Shirley to the effect that *The Dinkum Bloke* had not lost money, the journal refused to print an apology, or indeed any statement by Longford as to the correct situation, and as such must stand complicit with the M.P.D.A. for an action, deliberate or otherwise, which had a crippling effect on Australia's major producer in his final real attempt at independent production.

After the winding down of his company, Longford worked as Director of Productions for the Commonwealth Government for a while, making propaganda films around Australian primary and secondary industries for the British Empire Exhibition at Wembley. He then made three films with the financial backing of Charles Perry. The first of these was *Fisher's Ghost*: Longford clearly had a taste for tales of mystery and moralistic melodrama, quite apart from his 'push' and 'selection' stories, as this film and his 1930s version of *The Man They Couldn't Hang* show. In *Fisher's Ghost* he fleshed out the simple legend with heavy emphasis on the murderer's confession:

> There is no Hell save memory and remorse; no peace on earth but death's long dreamless sleep . . . I killed Frederick Fisher, but in my haunting dreams he has died at my hands not once but a thousand times.

The film opened at the beginning of October 1924 at Hoyts, *Everyones* remarking that during a period of hot weather when other cinemas were doing poorly, the De Luxe was packed to standing. This popularity continued into a second week at the Shell Theatre, and Herb Finlay was to say at the Royal Commission that the genuine popularity of Australian films was proven to him when he toured the backblocks with *Fisher's Ghost* and saw it outsell the Harold Lloyd film he was also promoting.

Trade comment was favourable, *Everyones* saying that *Fisher's Ghost*, despite limited capital, presented 'an able front to those who are of the opinion that pictures cannot be made in this country'.[40] The film was released in London in 1925, and the British trade press as usual praised Longford for his handling of actors (who were in this production mainly from the theatre) and for Arthur Higgins's photography, though *Everyones* managed to weaken a highly complimentary review in *Bioscope* by focusing, in a self-righteous way, on its comment, 'considering that the film was made in Australia the technical standard of the production as a whole is surprisingly high'.[41]

It was an ironic accident that the very same week that *Everyones* was reviewing *Fisher's Ghost* as 'not . . . an equal to the big majority of feature films released here' it was also reviewing as a 'good feature' and representative of American imports *The Lure of the Yukon*, directed by Norman Dawn, starring Eva Novak and released by Australasian Films. Longford was to reach the nadir of his career two years later at the hands of that particular combination, and even in 1924, by Longford's account, he was receiving poor consideration by Stuart Doyle of Australasian Films. Doyle, only two years before he approved the cannibalistic references in *For The Term Of His Natural Life*, told Longford that he was sickened by the 'gruesome' quality of this mild tale of the supernatural, and refused it a first release. In order to understand this rejection though, it is again necessary to go beyond Longford's personal-conspiratorial interpretation. Doyle was following common practice among American exhibitors in rejecting films with the slightest touch of horror content as 'gruesome', 'sickening' or 'repulsive'.[42] Another clue lies in W.A. Gibson's evidence to the Royal Commission. Gibson, who liked *Fisher's Ghost*, said he was not surprised to hear 'that Mr Stuart Doyle refused to take because it contains references to the Kelly Gang.'

Longford complained that as a result of the refusal Hoyts could offer him rockbottom prices which he was forced to accept. Thus a film which cost only £1,000 but netted Hoyts over £1,200 in the first week's showing, gave the producers a mere £30 rental for that week, out of which they had to pay £20 for publicity.[43] Doyle argued at the Royal Commission

Hoyt's De-Luxe Theatre
SYDNEY

thought so much of this sensational Australian-made picture that they booked it as their A Grade Feature, and will advertise it on an unprecedented scale.

This amazing story of something that really happened, filmed by way of a change, and taken on the spot where it actually occurred.

Do You Believe in Ghosts?

'FISHER'S GHOST'

Produced by Raymond Longford, who personally is convinced it is the supreme photoplay achievement of his eminently successful picture producing career.

BETTER THAN "SENTIMENTAL BLOKE."

Released by
LONGFORD-LYELL PRODUCTIONS,
129 BATHURST ST.,
SYDNEY.

On an equity basis to all showmen, which means we don't demand a high price, but will stake our existence on the picture's exceptional merit.

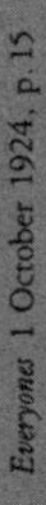
Everyones 1 October 1924, p. 15

Everyones 8 October 1924, p.8

Publicity for Longford and the American film-maker he could 'not equal', Norman Dawn that he had released the film 'in many theatres throughout Australia', but when cross-questioned it became evident that, as with a number of Longford's films, such as *The Sentimental Bloke* and *The Dinkum Bloke*, Union Theatres only took the film after it was a proven commercial success. Doyle claimed in response to this that *he* in fact was responsible for the success of *The Sentimental Bloke* since 'any detrimental effect because of being shown at the Theatre Royal . . . was more than overcome by the tremendous publicity we gave it'!

Longford's next film for Perry, *The Bushwackers*, was, like *The Dinkum Bloke*, a story of true sacrifice by a 'Sentimental Bloke type', giving the producer plenty of scope for pathos. *Everyones* noted that 'the film was of sufficient importance to Australasian Films as to warrant them purchasing it outright — a rather unusual proceeding on the part of this exchange'. It was actually the first time Australasian Films had done so and the trade press said that Longford was entirely satisfied with a deal which freed him from 'the necessity of creating a separate organisation to deal with this film, and means that instant preparations may be commenced on another picture'.[44] At the Royal Commission, however, Longford said that the 'picture was purchased outright by the combine at less than the cost price' because 'the combine wished to engage me . . . in succession to Mr Whyte who . . . had left the country without completing his second picture called *Sunrise* for the combine'.

This typically conspiratorial interpretation of Longford's is almost certainly wrong, because Stuart-Whyte was still working on *Sunrise* in the new Bondi Studios in late July 1925, the same time that Union Theatres were releasing *The Bushwackers* in Sydney,[45] having bought the film two months before that. However, there is no doubt that Longford's accusations against Australasian Films and Union Theatres (which were made public at the Royal Commission, but were obviously circulating around the trade long before that) were associated in the public's mind both with the production of *Sunrise* and the purchase of *The Bushwackers*. Referring to *The Bushwackers*, *Everyones* commented in May that 'following on the recent agitation in the public press, this deal would seem to be the first step towards the cementing of better relations between the Australian producer and the releasing house';[46] while in June the first trade press comment on the production of *Sunrise* said that the making of a second film by A.F. disproved the 'many people' who said they produced *Painted Daughters* only to placate public opinion.[47]

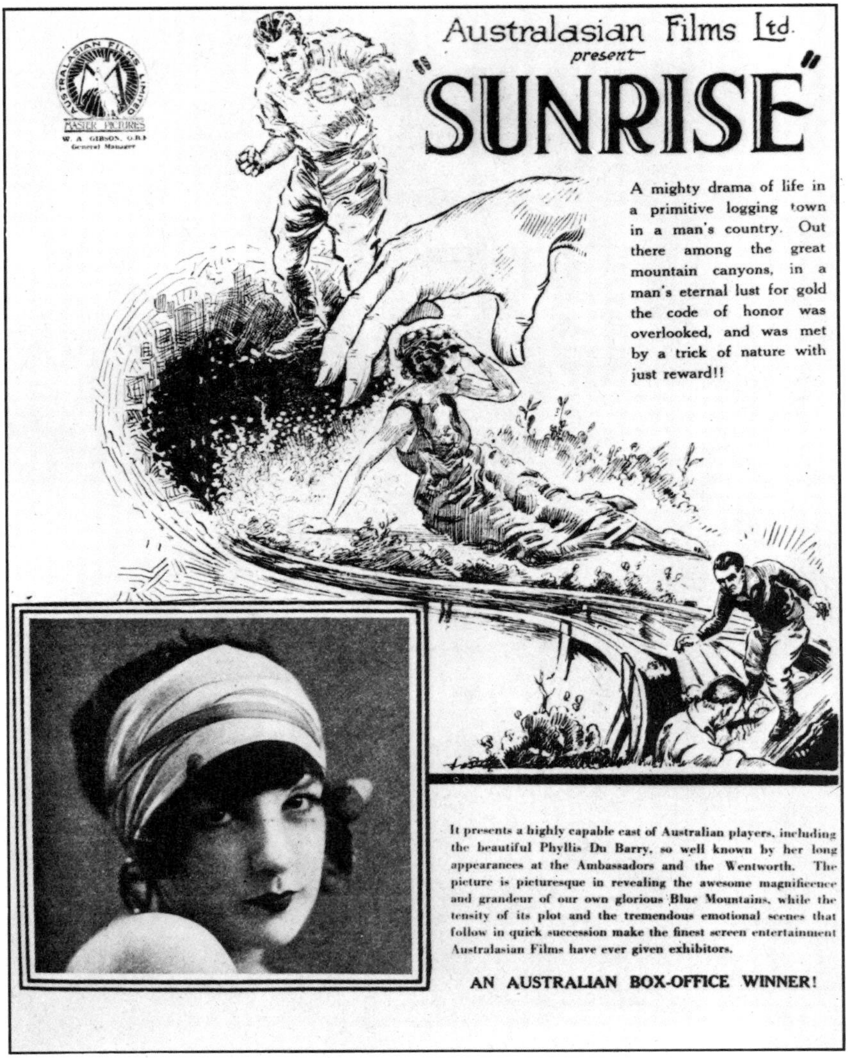
AUSTRALASIAN FILMS LIMITED
MASTER PICTURES
W. A. GIBSON, O.B.E.
General Manager
Australasian Films Ltd.
present
"SUNRISE"
A mighty drama of life in a primitive logging town in a man's country. Out there among the great mountain canyons, in a man's eternal lust for gold the code of honor was overlooked, and was met by a trick of nature with just reward!!
It presents a highly capable cast of Australian players, including the beautiful Phyllis Du Barry, so well known by her long appearances at the Ambassadors and the Wentworth. The picture is picturesque in revealing the awesome magnificence and grandeur of our own glorious Blue Mountains, while the tensity of its plot and the tremendous emotional scenes that follow in quick succession make the finest screen entertainment Australasian Films have ever given exhibitors.
AN AUSTRALIAN BOX-OFFICE WINNER!

Everyones 20 October 1926, p.9

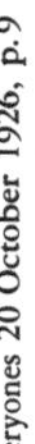

Spectacle and episodic action: *Sunrise,* a Longford vehicle by necessity, not conviction

National Film Archive

More Union Theatres melodrama forced on Longford: *The Hills of Hate*

But the purchase of *The Bushwackers* did enable Longford to go into instant production of his next, and last, film for Perry. The controversy was not over, however, since Longford accused Union Theatres first of rejecting the film, *Peter Vernon's Silence*, and then, after it was accepted by Paramount, of resisting its release for a year, finally showing it 'at a third-rate city theatre [The Empress, Sydney] with inadequate publicity and very little, if any, newspaper publicity'. Under cross-questioning at the Royal Commission, Doyle replied to these accusations by saying that the Empress was an A-grade theatre, even if not a very special one; that *Peter Vernon's Silence* was one of the poorest of Longford's films, which the Empress audiences became abusive about; and that the question of its early first release was in Paramount's hands since they could easily have included the film in their block-booking packing. Since this had not been done, the film had to wait for a vacant theatre — a fact which Doyle, remarkably, denied was evidence of the stranglehold American companies had, via block booking, on Australian production. Certainly the film received very little publicity, meriting only one full page advertisement in *Everyones*. Reviews of the film supported Doyle's opinion. *Everyones* praised the photography, but argued that the story was 'very weak and unconvincing', and *Film Weekly*, noting that the scenery was beautiful — with some of the first snow scenes in an Australian production,[48] added that the plot was 'entirely too melodramatic to be convincing'. Plot synopses reveal a familiar Longford theme: self-sacrifice by the lower-class hero, exploitation by the upper class.[49]

The Last Challenge

The final stage of Raymond Longford's silent film-making career was described by him to the Royal Commission as follows:

> At the completion of this picture I was appointed Director of Productions for Australasian Films, i.e. the combine, and put in charge of their Waverley studio. My first work was to complete the picture which Mr Whyte had left unfinished. I was next given a story called *The Pioneers* to produce, which had been done before, followed by a story, *The Hills of Hate*. Both these books were selected by the directors of the combine, they were produced at an inadequate expense, and in many cases the cast for the picture was chosen despite my protests.

Recognising that these films were 'absurdly cheap and inadequate to secure even an English market', he persuaded Australasian Films to purchase *For the Term of His Natural Life*.[50] However, he was asked to stand down in favour of Norman Dawn on the grounds that 'if produced by an American, with American artists, it would be sure of an American release. Mr Balcombe further assured me that if I fell in with their views, I would lose nothing by the sacrifice, and would still continue to produce for them'. In fact, however, they let his contract expire.

The scenario is a familiar one. In all the publicity about Longford being appointed producer for A.F. Master Pictures two chronologically distinct features were emphasised: the pioneer film-maker and the multi-million dollar industry. But there were two different versions of this, the trade's and Longford's. The first version, adopted by the trade and W.A. Gibson (the trade's reports were little more than verbatim Gibson), emphasised the 'first in the field' qualities of Longford: producer of the first long-run film, the first Australian studio, the first indoor sets, the first air-war picture, the first Australian comedy, the first historical picture, the first overseas location. All of these, for instance, were encapsulated within an *Everyones* lead article entitled 'An Australian Film Pioneer',[51] which also mentioned his romantic pioneering life as a young man roaming across many continents and oceans. This was only half of their equation, which is the same optimistic contrast *Picture Show* began with six years before.

Longford, it was said, was a 'battler' for Australian films 'against weighty opposition' and 'innumerable difficulties', but now, with the vast modern facilities of A.F. behind him he should be able 'to show his mettle'[52] and make films of world appeal. By a process of evolution the 'lag' that *Picture Show* had noticed between pioneering production and modern distribution and exhibition was, in the most natural way, about to be made up.

Longford was also an evolutionist, often speaking with supreme self-confidence of his natural abilities in the 'struggle for survival'. So, in his version, he too spoke of his fight against great odds and the need to 'battle on by myself without encouragement'.[53] But whereas the trade spoke of a natural evolution towards the very best synthesis of individual spirit and civilised organisation, Longford referred back to a more romantic and pristine age, the time before the Great War when competition was more open than 'in this commercial age' of great crushing juggernauts financed by American capital. In his view, then, the battle was an open and endless one between the pioneer and the combine, and only government action could carry enough weight to restore that pristine economy in which, he was quite sure, as one of 'the three foremost producers in the world', he would triumph.

The Royal Commission noticed this constant polarity in Longford's world view: 'To judge from your statements right through, the combine has been chasing you as though you were a mechanical hare?' He replied, 'Absolutely; they recognise that I can make pictures.' Longford argued that there was nothing inconsistent in his old enemy now employing him to make films: 'the fact is that they engaged me to kill the business. That opinion was expressed to me at the time.'

What is the evidence one way or the other? Longford argued that A.F. could not have been serious about their new production policy because of the absurd cheapness of the films, and because they consciously went against two of his fundamental principles: the right to choose his actors and his story. In relation to the first point, it is certainly true that A.F. spent very little. At a time when publicity was regarded throughout the trade with mystical veneration, it is hard to find any films of any production company, no matter how small, throughout the 1920s which were less publicised. For the two Master Pictures, *The Pioneers* and *Hills of Hate*, there were *no* advertisements at all in *Everyones*, the leading trade journal. While searching for contemporary accounts of the productions, in *Everyones* I have been able to find only one mention of *The Pioneers*, a total of one column inch, and three mentions of *Hills of Hate*, the largest of these at two column inches. The fact that out of the five column inches *total* publicity I found in *Everyones* for *Hills of Hate*, over half was about Dorothy Gordon as leading lady, may raise a point about the second of Longford's complaints: that the cast of the film was engaged without his consultation, and the star part chosen by Hugh D. McIntosh to buy off his newspaper's attacks.

McIntosh, a parliamentarian who owned the *Sunday Times*, a high-quality Sydney newspaper, had been criticising certain aspects of the film industry to the Tariff Board, in the New South Wales Legislative Council, and in the pages of his paper. His main complaints were that Hollywood was Americanising Australia, and that American companies were paying no tax in doing so. As a result there were two huge sources of profit. First, by establishing Australian subsidiaries which were charged in advance the total estimated profits they were likely to make, the home American companies creamed off most of the gross takings without paying tax — since only the Australian companies were subject to tax and were ostensibly making nothing to be taxed on. Secondly, as a broader argument, not only were these films 'prostituting our language, destroying our ideals and gravely menacing the wellbeing of the Empire' by endlessly presenting to Australian youth 'super-American citizens and apologetic eye-glass lunatic-looking Englishmen in the films', but also 'because trade follows the film' they were having a distinct effect on trade. McIntosh spoke of a deputation of Bradford woollen manufacturers to the British Prime Minister who complained of 'the pernicious influence of these pictures in the far East . . . where they had to alter the whole of the costumes and woollens because the Eastern people wanted to dress like movie heroes'.[54]

The example McIntosh quoted was one of many at the time: Japanese tailors were said to be going to American films to learn how to cut according to Western styles; in Brazil American cars were said to be selling thirty-five percent more after being featured in American films, and American-style bungalows were increasingly built overseas for the same reason.[55] The 'trade follows the film' argument prompted considerable government action. On the one hand it was an extremely important factor behind the attempts at quota legislation in all parts of the world in the 1920s to establish local film industries; on the other hand it prompted Congress to set up a Motion Picture Section in the Bureau of Foreign and Domestic Commerce in 1926 under Herbert Hoover, with the object of promoting the rental of American films overseas in order to secure trade.

In the light of this, and of American control of world screens through dumping and block-booking, it was fatuous of *Everyones* to reply to McIntosh's complaint of an American stranglehold on local film industries that good films create their own market and that 'if . . . the Slavs succeed in making one better it will supersede the American offering and will in turn give way to something still better'.[56] To his accompanying complaint that attempts had been made to strangle him, too, by withdrawing all cinema advertising from his newspaper (a very serious threat to a quality paper which did not make much money), *Everyones* had the equally disingenuous response that 'papers of the calibre of the *Sun*, the *Sydney Morning Herald*, the Melbourne *Age* and *Argus* are above all suspicion in the matter of being subject to advertising pressure'.[57]

Far more significant was the fact that Stuart Doyle of Australasian Films was himself to move towards a multi-media control, by gaining considerable influence in radio and newspaper spheres[58] and also, in terms of the 'trade follows the film' argument, that he and his brother Ralph (managing director of United Artists, A/sia, Ltd) set up a company, American Modes Ltd, 'importers of clothing and wearing apparel of all kinds'. The Doyle brothers, respective managing directors of major Australian distributing organisations, had this direct financial stake in the abundant importation of American films.[59]

It is clear, then, both that the trade in general reacted very sharply to McIntosh's statements (*Everyones* threatening his parliamentary career with 'all the forces of the screen'), and that Stuart Doyle had a substantial interest in the continued domination of American films. Doyle also at this time spent a lot of time and money publicly denying American tax evasion (a position he was to change dramatically in the 1930s), while *Everyones* fulminated that the matter of tax was 'a phase of the business which concerns no one but the companies themselves'.[60] McIntosh certainly stirred a hornet's nest, and in view of the open threats to him in the trade press it is not hard to accept his claim that the trade had tried to buy him off by promising to re-advertise if he shut up. *Everyones* also admitted that the recent interest in local productions was the result of complaints against American monopoly and tax evasion to the Tariff Board.

In the light of all this, Longford's allegation does not seem preposterous. It is also consistent with his argument that Australasian Films inevitably responded with deliberately half-hearted attempts at film production whenever there was strong public criticism. And that would account for the minimal publicity for the Longford films. In the context of this argument the concluding statements in the trade press about Longford's appointment by Australasian Films read as though blame for the expected failure was being transferred from the juggernaut to the pioneer. On the one hand *Everyones* argued, 'If local pictures made under these conditions fail to find favour with the public it will not be the fault of the far-seeing directors of Master Pictures, who are sparing no expense and pains so that their enterprise may be justified'.[61] On the other hand the journal stated ominously that the future of Australian production was solely in Longford's hands and they hoped 'he will not abuse the trust placed in him'.[62]

The extent of that trust was displayed when, after working with his son Victor on the script of *The Term* for a year,[63] he was dismissed. Longford was never able to surmount his conspiracy argument. When asked at the Royal Commission why Australasian Films should spend £50,000 on *The Term* if they wished to kill Australian film production, he said, 'I cannot say . . . The situation has me puzzled', adding, however, that 'It would be a very small amount to spend if they desired to kill the industry'. Further, Longford did *not* blame the American distributors in Australia:

> I have the greatest respect and admiration for Mr Hicks, and I do not blame him. We are not up against Universal Films or Fox Films . . . Mr Jones of the First National has been a personal friend of mine for years. Mr Crick, of the Fox Corporation, is also a friend of mine; in fact I am friendly with all the film people except Australasian Films Ltd.[64]

Longford tended to see the world in individualist terms; hence he explained his career in terms of solo pioneering and personal vendetta. He had one final example of it to recount to the Royal Commission: of how a new production company was proposed at the end of 1926 which offered Longford £2,500 per annum as producer; how Fred Phillips then offered him a directorship at the same salary and how, after turning the latter down because of prior commitment, he was told by the company accountant of a proposed merger with Australasian Films Ltd who wanted Frank Hurley instead, since Longford was not acceptable to that company. He ended up with neither of the jobs.

As with so many of Longford's stories of persecution, there is not a lot of evidence to support or refute his claims. Fred Phillips did not mention in his testimony having intended Longford for the head of his productions. Indeed, it is clear that he had been planning for a very long time to appoint a top-rated American director. On the other hand it appears that Phillips did try to get Gayne Dexter, editor of *Everyones*, as a director of the company, so perhaps he did also ask Longford for the technical help he was much more equipped to give than Dexter. It is also likely that Hurley, who was a friend of Doyle's, and regarded as having an international reputation, would have appealed to Australasian Films more than Longford, and we do know that a very large building and production enterprise was being planned by the company at this time, with Hurley as production head — though that in itself might be a further indication that Australasian Films was not trying to 'kill the industry'. Until much more information about the daily dealings of Union Theatres and Australasian Films is known — their association with the other big exhibiting circuit,[65] as well as major independents like Howe, their detailed relations with the American distributors, their estimation of and strategy towards the Royal Commission and the proposed quota legislation, and their policy regarding the regenerating British production industry — it is impossible to fully explain the decisions which Longford interpreted as conspiracy. What is certain is that these broad forces, and the others that have been mentioned in this chapter, were the main motivating factors and that Longford's personal career was no more than a secondary factor in their decisions.

The fact that so few of Longford's accusations can now be either substantiated or refuted can be blamed in no small part on the Royal Commission itself in its refusal to follow them up. Even though the evidence of Doyle and Gibson was shot through with contradictions and inconsistencies, the Commissioners by and large preferred to take their comments on trust. Virtually none of the men Longford mentioned as being able to testify — Baker, Percival, Musgrove, Perry, Earl, Court, Higgins — were called to do so. It may be that some of them would have refused to speak, but that does not excuse the Commission's failure to ask pertinent questions of those they did interview, such as Fred Phillips or Dan Carroll.

At the Royal Commission Longford had said, 'I know if we fail this time we are gone'. That was how it was to be. In November 1927 Longford threw down a last challenge to the local industry. Earlier that year W.J. Howe and other exhibitors had compiled in the pages of *Everyones* a list of ingredients necessary for a successful Australian feature film.[66] Longford proposed to make it. He pointed out that there were only two 'specimens of Australian literature widely known to the outside world'.[67] One of them, *For the Term of His Natural Life* he had suggested to Australasian Films. They had bought it but had rejected him. Now, consistently, he had bought the world film rights to the other property, *Robbery Under Arms.* Nodding at Stuart Doyle, he pointed out that there was nothing 'morbid or gruesome' in it. Nodding at Howe and all the others in the trade who had insisted at the Royal Commission that for an Australian film to be shown it only had to be 'the goods', he asked them to invest in a film to be made for £15,000 which had all the ingredients they had asked for, was based on a popular classic and was to be made by Australia's leading director. Howe replied that film production was not in the ambit of his association, and the Queensland showmen, saying that local production could not succeed until distribution was out of the hands of the monopolies, were also unwilling to invest.

Although Longford was highly optimistic about the Report of the Royal Commission when it came out in 1928, by March 1929 when the main resolutions on an Australian quota had not been implemented through the intransigence of the State governments, and the promised production awards which *were* in the direct provenance of the federal government had not been implemented either, Longford lashed out. The scenario in *Everyones* (which was no doubt delighted that Longford was shifting his attack from the combine to the parliamentarians) was the familiar one: on the one hand the solitary pioneer with so many 'firsts' in production who had for so long 'rubbed against the raw edges of life' and now 'finds himself driven abroad in order to keep his arcs burning'; on the other hand the juggernaut. But it was now a different juggernaut: the dead hand of government 'bureaucracy' and 'inertia'. Taking up the cry the trade press had been issuing regularly for months, Longford argued that government interference via the Royal Commission had scared capital away from production. Men who would have invested were keeping their money in their pockets until they knew under what conditions the annual awards would be made.

> Today the position is so hopeless that the men in the game have to get out. Not the combines or the circuits but the Commonwealth Government has ruined us.[68]

And so Longford sailed away to England with the rights of *Robbery Under Arms* in his pocket, and, inevitably for him, new windmills to tilt at. Less than a year later he was back, flaying a new opponent:

> For years and years I fought for the English industry. I battled against the Americans. But now, after seeing the English film men at work, I am prepared to admit that I backed the wrong side.[69]

This time it was not Stuart Doyle who had kept him waiting for weeks outside his office, but British executives. Once again *Everyones* was delighted to print his denouncement of quota-bred mushroom companies and his praise of 'the kindness of the American executives — the very men I fought for years'. Within a few months he was engaged in a new slanging match, this time with another Australian producer over the possibility of a quota and a national sound studio. In June 1930 Longford, on the edge of obscurity, still spoke bravely of his dream, of a local production industry:

> I can only see that object achieved by the construction of a sound proof studio, the installation of necessary machinery and the long withheld support of *all* picture producers that will make what is now a pathetic joke into what I have always believed it could be — a great Australian industry.[70]

Raymond Longford's vision of the potential of an Australian film industry was always a Romantic one: the struggle of heroic individual pioneers and bitter artists of genius against the crushing forces of modern civilisation. And even after his death the Romantic image remained of the artist, ahead of his time, dying in penury. The Melbourne *Herald* said in 1976, for instance;

> Henry Lawson was broke at the end of his life — now he stares at us from every $10 note. The irony of the poet's posthumous canonisation is echoed in the belated recognition of the man who was the Lawson of the Australian cinema — Raymond Longford. Longford, Australia's great pioneer film maker, ended his working life as a watchman on the Sydney waterfront. Now Melbourne's newest cinema will be named after him.[71]

The real irony is that it is yet one more example of the media's use of the Longford legend to evoke a complacent *synthesis* between the pioneer and modernity. Longford's own version, of an irreparable breach, never left him. One of the industry's last insults to Longford was in 1955 when the Sydney Film Festival screened *The Sentimental Bloke* and neglected to invite him to the screening. Longford's public response was typical: reminiscences of an age past, his pioneering and creativity ('the close up . . . I was the first film producer in the world to use it. American film authorities now admit I anticipated Griffith by some years') together with a final bitterness against the impersonal institution: 'I wasn't asked . . . I didn't even know they were going to show it. Pioneers are forgotten men.'[72]

5

The 'Practical Way': Beaumont Smith

In late 1919, at a time of supreme optimism for Australian production, *Picture Show* described Beaumont Smith as pre-eminent as a producer of Australian successes. It was an attitude which was never to alter. The disparity between the success of Beau Smith and the failure of Raymond Longford is a mark of the different treatment they received from the film trade. The question remains, however, as to why Smith was always given an exemplary status by the trade whenever it wanted a stick to beat other producers with, particularly when there was pressure for quota legislation.

Unlike Barrett who was an all-round pioneer of the cinema, and Longford who was something of an international peripatetic before taking up acting and film making, Beau Smith had been an entrepreneur of the popular and more serious arts in Australia from his early days.[1] His theatrical career began when he became publicity manager and secretary to William Anderson, who was an exception among theatrical proprietors in giving space to Australian dramas. In 1912 Bert Bailey and Julius Grant created an amazing success (and made their fortune) with *On Our Selection*; according to *Everyones*, Beau Smith 'although it is not generally known . . . was responsible for the stage version of *On Our Selection* which is freely admitted to be the forerunner of the real Australian drama'.[2]

After acting as a buyer for Anderson in London, he set up his own dramatic company, producing *While the Billy Boils*, which he later made into a film, and *Seven Little Australians*, which Louis Paul described as the 'most notable of staged plays concerning Australian city life'.[3]

Smith's fortune, however, came from side shows not the theatre. While searching Europe for 'novelties' he was impressed by the entrepreneurial possibilities of a group of Austrian midgets. An extensive tour of Canada, Africa and Australasia with this 'Tiny Town' brought him a fortune which enabled him to enter theatrical and, towards the end of World War I, film production in a considerable way. By the end of 1919 Smith had established the very popular *Hayseeds* series on film, and made box office successes with *Satan in Sydney* and *Desert Gold*, together with the less successful *Barry Butts In,* which was an attempt to launch the Australian vaudeville comic, Barry Lupino into film stardom.[4]

In November 1919 Smith, like Barrett, was inspired by the optimism of the trade and the success of *The Sentimental Bloke* and began a major venture into Australian film-making. However, unlike Barrett, Smith was intending to make his 'true-to-Australia' films in America! He had already bought the film rights to the works of Banjo Paterson and Henry Lawson (each supposedly for £500), and he intended to make *The Man from Snowy River*, and if that was successful, *While the Billy Boils*. The problem of Australian scenery was to be solved by Smith shooting in Australia before leaving several hundred feet of panoramic 'scenics' which he intended to intercut with action close-ups taken in the United States. He had also chosen for his American locations an area outside Los Angeles with 'long rows of gum trees and wide patches of scrub, exactly as they are found out-West'.[5] He intended to select his cast entirely from the many Australians in Hollywood, and would take with him 'a complete Australian equipment . . . even including the saddles the boys in the bush use'. In this way, he claimed, with a showman's concern for visual detail and disdain for cultural subtleties, the 'possibility of the characters of *The Man From Snowy River* being somewhat Americanised does not not arise.'

Bizarre though the venture sounds, it was yet another of the many variants which Australians tried for reaching a world market with their films. Some producers imported American directors and stars, others tried producing 'international' stories; Longford aimed simply at 'quality' Australian subjects. Smith's solution was to reverse the Baker–Carroll venture, and use Australian producers and stars in Hollywood. The idea had a good deal of practical sense behind it. As Smith pointed out, he, like all Australian producers, had learnt the trade by intuition and experience. Now he would learn current American techniques by going there and engaging directors 'who knew the business back to front'. Most important of all, he would distribute his own films in America. A key problem for both British and Australian films in this period was the *ad hoc* selling system employed in the only market that really mattered.

Picture Show bestowed as many laurels for enterprise on Beau Smith as it had on Snowy Baker: 'Mr Smith is as game as they make them. I have not the least doubt that he will make good in Los Angeles'. However, in May 1920 Smith was back in Australia, complaining that the costs of film-making were exorbitant due to 'the American habit of overcharging everyone connected with the film business. Over there producers don't bother much with economy. Mostly they have other people's money behind them, and in that case don't care how much a picture costs as long as it turns out well'.[6] As a shrewd independent producer, Smith was quick to notice the escalation of costs which spread out to every quarter of film-making from this practice — even to the hiring of minor props — making it very much cheaper to produce the films in Australia. Though Longford and others were to point angrily at Australian companies allowing American directors to throw money around during production, the cost of American film-making was normally conveniently forgotten by those in the trade who argued that because Australian films cost less money than American, they could never be as good. And, ironically, they always then turned to Beaumont Smith as a local film maker who knew his place and produced films cheaply for the home market. But this image was just as much part of the moulding of the Beau Smith the trade desired — and eventually got — as the director himself wished.

Smith certainly returned from America with the firm opinion that Australian films would 'have to be particularly good to compete outside'. But this is not to say that he had at this stage lost interest in the international field and committed himself to second-rate pictures. He had, after all, cut *The Sentimental Bloke* for the American market while over there, and had learned about new techniques, particularly in studio lighting. As he pointed out, he still held the rights to the works of Lawson and Paterson and, armed with the new lighting equipment he had brought back which would allow him to shoot in all weathers, he intended to go into major production.[7]

'Marketable Angles'

Smith cast *The Man From Snowy River* immediately. His casting policy was to be consistent throughout his silent-film-making career and displayed his shrewdness concerning the current state of Australian cinema as well as his theatrical background. For his male stars he usually relied on men with long stage experience, which in Australia implied considerable versatility. Cyril Mackay, who played the male lead in *Snowy River* had been on the boards for years, in both England and Australia, had played forty different roles in only six years while he was with J.C. Williamson, and maintained that he had no preference for particular types, since 'there are so many parts I have loved equally well'.[8] John Cosgrove, who played Saltbush Bill, had been on the stage for nearly thirty years, playing every city in Australia, as well as touring the outback by Cobb and Co. coach.

(i) (ii)

(iii) (iv)

Actors against type: Cyril Mackay in (i) *When London Sleeps* and (ii) *The Man from Snowy River;* John Cosgrove in (iii, far left) *As You Like It* and (iv) *While the Billy Boils*

(i) *Theatre Magazine* 11 September 1913; (ii) *Everyones* 1 September 1920, p. 10; (iii) *Stage and Society* 19 May 1925, p.19; (iv) *Picture Show* 1 October 1921, p.26

(i)

(i) *Picture Show* 1 June 1921, p.8; (ii) National Film Archive; (iii) *Picture Show* 1 January 1922, p.41

(iv)

(v)

(iv) National Film Archive; (v) *Picture Show* 1 September 1921, p. 34

Acting versatility: comedian Tal Ordell (i) in (ii) *On Our Selection.* (iii) *The Gentleman Bushranger,* (iv) *While the Billy Boils* and (v) *Silks and Saddles*

He was also cynical about film's tendency to 'typing', having for years played Shakespeare, melodrama and light comedy all in the same week: 'There was no talk of types then as there is today. We played any part we were given, and had to adapt ourselves to it — not make the part adapt itself to us'.[9] The parts of John Carewe and Stingy Smith were played by two more experienced stage actors, John Faulkner and Tal Ordell. Faulkner had stage and screen experience in three continents. Tal Ordell, whose talents extended to playwriting, vaudeville, 'lightning-artistry', and later film-making, had been a well-known character actor for J.C. Williamson. He was used consistently by Smith for his versatility, playing with equal ability, elderly hayseed, young blade or heavy villain.

In contrast, and in recognition of the new medium and its place in the Hollywood domain, Smith tended to adopt new young female stars in many of his productions, and cast them according to type. Whereas, for example, Barrett chose Marie La Varre, with her composite background of legitimate stage, Hollywood and vaudeville to play the vamp in *The Breaking of the Drought*, Smith in contrast cast Hedda Barr, a young Hollywood film actress on holiday in Australia to establish the typical city vamp type in *The Man from Snowy River.* And for his innocent country-type lead he gave Stella Southern ('star of the south' — real name Billie Winks) her first part. Smith selected Southern, according to reports in true Hollywood fashion, straight out of a millinery shop because he was 'looking for a type'.

Descriptions of Beaumont Smith productions tended to emphasise both how well he integrated his company with the local community while on location, and the all-in-the-family fellow feeling within the company itself. This no doubt had a lot to do with the theatrical mores of Smith and his experienced stock actors which, as they tended to stay together for a number of productions, created a valuable launching pad for young actresses (and the occasional young male star like Gordon Collinridge).

For *The Man from Snowy River* Smith continued his policy of 'learning the game' from American directors by employing John H. Wells who had some years experience in Hollywood studios. But Smith always kept 'the Australian details' in his own hands, which meant that he wielded considerable control over his productions, not only as producer, but as scenarist, financier and distributor as well.

The scenario gives us valuable insights into Smith's writing and production methods. Like Longford, he was faced with the problem of turning a poem into a narrative film. An American critic had commented on Longford's *The Sentimental Bloke* in December 1919 that 'the picturization of

(i) Hedda Barr

(ii) Stella Southern

Stage and Society

A

Happy

New Year

Miss Stella Southern

The Charming Theatrical Artiste

A BONA-FIDE USER OF MERCOLIZED WAX FOR THE SKIN, STALLAX HAIR SHAMPOO, AND BARRI-AGAR FACE POWDER, THE SUMMER GIRL'S TOILET PREPARATION

Buy to-day from your Chemist or Store. Specify Dearborn's.

PRICE 6D.

(i) *Picture Show* 1 September 1920, p.7; (ii) *Stage and Society* 1 January 1925, cover popular poetry provides a field of legitimate endeavour for scenario writers'.[10] The common opinion of the trade was less innovative. *Picture Show* had felt that neither *The Sentimental Bloke* nor *Ginger Mick* was 'a moving picture in the ordinary sense. It is a poem illustrated by local scenes and types'.[11] And later detractors of Australian production were to argue that the success of these films was no more than a flash in the pan, not repeated by later films in the genre such as *How McDougall Topped The Score* or *Around The Boree Log*, since they were poetic oddities which could never be repeated. Beau Smith, for whom formula and continuity of production were paramount, determined to avoid these problems, and at the same time add the 'much needed woman interest'. *Picture Show* had remarked that Paterson's poem 'is vivid and racy, but hardly contains enough story to suffice, as it stands, for a film', and Smith's first decision, also made by Longford to a much more limited extent, was to combine characters from a number of Paterson's short works. But that was only a beginning.

Everyones was later to speak of Beau Smith's 'cunning that speaks of showmanship of the highest degree',[12] and this was revealed in the continuity he developed for the famous poem about the colt that got away. In 1927 *Everyones*, in its series 'Helping Hand to the Australian Producer',[13] asked leading exhibitors whether the most marketable 'angle' was: (a) bush drama, (b) society drama, (c) racecourse drama, (d) surf story, (e) pioneering story, (f) historical story. It also asked whether as selling angles a film should include: (a) athletic stunts, (b) emotional drama, (c) problems of mother love, (d) outback episodes, (e) society or theatrical episodes. W.J. Howe replied that a producer should include as many of these angles as possible. This is what Smith, sensing the direction of the trade even in 1920, set out to do.

The film began with the conventional opposition of city and bush as Jim Conroy is in the clutches of the city vamp, Helen Ross. This allowed the treatment of 'society' life and water 'scenics' as well, as the society set is 'pleasure-making' on a yacht while 'Sydney Harbor sparkled in the warm sunshine'. As in *The Breaking of the Drought* which Franklyn Barrett had just made, the opposition of city and bush is clarified by a visit to the boy by his squatter father who refuses to give him more cheques. At this, the 'mercenary woman' leaves him, and Jim returns to the bush where, again like *The Breaking of the Drought*, the boy's society vices are purged by competing against nature. This is the point for inserting 'the colt that got away', and Jim, 'a true son of the bush in spite of his fling in the city' brings it safely back.

The colt, however, turns out to be John Carewe's racehorse, which is all that stands between him, his daughter and bankruptcy. This allows Smith to introduce the emotional drama (Jim's fight for the girl and her father's property, which is presented as an internal struggle between love and pride) and the racecourse drama as well. As in Wells's next film, *Silks and Saddles*, a villainous jockey is replaced by the star at the last moment. Next, Smith introduces 'athletic stunts' (since Jim is wrongfully imprisoned and makes his daring escape on the racehorse, chased by a trooper) and 'outback versus society' episodes when Helen, as (significantly) the lower-class daughter of the villain's housekeeper, returns to the country and cunningly separates Jim from Kitty, the 'real bush girl'. All that is missing from Howe's list of marketable 'angles' is 'mother love' (provided here, in attenuated form, between Mrs Potts and Helen) and is replaced by the mateship of father and son. The end is a triumph for bush community, as not only do the villains pay and Conroy's property is saved, but also Jim is re-united with his father and marries Kitty.

The pace with which the film moves from city setting to 'the colt that got away', to love story and skulduggery, to bush race-meeting, to chase by troopers and final resolution, while incorporating numerous other exciting incidents on the way such as Kitty's rescue from a bushfire by Jim, is the hallmark of Beaumont Smith productions. In the trade he was regarded as having the Hollywood touch: rapid rhythm which avoided breaking the pace of continuity with beautiful location shots. The 'typical' scenery became *part* of the action, in, as *Picture Show* described it, a 'whirl of events that will overcome any minor deficiences the picture may have'.[14] When *Film Weekly* in 1926 offered its advice in 'Talks to Australian Producers' that 'Action is of vital necessity to any photoplay, and anything that interrupts continuity interrupts action',[15] it was basing that advice on the favourite, Beaumont Smith, and his assumed imitation of Hollywood.

Smith also liked to argue that here was another 'absolutely real, honestly Australian' film, 'without any artificiality, burlesque, or exaggeration of types. There are no bushrangers', not an insignificant detail when appealing to Stuart Doyle, 'there are only true Australian people'.[16] This was precisely the same claim Longford had made for his 'Selection' films. But when Longford portrayed a bushfire in *On Our Selection* he did so without heroics, as part of a slow rhythmic and endless struggle of small communities against nature to care for simple things — the boundary rails and slab huts that the cast had built themselves. When Smith included a bushfire in *Snowy River* it was simply a melodramatic sign for the hero's

"The Man From Snowy River"

In Six Masterly Reels, with every part admirably portrayed by

CYRIL MACKAY, STELLA SOUTHERN, TAL ORDELL, HEDDA BARR, ROBERT MACKINNON, NAN TAYLOR, JOHN COSGROVE, JOHN FAULKNER, CHAS. BEETHAM, DUNSTAN WEBB, etc.

Written by BEAUMONT SMITH, and produced in conjunction with JOHN K. WELLS.

Picture Show 1 August 1929, p.46

OUR NATIONAL DUTY.

BEAUMONT SMITH'S IDEALS.

[Mr. Smith, producer of "The Man from Snowy River" and other local films, has a definite creed to govern his work for the screen. Below he gives his articles of faith, and describes the character types he aims at placing on the screen.—Editor's Note.]

I believe to-day that every Australian film producer has a great national duty. It is to infuse into every film he produces a truly Australian national sentiment.

* * * *

He must produce Australian films with TRUE TYPES of Australian manhood and womanhood—types that will make the younger generation (and the older generation, too) anxious to imitate; types of Australian men who are strong, masterful and fearless, but gentle at heart withal; and Australian women who are really womanly, wholesome and true.

* * * *

American ideals have been placed before us on the screen so long that we are in danger of becoming Americanised. The time has arrived for Australians to be fully Australianised.

* * * *

In no small degree, it is in the hands of Australian film producers to bring that about.

* * * *

The picture theatre is the new cradle of national sentiment—the great national school that is attended by all, whatever their age, class or creed. Unconsciously, the public is educated, morally and mentally, by the screen.

* * * *

Therefore, all good Australians should patronise picture theatres that screen good Australian films, and so encourage Australian producers to make them, and picture showmen to exhibit them.

Picture Show Trade Supplement, 1 September 1920, p.72

bush manhood and the maiden's 'natural' vulnerability. The injection of 'thrills' of this kind was a hallmark of Smith's style which Longford parodied in *The Sentimental Bloke*, but the trade particularly appreciated. In *Desert Gold*, essentially a racecourse story, he inserted a fight to the death at a cliff-edge in Katoomba, and staged a 'thrilling and risky race between a motor car and a train' through the Blue Mountains. In *The Betrayer* there were desperate fights between Mackay and Cosgrove shot 'for realism' as they rolled downhill 'right into the mouth of the awe-inspiring Devil's Cauldron'; while for the English presentation of the film, as though this was not enough excitement, he inserted the car and train chase from *Desert Gold*. For *The Gentleman Bushranger*, he shot a fight in the rigging of a ship, a mine rescue, and tree-climbing acrobatics by an Aboriginal. Sometimes even the trade suspected that it was one of these incidents, rather than an original work such as Paterson's poem, which motivated the entire film. Several months before making *Hullo Marmaduke*, Smith had taken some exciting film of the sinking of HMAS 'Australia'; he then shot a desperate fight between hero and villain in a ship being scrapped at Cockatoo Island, and with the ultimate and penultimate scenes of his film already in the can, was ready to write and shoot *Hullo Marmaduke*.

The Man From Snowy River opened at Union Theatres' Strand and Lyric in September 1920. *Everyones* called it 'scenically, and in both photographic and acting senses . . . the best Australian movie yet',[17] arguing that the personalities of Paterson's verses had been 'skilfully interwoven with a story into which the woman interest is cleverly introduced'.

In the same issue of *Picture Show* that announced the departure of Baker and Lucas for the United States and the need to concentrate on production for the local market only, Beaumont Smith published his ideals of cinema production.[18] But despite the emphasis on local support and the Australian sentiment, Smith at this stage (and whatever the trade might have said later) was aiming at an international market with costly films based on expensive scripts. *The Man From Snowy River*, which the trade recognised as being easily his most ambitious film to date, was designed 'to be of a standard that can readily ensure its acceptance, not only in Australia, but also in America and Europe'.

It was also insisted at the time that *While The Billy Boils* was to be his second 'high standard' production 'intended for release abroad as well as in Australia',[19] and that Smith was combing Australia to find 'capable type-actors' to play the host of characters who were again to be taken from a number of Lawson's works. In fact it was not filmed until after his next production, *The Betrayer*. Smith said there had already been too many bush films. He may have been reacting to the recent failure of the Baker–Lucas venture, but the more likely reason was the sickness of Henry Lawson who was due to appear in the prologue of the film. When this proved to be more than a temporary illness, Smith managed to get a brief interview with Lawson in his sick bed before he died and inserted it at the opening screening to give the film a much enhanced value. Trade comments about *While The Billy Boils* were almost identical with those about *On Our Selection*. The Longford film was described as not caricature 'but about the indomitable chap who just keeps on slogging . . . funny, but it would be tragic in places if the real Australian knew how to be tragic'.[20] Similarly, *While the Billy Boils* was supposedly 'not the caricatured bush and caricatured bush people, but the strong men and women who work hard . . . His film has retained the true Lawson power of showing the tragic that so often underlies the commonplace, as well as the laughter that goes hand in hand with it'.[21]

But despite the trade's quite systematic attempts to link the work of Longford and Smith at this time, the familiar hallmarks are visible from production news and reviews. We hear of 'clever weaving' of characters into a good scenario in which 'the incidental scenes have a big attraction of their own', and a scrutiny of the plot reveals close similarities with *The Man From Snowy River*. Once again there is a man who works incognito on a bush station after years of absence because of a quarrel with his father; a man in the toils of a city vamp (this time the hero role is divided between two brothers, which gives more room for complications of 'emotional drama' concerning the pure country girl they both love); a wrongful arrest; 'fights, chases, and all manner of excitements until the whole matter is cleared up, and the hero is free to lead his beloved to the clergyman'.[22] There is nothing to suggest that production, completed in four weeks at Windsor, was any closer to Lawson's spirit than *The Man From Snowy River* was to Paterson's.[23]

Spectacle Melodrama

The Betrayer, made in New Zealand, was again aimed at the international market. 'The undertaking will be a very expensive one, but I have so much faith in the future of Australian picture production, done on the right lines, that I consider that the outlay will be fully justified'.[24] Smith emphasised that, as with *Snowy River*, 'the techniques of production should compare well with American films'.[25] And once again he announced his intention to scour the nation for 'the necessary types'.

Though Smith argued that *The Betrayer* would be a different class of picture from any produced in Australia before, with 'no horses or cows or sheep or kangaroos . . . or buck-jumping or racing or bushfires', his own description of the film as 'fresh and clean as the islands themselves and the sunshine which blesses them' was remarkably similar to his 'clear as the air of Kosciusko' comments about his last film, and in fact the kangaroos and buck-jumping were simply replaced by the appropriate New Zealand 'touches of local colour . . . Maori hakas, poi dance, Maori wedding, Maori funeral'. The plot, in which the hero (again Cyril Mackay) and his mother adopt a quarter-cast Maori girl (again Stella Southern) and take her via Sydney society life to the treacherous breakers at Coogee Beach, managed to include most of Howe's marketing 'angles' *plus* the 'surf-drama' and 'mother-love' almost, but not quite, achieved in the previous film. To this was added 'the charm lent by delightful views of geysers, hot pools, and native bush in the vicinity of Rotorua' and 'some glorious views of the ocean beach at Coogee, near Sydney'. These were shrewdly chosen to capture audiences in both New Zealand — 'the first modern photoplay that involves Maori life and scenery in the thermal regions', and Australia — one of the very first films with 'Australian girls displaying their skill in the water and gallant life-savers all ready for rescues'.[26]

As with his previous film, Smith mixed spectacular scenic shots with hair-raising actions in a tightly controlled episodic plot line. Probably the most significant thing about Beaumont Smith's film-making, in terms of his popularity with the trade, was this close connection with popular melodrama. Nicholas Vardac has argued that the stage melodramas of the late nineteenth century 'depended essentially upon the sensational action, the spectacular scenic conceptions, and the cleverness of the overall episodic pattern'.[27] It is for exactly these three categories that time and again the trade praised Smith's films — with the single difference that however spectacular the nineteenth century might try to be with its rail and riverboat races, its cliff-edge struggles, and its Red Indian ceremonies, Beau Smith could do them all with more 'realism' on the screen. This is essential to understanding both the perception of silent cinema as a popular art form by the trade and its constant praise for screen 'realism'. The two key qualities of the popular stage had been its combination of rapidly paced, highly improbable melodramatic actions with an almost fanatical concern, via scenic spectacle and visual 'sensation', for 'realism' — and the harder that was to achieve in terms of avalanches, train crashes or bushfires, the more it was tried. Cinema developed out of this very popular amalgam, and Hollywood based its new screen acting styles of understatement and typing on this emphasis on dramatic external visual values. Pantomimic personal gesture was no longer required when drama was carried by rapid movement of bodies and scenes, and narrative development by 'business' and effects rather than dialogue or complex characterisation.

Even without the specific Hollywood orientation it is likely that Smith, with his long stage experience, and likewise those at the head of the cinema trade, would have developed in the same way. Australian popular theatre had followed the American and European model of improbable action and realistic spectacle. In the years just prior to the coming of cinema, the visual 'sensations' presented on the stage, with attacks on real mail coaches, real racehorses, real sheep, and skeletons with real crows to pick their eyes out, bushfires, cliff-edge fights and so on, had actually increased in the productions of Alfred Dampier, Bland Holt, and others. Smith's perception of his audience and what they wanted, his notion of film rhythm and syntax, his concern for 'authentic' spectacle and never-before-seen customs, and indeed a number of his plots, developed out of his theatrical background in melodrama. It was essentially because he came from this tradition that the trade valued him so highly.

In *The Betrayer* Smith added another ingredient to catch the public's notice, despite all the 'fresh and clean' publicity for the film: the interracial sexual piquancy, of a hero who was twice intimate with Maori women. This confrontation and blending 'of the ancient and modern customs' in *The Betrayer* reveals another characteristic feature of Smith's films. Both the comedy and the drama in his productions draw heavily on a confrontation of cultures: in *The Man From Snowy River*, vice-ridden city and virgin bush purity; in *The Betrayer*, compromised modern society and innocently wronged native culture; in *Townies and Hayseeds*, 'highbrow' city folk and absurdly caricatured country people; in *Pre-Historic Hayseeds*, modern city dwellers and stone-age people; in *Hullo Marmaduke*, effete English gentry and rough pioneering Australians; in *Adventures of Algy*, gentle, crossword-playing simpleton and a Maori girl, wise in all the arts of her age-old culture. Sometimes these are coupled with other oppositions, such as the conventional city banker villain against the countryman hero of *The Betrayer*, and frequently the resolution is reached when the primitive girl marries the modern hero (as in *The Betrayer*, *Prehistoric Hayseeds*, and *Adventures of Algy*).

Without going far into the question of oppositions of 'modern' and 'traditional' in Australian cinema (which will be the subject of a later chapter) it is sufficient to say here that Smith had in this device a principle similar in kind to generic conventions which, coupled with a facility for continuity work and a profusion of scenic shots, enabled him to produce formula movies very quickly. *While The Billy Boils* was completed in four weeks, as was *The Gentleman Bushranger*; *Townies and Hayseeds* took four weeks exactly from the first day of production to screening, and was sold for Australia-wide release in less than five; one-fifth of *Joe* was, according to *Everyones*, shot within two hours of one day.

If Smith did not take long to make his films, nor did he, as the trade constantly noted, delay between films. After his four weeks on *While The Billy Boils*, Smith went straight into production of his next film, *The Gentleman Bushranger*, which, despite rain at Bowral, was ready in another four. *Picture Show* complimented him, saying, 'For quick work, Beaumont Smith surely holds the record'.[28] Once again the cast included 'Players both well known' (John Cosgrove, Tal Ordell, J.P. O'Neill, Ernest Hearne) and 'not so known', with two new female leads, sixteen-year-old Monicka Mack and the champion horsewoman, Dot McConville. The plot had the male and female leads as 'new chums' (recent immigrants to Australia) persecuted across sea and land by hardened sea-ruffians and bushrangers, and it contained the usual dose of 'marketable angles'. It even aspired to one 'angle' which he had not used before: 'theatrical episodes', when he introduced a touring theatre company which had humourous scenes with the bushrangers.

However, on this occasion something went wrong with Smith's formula (possibly the bushranging element was not to the liking of Union Theatres) with the result that first release was delayed by several months, and consequently Smith was unable to start a new production. He took the film to New Zealand, and *Everyones* noted in February 1922 that this was probably the first time an Australian production had its initial release there.[29]

Faced with this setback, Smith did as he had done in 1919 after the failure of *Barry Butts In* and left Australia, this time for England and Europe. It is clear that all was not well with his financial situation since he gave as the main purpose for his journey the selection of 'novelty attractions for Australia and New Zealand'. Hoping to find another pot of gold like 'Tiny Town', he stated that he was in future going to cater to the 'novelty entertainment' public.

As for film production, he said that unless he could sell in England at the very least *The Man From Snowy River*, *The Betrayer* and *The Gentleman Bushranger* and gain some 'assurance of an outside market' through a partnership arrangement with an English company, he would 'discontinue production indefinitely'. 'We cannot now produce solely for the local market, cost of production is too high'.[30]

(i)

(ii)

Picture Show (i) 1 April 1921, p.70; (ii) 1 February 1921, p.20

The confrontation of ancient and modern customs, with a touch of inter-racial sexual piquancy: *The Betrayer*

Everyones 8 March 1922, p.15

'False arrests, police chases, fights, desperate horse races, magnificent scenery': marketable angles by Beaumont Smith

In December 1922 Smith returned disillusioned and announced an end to his film-making. In the course of attempts to sell his films in England, he had encountered head on the consequences of American dumping and the block-booking system. American films, which were able to get back their costs in the home market alone, could be sold in foreign markets at whatever price was necessary to control the trade, while Australian producers were forced to ask higher prices in an attempt to break even. Commenting on this, Smith mentioned one London distributor who had bought the rights of four American films, including one brand new copy, for £317 each. 'You will see, therefore, that whilst medium American pictures can be purchased at prices like this, English and Australian productions cannot be successfully carried on'.[31]

In addition, there was the block booking problem which was worse in England than in Australia, regularly tying up films and outlets for a year or more. A practical businessman like Smith, who produced formula films with an eye to the current market recognised a whole range of disadvantages to the producer in such delays. First of all, there was the problem of film fashions, especially strong in the English trade. 'For example, a racing picture may have made a big success. Immediately the buyers all demand racing pictures, and aren't anxious to look at others'. In this situation they would buy an Australian racing film like *Silks and Saddles* at a good price. But this then had to lie on the shelf for over a year. By this time 'the public may be demanding a new type of picture. The racing drama is no longer what it wants'. Nor could the Australian producer wash his hands of the problem by selling his films outright because no English distributor seemed to have the money for straight cash-down deals. Secondly all the money spent on publicity for the film's trade showing was wasted when the film did not appear publicly for another year. 'In the long interval it has been forgotten. Each showman has to start afresh on his exploitation'.[32]

However, despite observing the *systematic* causes of the film trade slump in England, Beau Smith, like so many of his businessmen friends in the Australian film trade, was not anxious to blame the Americans. Like them, he preferred to blame the government which, he argued, had been a major reason for the slump in every sphere of the film business, because the Amusement Tax, in a time of rising property values and higher theatre rentals, squeezed the exhibitor out of the business. This, he said, was also the main reason why there was no money to buy his pictures.[33]

Everything seemed over for Beau Smith as a film-maker. He had made a series of attempts to produce for the international market and to arrange distribution of them in America and Britain. In each case certain facets of the American industry — high production costs, closed home market, control of overseas markets by dumping and block booking — had defeated him. But if Smith recognised all these as being different facets of one system — and his comments here suggest that he did — he was never prepared to say so, either in the trade press or at the Royal Commission of 1927, from which he was notably absent. Much of the reason for this seems to lie in the business links between Smith and various exhibiting circuits in the years that lay just ahead. Smith was, in fact, destined to make more films.

His attempt to find novelties had been equally disastrous, due to post-war European poverty and social breakdown, particularly in Austria where he had originally found his 'Tiny Town'.[34]

Producer to the Trade

It was under this double blow that Beaumont Smith became the producer he is best remembered as, which the trade had been trying to make him for some time, and which it certainly wanted: the producer of very cheap caricature comedies, taking up where his earlier 'Hayseeds' had left off. As early as 16 May 1923 he was producing his next film,[35] *Townies and Hayseeds*, and by 23 May it was said to be nearing completion. On 30 May, *Everyones* announced that, 'as is always the case with this producer's pictures, there will be no delay in placing the feature on the market'. For this picture, an early release was more essential than ever before because, apart from the caricatured interaction of a supposedly 'typical highbrow' city family with a 'rough-and-ready bush family', much of the humour came from topical gags in the titles and the appearance or impersonation of in-the-news personalities and cartoon characters. This was quick, cheap and *very* parochial production, shot around Sydney and in the Rushcutters Bay studio, but with Melbourne scenes added before its release there.

Union Theatres had nearly always released Smith's films promptly, but during this period he seems to have been working under an *assurance* of release from Stuart Doyle, and produced the right kind of films 'on prompt'. At the time when Union Theatres were neglecting Longford's *The Dinkum Bloke*, they were giving massive publicity to Smith's films, both in the general trade press and in their own magazine, the *Photoplayer*. During this time the trade press made frequent references to Stuart Doyle's support of Smith's films, of instant deals and no haggling, and *Photoplayer* strongly supported the swing back to Hayseeds-type production. Somehow, the journal said, Beaumont Smith had 'departed from the laughing side of picture production and went in for more serious dramas', but now 'he has came to the fore again, with *Townies and Hayseeds*'.[36] *Everyones* also praised the return to the Hayseeds format, reminding the trade that these 'were amongst the most successful local pictures that we have ever seen'.[37]

At a time when the struggling Longford–Lyell company was failing to interest Doyle, *Everyones* announced that within ten minutes of viewing *Townies and Hayseeds*, 'Stuart Doyle . . . offered to present it at the Lyceum and Lyric Theatres as a first release, to be followed by the whole of Union Theatres in New South Wales. Terms entirely satisfactory to Beaumont Smith were arranged', and the film would have virtually immediate release. 'Union Theatres Ltd are also prepared to book the picture right through Australia' and Henry Hayward was doing the same for New Zealand.

The trade began to see Beaumont Smith as its prodigy:

> *Everyones* mentioned recently that it was something of an achievement for Beaumont Smith, and photographer Arthur Higgins, to produce, photograph, cut, edit, print and place on the screen *Townies and Hayseeds* in four weeks. The achievement now grows greater for in less than five weeks from starting date the first releases of the film have been booked throughout practically the whole of Australia.[38]

The same jack-of-all-trades qualities which were said to be the failure of Franklyn Barrett and other less-favoured Australian producers were seen as shining qualities in Beaumont Smith. Reviews in the trade were carefully pitched:

> Produced in a record time, and ostensibly for the purpose of creating harmless entertainment and plenty of laughter, this feature appears to have succeeded in all it set out to accomplish.[39]

At a time when the directors of Union Theatres and Australasian Films were becoming increasingly concerned about hostility from pressure groups and parliament, and the trade was calling to the distributors to combine together and appoint a champion to fend off hostile legislation, *this* was the kind of Australian production it was supporting, at the same time using Smith's problems with petty officialdom while shooting *Prehistoric Hayseeds* to blame government bodies for the ills of Australian production.[40] Smith was adopting his well-tried methods, but at a lower level; pace, inserted cameos, climaxes like Pa Townie's suicide attempt at the Gap, 'a score of well-chosen types', with lesser vaudeville actors as male leads.

Prehistoric Hayseeds was shot in three weeks and released in eight and Union Theatres' publicity, which had been extensive for the previous film, was increased still further. All the film journals carried big articles and

Rollicking Australian Comedy.

"TOWNIES AND HAYSEEDS" IS OUT OF THE "BOX."

Most Australian pictures have been dramas of a sensational type. Few producers have explored the field of comedy. When Beaumont Smith first entered the moving picture field he produced a series of comedies entitled "The Hayseeds." But somehow he departed from the laughing side of picture production and went in for more serious dramas, making "The Man from the Snowy River," "The Betrayer," "While the Billy Boils," and several other well known films.

However, after a year's absence from producing circles he has come to the fore again with a film that is funnier than his friends ever dreamed he could make. It is called "Townies and Hayseeds," and in a satirical vein he deals with the humor and peculiarities of city people, especially when they visit their country cousins.

He has created what is a typical Australian city family, and it consists of Pa Townie, Ma Townie, and their brood of children, all named after capital cities—Sydney, Melbourne, Adelaide, Brissy, Perth, and Hobart.

Pa Townie's holidays having fallen due he decided to take his family into the country and fill them up with fresh air and milk. They go to stay with Dad Hayseed and his extensive family. The Townies have some quaint ideas of country life, and they cause the Hayseeds endless merriment. You can well imagine the hundred and one eccentric, ignorant things City people do on a farm. After a riotous month the Townies return to Potts Point, bringing Dad and Mum Hayseed with them. Here more contrast is given to the picture by the do'ngs of Dad and Mum in fashionable circles.

A pleasant, simple, triangular love story runs through the picture, and the ends of the triangle are, Adelaide Townie (named Adelaide because she was "so" cultured), a Pommy named "Choom," and a returned Aussie soldier named George.

The picture is right up to date, and contains some satire. It is said that a character representing William Morris Hughes blows into one important scene. The character is one carrying a bag containing £25,000, so we can't think of any other person round Australia who has got so much loose money about him.

The "Suicide Club" at the Gap is a very original scene, and will cause merriment for a long time to come.

The picture is beautifully photographed, and delightfully acted by a score of well-chosen types. Beautiful little Lotus Thompson plays the heroine (Adelaide Townie), whilst the leading comedy roles are undertaken by Mr. George Edwards ...ll known on the stage), ... of ...m- ... is ...l at and ...atres, next

"Choom" arrives a

(ii)

Union Theatres' continuous support for Beaumont Smith's 'Hayseed' films

(i) *Photoplayer* 30 June 1923, p. 15; (ii) *Everyones* 18 July 1923, p. 30

IN FUTURE'S STORE

Cave Men are Coming to Sydney

GOOD FUN PROMISED IN "PREHISTORIC HAYSEEDS"

Fashions change. That is not meant as an original remark, but as a statement of self-evident fact. And it does not refer to feminine clothes or masculine fancies, or any of a dozen other things to which it might.

For the time being, it may be applied to the songs that we sing. Consider our musical optimism of a few months ago.

We were advising ourselves and each other to "look for the silver lining," to "pucker up and whistle till the clouds roll by," and to otherwise treasure merriment above all. Nowadays, however, when the bathroom nightingale is announcing to an unsympathetic world that he's "blue—and broken-hearted," while his wife murmurs her sadness that the "leaves come tumbling down," Sydney frequently needs a tonic of cheerfulness.

In "Prehistoric Hayseeds" that tonic will be provided. It is a picture to make the blues turn red with laughter; it is funny and it is Australian.

Several years have passed since Beaumont Smith made his first "Hayseeds" picture. When it appeared, audiences were immediately convulsed with the adventures of Dad, Mum and the rest of the family. It caricatured the bush, but the picture proved just as popular in country shows as it was in the city.

Periodically other "Hayseeds" films have since been produced, bringing the total number up to six. Each one has been successful, bu
seeds" promises to

Beaumont Smith
as well as filming
entirely new set

to back up the Hayseeds. No longer are the bush folk seen by themselves on their farm or entirely surrounded with city people. They have the task of enlightening some Stone Age survivors and showing them the ways of the modern, wicked world.

It all happens through the visit of a certain young man to Stony Creek. He and Dad go exploring round the district, and having found a cave, they attack one of its walls with a pick-axe. To their amazement the pick goes right through the wall, leaving a gaping hole through which they look upon an unknown world. It is the realm of prehistoric people.

They enter it, and their strange adventures begin.
he other side
Mr.
ll,
ge
or-
, in
does
d. So
and
, when
up that
out-of-
he took
r. Wup's

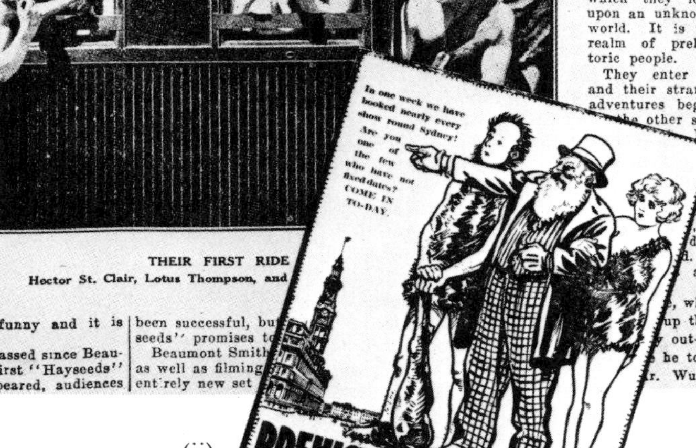

THEIR FIRST RIDE
Hector St. Clair, Lotus Thompson, and

(ii)

(i) *Photoplayer* 17 November 1923, p. 15; (ii) *Everyones* 5 December 1923, p. 24

Picture Show 1 November 1923, p.38

The sad decline of *Picture Show*, marking its final issue as an independent magazine with this tribute to the trade-dominated Beaumont Smith, just as it had marked its first issue with the making of *The Sentimental Bloke*

(ii)

(i)

Everyones (i) 21 November 1923, p.12; (ii) 28 November 1923, p.21

Advertising *Prehistoric Hayseeds* with elderly yokel and the legs of Lotus Thompson constant production details weeks ahead of release. Even *Picture Show* which was about to fold and had long ceased its editorial push on behalf of Australian production, marked its sad decline with a double-page spread about the ludricrous antics of Smith's prehistoric Wup family. The cast of Smith's film was to be seen wandering about Sydney's Central Station and city streets where Smith himself sought publicity with a lot of very public filming; and finally, in the few days before the film's release, the campaign was stepped up, with window displays, street stunts, a very tall 'hayseed' roaming about the city and suburbs advertising the film, and 'one of the finest lobby displays' seen at the Union release theatre 'wherein reposed a beauteous damsel garbed in "Prehistoric" raiment'.[41]

It is worth reflecting on all this display, because it gives a very clear idea of what the moguls of Australia's monopoly cinema circuits considered to be 'good' Australian cinema. All this publicity was for a film about which the trade could say at best that though Smith 'has not yet attained greatness' he was to be commeneded for 'effort to keep the feeble spark of local production glimmering'[42] with a sequence of humorous incidents which located the prehistoric people in a series of 'contemporary problems' such as feminism and alcoholism. In a weak gesture to the Hollywood mirage, it was said that Gordon Collingridge looked like Thomas Meighan, while Lotus Thompson as the Golden Girl, who was soon to be complaining about the exploitation of her legs in Hollywood, was 'pretty enough to wear the stone-age costume triumphantly, and feminine enough to put plenty of romance into the production'.[43]

Beau Smith had set up his own distribution exchange early on, and for his latest films adopted the new policy of disposing of any state's rights not covered by Union Theatres. By selling outright rather than waiting for percentage returns, he got instant money and could go into a new production schedule straight away. He announced in November 1923 that with this system he hoped to release four films a year, and in fact had three new films on release by November 1924.

The first two were a step back towards his more ambitious production. *The Digger Earl*, which took three months from first production to first release, starred Arthur Tauchert, Gordon Collingridge, Lotus Thompson, Dunstan Webb, and introduced Heather Jones as the new leading lady. It was described as his 'first dramatic picture' for some time. The plot embodied the familiar Smith device of contrasting old and new cultures, and featured Tauchert as an Aussie joker who changes places with an English earl. *Everyones* rated the film highly for story and continuity, but added the rider 'for a *local* production'. Smith had hopes for foreign sales and had been in touch with a London distributor, but nothing came of it.

His next film, *Joe*, was again based on an opposition, this time the formula from *The Man From Snowy River*; the country, age-old and created by God (where women mended and washed in the gloom of bush huts), against the city which was new, brash and constructed by man (where women's husbands were seduced, jazzed and feasted amongst its bright lights). Both films gained wide release from Union Theatres in New South Wales, South Australia[44] and Brisbane, and from Tallis and Thring in Western Australia, with other state and suburban rights sold to independents. *The Digger Earl* was advertised as being the best of Smith's films to date, while *Everyones* described *Joe* as, though simple, 'the most convincing thing Beaumont Smith has given the screen'. [45] Familiar signs of Smith's earlier work are suggested in trade comment on the blending of fine bush scenics with the considerable narrative elaboration of Henry Lawson's 'trifling thread' of a story; but in this case more may have been achieved by the leading actors. Marie Lorraine was described as 'one of the most promising amongst Australian feminine leads on the screen in this country', and there is a hint of *The Sentimental Bloke* in the praise of the natural acting and 'blending of humour and pathos' by Arthur Tauchert.

Smith had almost completed the scenario for *Hullo Marmaduke* before *Joe* got its first release, and had already shot its climax some months before. The plot, like that of his next film, concerned the adventures of a typical 'johnnie of the silly-ass type' (played by Claude Dampier and other comedians from the Fuller vaudeville circuit)[46] who has numerous adventures in the Southern Continent and eventually makes good, getting away in *Hullo Marmaduke* with the daughter of the murdered heroine, and in *Adventures of Algy* with the Maori maiden. Lucille Lisle, 'a real find' as youthful feminine lead was much appreciated, and *Everyones* pointedly remarked that the production was likely to succeed because it was 'well advertised in advance' by the successful Union Theatres–Beaumont Smith Exchange team (including some free publicity from M.P.D.A. secretary Voltaire Molesworth in his role as editor of *The Daily Guardian*). The film was released at Union's Lyceum and Lyric Theatres, *Everyones* noting that, 'Mr Smith has a way of completing his pictures quickly and arranging for their release while public interest is keen',[47] and in this case at least Stuart Doyle had booked the film for wide Australian release even before the trade screening.

At the end of the production of *Hullo Marmaduke* Beaumont Smith

RELEASING ON SATURDAY, AUGUST 23 AT THE LYCEUM AND LYRIC WINTERGARDEN FOLLOWED BY THE RIALTO, THE MAJESTIC, KING'S CROSS, AND OLYMPIA.

Owned and Controlled by BEAUMONT SMITH FILMS, Banking House, 228 Pitt St., Sydney.

LOOK OUT FOR OUR NEXT, "VENUS OF THE SOUTH SEAS," WITH ANNETTE KELLERMAN, LYCEUM, AUGUST 30th.

Everyones 13 August 1924, p.25

(i)

(ii)

National Film Archive

(i) 'The country, age-old and created by God . . .': Beaumont Smith's *Joe*
(ii) The Englishman as monocled fool — an 'Americanism' much complained of by Australian anglophiles: *The Adventures of Algy*

Everyones (i) 19 November 1924, p.11; (ii) 14 April 1924, p.17

Doyle- Gibson publicity for *Hullo Marmaduke* had 'unsolicited' support from M.P.D.A. colleague Voltaire Molesworth.

announced he would take a holiday after eighteen months without a break in production. An indication of his driving business enthusiasm is the fact that his 'holiday' consisted of a four-month tour of New Zealand to exploit his previous four films, none of which had been released there, and to shoot another film. When he got back from New Zealand in April 1924, he had conducted screen tests and shot over half of *The Adventures of Algy*, introducing a new feminine lead, Bathie Stuart who was chosen especially for her 'specialised knowledge of Maori manners and customs' which, in Beaumont Smith style, had been 'skilfully woven into the film which also has a strong dramatic undercurrent running right through it'.[48]

While Smith was away in New Zealand the public debate about local production had come to a head with an Australian producers' deputation to the Minister of Customs in February 1925, led by Franklyn Barrett and Arthur Shirley, demanding protection via a quota. The response of the trade and trade press was immediately hostile, with lengthy attacks from the M.P.D.A., the New South Wales Federated Picture Showmen's Association, and Stuart Doyle for Australasian Films and Union Theatres on the unbusinesslike attitudes of Australian producers. In the public debate preceding the deputation, Doyle had been driven to announce that his company intended to go into production itself with *Painted Daughters*, and claimed that they had already given every Australian producer of merit a ready outlet 'whenever the picture has been possible to present to the public'[49] — by which he presumably meant Beaumont Smith's, since Union Theatres had released incomparably more of his films in recent years than anybody else's.

After the producers' deputation, Doyle was able to devalue its status by saying, 'I notice that the deputation to the Minister did not include the two principal Australian producing factors, namely Beaumont Smith and Australasian Films'. W.J. Howe replied to the deputation in kind on behalf of the exhibitors:

> The Australian producers, like Mr Beaumont Smith, who have gone about their business in a practical way, have produced Australian pictures at a profit, and to suggest that extra taxation should be placed on the industry is to spoon-feed unskilled producers, who for the sake of a subsidy, would produce an inferior picture.[50]

Just how far Smith was going about his *own* business in a 'practical way' or how far his business had been shaped to the wishes of the trade is clear from a statement he made on his return to Australia in 1924, which reversed his earlier ambitions and was an obvious response to the deputation:

> Pictures can be made profitably for the Australian and New Zealand markets, providing they are made by men who know the meaning of economy and have imagination and a sense of showmanship . . . local film producing, to my mind, is useless unless one can see the return of one's cost in the country of origin. An Australian or New Zealand film requires great novelty to be acceptable to the people of Great Britain or America.[51]

The only trace of the old Beau Smith, shrewdly angling his productions to a broad market, was his comment that he had written the scenario of his new film around scenes in both Australia and New Zealand to capture audience interest in both countries. Anything else, he added in an implied comment on his Hayseed films, was 'too local' to gain a sufficiently large market.

By a process of help, friendship and cossetting of the declining ambitions of Beaumont Smith, the trade had got the compliant producer it wanted and had predicted for a long time. A quite precise indication of this status with the trade, *and* of its strictly limited nature, was given eighteen months later when Gayne Dexter, editor of *Everyones*, in the midst of the mounting disputes about quotas and local production, said that the proper way ahead for Australian films was via humorous two-reelers, run as support films, and suggested to Smith that he should make them since, 'didn't you make more out of your two- and three-reel *Hayseeds* than you did out of any of your bigger pictures?'[52]

Following the interchange between producers and the rest of the trade in early 1925, *Everyones* added its support against Barrett and Shirley by asserting that;

> no recent film of average standard has been denied a screening. We hear no complaints from Mr Beaumont Smith, who boasts of having made and released seventeen during the last ten years or so . . . and from what we know of Mr Beaumont Smith, he is not likely to risk the depletion of his hardly earned capital without a sporting chance of its returning to the fold.[53]

Everyones had a tendency during these years of outside 'interference' with the trade to lend its leading articles to the cause, and it did so now with an article on Beau Smith which began

> whilst Rome burned, Nero fiddled, and whilst many people have been occupying their time in the compilation of long epistles to the *Sydney Morning*

EVERYONES
WITH WHICH IS INCORPORATED
AUSTRALIAN VARIETY & SHOW WORLD

Consistent Beaumont Smith.

WHILST Rome burned, Nero fiddled, and whilst many people have been occupying their time in the compilation of long epistles to the "Sydney Morning Herald" on the subject of local pictures, Beaumont Smith was quietly going on producing them and what is vastly more to the point, getting them released.

This young man from Adelaide, like Peter Pan, refuses to grow up, and though he is by no means the pioneer of Australian motion picture producers, he is the daddy of them all by reason of the number of films he has produced.

To date he has produced seventeen films—and this without a penny of introduced capital. He is his own financier and has not found it necessary to float a company to stand behind his products. There are many who sneer at some of them, but it is a fact that they have all made money for Beaumont Smith and the showmen who have screened them, and what more could any man ask.

The first one, "Hayseeds No. 1", is still asked for in the country and were it possible to re-issue this film—it is now ten years or more since it was taken—it would still have a popular appeal.

Exactly what there is about the Beaumont Smith films it is hard to say. There was with some of the earliest a crudeness that was apparent, yet they are all devised with cunning that speaks of showmanship of the highest degree and as such they get over flaws and all and the general impression defies criticism.

The introduction of the sinking of the Australia into the final reel of his last success, "Hullo, Marmaduke," was a touch of genius, which only Beau Smith would be guilty of. It made the final scenes unforgettable and entirely erased from the mind any flaws there may have been in the earlier part of the story. Possibly there were none, but what-

MR. BEAUMONT SMITH.

horribly when he found that collection of individuals looking the other way when the incident appeared.

Paradise with a team of actors—there to commence the first of the "Hayseeds" series which was finally to

Everyones 20 May 1925, p.3

> *Herald* on the subject of local pictures, Beaumont Smith has been quietly going on producing them, and, what is vastly more to the point, getting them released.[54]

Their explanations of his success were typical of the trade. First of all, he was a successful individualist, an entrepreneur 'without a penny of introduced capital' who did not put at risk other people's money by floating mushroom companies in the way so many other producers were prepared to do. Relying on his own resources, he made films which, whatever the sneers about their crudity, 'all made money for Beaumont Smith and the showmen who have screened them, and what more could any man ask?' Secondly, there was his genius for showmanship which covered the flaws of construction. As evidence *Everyones* cited the

> introduction of the sinking of the 'Australia' into the final reel of his last success, *Hullo Marmaduke* . . . a touch of genius which only Beau Smith would be guilty of . . . and entirely erased from the mind any flaws there may have been in the earlier part of the story.

Thirdly, there was his flare for publicity, enabling him to turn his temporary police censorship problems with *Satan in Sydney* to priceless advantage. Fourthly, there was his intention to make films efficiently and economically, enabling a cheap hire-cost to the exhibitor: 'So far he has not created an epic. He has never set himself out to do so. He aims to produce marketable pictures for Australian audiences and so far has succeeded admirably'. Fifthly, there was his search for 'types' to portray reality, as in *Adventures of Algy* where, instead of 'the anaemic blonde and the sloe-eyed brunette so usually sought after by directors', he had discovered a woman embodying the colourful culture of the Maori past'.

Entrepreneurial individualism, showmanship, spectacle, clever publicity, the search for 'types' and scenic 'realism', cheap production for a local market: key concepts all of them, were used again and again by the trade during these years, and as such defined the attitude of the film producer the trade had created, Beaumont Smith. It was a trade which endlessly called 'Hands Off Our Industry', and the punch line of the article, the key intention for which Smith was no more than a vehicle, came at the end:

> Whilst there are men like Beaumont Smith in the film producing business in Australia, the industry will not need the extraneous aid of near politicians and others who would be as much out of their element as a flea in the desert of the Sahara.

At the climax of this off-screen melodrama came *The Adventures of Algy*, released by Union Theatres six weeks earlier than expected. The trade review was predictable: a slight tale arranged into clever continuity, interweaving fine New Zealand scenery and Maori ceremonies. In essentials it had all been done before — the conventional slapstick element of the frightened fortune hunter beset by a formidable host of would-be wives — and been said before — as had the conclusion of *Everyones* review: 'Mr Smith is to be commended for his efforts to keep the game alive'.[55] *Truth* predictably praised the interweaving of comic incidents and 'entrancing scenery', Sydney's *Sunday Sun* liked the blend of exciting incidents and love motif with locations in three countries, and *The Sydney Morning Herald* specially praised the 'elaborate ballet scenes' on the Tivoli stage and the 'glimpses of dancing amid the actual carved huts of the Maoris'.

These particular inclusions illustrate the wide-ranging showmanship of Smith, and his sense of 'total' theatre performance, because the Maori dancers could be used outside the film, as a prologue, as well as in it. Stuart Doyle had recently pointed out in the trade press that 'high-class vaudeville turns as an adjunct to pictures are a firmly established fact, and mark the high-water mark of modern methods of presentation'.[56] Doyle, who was as keen to attract high-class clientele to his increasingly magnificent picture theatres as he was to emphasise his service to Australia by employing local artists, emphasised that this trend in presentation was a result of the change in the picture show from 'a thing of old iron and derision' to a 'super theatre with all modern comforts and conveniences', and also to the fact that this kind of venue discouraged the more 'vulgar' type of vaudeville performer 'who was not too particular as to his choice of material and the manner in which he put it over'.

Smith's sense of showmanship allowed Doyle to book Princess Rangiri and her nine Maori maids — 'a distinct novelty', and distinctly not too vulgar for the performance of *Adventures of Algy* before their Excellencies Sir Dudley and Lady De Chair. This combination of vaudeville with linked cinema, which Doyle and the trade promised to be of enormous importance 'for those who are aiming for the progress of the entertainment business', had of course been a part of Beaumont Smith's career for many years. It had been implicit in his production at least since the Maori dances in *The Betrayer* and the travelling theatre in *The Gentleman Bushranger.* It was yet another example of the way Smith and the trade breathed together.

While the film was running to good houses, Smith was doing screen tests in Queensland for his next film. At the end of July he announced

(i)

ADVERTISING RATES
(AUSTRALASIA)
Display, per inch 5/-
Half Page £5
Full Page £10
Address—
Advertising Manager,
"Everyones,"
114 Castlereagh Street,
Sydney, N.S.W.

EVERYONES

WITH WHICH IS INCORPORATED
AUSTRALIAN VARIETY & SHOW WORLD

SUBSCRIPTION RATES
POST FREE
(AUSTRALASIA)
12 Months 20/-
6 Months 12/6
3 Months 6/6
Address—
Advertising Manager,
"Everyones,"
114 Castlereagh Street,
Sydney, N.S.W.

Super Vaudeville in Picture Theatres

RECENT mails from England have contained the information that a new form of public entertainment was rapidly coming into vogue, by the introduction of vaudeville in some of the smaller picture theatres which have hitherto held aloof from this form of presentation.

The system, of course, is familiar to all Australian playgoers as high-class vaudeville items have for the past few years been conspicuously featured in our principal houses, but in England the idea is so radical as to be looked upon by the performers as a means of saving the situation which was rapidly becoming serious by reason of the great scarcity of work.

There has, however, in Australia been a really drastic change of policy on the part of the large picture houses by the inclusion in their programmes of headliners imported from overseas at salaries which would a few years ago have been considered by moving picture men as providing the shortest possible cut to bankruptcy.

The inclusion of acts of this calibre have stilled for ever the old conservative idea that it was incompatible with the dignity of a performer to appear in a picture house. Indeed with the advance in methods of presentation, the very reverse has happened, and performers now consider it an honour to appear where a few years ago they would not have deigned to tread.

This paper called upon Mr. Stuart F. Doyle, of Union Theatres, last week, with the idea of getting from him his views on these changes.

Mr. Doyle said in response to our queries:

"High-class vaudeville turns as an adjunct to pictures, are a firmly established fact, and mark the high-water-mark of modern methods of presentation. There are many contributing factors to this. Public taste in entertainment has progressed considerably, and the old time "picture show" has ceased to be a thing of old iron and derision, and in its place has arisen a super theatre with all modern comforts and conveniences.

"The change is not only confined to the form of presentation and the style of theatres, but in the performers themselves a distinct change

Mr. STUART F. DOYLE

often ruined by bad deportment and dressing, and these little things are sometimes forgotten by those who seek engagements with us. We cannot afford the time to produce acts, though we often have to reject promising material because this very necessary thing has been overlooked."

Mr. Doyle, while in New Zealand recently, booked Princess Rangiriri and her nine Maori maids—a distinct novelty which should be of the greatest interest in this country, and a fact which shows that the origin of an act is no deterrent to its success.

With the publicity which is put behind an act by the picture men—for in no other form of entertainment is the punch utilised by the live wires of the industry to be seen—a good ordinary act with an exploitation angle often emerges as a headliner, for publicity is often 50 per cent. of the worth of an act. A good act without publicity is worthless from an entrepreneur's point of view, and still more worthless from the point of view of the general public to whom familiarity is nine-tenths of the attraction, and familiarity is only gained after judicious publicity.

Therefore, this new form of entertainment—which in England is known as Kinevaudeville, is serving a dual purpose in providing superlative entertainment for the amusement seekers and extending a possible avenue of employment to local acts who might otherwise be forced to try their luck overseas.

The whole question of extending the activities of the vaudeville act in pictures is in its infancy, but its possibilities, worked on a scale which would embrace city and suburban and country, are enormous, and should not be ignored by those who are aiming for the progress of the entertainment business generally.

IF THIS SQUARE IS MARKED WITH A CROSS IT MEANS THAT YOUR YEARLY SUBSCRIPTION IS DUE.

(ii)

BEAUMONT SMITH
presents his Australian
New Zealand Comedy Romance
THE
"ADVENTURES
OF ALGY"
featuring
CLAUDE DAMPIER
with
Bathie Stuart
Eric Harrison
Billie Carlyle etc.
The Year's Greatest
Novelty Film
NEW ZEALAND &
AUSTRALIA are
waiting for it
on the tip-toe of
expectation

Released by
BEAUMONT SMITH FILMS
Banking House
228 Pitt St Sydney
NEW ZEALAND OFFICE, DE LUXE THEATRE COURTENEY PLACE WELLINGTON

Everyones (i) 17 June 1925, p.3; (ii) 20 May 1925, p.29

(i) Stuart Doyle; (ii) 'Fine Picture palaces' and a discriminating public: Smith's *The Adventures of Algy* as a mere vehicle for the business pretensions of Stuart Doyle he was about to start on the very epic *Everyones* had said he would not make: 'the filming of the history of Australia from the earliest days of Captain Cook's momentous discovery to the present day'.[57]

The film, to be called *The Birth of Australia*, was to cost £15,000, 'by far the largest sum yet expended in this country on a film production'. Perhaps Smith had been influenced by a personal message from Jack Gavin in Hollywood to 'spend an extra thousand or two on the production . . . and assure success not only in Australia, but elsewhere in the world'.[58] However, this was not the Beau Smith beloved and created by the trade, and after 5 August, when a brief announcement appeared that Smith was searching for types to represent the various historical characters and that great help had been promised by 'various public bodies throughout Australia', there was uncharacteristic quiet in the trade press. Apart from his appearance at the Tariff Board hearing, also reported in *Everyones* on 5 August, in which he disagreed with increasing tariff duties on American films but hinted, in a guarded way, that some kind of quota might be the answer for local production, he went out of the news.

Then, in November 1925, *Everyones* afforded him the unusual privilege of a second leading article within six months, announcing that with Frank Thring, Smith had become resident managing director in New Zealand of J.C. Williamson Pictures, who planned to build a chain of modern theatres 'to give the public of New Zealand the very best in pictures and vaudeville'.[59] 'Presentation' was to be a major feature, as was the latest of architectural design in the construction of fine picture palaces for the public. Beaumont Smith was entering the domain of Stuart Doyle.

The reasons for what *Everyones* called the 'uncanny' rapidity of the change from independent producer to exhibitor are not totally clear, and one's interpretation would depend on whether one agrees or not with Longford's attitude to Union Theatres. Longford would certainly have said that this was a deal to 'buy off' Smith from entering a more ambitious phase of production which the trade did not want. Certainly there were rumours of this kind of deal circulating which the Royal Commission was to pick up and ask none-too searching questions about. J.C. Williamson, to whom Smith moved, Union Theatres, who distributed and released his films, and Fullers, from whom he took a number of his actors, were associated concerns,[60] and with Smith's broad talent for presentation and publicity, and with Union Theatres now producing their own films, it could be argued that he was of far greater use to the trade in his new job than his old. Certainly he made a great success of it. It should also be remembered that what Doyle called Smith's 'sound business acumen and administrative powers' had won both the respect and close friendship of many of the trade's most prominent men, including Doyle himself, the Carrolls, and J.W. Hicks, Jnr of Paramount Films.

It is not necessary though to adopt Longford's conspiracy theory about Union Theatres. The move was very much in Smith's interests, and was not in the least discontinuous with his career, if one remembers the entrepreneur of 'Tiny Town' who had said just two years before that he intended giving up production.[61]

On retiring from film-making he said that he knew the hardships of pioneering film production 'and it will be my ambition to do all I can do to encourage all worth-while local productions'. Again, it had all been said before, by Stuart Doyle and W.A.Gibson.

Longford's conspiracy thesis, though, tends to lead us too quickly and easily to a romantic contrast between film hero and film lackey, most spectacularly marked by the last days of the two most prominent of Australian silent-film-makers: Longford ending penurious as a wharf nightwatchman looking for rats, Smith concluding his life in affluence surrounded by one of the finest private collections of Australian paintings. But Longford was not a Romantic hero, however much he might have liked to be, and Beaumont Smith was certainly no lackey. The difference between the two men's fortunes was that, in an industry which was heavily commercial, Longford aspired to be one of the world's greatest film directors, and Smith wanted to be a wealthy man. Given that he had the business drive, acumen and ruthlessness to later take £3,000 off Charles Chauvel for using Paterson's 'Waltzing Matilda' (after buying the rights to the complete works for not more than £500 twenty years before), and to eventually acquire a quarter share in the New Zealand company he was now entering, which he sold for a fortune twelve years later, we can see that Beaumont Smith was not a man who needed to be pushed in the direction of his ambition.

6

The Return of the Big Australians: Arthur Shirley, Louise Lovely and Jack Gavin

Picture Show 1 May 1920, p.26

Three Australians who, in varying degrees, achieved stardom in Hollywood, returned to produce films in Australia in the 1920s. Louise Lovely, after a career in vaudeville and films in Australia, was the most successful of the three in Hollywood, ultimately becoming a major Fox and Goldwyn star. Arthur Shirley, who also had prior stage and film experience in Australia, had worked in Hollywood with Bill Hart and played in *The Fall of a Nation*, the follow-up to the D.W. Griffith classic. Jack Gavin had been the most successful as actor and producer before leaving Australia, directing and starring in a number of financially successful bushranging films. But he was the least successful of the three as an actor in Hollywood, often out of work or playing extras, and in the best times taking character parts on a fairly regular basis with the Hal Roach stock company.

Gavin had far more experience of Hollywood film production than the others, having produced a fair number of cheap Westerns. However, both Shirley and Lovely were totally confident of their ability to produce,

(i) Jack Gavin

(ii) Louise Lovely

(iii) Arthur Shirley

(i) *Everyones* 22 March 1922, p.3; (ii) *Picture Show* 1 November 1922, p.1; (iii) *Everyones* 22 October 1924, p.3

arguing that they had had years of production experience, as well as training as actors in the art of make-up and screen interpretation.

Lovely, Shirley and Gavin had all made many friends in Hollywood and admired the system there, but all three were more or less at the end of their active Hollywood careers. Each of them returned in the early 1920s with great hopes of using their Hollywood experience on a grand scale in Australia, with big studios, American stars and experts, and the idea of cracking a Hollywood market they believed they knew so well.

Their priorities and interests varied. As an actress, Lovely wanted directors and technical experts brought from America, but not stars. Gavin, on the other hand, seeing himself primarily as a film-maker, argued that stars should be imported, but that no Hollywood director had anything much to teach him. But the general principle, popular with the trade at the time, of going to Hollywood, 'learning the game', 'making it', and returning to produce films of world quality was the one that fired the ambitions of each of them.

None of them succeeded. By the end each had learned the harsh lessons of a systematic bias against Australian producers which some of their colleagues who had not 'made it' had learned a long time before. For all their initial Hollywood orientation and ambition, each became involved in a very *Australian* directed development: Lovely and Shirley through their association with Alex Hellmrich's attempt to set up the first significant Australian exchange for Australian films; and Gavin, in association with Herb Finlay, directing cheap films for a purely local market.

Arthur Shirley

Arthur Shirley was the first to return, in early 1920, with a script which had been written in an hour by an American author 'of the Jack London type', Pat O'Cotter. It was for a film with a South Pacific background, *The Throwback*. The trade press trumpeted the arrival home of 'the big Australian', and Shirley's plans were pitched at an appropriately grand level. He had hardly arrived before he announced his intention of building a big studio 'of the Californian Spanish type', incorporating four closed stages and 'right-up-to-date' lighting equipment. He brought with him Lawson Harris as business manager, and said that an American director, cameraman, scenarist, art director and female star had already been signed up. He gave two reasons for relying so heavily on American talent. Firstly, 'we've got to employ the people who know the game better than ourselves until we also know it well'. Secondly, because 'a picture turned out here might be the most wonderful thing ever made, but it would be hard to get American exhibitors to look at it unless there were some familiar names connected with it'.[1]

> The pictures will not be essentially Australian . . . to make the interest always entirely local would be to kill the chances of the productions in other countries. And I am aiming at competition in the world's market.

The trade was impressed by the energy and ambition of this 'big, capable-looking man' with a pocketful of encouraging letters from American distributors, and whose overall theory for film closely matched that of many people inside both the trade and governments of the time. 'What the country needs', Shirley argued,

> is capital and population for its proper development. We can't have the capital till we get the population, and we can't get the population until we advertise the country. The best way of doing that is through moving pictures.

The complicated part of this equations — how to make profitable films without the population — was not asked at the time.
Nor was the contradiction noticed between Shirley's desire to advertise Australia and his determination that his films should 'not be essentially Australian', because far more pressing economic factors were quickly laying waste his grand design. Within a few weeks his custom-made studio design was shelved, and he purchased instead a stately old building in Rose Bay which needed extensive, costly and time-consuming alteration. The delay and cost associated with his sets were to be major factors in Shirley's failure and bankruptcy, but at this point, in July 1920, he had lost little of his ambition for 'Moving Pictures Made in Australia for the World'. He began securing 'types' for his first film, and issued a glowing prospectus which spoke more of the huge profits earned in the years up to and during the war, than of the changed conditions and costs since then. *Everyones*, much impressed, urged Australia to stand behind the 'experienced, energetic, enthusiastic' Mr Shirley to build 'a great movie enterprise'.[2]

Already, however, the plans of 'that big Australian' were becoming less energetic. Interiors were shot at private homes, not in the new studios. Ernest Higgins was the cameraman, not the Hollywood expert 'of twelve years experience' originally announced. Endless delays on the studio sets prevented the major interiors being shot. There was the expense of building a Hawaiian village at Newport, and the departure of Lawson Harris to his own film enterprise. By June 1921, *Picture Show* admitted that 'Arthur Shirley's picture is taking as long as a serial to reach its end'.[3] By September

Arthur Shirley Productions Ltd had gone into voluntary liquidation, and Ernest Higgins had taken over financial control, employing Shirley to finish what the trade press was still hopefully calling a local production so 'lavish' as to place it 'among the most important contributions to the silent drama achieved in this or any other country'.[4]

But from this point on the most lavish thing about the production was the court cases it elicited: vamp star, Vera Ramée suing Higgins for unpaid salary; Shirley unsuccessfully suing Higgins for breach of contract; Shirley unsuccessfully charging Lawson Harris with 'grossly offensive words'. Yet by the end of 1922 *Everyones* was still carrying desperately grandiose advertisements on behalf of Shirley: 'Big in heart, as well as in body' and with 'broadness of mind', he 'had the courage to fight for his convictions against all comers' on behalf of a film which 'an army of big men in America' were only too 'willing to handle . . . throughout the world'.[5]

In January 1923 *Everyones* printed more Shirley publicity: '*The Throwback* is finished and promises to be one of the biggest features of its kind ever made in Australia . . . the market in America is assured.'[6] The truth was, however, that Shirley was bankrupt, and *The Throwback* was never to be released, if indeed it was ever finished.

Shirley started again on a much smaller scale, and between October 1923 and October 1924 produced *The Mystery of a Hansom Cab* for a Melbourne syndicate, Pyramid Productions Ltd. As the advertisements for the film make clear, however, certain things had not changed. Shirley was still producing 'untypical' Australian films. *The Mystery of a Hansom Cab* was an old 'society' murder mystery by Fergus Hume, which had been enormously popular both as a novel and play in Sydney and London in the 1890s. Shirley was also still oriented to films 'Made in Australia for the World' and still drawing upon his American 'stardom' to buy financial backing and trade acceptance.

By allying himself with the distribution agency of Alex Hellmrich, Shirley had become part of the most ambitious attempt to market the films of Australian independents by an Australian distributor in the 1920s. Hellrich rejected the standard trade opinion that Australia was weak in scenarios, actors, technicians, or any other facet of the film-making process. The only thing which had handicapped the pioneers was lack of money.

> If capital is put into the business, then local producers will soon develop and these, whether brought from abroad should be men who can absorb our local atmosphere, mainly Australians with overseas experience, and who can be offered sufficient inducement to return. We have one such here now, in Arthur Shirley.[7]

(i)

(ii)

(iii)

(iv)

Picture Show (i) 1 May 1920, p.27; (ii) 1 July 1920, p.57; (iii), (iv) *Everyones* 22 October 1924, p.28

The declining ambitions of Arthur Shirley: (i) Plans for the Californian Spanish-style studio he hoped to build in Sydney and (ii) the Rose Bay property he bought. (iii) After his bankruptcy Shirley was confined to the cramped space of the Australasian Films' studios at Rushcutters Bay. (iv) The setting up of *The Mystery of a Hansom Cab*

National Film Archive

Cameraman Ernest Higgins and Arthur Shirley in production

In fact by then there were two for Hellmrich to use, because Louise Lovely was back in Australia, already negotiating with Stuart Doyle about making a film. *Everyones*, in September 1924, said that this kind of collaboration could arouse real interest in the local industry, and 'one of the most convincing arguments to bring before capitalists is the fact that a star of international reputation is being featured in an Australian production'.[8] Within a week Louise Lovely was personally addressing the capitalists of the Sydney Millions Club about the need for funding a new Australian Hollywood. When, in addition to Shirley's backers, she gained the support of E.J. Carroll, even the reluctant *Everyones*, which had just been accused by Franklyn Barrett of being against Australian production, 'felt considerably cheered' about 'the enormous possibilities which lie at Australia's gates . . . in the motion picture industry'.[9]

In this climate of opinion Hellmrich established his new Australian policy. He based a lot of his hopes on the recent success abroad of *The Sentimental Bloke* — which, of course, had been produced with an entirely different conception of film-making. He was jointed in partnership by Allan McGowan who, with twenty years in the trade behind him, argued that *The Mystery of a Hansom Cab*, produced for £10,000, was 'the finest thing I have ever seen — that is, for an Australian production',[10] and, in a moment of euphoria, proclaimed that the film trade had reached a peak of cameraderie 'conducted on a better footing with a spirit of "help your fellow man" which you seldom find in other walks of life'.

In fact this was one of the moments of most open conflict in the trade. The Australian Picture Producers Association was bitterly demanding the government's support against the American combines and asking for an Australian quota; and *Everyones*, sidestepping all the systematic reasons for the conflict, was chiding the producers for not sitting down in a spirit of harmony and unity 'to calmly and impartially discuss the whole matter'.[11] McGowan's vision of unity and *Everyones'* may have been from different sides of the production–exhibition divide, but cooperation was needed every bit as badly by the Hellmrich company to get first release screenings for their films, as it was by *Everyones* which feared major government intervention unless the trade closed ranks and put its own house in order.

Of its own position it argued that:

> *Everyones* is out for the best interests of the industry. It could not exist for five minutes were it to try to single out one small unit of the business and boost that to the detriment of any other section.[12]

It too, it claimed, was behind the pioneer producers. But when 'the Big Australian production' came, made by the 'Napoleon' of producers 'it will need nothing to put it on a pinnacle. It will be there'.

The fact was, as the future history of the Shirley and Lovely films was to show, that the trade could very well succeed in a situation where nearly all the power was in the hands of one closely combined section: the distributors and big exhibition circuits. And it was perfectly possible for the leading trade journal to survive on the advertising of these big forces without being at all concerned with the fate of that 'one small unit of the business', the producers. As for 'Napoleons', the big Australians were not big enough, and none of McGowan's spirit of 'help your fellow man' was forthcoming from the big forces when they needed it.

Shirley made two 'society' films, *The Mystery of a Hansom Cab*, and *The Sealed Room.*[13] The films were praised by Prime Minister Bruce 'as an incentive to the establishment in this country on a successful financial basis of the moving picture industry'.[14] But the general opinion, for instance among the Royal Commissioners, and indeed of Hellmrich himself in his evidence to the Commission, was that they could only harm Australia's reputation for film production.

Louise Lovely

Louise Lovely produced *Jewelled Nights* on a tight contract which required her to complete the film within twelve weeks or bear the extra expense. In fact the film took six months to finish. This was partly because Lovely, like Shirley in the first instance, worked in emulation of the Hollywood model. *Jewelled Nights* was planned as a 'super' feature, and included a cathedral interior, 'one of the costliest sets ever built in Australia' which took a month to construct. Also, following Hollywood practice, but unprecedented for local production, two complete negatives were made, one for Australia and England, the other for America.

The other major reason for delay was due to conditions which were not at all like Hollywood. Whereas Shirley shot *The Sealed Room* at Australasian Films' Rushcutters Bay studio, using their cameraman Lacey Perceval, Louise Lovely had to film her interiors in an ice rink, and shoot only at night before moving to another venue 'where the same difficulties were encountered'. The film cost £9,500, but she told the Royal Commission that with her own studio the film could have been shot for £5,000, without cutting any of the special effects.

(i)

(ii)

(iii)

(iv)

Hellmrich-Conrad publicity: (i) 'Louise Lovely in the wedding gown as worn by her in "Jewelled Nights", leaves Hoyts' De Luxe Theatre, Melbourne, to take up a long run season at Hoyts' New Gaiety across the street. Thousands of people blocked Bourke Street for one hour to witness this unique advertising. A Gordon Conrad stunt.'
(ii) Alex Hellmrich; (iii) Gordon Conrad
(iv) 'When Albert Myers (Civic Pictures, Warrnambool, Vic.) arranged for the screening of "The Mystery of a Hansom Cab" — released by Hellmrich and Conrad — he went all over the district for find a hansom, but none was available. Nothing deterred, this astute exhibitor utilised the contraption shown above, with remarkably successful results.'

(i) *Everyones* 11 November 1925, p.12; (ii), (iii) *Picture Show* 1 August 1922, p.69, 1 December 1920, p.66; (iv) *Everyones* 30 September 1925, p.37

The Mystery of a Hansom Cab and *Jewelled Nights* were released with considerable publicity by Alex Hellmrich, who argued that though Shirley's film was inferior to Chavel's *Moth of Moonbi*, which he also handled, it was a success in Melbourne for a month due to his personal exploitation. Shirley's two films in fact do not seem to have had much trouble with first release. This is a point to remember when formulating conspiracy theories about the Australian combines because Shirley was one of the leaders of the producers' deputations to the government — though he did expressly exclude Australasian Films from his criticism, arguing that they were 'the only firm in Australia that will take Australian pictures'.[15]

This was not, of course, Longford's opinion; nor was it Alex Hellmrich's, given his experience with *Jewelled Nights.* Despite intense publicity the film was not a success for Louise Lovely. The first release, which according to Hoyts' managing director, George Griffiths, broke all records for his big theatre, brought in £1,565 18s 6d, but Lovely only got £382 of that. Hellmrich was unable to secure an adequate release in the suburbs of Melbourne. Hoyts released it in seven suburban theatres for £450, but other suburbs were controlled by Associated Theatres (prior to their amalgamation with Hoyts) who only offered £155 for screening the film in a total of nine theatres. It is an interesting case of monopoly control by other organisations than Hoyts and Union Theatres — in this case the influence which powerful local ratepayers had on local councils who refused the film alternative venues. The trade journals constantly attacked these suburban pools for their monopoly practices because they threatened the easy profits of the big distributors. But this was a case where they worked against local producers too.

However, the large combines were also party to the failure of *Jewelled Nights.* Doyle agreed to take the film for release by Union Theatres in other states, but at basic rates, and he refused to give a release date. Hellmrich complained that this was really a kind of passive resistance because his overheads continued while nothing was coming in from the film. *Jewelled Nights* returned only half its production costs in Australia, and Hellmrich, unlike Shirley, argued in 1927 that Hoyts and Union Theatres were 'deliberately keeping Australian and British pictures off the screen'.[16]

Louise Lovely Productions had floated a company with a share value of £10,000, of which only about £7,000 was subscribed. The film had cost £9,500 to produce and advertise and had returned under £5,000. Despite her hard work exploiting the film with personal appearances in the country as well as cities, and her belief that *Jewelled Nights* was the

ARTHUR SHIRLEY

THE BIG AUSTRALIAN
Who Rose to Film Stardom in AMERICA
in

"The SEALED ROOM"

Story and Direction by — ARTHUR SHIRLEY
Made in Australia for the World
Distributed by PYRAMID PICTURES Sydney Australia

Breathes there a man with soul so dead,
Who never to himself hath said
This is my own, my native land?

PRIME MINISTER

S. M. BRUCE, twice Prime Minister of Australia, says:

Dear Mr. Shirley,

I attach hereto copy of a letter which has been addressed to the Official Secretary to the Governor-General to my colleague, the Minister for Trade and Customs.

I note with great pleasure His Excellency's commendatory remarks with regard to the picture, "The Mystery of a Hansom Cab," and wish to extend to you, and to the other principals in the production of this film, my congratulations on the success of this All-Australian picture. I hope its success will serve as an incentive to the establishment in this country on a successful financial basis of the moving picture industry.

Yours Sincerely,

S M Bruce

Prime Minister.

We will Not say that "The Sealed Room" is the Greatest Australian Picture ever produced, as there have been so many "Greatest Australian Pictures," but we will say without Fear or the Slightest Hesitation that "The Sealed Room" is Greater than "The Mystery of a Hansom Cab," which was proclaimed by Press, Public and Exhibitors throughout Australasia as a "Truly Great Production."

Booked by UNION THEATRES LTD. for their ENTIRE CIRCUIT. SYDNEY LYCEUM and EMPRESS THEATRES, Commencing SATURDAY, JULY 3rd.

Distributed throughout the World by

PYRAMID PICTURES

NATIONAL BUILDING, 250 PITT STREET, SYDNEY. Telephone M 3570.

Telegraphic and Cable Address: "PYRAMIDS, SYDNEY."

NOW IN COURSE OF PREPARATION

"1840"

AN HISTORICAL ROMANCE OF LOVE AND ADVENTURE IN EARLY AUSTRALIA, FROM THE BOOK ENTITLED, "CASTLE VANE," BY J. H. M. ABOTT.

Everyones 26 May 1926, p.27

best film produced in Australia, Louise Lovely could not go on. In November 1926 her husband, Wilton Welch, went to London to try to sell the film and find backers for further scripts he had witten in order to secure financial guarantees that future costs of production would be met. This was not forthcoming, and his plans to build up-to-date studios in Australia came to nothing. Louise Lovely stayed in Australia, hoping to convince the Royal Commission to recommend a quota system and a national studio. They made no more films.

Arthur Shirley, despite limited success with *The Mystery of a Hansom Cab* and the announcement of a new production, *1840*, was unable to continue because of lack of capital. Shirley had maintained his policy of making 'untypical' Australian films to the end. *The Sealed Room* was 'by no means Antipodean in character but possesses universal appeal'.[17] The trade's idea of appropriate 'Australian' pictures is evident from *Everyones* approval of Shirley's melodramatic tale of anarchists and revolutionaries in a fictitious land, but with 'exceptionally fine' shots of the Blue Mountains thrown in for local content. *Everyones* remarked that whereas Australian films hitherto had been too local this film would appeal overseas *and* attract 'all classes of audience'.[18]

'All classes', of course, included 'better classes', and this may offer a clue to the trade support for Shirley in comparison with Lovely and Gavin. The same issue of *Everyones* carried an editorial article which spelled out the argument more fully. Written in response to renewed tax threats from the Government, this article is virtually unique in the trade press of the 1920s in taking the matter of disputes with government beyond the self-righteous complaints of trade 'professionals' against 'ignorant' laymen.

In a piece of typical conspiratorial thinking,[19] *Everyones* isolated three distict groups the trade had to fear. Firstly, there were the parliamentarians who tried to oppress the trade with their taxes and talk of quotas, but who were 'sincere in their beliefs' and were only used to 'fire off the bullets' prepared for them by other men lurking 'in the shadows'. The parliamentarians were 'deliberately blinded' by this second group which contained 'powerful interests' and 'funds and men of ability' with 'warped brains'. These sick people, who were 'insanely jealous' of the American film industry because of their own 'failure to do what the Americans have done' . . . sought 'for their own purposes . . . to stultify and hamper the progress of the Motion Picture Industry'.

The *third* group is the one to which *Everyones* believed 'the industry should direct its salvo of eloquence'. This consisted of the older generation of the

National Film Archive

Society maiden goes bush: Louise Lovely in *Jewelled Nights* affluent classes who still regarded 'the movies as occupation for housemaids' and 'who preferred to lounge in clubs and by their firesides'. These 'fathers of the present generation' were untouched by the cinema's publicity men, and sat 'in solemn council on affairs of state', accepting at face value what 'those whose business it is to distort the truth' told them of the evils of the cinema industry. This class had been weakened but not eliminated by the triumphant march of democracy. It constituted 'the backbone of conservatism' and because of its sheeer ignorance was 'a cog in the wheels of progress'.

What was to be done? This third group never attended the movies because their minds had been trained that 'cheapness means mediocrity'. However, as great new picture palaces were built, combining 'ease and comfort' with 'advanced forms of presentation' this 'class' was 'gradually being drawn towards the cinema as a national form of amusement', and soon there would be 'born a much better understanding of a much-maligned industry'. To ensure this 'great reform' it was imperative that cinema presentations and publicity were of a high quality. 'Dignity of method is the only means by which their interest may be awakened'.[20]

This is an important article, the last written by *Everyones* outgoing political editor Frederick Ward, who was socially connected with most of the trade's leading figures and professionally connected with Doyle and Gibson. It was, as seen earlier, crucial to these men that a 'better class' of audience be attracted by screening the 'right' kinds of films with superior presentation in palatially comfortable theatres, and Ward here was adding a political rationale to their economic one. It seems clear that though Shirley, as a political animal, belonged to Ward's dangerous second group, his Hollywood experience and sympathies as well as the 'class' of film he produced attracted the sympathies of the trade in their efforts to appeal to that powerful third group who had already approved of the subjects of his films when they were played to the dignity of the 'legitimate' theatre a generation before.

By now, however, Shirley had lost his financial backing, and though he tried to continue as sole proprietor of Pyramid Pictures, *1840* never got past the scenario stage. *Film Weekly*, in September 1926, spoke of a deal between Shirley and 'a very prominent motion picture theatre man', who, in the event of the former making at least three or four pictures a year, would 'guarantee them a screening in Melbourne, and subsequently play them over a considerable chain of houses'.[21] This may have been a response by Hoyts to Union Theatres' big plans for *For The Term Of His Natural Life.* Interestingly enough, *1840*, like Norman Dawn's film, was to be about convict days — and an insight into the variations of social position and target group of the various film journals is that *Stage and Society* (which had incorporated *Picture Show* and was very much aimed at Ward's third group of 'high culture' conservatives) was pleased with the fact that the film would not 'slavishly imitate the American product and lack any stamp of nationality'.[22] But if Shirley *was* aiming at a 'typical' Australian production here, it was quite out of character for him, and it is much more likely that he wanted to cash in on the international popularity of recent Hollywood films on the Yukon gold rush with an Australian feature on the 'Roaring Days'.

At any rate, no money was forthcoming, and Shirley did not even wait in Australia for the Royal Commission. He left in January 1927 to exploit his films in Britain, where he encountered custom duty trouble, further court cases, and where, after an abortive attempt to produce films 'Made in Rhodesia for the World', he remained. Like Longford his silent-film-making career ended firstly with hope of the British quota system, but finally in disappointment, and a slashing attack on the 'hide-bound conservative attitude' of the 'addled-brained idiots' who made up the majority of the British film industry.[23]

Jack Gavin

If Shirley with his 'society' films and Lovely with her tale of a society maiden who goes bush were getting at least some backing from the big combines, Jack Gavin was getting none for his bushranging tale. Gavin's initial reception by the trade was enthusiastic, probably because he said 'I learned almost everything in Los Angeles' and complained of the backwardness of the Australian producing industry. *Everyones* gave him its lead article on each of his returns from America. The journal noted Gavin's comments that few people in Australia 'have had any real experience in film work' and commented on 'a marked improvement in the big fellow's manner and method. Not only does he appear to have gleaned all that is necessary for motion picture production, but his very appearance and conversation convinces one that his education has been complete'.[24]

Once again the trade press was much impressed by the man who had 'made it' in Hollywood, and had returned, apparently no longer the crude producer of rough bushranging tales. *Everyones* followed up its announcement that 'Gavin will have "The Goods",' with numerous announcements that he was about to turn out important and 'pretentious' features.

However, despite frequent claims that 'moneyed syndicates' were behind him, financial backing was not forthcoming, and Gavin's intention of serialising *The Kelly Gang* would not have impressed the trade. It looks as though Gavin was relying on his old pre-war policy when, as he put it, 'showmen would come along and pay in advance for the film before the story was even finished',[25] because no more was heard of these productions, nor of the numerous scenarios Agnes Gavin was supposed to have written.

Gavin returned to Hollywood. There he tried to interest the Horner Production Company into coming to Australia. *Everyones*, which like Gavin would have been more than happy to see Australian productions by Hollywood companies, wrote hopefully, that due to the 'over-supply' of film-makers in California, Horner's 'appearance in this country is only a matter of weeks'.[26]

Nothing came of this scheme, and Gavin stayed in Hollywood acting in small character roles. *Everyones* gave him a lot of publicity and regularly printed his opinions on both Hollywood events and the hopes for Australian production. In July 1922 Gavin repeated his hope that, as a result of the slump, Australia would be invaded by Americans 'with a view to producing direct for the markets of the world'; and it is clear that at this time he pinned his hopes as a producer on the 'natural' expansion of the Hollywood production system to his own country. At the same time he offered his personal advice to 'Beaumont Smith, Raymond Longford, and the rest' to spend more money and asssure a world sale for their films. Like Shirley, he was still imbued with Hollywood-scale ideas for Australia, and argued that only when the 'huge production budgets' he was used to there were applied in Australia 'will there be some chance of competing with the country that supplies the world with 80 per cent of the pictures'.[27] Further, like Shirley and Lovely, he pointed out that to get the essential American release, the film would have to carry the names of American stars or producers. Like E.J. Carroll, who backed Louise Lovely partly because he thought that Pauline Frederick was about 'to set the ball rolling' by acting in an Australian film, Gavin argued that a Frederick film would 'add a wonderful impetus' to Australian production.[28]

Noting, in an article printed in *Everyones* in Spetember 1925 that 'Louise Lovely and Arthur Shirley have secured substantial backing from an Australian syndicate', he added that 'the time must be very near when continuous picture making will be an established fact in the Antipodes'.[29] Within two months Gavin was back in Australia, and *Everyones*, under the title of 'The Man Who Made Good', gave heavy publicity to his plan to make an Australian film 'in the way in which it is made over there, by methods with which I am familiar, and are a long way ahead of the old methods we used to employ'.[30]

Once again, however, his grandiose plans failed to secure backing. In early 1926 he formed an association with Herbert Finlay who was to tell the Royal Commission that 'After careful consideration of the statements in both daily press and trade journals that Australasian Films and Hoyts would entertain Australian pictures, we decided to re-engage on local production and arranged to produce four pictures a year'. Between July and September 1926, Gavin directed *Key of Fate* with a local cast but plot of 'universal appeal' for £1,000 with Finlay. Renamed *Trooper O'Brien* the film was taken to both Union Theatres and Hoyts. Doyle did not even give them an interview, but Hoyts negotiated.

Finlay argued that these negotiations depended on a dispute between Union Theatres and Hoyts which arose as a result of the latter not taking some American films that Australasian Films were handling, which meant a loss of 'about £400 a week in film hire to Union Theatres'. However, the normal booking consensus between the two combines had been restored, and consequently Griffiths of Hoyts, sure of his supplies, dropped the negotiations over *Trooper O'Brien*.[31] Doyle refused the film on the grounds that his company was 'not operating the class of theatre in which it would have an appeal'.[32] 'Unfortunately', Finlay noted, 'we found that their statements in the press did not coincide with their actions in trade'.[33]

It is ironic that news of the 'surprise run' of *Trooper O'Brien* at the mainly suburban Australian Picture Palace in Sydney in May 1928 was juxtaposed in *Everyones* with an artist's sketch of the new Union Theatres Sydney State cinema, because the two things were integrally connected. Much of Gavin's and Finlay's success in the early days of film production had been with bushranger films, and their mistake now was to stick to that formula of the 'tin roof' days which Doyle was ostentatiously rejecting with palatial theatres like the State. The fact that Gavin and Finlay were now aiming cheaply at a purely local market was not the problem — Union Theatres had supported Beaumont Smith just as long as he did that. The real problem, as Doyle's comments about 'class of theatre' indicate, was the bushranging emphasis of *Trooper O'Brien*. The Ned Kelly sequence was no more than an insertion in the film — and *The Sydney Morning Herald* condemned it as such for destroying the film's continuity. But it was the Kelly image that the producers in their advertisements, the trade with its lobby displays, and *Everyones* in its review all emphasised. And quite apart from

ɪo to Press.

e Sorlie arrived by the Orvieto from ch Sydney on June 7.

• •

ɛaland Publicity Department has eeney as a means of advertising the completed a visit to Heeney's birth- shots of his father and mother at learned to fight and other scenes life. The takes formed a 1000-footer this week. Arrangements have been the picture throughout U.S.A. prior ith Tunney.

• •

Hamilton state that a New Zealand tion to the average American comedy Miss Dale Austen, recently home ed in M.-G.-M. studios will be fea-

• •

Williamson Films Ltd. will be vacat- Street shortly and will occupy space heatre Buildings, Flinders Street. their supplies as a separate concern, ill be incorporated with the already dan Films. Arch. Young, manager, or, and the booking department will

Local Film, "Trooper O'Brien," Surprises in Sydney Run

One of the surprises of last week was the way the local film, "Trooper O'Brien," scored at the Australian Picture Palace, Sydney, which caters to a half-city, half-suburban audience.

PRODUCED by Bert Finlay, the picture has taken nearly 15 months to be put into shape. Principal players are Gordon Collingridge, Merle Ridgway and Jack Gavin, while the story has a lengthy Ned Kelly sequence interpolated as a narrative told by Gavin, who plays the part of Trooper O'Brien.

On rental plus percentage the film played the Australian Picture Palace on Wednesday, Thursday and Friday of last week with a bushranging lobby display. The managerial verdict is given in a letter from Manager L. B. Grogan to Mr. Finlay:

"I suppose the best evidence of how the picture shaped is in the facts: your cheque represents the payment of a cut nearly three times as great as the hire fixed in the first place on high normal takings. And also it might be noted that the third night, Friday, late shopping night as a rule, came very nearly being the best of the three.

"Apparently our constantly growing crowd thought "Trooper O'Brien" the goods and flocked in accordingly. We always have a three days run here for genuine local productions of that kind."

Bookings for "Trooper O'Brien" are now being arranged.

Car Parade for Movie Ball

CAR owners in the industry are reminded that on Friday, June 15, they are asked to assemble at the Palais Royal with their cars at 11.30 a.m., and take place in the car parade in connection with the Movie Ball. Prizes will be awarded for best decorated cars. If you cannot decorate a car, come along and carry a pennant.

Sydney's Next Cinema Will be the Stately State.

GIRDERS are rising in Market Street, Sydney, for the State Theatre, which Union Theatres will open next Easter. This is the first published illustration of the new cinema which will be the most beautiful theatre in the British Empire, it is claimed. The building embraces both the State Theatre and the Shopping Block. The theatre, seating 3,500, is built well back with entrances on both Market and George Streets. One hundred and fifty shops arranged on the arcade principle will occupy the 14 floors in the front, and will be served by 8 express elevators of the latest design.

Everyones 30 May 1928, p. 18

this connection between the genre of film and the big circuits' concern with pulling in an up-scale market, there was another connection which Herb Finlay shrewdly guessed at in his evidence to the Royal Commission.

Finlay noted that there was a contradiction between Union Theatres claim to have recently made 'Australia's First Real Attempt to Produce Australian Pictures' and their other proud boast to have been the leaders of the Australian industry for fifteen years. He argued that the fact of these years of dominance with massive funds to make films and a string of theatres to show them in 'should prove that they did not desire to produce Australian pictures'. Finlay also had 'the sinister suspicion that the Americans retain their grip on Australia under threat of entering the exhibiting field. An Australian in the employ of one of the American agencies informed me that if Mr Griffiths, of Hoyts, carried his methods too far, the Americans would undoubtedly enter the exhibiting field'. And First National had gone as far as negotiating to build cinemas in Perth to put pressure on Union Theatres.

That Finlay was not far off the mark is suggested by Griffiths' request to the Royal Commission for government legislation to prevent American control of Australian cinemas; and it is corroborated by Stuart Doyle's evidence to the New South Wales Government Inquiry into the Film Industry in 1934. Doyle argued that in 1927 and 1928 'pressure was brought to bear by American Film Distributors, who were then doing business with Union Theatres . . . to raise extra capital and build theatres' for the presentation of their films. In particular, John W. Hicks of First Lassky–Paramount 'insisted that the State Theatre, Sydney and the State Theatre, Melbourne should be built, or they themselves would build theatres of equal importance for the purpose of placing Paramount Pictures therein'.[34]

Doyle was, of course, trying to appear whiter than white, since we know that the policy of building large theatres had appealed to Union Theatres for many years previously in order to attract the 'better class of market'. The incident of the juxtaposition of the *Trooper O'Brien* review and the picture of the State Theatre dramatised very clearly the big pool of national and international capital into which Gavin had thrown his film with innocent appeals for support.

Ironically too, that self-same struggle of American and local capital also helped *Trooper O'Brien* cover some of its production costs, since the film was one of the few Australian productions bought up by the Universal company in 1929 to fulfil its quota obligations in Britain. All of these were cheap productions, all were bought by American companies to beat

"Better Pictures Mean Better Theatres"

MR. JOHN W. HICKS (Jnr.), Australasian Managing Director of Famous Players Lasky, who returned last week from America from the Annual Convention held by that organisation, whilst most anxious to impart all information regarding his tour, was a trifle reluctant to relate the details of what is, after all, a set function, the details of which do not vary year after year.

"You do not want me to say the same old thing," said Mr. Hicks. "That I had a great trip, that I have come back full of new ideas. That production is still on a very high plane, and matters are pushing ahead. I have told the showmen that on many occasions. After all, my trip is merely incidental to the year's work. I can only tell you what I told you when I returned from last year's conference.

"Of course, one or two things of moment have transpired, but I am sure you wont mind if I keep them under my hat, so to speak."

The slight air of mystery with which Mr. Hicks imparted this last little bit of information, set us on the qui vive, but no amount of diplomatic conversation could elicit the subject of Mr. Hicks' mystery. Whatever it is he keeps under his Stetson, he is keeping it well covered until such time as it is politic to release it.

"I am sure the showmen don't want to hear me speak about myself," said Mr. Hicks, "but I tell you what I would like to do, and that is to talk about Jim Thornley, lately general manager of the Capitol Theatre in Melbourne by arrangement with Famous Players-Lasky.

"Jim Thornley left with me on the 2nd March, and for the time being he has become an integral part of the Publix Theatres with a view to learning all there is to be known about theatre construction, lighting, seating and stage presentation. Whilst there he will join a school for managers and he will learn thoroughly and from the beginning, every angle of the business as adopted in the United States for the better presentation of motion pictures. He will travel to Philadelphia, Chicago, Buffalo and other centres, and east to New York and Brooklyn.

"He is going with a view to learning every minute detail there is to be learned from the men who have pioneered the business of motion picture production and motion picture presentation from its infancy. He will have the advantage of the knowledge gained by those men who, beginning from the very humblest beginnings, have brought the picture business to the pitch it is to-day, and he will also have an opportunity of studying in detail the construction of those palatial theatres which have sprung up all over the United States, and which are a solid tribute to the strength and dignity of the motion picture as it stands to-day.

"Look at this."

Mr. Hicks threw across a volume of "The Architectural Forum," a ponderous tome of several hundred pages on art paper entirely devoted to architecture in modern picture theatres.

"Cast your eyes over these pictures and then tell me whether you think they establish the fact that the motion picture business has reached the highest standard."

The volume was packed from cover to cover with photographs of

JOHN W. HICKS, JNR.

some of the most remarkable examples of architecture, all colossal buildings devoted to the presentation of motion pictures on a scale hitherto undreamt of, even in Australia with the high standard as set by the Prince Edward and Capitol Theatres.

"Jim Thornley will meet the men who designed these theatres. He will not merely meet the clever architect who is carrying out an artistic scheme, because over there they do things differently. After the architect has designed the building in accordance with the requirements of the owners, then the experts in the various subsidiary branches are called in and they co-operate with him in the final plans. For instance, no theatre is ever erected without a consultation with a seating engineer who has spent his life devising correct methods of seating an audience.

"It may interest you to know," said Mr. Hicks, "in this regard, how they do things on the other side in what might be considered a trifling point. For instance, supposing the standard theatre seat is 19 inches wide. In order to take advantage of every available inch of space they work on the law of average, and for, say, every three seats at 19 inches they will slip in one at 18 inches. After all, it is only reasonable. You and I might go together, and where I might find a tight fit you will have plenty to spare. Work that out and you will find the law of average a good factor in the economical seating of an audience.

"Jim Thornley will also have met the engineers who devote a great deal of time to the artistic lighting of the stages and auditoriums, and after thoroughly exhausting all avenues of research in America he was due to sail last Saturday to England and the Continent of Europe, there to study the methods ruling in those countries. He is scheduled to return in August.

"No. I cannot say at the moment exactly what Mr. Thornley is to do on his return. All I know is that he will be thoroughly equipped with knowledge and that this knowledge will be at the disposal of the motion picture industry, and all those who desire to see the better presentation of better pictures.

"My sole thought, and the sole thought of the organisation which I have the honor to represent in Australia, is better and better pictures, and with better pictures comes better theatres.

"Look around you, and see the effect of the scare which was thrown around town about a year ago. You will remember at that time everyone was talking about building, building, building. People said, 'John Hicks has come back with a million pounds to build a theatre,' when I returned from my last trip to America. I didn't contradict them. No, sir. I neither affirmed nor denied, but rumor went on talking and now, see the result. I guess there isn't an available site in Sydney that isn't earmarked for almost immediate erection of a monster picture house, and that's just what I like to see.

"Better theatres mean a better state of things for the whole of the industry. There are a whole heap of fellows making pictures, and unless they get adequate theatres in which to show them, then there has been a whole heap of money invested to no purpose. After all, it is only a fair thing. If a man invests his good money in a motion picture, then he should have an adequate theatre in which to show it. He cannot do either himself or his stockholders any justice if he has to show it in some little out of the way hole and corner place, badly ventilated and badly equipped, and holding only a small proportion of those who want to see it.

"You would be surprised at the number of people who don't go to motion pictures. They are by no means a rarity. Quite a number remain rigidly aloof, but these people would become regular attendants if there were theatres which would worthily uphold the dignity of the motion picture.

"The Prince Edward has started it, and now I guess there will be a number of motion picture theatres going up in the big centres on that same scale, dignified, palatial buildings, in which it is a pleasure to sit, and when the time comes that these theatres are erected, a great deal of prejudice which exists in the minds of the public regarding the motion picture industry generally will be removed, or at any rate we shall be a long way on the road to the millennium in the industry."

Mr. Hicks is only voicing that which becomes more apparent every day. Many excellent pictures are being ruined because there are not enough big houses in which to properly exploit them. Each day sees the completion of some picture which is planned on a big scale and which demands different treatment to that style of offering which we have learned to class as a "programme picture."

Either by its lavishness or its direct appeal to the finest chords in human nature it calls out for dignified presentation. The old methods do not fit in with its theme. It needs atmosphere and environment and a treatment calling for big money in its handling. The support must be carefully chosen, the musical accompaniment must be first class, and the interpolated acts must harmonise in dignity and suitability. All these adjuncts mean the expenditure of big money which cannot be taken in the theatre of yesterday.

Therefore with the consummation of the big ideals which are being promulgated at the present moment will come a better understanding of what is best in motion picture presentation, and with it a more enlightened public and a better status for an oft maligned industry.

At least we hope so.

Everyones 26 May 1926, p.5

John W. Hicks returns from America, already hinting at the pressure he will put on Union Theatres to build better cinemas.

Main Entrance to the Roxy, the World's Largest Theatre.

A view of three of the many ticket sellers' boxes in the main entran

... rising upon tier, 6,200 seats, all having an unobstructed view of stage or screen.

"THE ROXY"

THE WORLD'S GREATEST THEATRE.

Aptly named "The Cathedral of the Motion Picture," "The Roxy" Theatre, New York, is truly the most sumptuous and stupendous theatre ever erected.

By securing control of this, the world's largest theatre, together with a chain of 5000-seat, first-run houses situated throughout the U.S.A., William Fox is now in a position of unassailable strength in the motion picture industry.

The control of these theatres demands that Fox must make the world's greatest pictures, possessing 100 per cent. box office value, for the world's greatest theatres.

Knowing this, Exhibitors of Australia and New Zealand can be certain that the Fox Product must, and will, dominate the field of the motion picture.

Portion of Grand Foyer, showing entrance to main auditorium.

Grand Foyer, showing portion of Dome and Chandelier.

The ceiling of the Roxy is illuminated by concealed lights, which emphasise architectural details.

Film Weekly 28 July 1927, p.5

Picture palaces, the Australian ideal: the Roxy, New York and the State, Sydney

Splendors of Sydney's New State . . . . . .

The State is a theatre of contrasts. The entrance hall is planned on medieval lines, and reflects the magnificent grandeur of centuries ago. In the Grand Assembly the Louis scheme, which is brought into effect in the auditorium, runs riot. Period decorations, pictured left and below, endow the theatre with a luxurious detail, which is brought into effect by chandeliers and concealed lighting. The immensity of the auditorium can only be realised from the stage.

Special permission had to be obtained by Union Theatres for the importation of Czecho-Slovakian experts to erect this immense chandelier. Many tons in weight, the strain is borne by a steel rod around which cluster a myriad of prisms.

One of a hundred points of artistic interest. A cameo of a Japanese landscape with volcano in the background, a stream trickling down, and stunted pine and oak trees a hundred years old growing in the foreground.

The Pioneer Room for men, a novel and striking effect.

the quota, and they were greatly responsible for the British hostility to Australian productions which disappointed the hopes of Longford and Shirley at this time. The trade journal, *Film Weekly* had noted the 'paltry hundreds of pounds' which the film had cost when it commented on this quota sale — a remark which, according to Finlay, seriously affected his negotiations to sell the film in New Zealand, Queensland and Victoria.

Hopes Ended

And so ended in petty recriminations the great hopes of the 'big Australians'. Lovely, Shirley and Gavin had assumed, at the beginning of the 1920s, a ready international market based on the free competition of films, in which 'big pictures of quality' made by Hollywood-trained Australians would do well. By the late 1920s they had learned that things were more complicated. Their response is interesting.

Louise Lovely, though still believing in producing for an international market and importing American experts, was now calling for an Australian quota and a government run studio. She had had enough experience of people refusing to invest because of 'so much talk about Australian pictures not being able to get in', to argue that if poor American pictures were forced on exhibitors by block booking, why should not legislation force Australian pictures on them? John Gavin had also seen investment scared away by the block-booking system, and though still admiring American methods and arguing that only great names would sell pictures, he was now acute enough to point out: 'The exhibitor here says that the public do not want Australian pictures, but the public have not been asked whether they want them'.[35] He advocated twenty per cent Australian quota, arguing that it would unloose Australian capital and also force Americans to come to Australia and create a second Hollywood. This aspect of his early hopes had not changed. As though it were a culmination of his entire career, he now looked forward to an industry which would both produce 'American pictures in Australia depicting cowboy and Indian scenes' and 'good Australian pictures' which would appeal to Americans 'fed up with their own pictures'. But a quota was essential and, further, 'It is a matter of impossibility for exchanges representing American producers to be in favour of Australian productions'. This was also Arthur Shirley's opinion, when he argued for a quota and different distribution methods, directed by men who 'have no connection with our American competitors'.[36] Shirley, unlike Finlay, still insisted that an international market was necessary since the local market was too small to recoup production costs, but by now he had lost his belief in the imported expert, arguing, under the pressure of financial necessity, that 'in this country . . . artists capable of filling all roles, cameramen equal to the world's best, mechanics, and others required for successful production, are available at reasonable salaries'.

Herbert Finlay also argued that Australia had adequate film personnel 'to produce twenty good average pictures a year',[37] and knew from his experience of travelling the country with Australian films that they could make money. He, too, argued that distributors' control of the market prevented a profitable Australian producing industry. But, without the others' Hollywood sympathies and experience, his solutions were more articulated than theirs and more radical. He advocated a government subsidised national film exchange, headed by experienced Australian exchange managers, which would be responsible for advancing money 'to producers of approved films' to enable them to undertake continuous production; for distributing their films; for registering all production deals, contracts and companies; for encouraging local investment; for undertaking national publicity of the films; and for informing the government 'of any restraint or unfair policy adopted in the industry'. This scheme, he believed, would lead to the creation of 'an Australian type of picture acceptable to our own people', would 'unite all independent producers and enable us to present a powerful front to those concerns which do not wish to see a big industry grow up in our midst beyond their control'.[38] His analysis of the situation was very similar to Alex Hellmrich's, and his solution was close to the Hellmrich agency writ large, except that the latter felt that, with the help of a quota, he could float the required company without government subsidy as a matter of private enterprise.

Among these different Australian men and women, producers and distributors, who set out with high hopes of building an Australian industry, there were, even at the end of the period, sufficient differences of opinion to have led, under different conditions, to very diverse orientations. But in the specific situation of trying to produce and distribute Australian films independently in the 1920s, their differences of strategy were little more than minor variations on a common opinion, 'that Union Theatres Limited, Hoyts, and others are not out to help the screening of Australian pictures'.

National Film Archive

7

Northern States and Southern Seas: Charles Chauvel and Frank Hurley

Charles Chauvel

If Longford was Australian cinema's great Romantic, Chauvel was its organisation man. This is not intended as a rebuke. In many ways Chauvel was Australia's most successful producer of quality films, and his recognition of what was needed in Australian films in the 1920s was shrewd and up-to-date without being glib or imitative of Hollywood.

Chauvel's formula was based on two fundamental principles: First, Australian film producers should learn and re-learn Hollywood's skills, because that was where the art was at its most sophisticated. Secondly, Australian film producers should make *Australian* films of the wide open spaces to appeal to the world market. As a grazier's son with acute business acumen, he realised that films with traditional Australian bush values could appeal for their financing to squatters. But his experience of Hollywood also suggested to him that films with a specific local 'slant' could become American best sellers, hence there should be no contradiction between either funding or making films which were authenically Australian *and* had an international appeal.[1]

There are, then, two aspects to Charles Chauvel which, in his opinion at least, were not inconsistent; the apprentice who went anywhere he could to learn the skills of the trade; and the bushman from Queensland who made his films, financed his films, and initially screened his films in his own northern state.

The apprentice

From the beginning Chauvel impressed the trade with his determination to learn. His wife Elsa describes how Charles first came to Sydney and pestered Snowy Baker at his physical culture school because he recognised that Baker's would be the first organised venture using American experience to try and establish Australian production on a sound footing. At the Carroll's Palmerston studio he worked as assistant property man, bit-

(ii)

(i) *Green Room*, 1919; (ii) *Picture Show* 1 September 1923, p.50

Charles Chauvel with Douglas Fairbanks on the set of *The Thief of Bagdad*
(ii) The Baker-Lucas operation relied on an extensive fleet of cars when on location, which it became Chauvel's task to supervise.

part actor, set designer and transportation man. In these early years he also acted in Kenneth Brampton's *Robbery Under Arms* and helped produce Franklyn Barrett's last film, *A Rough Passage*. But neither this experience nor the studio knowledge he picked up from the Americans was sufficient, and soon *Picture Show* was announcing that this 'ambitious young Australian' with an initiative rare among his peers, was going to 'the Mecca of the moving picture world'.[2]

Chauvel was in Hollywood on this occasion for about a year and a half, during which time he worked at the Hal Roach, United Artists and Universal City Studios, did property work on Snowy Baker's first American film with the Phil Goldstone company, went on vaudeville tours as Baker's stooge[3] and observed Fred Niblo's production and editing methods in the making of *Strangers of the Night*. He was the eclectic young film enthusiast and odd-job man, transferred from Palmerson to Hollywood. But Chauvel was also noting the trends in the cinema trade which were of significance to his future role as an Australian producer. He argued that Hollywood was recovering refreshed and renewed after the slump caused by the extravagance of the old 'star' system. Independents had come to the fore during the time he was in Hollywood offering 'new ideas, new angles of expression . . . new atmosphere and have won in the box offices.[4] Having watched Douglas Fairbanks in the making of *The Thief of Bagdad*, Chauvel knew that Hollywood had an unassailable lead in resources and talent in the making of spectacular costume dramas. But not all the independents worked on that scale. He saw that among the biggest box office successes of 1923 were *Nanook of the North* and *Hottentot*: films with the technical quality the Americans expected, but in addition 'new screen values' and 'a novel twist' in being located abroad. 'The buyers who have to supply the theatres of the world with pictures are searching for new atmosphere . . . I believe that Australia can supply a certain type of picture, typical of her life, that will have a world market'.

The other thing that Chauvel learned from Hollywood at this time was its organisational efficiency; from the first setting up of a screen story through to its editing and public presentation. He returned to Australia in October 1923 with the message that 'Australian picture makers must look to their organisations and inaugurate most practical business methods and principles that will gain the confidence of Australian capital'.[5] This concern of organisation impressed hard-headed Australian businessmen, and it is significant that Chauvel on his return secured not only pastoralists' money, which other, less-respected film-makers found relatively easy to get, but also the financial backing of some of the leading Queensland exhibitors.

This direct association with the Federated Showmen's Association was something no other Australian producer achieved on any scale. On the one hand it helped him in exploiting his films in Queensland; on the other it may account for the much greater sympathy towards local production shown at the Royal Commission by Queensland exhibitors than any of the others. With a mixture of graziers, city businessmen, prominent politicians and leading exhibitors, Chauvel achieved a wide consensus which was essential to the success of local production, and which was the very thing Longford most lacked.

At the same time, however, Chauvel was always impatient with local problems which made the dreams of organisation and efficiency somewhat redundant. The lack of money, for instance, forced him to build and rebuild open air 'indoor' sets on vacant industrial land because of inadequate lighting systems; and to produce, direct, scout locations, personally construct sets, and act in his films.[6] He was aware of working at a great distance from Hollywood which made him ignorant of the latest technical developments. The many defects of his two early films which were widely criticised, in particular the editing, which was poor even by Australian standards, drove him back to Hollywood after the failure of his production plans in April 1928. It was typical of Chauvel that he should leave for America at a time when lesser Australian directors were beginning to float plans for 'quota quickies' in the light of the Royal Commission's recommendations for Australian production. Chauvel felt that poor quality productions were the quickest way to alienate exhibitors, and that his failure was partly due to a number of mushroom companies producing films in 1926 and 1927 which had ruined the reputation that Australian productions had slowly been building up with exhibitors.

He went to Hollywood to learn editing, cinematography and scenario writing. Recognising that he was at least six years out of date, he re-edited *The Moth of Moonbi*, reducing it from nine reels to six. He also intended to take a course in cinematography to give him enough grounding to understand, as a director, 'more fully the camera's scope and its possibilities'.[7]

His main concern was with scenario writing because he recognised that neither the purely technical side, nor the bush themes alone, would sell Australian films in America. That required 'vital screen vehicles'.

> The screen story is the beginning and end of picture making, and with this in view, and realising the material that we have in Australia, I am devoting the bulk of my time here to the study of scenario construction.[8]

He was working with one of the most successful Western scenarists in Hollywood, Ford Beebe, not only because 'both of us have been reared in the outback of our respective countries' but because Chauvel felt that this was the closest that he would get to learning scenario writing which was appropriate to his local outback films and yet international in quality as well.

As on his last visit to America, Chauvel was closely watching the Hollywood market and its relevance to Australia. He saw the traumatic effect the change to sound was inevitably having on Hollywood, and decided that while the American industry gave all its attention to 'how, slowly and with safety, efficiently and yet economically, to change the gearage of its huge machine',[9] British and Australian producers should take advantage of the millions of dollars spent in American sound experiments, and make a quick and efficient move into sound production to grab the American foreign market which accounted for 40 per cent of their total income.

But he also had a warning for Australian producers of one potential result of these American changes. He observed that with the coming of sound, the future of Hollywood lay with the big combines, heavily tied to Wall Street and big radio and electric corporations. He pointed out that Hollywood would have to seriously retrench and cut back on overheads. The day of prodigiously wasteful direction was over, and many directors and stars would be out of jobs altogether. The warning to Australia was that some of the 'army' of unemployed directors and stars walking Hollywood's streets would be glad to come to Australia, carrying their old, extravagant methods with them.

> In this fact lies the danger for the next more serious and determined step towards the establishment of Australian picture production. If our next move is to be quickly followed by a heavy loss to investors, which means a loss of confidence as well as cash, the damage will take a long time to repair.

Arguing, as he had at the Royal Commission, that Australia needed to import scenarists, experienced cinematographers, editors and other carefully chosen technical experts rather than 'expensive megaphone-wielders' from the United States, Chauvel was talking as much about the history of recent Australian production as of its potential future. Like Longford, though he made the point less bluntly, he felt the importation of Norman Dawe and Eva Novak had done little for Australian production other than show it how to spend a lot of money.

2. *The bushman*

It has sometimes been said that the characteristic values of Australian cinema had a direct genetic basis in the graziers and pastoralists who financed the films. C.J. Dennis complained in 1925 that the production company behind Longford's successful films, was composed mainly of squatters who knew nothing of picture production. Longford proved him wrong by pointing to the city accountant, jockey club and merchant backgrounds of the Southern Cross directors. It is true that some small production companies found it relatively easy to extract money from graziers with traditional values and sentiments — Phil K. Walsh's film *Birth of a White Australia* is a case in point. By and large, though, the connection between the high valuation of the country in the films and *city* money made that question of causality much more problematic.

However, Chauvel's films are the one outstanding example which do seem to present a transparent connection between grazier background, country money and country values in the films — though the relative failure of Chauvel's films to gain screenings in the country *market* brings us back very quickly not simply to the city connection, but to the international metropolitan one as well.

Born into a well-respected grazier family, Chauvel worked as a cattle drover and jackaroo on a Queensland station before joining Snowy Baker who valued him for this experience with horses. On his return from his first American trip he set up Australian Film Productions Ltd 'to produce films in Queensland based upon the industrial and pastoral background'.[10] Much of the money that came in was from Queensland countrymen, and there were a number of pastoralists and graziers in the first batch of directors, including Chauvel's father. From the start, and with his American experience in mind, Chauvel resolved to 'go Far West' for his principal scenes, with views depicting large mobs of cattle 'deemed essential to the picture'.

For his first film, *The Moth of Moonbi*, Chauvel, who was then one of Australia's youngest directors, relied on the help of an experienced cameraman, Al Burne, who had worked with the Carrolls as well as in Hollywood, and who acted as co-producer. Arthur Tauchert brought his own wealth of knowledge to an otherwise fairly inexperienced cast. Young actors like Marsden Hassell were chosen because, Chauvel said, 'I believe he typifies the young clean-cut and manly Australian in a way that few stage juveniles can possibly do'.[11] It was this kind of virile hero whom he believed would capture the foreign market, rather than the Hayseeds caricatures which had so often been attempted.

The local press was impressed with the idea of 'a Queensland Company, with Queensland capital . . . producing Queensland films', and Chauvel assured his backers that

> the most ideal conditions exist here for film production, and that, with the support of capital and the careful choice of material and personnel and efficient methods of distribution, film production in Australia can be established upon a very sound commercial basis'.[12]

The plot was conventional; contrasting 'the free life spiced with adventure' of the cattle industry with, on the one hand the material lust of cattle duffer Black Bronson, and on the other hand the 'life is so short and so full of good times — come, let's dance' seduction of the cities. The heroine spans this gap, moving from being a bare-shouldered country waif to the deshabillé sophistication of city drinking, dancing and boat parties, before returning to 'the cattle country — back where she belonged . . . the only place of sanctuary and forgetfulness left for a moth with singed wings'. The plot, in which Tom is taken for a city weakling before proving himself as a jackaroo, has some similarities with Baker's *Jackaroo*. The acting style is laboured, partly through inexperience and partly through Chauvel's adherence to the Hollywood 'types' system, the editing is very crude in places, and apart from one or two shots of the beautifully soulful heroine, the camerawork is not particularly distinguished. *Everyones* complained of 'faulty lighting' in a film that was only 'fairly entertaining'.

Announcing his second film for 1926, *Greenhide*, Chauvel said that the way to film success was to 'present dramas of the great outback set amid the natural beauties of the country . . . which hold a world of romance and glamour to the dwellers of the cities'.[13] Despite his claims that *Greenhide* would be completely different in story from both *The Moth of Moonbi* and 'the usual cut-and-dried film play', the plot is again based on the conventional opposition of bush — 'land of silent, slumbrous strength' — and a city of flappers, bathing belles and spoilt young women. In *The Moth of Moonbi* the station owner was 'rough and hard like his station, but a man among men — with a heart as big as his lands were wide'; in *Greenhide* the hero is 'as rugged as the stony hills themselves, with a wallop in both fists', but with sufficient heart beneath the woodenly acted exterior to make room for the 'alluring child of the city'. She in turn is sufficiently lured by the 'dreamland of intangible things' to seek romance 'over the rim of the world', but is suitably reformed by the real bush from her charleston garden parties and desire to 'be sheiked by a real live bush-

National Film Archive, reproduced by permission of Elsa Chauvel.

From bare-shouldered country waif to the deshabille sophistication of city drinking and boat parties: frame enlargements of Doris Ashwin as the moth with singed wings: *The Moth of Moonbi*

(i)

(ii)

Eggs and Exploitation.

THE accompanying picture shows a very attractive lobby display arranged by Mr. J. M. Cahill, at the Capitol Theatre, Coolangatta (Q.) for the locally made film "Moth of Moonbi." It created such attention from the passing crowds that the police had to clear the footpath on several occasions. The logs of wood concealed an electric griller on which the swaggie boiled his billy, and fried a couple of eggs. From eight till ten the gentleman shown consumed a dozen new laid, and on each occasion his meal was viewed by a large and admiring crowd. Needless to say the novelty of the stunt reflected at the box-office and record business was done with this excellent picture.

Mr. Cahill is also showing "Zeebrugge," for which attraction the local Council has permitted him to swing a 20ft. double sign across the roadway, which is illuminated at night.

Mr. Cahill states that business at his three theatres at Coolangatta, Tweed Heads and Murwillumbah has been a record one over the holiday season.

'Pioneer' sets: Chauvel and Al Burne shooting *The Moth of Moonbi*
(ii) Lobby display at the Capitol Theatre, Coolangatta

(i) National Film Archive, reproduced by permission of Elsa Chauvel; (ii) *Everyones* 3 March 1926, p.29

ranger' to wear a simple white dress and mend Greenhide's socks in a wooden shack for ever.

Chauvel's technical control is better in this film, with more efficient editing and interesting 180 degrees doubled tracking shots as horsemen move together through a panorama of white gums. The city 'interior' sets, however, visibly blow about in the wind, revealing the difficulty of producing low budget films shot away from the studios of Sydney. The trade tended to stress the 'pioneer' quality of Chauvel's work, mentioning the rudimentary sets with their curtain-controlled natural lighting as a case in point.

> One approaches the stage over packing cases, crates and odd bits and pieces of furniture, properties and actors . . . one wonders what class of work Mr Chauvel would turn out were he given the facilities existing in modern American studios.[14]

As leading actress, Elsa Chauvel recounted the discomfort of working in these conditions: the 'rain, dust, heat melting our make-up into sticky streams', the mirrors used to reflect the sun 'pitilessly, blindingly into the players' faces'.[15] And as director, Charles Chauvel complained,

> I had to wait on the weather. I had to pull a whole set down and re-build it, which doubled the cost of a particular scene. I could have made my interiors in ten days — with a proper studio — whereas I took a month'.[16]

Even under these conditions, Chauvel's drive for business efficiency was remarked upon. The company slept virtually next to the set, and were on location before breakfast 'thus utilising every atom of daylight' — the only lighting Chauvel had. On location, too, the production was marked by its efficiency. The whole company of technical men and artists had to be housed under canvas 500 miles from Brisbane, but the press commented on the recreation tent, the well-appointed cook's gallery, the good food, the water laid on from windmill tanks, the wireless, and the cows, horses and properties from Walloon station where there was a first-aid department installed. Since the location was thirty miles from the nearest railhead, Chauvel, an expert in transportation since his Baker days, organised a truck service to 'move his company to and from any chosen location as easily and as quickly as a circus goes and comes'.

Queensland exhibitors were particularly impressed by this pioneering enterprise, and by the resulting film with 'many Western touches'. The prominent local exhibitor R.F. Stephens praised 'its wonderful outdoor scenery and splendid photography' and regarded *Greenhide* as better than 'any Australian production of a like nature yet attempted', especially considering the 'limited cash outlay', 'embryo players' and difficult production conditions.[17]

The Sydney journal, the *Film Weekly*, was less generous, calling *Greenhide* 'good as an Australian film, but compared with the world's, it is only average'. The action was criticised as unconvincing and wooden, with most of the film's naturalness and quality coming from the scenery, the Aborigine and a dog.[18] Stuart Doyle was later to quote the *Sydney Morning Herald*'s 'scathing' critique of this 'third-rate' work as part of his own attack on local production at the Royal Commission.[19]

By 1926 the trade was losing some of its initial enthusiasm for Chauvel, *Film Weekly* announcing that it was 'astounded' by the 'unnecessary overhead expenses' of Chauvel's next planned production, *Geoffrey Hamlin*, which would depict the life and work of Australia's pioneers, and was planned as a British–Australian co-production. This was, of course, beginning to enter the preferred territory, both in cost and potential subject matter, of Doyle's own company. As was the case when Beaumont Smith had announced an expensive Australian 'epic', the film was never made. A further reason for hostility to Chauvel was no doubt his connection with Australian politicians and the quota issue. J.S. Kerr, M.L.A. had for some years been attacking the American monopoly of the Australian film industry and failure to pay adequate taxes on the profits. The same J.S. Kerr was secretary of Chauvel's Australian Film Productions Ltd and in early 1927, while complaining about distribution of *The Moth of Moonbi*, he had argued for an extension of the Victorian quota legislation to Queensland, and the adoption of a reciprocity policy with American distributors forcing them to take Australian films for American release in return for bringing in Hollywood ones.

Film Weekly lambasted these 'fantastic proposals', which it argued would injure cinema owners throughout Queensland and deprive many workers of their jobs. When Kerr wrote complaining of bias and inaccuracy in *Film Weekly*'s account of his speech, the editor held the letter back until it was 'out of date' and then said he had not printed it in his national publication, because the local Queensland press had published it. *Everyones* too, kept a gloomy eye on the presence of Kerr and Chauvel in Sydney 'for flirtations with both Federal and State politicians'.[20]

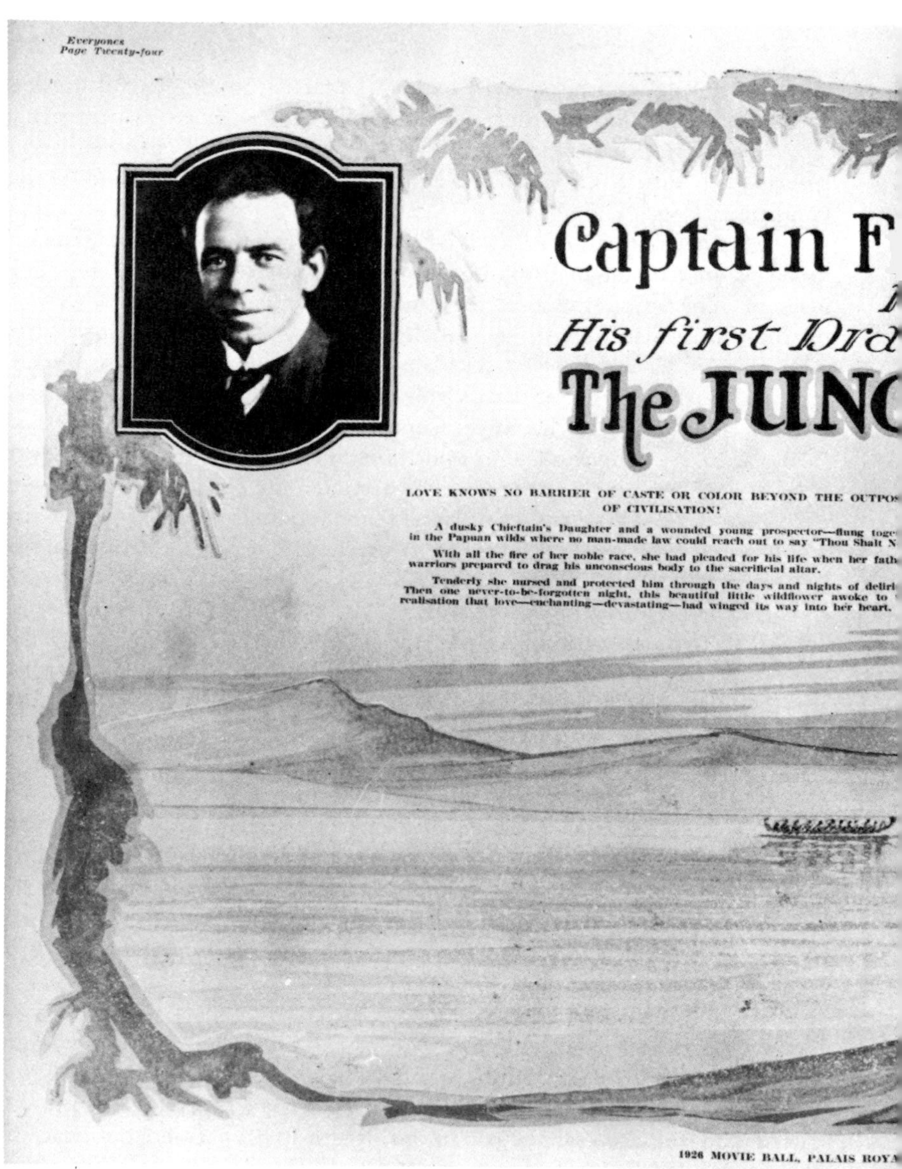

Melodrama as documentary: the realism of *The Jungle Woman* was held to 'cleverly suggest the psychology' (and potential sexuality?) 'of the native race'.

29th.

Everyones 19 May 1926, p.25

The Block-Booking Blockade

However self-interested Kerr's actions may have been, there were systematic forces operating against the success of Chauvel's enterprise. Elsa Chauvel's explanation for the lack of marketing success was that the 'metropolitan theatres were owned by American combines and country theatres were tied to them in a "block booking" which gave the local showman little freedom to take an Australian film, were he ever so willing'.[21] Against this octopus, she gives us the image of the two Chauvels, without an exchange to handle their films, touting them 'from village to village' with impromptu monologues and acted highlights to doubtful country grocers-cum-showmen.

Although the details are no doubt accurate, the general issues were not so simple or clear cut. In the first place, no American distributors owned Australian cinemas at this stage, though it was true that very many country exhibitors were tied up completely by the block-booking system. Secondly, Chauvel did have Australian distributors, Hellmrich and Conrad handling the films both for Queensland suburban and general release. Chauvel offered them the film in the hope that as specialist distributors of Australian films they would give more personal attention to his productions than the big companies who were unlikely to give them 'the same attention as some of their own subjects'.[22]

The fate of the these two films illustrates the degrees of subtlety of control which the major distributors had over Australian production. Whereas Longford's complaint against Union Theatres was that they refused him the crucial first release houses, Chauvel pointed out that it was possible for the combines to release a film in a big theatre and yet still kill it. *Moth*, which had taken five months to make at a cost of £4,400, was released within about three weeks of completion by the Doyle–Carroll Wintergarden Theatre in Brisbane. After good publicity but a poor rental in Brisbane, the film was given suburban release through Hellmrich and Conrad in Queensland, and was then released in Sydney. Chauvel complained that despite all the work of his exchange, the film was then crippled 'because the opening releases were so poorly handled and advertised, making the film a 'lemon immediately in Sydney and Melbourne'.[23] When asked at the Royal Commission if this was due to the American corporations, Chauvel replied, 'I could not say that. We got our openings through Union Theatres Limited'. By that time, in mid-1927, *Moth* had earned £1,300 profits.

Greenhide was handled personally by Chauvel in Brisbane and with its extensive publicity (£800) in the first week, did very well running throughout the Birch, Carroll and Coyle circuit. However, Kerr complained that

From the collection of Elsa Chauvel

Charles Chauvel economising: as a cattle duffer (left) in his own *Greenhide* what profits they made were less than that paid in entertainment tax to the government.[24] The film was offered to Union Theatres who wanted to delay a decision for six months, by which time the postponement in releasing the film would have killed some of the effect of the initial publicity. *Greenhide*, which cost £3,800, had, by mid-1927 returned £1,000 in Queensland and £600 from its Hoyt's circuit release. At this point, Kerr told the Royal Commission that the company would need to earn another £6,050 before regaining its production costs, and noted that but for the substantial material and locational support given in Queensland country districts, the cost of the films would have been much greater.

Unlike Longford, Chauvel did not at this time accuse Union Theatres of malicious intent — this was the time when they were spending a fortune publicising *For The Term Of His Natural Life* — but he did point out that 'if our pictures had received the exploitation that a big distributing firm would give to one of its own films, undoubtedly our returns would have been more satisfactory'.[25] Chauvel also encountered great difficulties with suburban city release because there was a surplus of cheap American films which exhibitors tended to prefer to the more expensive Australian ones. Country exhibitors were so tied up with block booking that Chauvel usually either had to pay for an American film to be taken off, or ask for the theatre to open on an extra and less popular night. This restriction was particularly significant to Chauvel because he had expected to make very big money in country areas.[26] Good money *was* taken when the films were shown, as the Queensland exhibitors were prepared to admit, but, particularly in the case of *The Moth of Moonbi*, not much of it went into the producers' pockets.[27] The final disappointment was Chauvel's failure to sell the films either in America or Britain where, as his agent in London, E.J. Carroll, put it, 'The American exchanges . . . control the situation'.

Chauvel's proposed solution to the problem was a moderate one, which took full notice of the low returns of the Queensland exhibitors he was associated with. While advocating a quota, to encourage immediate local investment, he suggested a very low one in the first instance (in marked contrast to the twenty per cent Kerr was demanding)[28] with adequate safeguards for quality. He also opposed any scheme, such as a government studio, which might encourage mushroom companies to foist poor films on the exhibitors. At the same time he recommended a reduction of the block-booking period to six months (whereas the Queensland exhibitors themselves asked for a three-month maximum) with a reasonable rejection clause to enable exhibitors to screen Australian productions without the producers having to 'carry the American picture on their backs'. He pinned his main hopes at this stage on a government subsidy of two pounds to match every pound privately invested, taken out of the £140,000 annually received from the import tax on foreign films, together with action through the M.P.D.A. to ensure reciprocal arrangements with the companies. Like Longford, he was very conciliatory at the Royal Commission, arguing for 'solid co-operation between producers, distributors and showmen'.

It was not until the early 1930s that Chauvel came to agree with the more conspiratorial aspects of Longford's criticism of Union Theatres. By then he was accusing Union Theatres of intentionally killing the local production industry under the influence of American importers, while pretending to launch that same industry with *For The Term of His Natural Life*. By this time control of the Australian industry, and the self-interested fights between the American and Australian combines had become sufficiently public for even *Everyones* to deplore the state of the trade.

Chauvel was to be the only Australian director of silent films who made a success with sound features, and from the business acumen displayed on his Hollywood visits we can see why. He rejected all the usual clichés 'that we in Australia possess all that is necessary for the production of motion pictures — background, story material, talent and unequalled light. May I point out that we also have many thousands of acres of fruit trees; we have the sugar, the tin and a population of jam-eaters. Yet how many firms have made a success of jam-making?'[29] What was needed for quality — and therefore successful — Australian production was 'organisation, plant and experience'. This included learning from American and German methods since 'they are still the seats of learning in the production of pictures'. It also required drawing the limited capital of Australia into one or two big production units, backing this capital with 'keen business acumen and a true sense of showmanship', and exploiting the new potential markets in Britain, the Empire and America which the sound revolution had opened. Organisation, market and financing should not be parochial — Sydney financiers should happily support films shot in Queensland or New Zealand. But the stories should be local: 'we can't afford to leave untouched the picture gold that lies beneath the surface of our great gold-fields, deserts, pearling fields, mountains, coral regions and all the other picture backgrounds of Australia'. Ten years later Chauvel had turned these ideas into very successful films which, though more international in subject matter, were still, in the background, essentially located in the Australian outback.

Frank Hurley

On 19 May 1926, *Everyones* advertised Frank Hurley's *Jungle Woman* with a four-page colour advertisement — unprecedented for an Australian director. An earlier issue presented a eulogy from Hurley of Stuart Doyle and the directors of Union Theatres Ltd. 'for their ever ready support of Australian productions'.[30] *Everyones* remarked that these comments from a 'world-wide' authority confounded those who were currently accusing Union Theatres of lack of interest in Australian productions.

The trade often used Hurley to confound critics of the combines and the big distributors. In August 1925, the very week the news appeared of Hugh D. McIntosh's attack on the pro-American, anti-British position of the Australian film trade, *Everyones* gave its lead article to Hurley, remarking that since discussion on the subject of Australian production

> is rife to the extent of being acrimonious, the advent of Hurley on the local scene was good evidence of interest in the local film and of the fact that such films which were soundly based financially were very welcome.[31]

The political pressure on the trade, and particularly on U.T.—A.F. during 1925 and 1926 accounts in part for the publicity given to Hurley's films, but by no means entirely because the combine was also releasing its own Master pictures, *The Pioneers* and *The Hills of Hate* at this time, with almost no trade publicity. Why was there support for Frank Hurley, who was making his films for the British Stoll Company, and not for their own director, Raymond Longford?

Leaving aside Longford's own interpretation, the most obvious reason for the support is the fact that Stuart Doyle was chairman of directors of Hurley's 'Pearls and Savages' Company which owned the Australian rights to *Jungle Woman*, and thus had a direct financial stake in its success — a fact which Hurley seemed anxious to hide at the Royal Commission.

But this does not explain why business executives as shrewd as Doyle and Hugh Dennison, managing proprietor of the Sydney *Sun*, together with directors from Kodak Ltd, Waddington's Theatres, and McRobertson's Sweets should have sunk their money in a £20,000 company to exploit films which were at that stage only documentaries, and therefore, on the face of it, not big money spinners.

There are a number of answers. In the first place, Hurley's films, from the beginning, had been publicised as appealing to the 'discriminating picturegoer' that Union Theatres—Australasian Films was keen to attract. Equally importantly, Hurley's films did not drive away the usual patrons.

Hunting Headhunters with a Movie Camera

Captain Hurley's Papuan Picture.

You have been charmed, thrilled and enlightened by pictures that have taken you to the far corners of the earth—that have shown you glimpses of far-off horizons and strange, fascinating places that lie off the beaten track.

Now, the genii that lies hidden in the mechanism of the motion picture camera is going to take you into the fastnesses of a land of mystery and dark doings that lies close to Australia. This land is Papua—a vast territory close to us when measured in mere miles, but far-off indeed when measured in terms of what we know about it and its people.

The actual is always more fascinating and more thrilling than the make-believe—no matter how realistic that make-believe may be—and that is why the pictorial record of Captain Frank Hurley's venturesome journey into the heart of unknown Papua will stir you and hold you entranced to the final flick of the last reel.

You have read the newspaper accounts of the expedition which penetrated into the mysterious depths of the bush country that lies back of Lake Murray—veritably in the heart of the unknown land hitherto untrodden by the feet of white men. The chronicle

Photoplayer 29 September 1923, p.15

Documentary as melodrama: Union Theatres' publicity for a Hurley film shot with a lightweight camera donated by Stuart Doyle

In October 1922, *Picture Show* commented that Hurley's *Pearls and Savages* had run to full houses and appealed both to the young, who 'ordinarily find their entertainment in hectic romance' and to 'the older folk who only attend a picture theatre when a production of this type is offered. The appeal of the 'educational' film is therefore not entirely high-brow . . . But the educational picture must be rendered interesting. With a sugar-coating the pill will be welcomed by people who want the sugar, as well as those who want the pill'.[32]

This raises a second, less obvious reason for the success of (and therefore the trade support for) Hurley's early documentaries. They were, for all their 'factual' quality, direct descendants of popular melodrama as it had developed from the nineteenth century stage to the twentieth century picture show. Melodrama, as mentioned earlier, consisted of two defining but apparently contradictory features: a highly romantic adventure story packed with rapidly changing incidents, and a pictorial 'realism' of setting. Hurley's 'documentaries' included these features of melodrama to a remarkable degree — or at least they did in the trade publicity. Union Theatres' publicity for Hurley's *Headhunters of Unknown Papua*, for example, assured the patron of on the one hand amazing film veracity which it was hard to believe was 'just a picture and not the real thing'; and on the other continuous melodramatic incidents:

> 'On again through miles of trackless bush, in the depths of which lurk bewizened warriors awaiting one false move of the trespassing white man to give them an opportunity of adding a new sort of skull to their grisly collection — perhaps! The great Ravi, or hall of mystery, at Kaimari, looms up on the screen, a vast structure made of mats, and full of evil memories. The stuffed heads . . . occupy an important moment or two in our film journey into this land of lurking dangers and half-hidden wonders.[33]

When Hurley made his first feature, *Jungle Woman*, it was advertised with the same combination of ingredients of melodrama: the 'realism' of the 'pest-infested scenery of the interior' of New Guinea, within which is woven 'a logical, easily moving romance of love and jealousy and sacrifice, and incidentally cleverly suggests the psychology of the native race'.[34]

The marketing possibilities of this new kind of 'educational' melodrama were still unknown. *Picture Show* commented that it would be a mistake to leave films like *Pearls and Savages* to schools and universities because there was potentially a big general public for them. Stuart Doyle clearly had major hopes of a big American market where, at the end of 1923 there were rumours that Hurley had secured world-wide release terms with United Artists 'on a basis that will be highly lucrative to the shareholders of the company'.[35] It was at this time that Charles Chauvel was writing in the Australian trade papers that 'exotic' tales like *Nanook of the North* were big box office there. Although the American deal fell through,[36] it must have seemed to Union Theatres that Hurley had gold-mine potential: a melodramatic narrative that would appeal to the traditionally working-class patronage as it had for the last hundred years, and an 'education' aspect that would draw the 'better class' of patron.

Doyle and Gibson were no doubt even further impressed with Hurley when news came in 1925 that Sir Oswald Stoll, head of easily the largest film company and studio in England, had been sufficiently impressed with *Pearls and Savages* to finance Hurley 'to produce a series of natural colour films of romance and adventure in the South Seas'. *Everyones* felt that if Hurley could persuade the shrewd Stoll to part with his money for an enormous project which would take an entire production company on 'the longest journey ever undertaken' to produce films, he could also establish the film industry in Australia 'on a scale hitherto undreamed of'. The fact that there was 'no wild-cat element about the scheme' was enough to turn the 'jack-of-all trades' aspects of these production, which were usually the basis of criticism, into shining qualities

> An Australian is to be given the unique opportunity of making good in three roles, that of producer, author and camerman, with brilliant prospects of a future should his efforts prove successful.[37]

Stoll was in fact cautiously adopting a standard policy of his company which gave a proportion of its output to stories shot in exotic locations, thus easing pressure on the over-used studio. He gave Hurley only £10,000 for the entire venture of making two films, including transportation, which cost £5,000.[38] Hurley made both his films on the £5,000 he had left.[39]

During production of *Jungle Woman*, trade news of the film reflected the traditional Hurley pattern. 'Realism' was emphasised — Grace Severi had to be *actually* bitten by a snake while shooting at La Perouse, Sydney; and potential backers were told that the film had 'the extraordinary effect when being viewed of not being an acted drama at all, but . . . actual incidents that are happening'. But it was also to be a 'maelstrom of dynamic emotions', a 'romance of the tropics', to which was added the exotic twist of love between white and black races.[40] The Union Theatres' publicity handout indicated the aspirations of Gibson and Doyle clearly: Hurley films would 'add a large number of new patrons to any picture theatre', and 'there is little doubt that he has before him opportunities of becoming one of the world's greatest producers' with 'fortune knocking at his door' [41] —and those of Union Theatres.

(i)

(ii)

National Film Archive

The tradition of exotic melodrama dear to Gibson and Doyle: (i) Hurley's *The Jungle Woman;* (ii) Norman Dawn's *The Adorable Outcast*

Everyones' review was less certain. The 'uncanny fidelity' of the native scenes were praised, but the melodrama was said to lack punch at the end, the journal rather obtusely wondering what happened to the native heroine after the bite of a venemous snake.[42] But the film did well in both Australia and Britain, returning Stoll his £10,000 on this one production alone. *Hound of the Deep* was released within six months of *Jungle Woman*, Union Theatres publicity again emphasising that it was 'the type of film that most showmen find very successful and with Frank Hurley's name and following introducing a new type of patron to their theatres'.[43] *Everyones'* review of *Hound of the Deep* brought the journal into line with Doyle's ambitions. Commenting that Hurley's melodrama was better constructed than *Jungle Woman*, it now believed that 'we will soon see him amidst the top notchers'.[44]

The deal with Stoll went no further, but a much bigger one was in prospect. U.T.—A.F. were seriously considering floating a new £1,000,000 company, Australasian National Production, to back a number of feature films produced at the Bondi studio by Frank Hurley, and to build a chain of cinemas in Victoria thus breaking Hoyts' monopoly there. As well as three directors from Australasian Films, former Prime Minister W.M. Hughes was to be financially involved. However, Union Theatres backed out, worried, according to Hurley, at the potential effect of the Royal Commission on the industry. Hurley tried to float his own company to make three more feature films, but failed to so.

At the end of his short career as a maker of silent feature films Hurley was as eager as he had been at the beginning to insist that his 'success in Australia has been due in no small measure to the assistance given me by Union Theatres and Australasian Films Ltd, which have never at any time denied any of my productions release in their theatres'.[45]

Yet his evidence to the Royal Commission, where he bitterly accused the Hoyts monopoly of keeping his films out, and the contradictions between his evidence and that of Gibson and Doyle, reveal a film-maker who, aware of it or not, was able to maintain that Australian films 'of the required standard' secured a ready outlet, only because he made the kinds of films which appealed to the monopoly controlled by his close friend, Stuart Doyle. Hurley was quite aware of the problems of both American and Australian 'combines', and indeed recommended a merging of Hoyts and Union Theatres to protect the local market and force a policy of reciprocity out of the Americans. But he did so while also fully aware that his production chances could only benefit from an even greater Australian monopoly in which Stuart Doyle was certain to be very close to the top.

8

The Three Sydney Sisters: Paulette, Isobel and Phyllis McDonagh

Film Weekly 16 December 1926, p.38

In recent years Paulette, Isabel and Phyllis McDonagh have been recognised, like Franklyn Barrett, as being among the more significant Australian film-makers. The Australian Film Institute has spoken of the sisters' 'colourful and impressive career'.[1] Film-maker Joan Long has said that the 'McDonagh enterprise was one of the most interesting in our film history'.[2] The Victorian parliamentarian Barry Jones, in the House of Representatives, referred to them as 'the most remarkable women in the history of Australian cinema'.[3]

It is interesting that they were also well accepted in their own time. Other Australian film-makers with whom they are now compared, like Longford and Barrett, did not achieve the same degree of acceptance without considerable qualification: Joan Long quotes a newspaper article of 1932, which referred to Paulette McDonagh as 'probably the most outstanding figure in the Australian motion picture industry today'; and although this was more lavish praise than normal, it was certainly not atypical. Indeed, it is difficult to find *any* serious rebuke of the sisters anywhere.[4]

The trade was unanimous in its praise. *Everyones*, in an article headed 'brilliant Australian girls' great photodrama', described Marie Lorraine's (Isabel McDonagh's) portrayal of the young wife in *Those Who Love* as a performance which 'ranks with some of the best characterisations ever given to the screen by the world's greatest stars', and the film generally as 'probably one of the best Australian pictures yet produced'.[5] Paulette was praised for the novelty of her scripts, and skilful weaving of the plots which, *Everyones* added with respect, had 'already gained American recognition'.[6] Phyllis, as business manager, was praised for the immensely careful planning of the production details which enabled so much quality filming to be obtained in a mere six weeks. Impressed by this 'business-like efficiency' George Griffiths, managing director of Hoyts Theatres, told the Royal Commission, 'We are prepared to find the money for them to do as many more pictures as they like on the same standard'; and according to Isabel, Stuart Doyle of Union Theatres showed them every encouragement in making and releasing their films.

General and unstinting praise and support like this was unique in the history of Australian film-making, and it requires explanation beyond the high quality of their work. Those films that survive are highly competent and contain a lurking power in their claustrophobic, half-incestuous, pattern of family relations which threaten the conventional endings. But other film-makers who made better films did not achieve a tithe of the praise the McDonagh sisters received. What could account for this extraordinary support?

To start with, they were respected, in *Film Weekly*'s words, by 'their fellow Australians for the courage they showed in pioneering this industry here'. Under the broad ideological umbrella of *laissez-faire* capitalism that most of the trade preached but few were able to practice, this meant that the ladies had successfully broken into the male pantheon, that place of pioneering spirit and 'fighting dash' of 'Australian sons' on which *Picture Show* had wanted to found a new local industry in 1919. In the politics of business life this meant that the sisters could make acceptable films without floating mushroom companies or bothering the great men of the trade for money, either directly or, worse, indirectly by agitating for quota schemes or import tax subsidies.

The myth of how these 'three young ladies' with 'little else but pluck and determination . . . set out on their own' to 'prove that pictures could be taken in Australia which would compare favourably with the product of other countries' was built up and sustained in the trade press.[7] The strategic significance of this myth to the trade is clear from an article on the McDonaghs in *Film Weekly* in November 1926. The trade always maintained that there were no real hindrances to Australian films except lack of quality. *Film Weekly* said that *Those Who Love* disproved the claim that Australian films only failed because of inadequate cash.

> Money — or rather the lack of it — was an important item in the production of this film. Yet the finished product lacks nothing, and is every bit as good as the average imported six-reeler. Why? Because the promoters have sound common sense and keen business-like ability . . . Studio expenses were reduced to a minimum — as Drummoyne House was used instead. Thus the three Sydney sisters have shown that good films can be produced at moderate cost, providing brains are used in the selection of the story, and in the apportionment of available funds.[8]

Likewise, in December 1926, *Everyones* noted that 'with very little else but pluck and determination, they went ahead, and the results of their enterprise have been more than amply justified'.[9]

There is no mention in the trade press that the 'very little else' of the McDonagh myth included a wealthy family that financed the production, that Drummoyne House was a palatial family residence which other directors, whatever their 'brains and common sense', did not have access to, or that the elaborate furnishings used — Venetian mirrors, gold-framed oil paintings, tapestries, furniture and ornaments — were the valuable property of their father. He, as physician to the J.C. Williamson company, had also provided social and professional contacts which were highly significant in their development as film-makers, their acceptance by the trade, *socially* as 'part of the family', and the release of their films by J.C. Williamson Ltd. Nor is there mention of the leisured life the McDonagh sisters led which enabled them to develop their own skills in film-production, and then employ them — thereby saving the cost of some of the more expensive personnel.[10]

The trade found that the myth of the entrepreneurial sisters who overcame difficulties with nothing but their spirit and intelligence was far more useful. Its attitude to the sisters themselves was avuncular: generous but without too much responsibility; whereas the *myth* was often useful to the trade's needs — as, for example, in a typical case of union-bashing when the Musicians' Union, badly hit by the advent of 'talkies', refused to allow sound synchronisation of a musical score for their third film, *The Cheaters*. The 'David and Goliath' theme was readily brought into play, with *Everyones* foreseeing a conspiracy in which the musicians would inveigle actors to walk out. It was, the journal wept, 'Tough that this should happen to the girls, because if anyone deserves encouragement, they do';[11] while Sir Benjamin Fuller, who had earlier rebuked the Royal Commission for daring to put W.A. Gibson 'in the prisoner's dock' to question him about his monopoly enterprises, now castigated the 'dog-in-the-manger' attitude of the Union to 'these brilliant girls, left fatherless' who 'have made their own way' and helped 'to establish Australian talkies as an industry'.[12]

A second reason for the trade's support was the sisters' respect for Hollywood. Paulette McDonagh has said how she lived with Hollywood films, morning, noon and night from schooldays on, watching 'how the actors moved, the backgrounds, how they put the film together. I watched where they took a close-up, where they took a middle-shot, a long-shot and what they meant. And I learnt to do films that way'.[13] Given that their first film appeared at the time that the public attack on 'Americanisation' through the movies was at its height, this was highly significant. The same week that *Everyones* carried news of J.C. Williamson Films taking *Those Who Love* for release throughout Australia, it also carried a big article on a banquet given by 'Prominent City Men' to honour Sir Victor Wilson, the M.P.D.A's new champion against the anti-American attacks. The speeches by Stuart Doyle and Dan Carroll 'in refutation of the charges' were given prominence. They argued, on the one hand, that the public did not want educating but knew that American films were the best for entertainment, and on the other hand that people *were* educated by American films, especially in so far as they gave precept and example 'with regard to making people dress more carefully' and 'with regard to the artistic furnishings of their houses'.[14] This question of elegance and dress was to be taken up at the Royal Commission by Gayne Dexter, proprietor-editor of *Everyones*, when he criticised Australian film actors and actresses for their lack of sophistication, ugliness and inability to dress immaculately when compared with their counterparts in Hollywood. It was, therefore, of considerable interest that the *Sydney Morning Herald* praised the McDonaghs' *The Far Paradise* for the smartness of dress and the easy confidence of physical movement, and that the trade regularly commented on the elegant furniture and sets of their films. *Everyones* also reported the speech by ex-Prime Minister Billy Hughes (who was at this time contemplating a directorship with Union Theatres—Australasian Films) at the banquet, in which he said that those

Film Weekly, August 1927

'Respect for Hollywood': publicity for the McDonagh films emphasised exotic and society themes despite the Australian location work.

National Film Archive

Elegant furniture and sets, smart dressing and the easy confidence of physical movement: frame enlargement of the McDonagh's *The Cheaters* who criticised American dominance in motion pictures and motor cars need only 'get into an American motor car to understand why. We can learn some very useful lessons from America'. The McDonaghs had 'got into' American motion pictures and learned their lessons — and the trade found that comforting in Australian film-makers at this controversial time.

A third reason for their popularity was the McDonaghs' use of a conventional melodramatic form and, as a corollary, the Hollywood system of characterisation by types. *Everyones* said that a good deal of the success of *Those Who Love* depended 'upon the faithful casting of the types incidental to the story'. Forgetting what it had recently said about true actors getting outside their own personalities in reference to *For The Term Of His Natural Life*, *Everyones* complained that Australian screen actors 'so often portray parts obviously foreign to their temperaments or understanding', particularly when 'actors from the legitimate stage are employed'.[15] True, much of the success of Longford's films depended on the versatility of former stage actors, but the supposed uniqueness of *The Sentimental Bloke* and its failure in America left the trade more convinced than ever that the Hollywood conventions were right. *Everyones* approved of *Those Who Love* and said that

> In planning this Australian film, these young ladies have followed very closely the conventional lines as laid down in the production of other countries. Thus we find a cabaret scene and a frolicsome beach party included amongst the sequences.

The McDonaghs' films were not merely good quality; they located their quality within conventions of continuity, acting and setting which the trade liked and knew to be popular with the public.

Hollywood itself at this time was looking for new story lines, and the fact that the McDonagh films were thought to supply them offers a fourth reason for their success. In August 1926, as release dates for their first film were being negotiated, Stanley S. Crick, managing director of Fox Film Corporation (A/sia), was saying that motion pictures must give up their familiar and mediocre plots in face of a more discerning audience.

> The oft-told story of the boy who loved a girl, only to fall from grace by being accused wrongfully of a crime, and being exonerated in her eyes when the villain is brought to justice, won't suffice any longer.[16]

He called for fresh faces, quality acting and novelty of theme — and this was precisely what the trade press constantly said the McDonagh sisters provided. One might disagree with *Everyones*' contention that the 'novelty of theme' was primarily a matter of 'simple human nature', and even more with the notion that these tales with their incestuous resonance avoid 'all complexes'.[17] But the plot of *The Far Paradise*, in which a girl loves a boy, only to fall from grace by being innocently involved with a villain whose death leads to the final reconciliation seems to have had a sufficient 'twist' within the standard narrative conventions to satisfy Stan Crick. And he, like others, was impressed enough with their earlier 'rather good picture'[18] to offer to handle it for them.

A Guide to Trade Success

In November 1926, next to news of the release date of *Those Who Love, Film Weekly* carried an article, 'A Straight Talk to Australian Producers',[19] which might have been written to eulogise the McDonagh sisters, and certainly illustrated clearly the reasons for their trade popularity. Australian producers were given eight tips, each of which seems to have been derived from trade conceptions of the McDonagh's work and/or the American model they followed:

'First, study the exhibitor — he's the man whose going to earn your money'. *Everyones* felt that the producers of *Those Who Love* had done just this, to the extent that the journal could recommend the film to exhibitors, not for the usual 'patriotic and sentimental reasons', but because 'as one of the best Australian pictures to date' it was certain box office.[20]

'Secondly, don't drag scenery into your productions for the sake of scenery — it carries no weight with the public. Every Australian film I have seen — with the exception of *Those Who Love* — has done this'.

'Thirdly, don't make your films too Australian . . . Australian films fail because of their bush stories and station locations. Get down to something of world appeal . . . big money and big productions'. From the first the trade had praised the McDonaghs for leaving the 'worn out' bush tracks, and though the films were cheap, Isabel noted in 1927 that while Australian productions should start simple, 'big pictures' on the American model would follow, at which point 'Australian audiences would soon get tired of the ordinary bush story'.[21]

'Fourthly, pay more attention to detail. Crude sets, impossible situations and faulty sequences are the biggest contributing factors to failure. Most Australian producers, too, pay little attention to casting.' The journal had earlier praised *Those Who Love* for 'outstanding' acting and 'excellent' continuity,[22] and had described the finish and detail as equal to 'the best that has yet been made by an Australian producer'.[23]

(i)

(ii)

National Film Archive

Leaving the worn-out bush tracks: shooting (i) *Those Who Love* and (ii) *The Far Paradise*

'Fifthly, are there no writers of subtitles in Australia? There seem to be only three kinds of titles in Australia — bad, damn bad and chronic' — but the writer had already praised *Those Who Love* in an earlier article for 'excellent' titling,[24] and the *Sydney Morning Herald* was later to speak of their 'unusually forceful captions'.[25]

'Sixthly, pay a little bit more attention to producing good photoplays instead of floating large companies': exactly what the McDonaghs, with 'little else but pluck and determination', were said to have done.

'Seventhly, Australia has wonderful cameramen — as good as any in the world. Give them a fair chance'. Earlier the writer had praised the excellence of their photography, and the *Sydney Morning Herald* was to say that for once Australian producers were sufficiently competent in the lighting of scenes and make-up to allow the camera to reveal 'the expression in the actor's eyes' and 'the contours in his face'.

'Eighthly, get a representative Motion Picture Producer's Association to further your interests . . . A body that is not representative only excites suspicion'. The reference was to the war between most Australian producers and the big Australian monopolies. But the sisters had uniquely friendly relations with the latter, and, unlike Shirley, Longford or Barrett were careful to avoid involvement in what the trade called 'unrepresentative' producers' deputations to the government.

All these features of a McDonagh production contributed to its trade description as a 'high-class picture'; and to the constant advice by the trade press that any Australian independent film which proceeded along the lines laid down by the McDonaghs would meet 'considerable success' and 'greatly assist the prestige of local production'.[26] The McDonagh sisters catered to the desire of Doyle and Gibson for the 'better class' of film, as understood by, made by, and made *for* 'the better class' of people. The McDonagh sisters' films could be screened to meet the Australian quota which the trade thought was impending, without, so the moguls believed, offending the desired up-market audience with the bush and bushranging elements that smacked of both an alternative set of values and the working-class days of a 'tin-roofed' industry.

It is ironic that at precisely the time the McDonagh sisters were being praised for low-cost but 'quality' settings of 'society' pictures, N.B.Freeman, Australian managing director of Metro-Goldwyn Films Ltd, was arguing that 'the society, or drawing-room, drama is decidedly on the wane, and . . . in future, pictures dealing with spirited and dramatic events in out-of-door locales will find first favour with audiences everywhere'.[27] For Freeman, the 'cycles in pictorial entertainment' running from outdoor tales

JUST CONCLUDED A WONDER SEASON AT HOYTS MIGHTY
REGENT THEATRE
SYDNEY.

The BATTLES OF THE CORONEL AND FALKLANDS ISLANDS

BRITISH DOMINIONS FILMS

AMAZING CHALLENGE TO AMERICAN FILM DOMINATIONS

These Two Mighty Empire Attractions—
"THE BATTLES OF CORONEL AND FALKLAND ISLANDS"
MARIE LORRAINE in "THE FAR PARADISE"
Now Available for N.S.W.
Apply to
BRITISH DOMINIONS FILMS
305 Pitt Street, Sydney.

MARIE LORRAINE IN THE FAR PARADISE

Everyones 1 August 1928, p.17

of the early days, through underworld romances to eternal triangle and society dramas, and finally back to prestigious outdoor action movies, had nothing to do with market exploitation. Rather, they were the spontaneous result of changing psychological states. The time for big action films had come because, firstly, they satisfied, with their 'quick thinking and quick action' a society 'living at a greater speed than ever before', and secondly because tales set in nature carried more of the required 'realism' than did 'the artificial surroundings of a studio set'. But the emphasis was on *prestigious* productions: 'the modern picture-going public has been educated up to a massiveness, to spectacular effects and to picture production of the highest order'. It was this massiveness and lavishness of cast that, in the eyes of Doyle and Gibson, distinguished their prestigious *For The Term Of His Natural Life*, then in production, from the early bushranging films — at the other end of the cycle — with regard to both the local audience and the world market.

So perhaps it is significant that by April 1927 the managing director of Union Theatres, Gordon Balcombe, was qualifying his praise of *Those Who Love* with comments like: 'a fairly good picture of its kind . . . fairly well received', and 'not much money spent on it'.[28] Perhaps it *is* the case that the trade was taking note of Freeman's words. It is true that hardly any 'society' films were produced in Australia for the rest of the silent period (and those that were, like *The Russell Affair*, were unable to get a release) as compared with 'outdoor action' films, whether 'prestigious' (like *The Term, Romance of Runnibede*, and *The Adorable Outcast*) or 'quickies' (like *Odds On*). The other two McDonagh films of this period also received much less emphasis than their first one — except in strategic political situations.

Those Who Love was released in Sydney by J.C. Williamson in December 1926 amidst a blaze of publicity that claimed it was 'by far the most popular Australian picture ever screened'. After a delay of about six months, the film was screened successfully in Melbourne, and, after another six months, in Adelaide. By then, however, some of the early eulogies and distinctions from other local films were wearing thin, and the McDonaghs met strong resistance from a number of exhibitors. On the strength of the rather limited profits from the film, and the offers of support from Hoyts, the sisters went quickly into production of *The Far Paradise* in early February 1927. But this film, which cost about £2,000, did not get a release at Hoyts' Regent in Sydney until mid-July 1928, followed by a release in Melbourne in October, and no release in Adelaide until two years after production began. The date of first release was significant. Hoyts and Union Theatres were at the peak of the 'film war' of that year in which Union Theatres had scooped the major American 'A-grade' services in Australia. Hoyts, in desperation, had turned to the previously maligned British industry, represented in Australia by British Dominion Films (soon to be bought out, significantly, by Greater Australasian Films).[29] The *Far Paradise* was handled by B.D.F. on the same bill as the British film, *The Battle of Coronel and Falkland Islands*, only a few days prior to Hoyts contracting with them for their whole year's releases for 1929. Possibly the 'film war' situation, or possibly the huge popularity of the B.D.F. double bill (which equalled the enormous drawing power at the same theatre of the Chaplin *Circus*/ Lang *Metropolis* double) explain the long-run status *The Far Paradise* acquired.

In December 1929, on the same day that *Everyones* announced the 'peace pact' between Hoyts and Union Theatres, it resurrected another political issue in relation to *The Far Paradise*. For some time the trade papers had been taking an indirect swipe at the proposed Australian quota system by attacking the British quota act for its 'unfairness' to Australian films. *Everyones* cheerfully detailed each case of the Universal company buying up Australian films for its British quota requirements as a triumph for American as opposed to British goodwill. The journal now detailed the case of the McDonaghs who, having been offered £1,500 for their film by Universal, turned instead to a British company, for motives of patriotism and profit. The British company then reneged, and Universal, having filled its quota requirements, 'cut to the bone' its original offer and accepted *The Far Paradise* simply as 'an act of goodwill'. This sample of inter-imperial reciprocity had, *Everyones* complained, 'cost the girls the best part of £1,500'.[30]

Apart from their use as political footballs, the McDonagh sisters gradually received less publicity in the trade press at the end of the silent period. Because of the delays on their earlier films they were unable to start on their third feature, *The Cheaters*, until June 1929, and by the time it was finished sound had made such inroads into local exhibition that they advertised it for release with sound synchronisation in early 1930 as 'the first Australian talking feature'. The film was not, in fact, released until much later. In the interim the trade press took the opportunity to use the film as ammunition with which to attack 'government interference' for causing the slump in Australian production in 1929; as a stick to union-bash over the musicians' ban in early 1930; and again as part of its ongoing attack on the government's 'theft' of import taxes to pay for annual prizes to Australian films, which, the trade complained, never seemed to be paid.[31]

There is no need to see conspiracy in all this. The suggestion is not being made that the 'myth' of the McDonagh sisters was merely a matter of cynical manipulation on the part of the trade, nor that somehow it made their films into something they were not. The McDonaghs' films were genuinely respected. But the respect was based on a meeting of opinion between the film-makers' formal and thematic preoccupations and the exhibitors' ideological and market ambitions. It seems to be true that when 'society' dramas were becoming 'outmoded' in late 1926, the big Australian combines adhered to the McDonaghs' film to secure themselves against the 'tin shed' past and the 'quota' future by drawing on a myth which located all the ingredients of pioneering capitalist values within suitably 'classy' settings. It also seems to be true that as the threat of government quota legislation receded, so too did publicity and support for the McDonagh sisters, until, by the end of the 1920s, they had become little more than vehicles for the trade's attack on the unions and the Government, the two forces it could never allow into its own self-proclaimed consensus of 'industry' and 'public'.

9

The American Invasion: Second Wave

Norman Dawn

For The Term of His Natural Life came to the notice of the trade through a remarkable piece of casuistry in the leading trade journal. Reproduced below are the two articles, published within a month of each other, from which most Australian exhibitors first learned of the film.

Everyones, 14 July 1926

Bushrangers and Convicts Taboo

Australian Film Stories Must Not Include Unsavoury Phases of History

THERE is a move on foot, so we understand, to obtain the Government's consent to the making of an Australian motion picture based on the exploitations of cannabalistic convicts of a day long past.

The original story had, at one period, a most remarkable sale in book form, whilst its success on the stage also measured up considerably. But these were in the good (or is it bad?) old days, when a morbid public literally devoured literature and drama of the kind.

In these more enlightened times, something better must be expected from our Australian writers, if their works are to be transferred to the screen for the approval or otherwise of our own country and that of other nations.

Australia was discovered by Captain Cook over 150 years ago. Its early days saw it little more than a convict settlement, and in later years a certain portion was overrun with bush-rangers and other notorious characters who brought a great amount of dicredit upon a promised land. The deeds of these notorieties were eulogised by some of our early writers, so that many of these gentry, who were really most hardened criminals, appeared in the light of romantic heroes.

This looked alright probably for the men who sought literary fame and cash emolument, but it served no other good purpose. The days of the transport of convicts, ticket-of-leave men, and bushrangers passed more than half-a-century ago, but there are writers with us who still continue to deal with these murderous individuals of the past, and it is time something was done to stop further breaches of good taste.

No other continent has gone ahead in such a brief time as has Australia. The eyes of the world to-day look to our fair country as a future home of prosperity and advancement, but whilst the stigma of the past occasionally presents itself the full credit due a progressive nation will never be obtained.

For several years there has been no marked effort made to revive these old convict and bush-ranging stories. Just at present, as above mentioned, a move is now contemplated. In the interests of Australian literature, we would advise those who are seeking to make capital out of the drab and sordid days of Australia, to look more upon the pleasant side of its possibilities. There is plenty of good material if you will only care to look for it.

Everyones, 11 August 1926

EVA NOVAK, film star, thawed the hearts of the solemn faced City Aldermen with a radiant smile as she responded to the toast proposed in her honor by the Deputy Lord Mayor of Sydney.

The same little lady will make Australian film history when that smile radiates from the screens of the world in a picturisation of one of Australia's literary masterpieces, "For the Term of His Natural Life," shortly to be commenced by Australasian Films Ltd.

The event was a significent one, though we doubt whether its full import was realised by those present at the Town Hall on Monday last. Civic receptions have on occasion been tendered to visitors from overseas, but this is the first time that such a function has been tendered to an American motion picture star arriving in this country under engagement to Australian enterprise.

Mr. Stuart F. Doyle, who supported the Deputy Lord Mayor in his speech of welcome, stressed the fact that though local enterprise had staked a vast amount of money in an endeavor to put Australia motion pictorially on the map, Australians were not short sighted enough to realise that they still had a lot to learn about the art, and it was for this purpose that the star and her assiates were being imported to support the local people already engaged for the production.

He also stated that as a result of the undertaking, hundreds of Australian artists and artisans would be employed, but that they had realised that to properly exploit a picture it was necessary to engage in the central role an artist who was known throughout the world and who had a reputation with the moving picture fans.

With all this "Everyones" is in hearty accord, and we welcome the project with avidity, and urge showmen to realise the full significance of the undertaking, and what it will mean to Australia in the years to come.

Mr. Doyle also referred to the criticisms which had been levelled at his company in selecting Marcus Clark's story, and assured his hearers that every care would be taken to see that the good name of Australia would remain unsullied, and that everything unsuitable would be deleted from the completed film.

But in this respect we think that Mr. Doyle is taking too much pains to mollify a few alarmists who are only shortsighted, and who are doing Australia an irreparable wrong in so loudly voicing their narrow views to the detriment of what is best in art.

Those of us who take the trouble to read, know that the early history of Australia is bound up with sorrow and suffering; that convicts and bushrangers made an unenviable page of its early history, but those who hold up their hands in horror in this contemplation do not stop to realise that this very fact is one to be taken with a deal of congratulation.

If this state of things were as bad as they picture, is it not a matter for rejoicing that only one hundred and thirty years after such a state of affairs existed, civilisation as represented by our capital cities today, exists on such a high plane?

The name of Australia is blazoned throughout the world by the doings of its sons and daughters, not only in the dark and bloody pages of war, but in the realms of Science, Literature and Art, and all in a brief passage of time.

Surely then if a people can rise to Nationhood from what looked like the uttermost depths it is a matter for rejoicing, rather than otherwise. The fibre of a people cannot be changed in a few decades; and to

our mind it proves beyond all reasonable shadow of a doubt that a nation or a people who can thus rise are of a calibre far above the reach of calumny.

Why then tamper with our literature?

Would we suppress Carlyle's "History of the French Revolution" on a similar plea and ignore the fact that France has risen Phoenix like from a past stained with murder, rapine, and a succession of crimes the like of which never figured in the calendar at a Quarter Sessions?

Do we want to ignore the History of England in its darkest days, or should we glory in the fact that through its dark and awful history its people have emerged tried and purified as in a fire until they occupy the place in civilisation they do to-day?

Why then close our eyes to the obvious.

Those who deplore the fact that in its early days Australia was a penal settlement, seem to be ignorant of the fact that the blame was England's and not Australia's.

We have never yet reconciled ourselves to the Biblical adage of the sins of the fathers being visited upon the children, which in itself is against modern teaching.

Why then mutilate what is a great piece of literature?

This remarkable volte-face, unique even in the trade press, was motivated by two particular events. On 21 July, *Everyones* announced that *For the Term of His Natural Life* was to be produced at a cost of around £40,000 by Australasian Films. On 28 July *Everyones* reported the beginning of an attack in Parliament by the Victorian senator J.F. Guthrie on the notion of importing Americans to make an Australian classic, and on the suggestion of giving world-wide publicity to Britain's 'barbarous treatment of criminals in Australia'.

Suddenly, *Everyones*, which had been presenting the standard Gibson–Doyle critique of low-class product in its first article, found itself in the wrong company. The trade's most important ideological strategy, as represented by its press throughout the 1920s, was to assume a consensus which emcompassed everyone from the American producers and distributors, through the large and small exhibitors, to 'the great public'. As long as this myth was maintained, the trade press could argue that any government 'interference' in the industry which cost any part of it more money was an attack on those to whom increased costs must 'inevitably' flow; which meant, first of all the exhibitors, and secondly the public. Consequently, any attempt to tax the profits flowing back to America from local exhibition — such as that by the Lang Labor Government — created hysterical accusations against the 'class' legislation which would force the worker to pay more for his hard-earned relaxation.

In mid-1926, however, *Everyones* found itself breaching that consensus, and heard its own arguments against filming *The Term* in the mouth not simply of any politician, but of Senator Guthrie himself, one of the leaders of the agitation to impose greater taxes on the Americans and change the orientation of Australian production from Hollywood to Britain.

A rapid change of position was required. One strategy was to attack Guthrie personally, which *Everyones* did over the next few months with a special intensity. The Journal devoted an editorial to Guthrie, accusing him of 'mischievous interferences' in the film industry, of ignorant 'vapourings' which carry 'just that smattering of knowledge which is dangerous', of being 'like a child' who cries for something (i.e. Australian production) but 'when he gets it does not know what to do with it' and abuses it (i.e. the new venture of Australasian Films). Brazenly ignoring its own editorial comment published just one month earlier, *Everyones* advised Guthrie that he should 'not attempt to deny early history, even though that history may be unpalatable'.[1] In September, when the Minister of Customs, Mr Pratten, announced new regulations to prohibit the exportation of any film 'likely to prove detrimental to the Commonwealth', *Everyones* fulminated:

> Thus is Australian enterprise stultified at its birth by the narrow-minded action of a Minister in response to the vapourings of a minority of persons possessed of loud voices and no breadth of vision.[2]

The same week *Everyones* announced a champion 'To lead the industry' against those who threatened Australian enterprise, 'A big Australian', Sir Victor Wilson, new president of the M.P.D.A. who 'Drinks his whisky, swears when he has to, smokes his pipe . . . and speaks our language . . . His task is to knit all factions of the industry. Solidarity rests on harmony within the ranks'.[3]

Before that could be achieved *Everyones* had first to restore the disunity it had itself created. Abusing Guthrie for saying the very things it had said was not enough — *Everyones* had to suggest it really had not said them in the first place. Looking carefully at the two articles above it is possible to see not so much a shift of paradigm, as an variation within it. The paradigm was that of progress from the bad old days to the world of 'civilisation', 'prosperity', 'advancement'. This was homologous with the trade élite's perception of its own particular history from 'tin sheds' 'to picture palaces' and as such this was far too central an ideological device to be changed. What *was* altered was the interpretation: from 'hide the past' to 'illustrate the past to show how far we have come' and with the useful addition, aimed at Guthrie's anglophiles, that the depravity of the past was all England's fault anyway.

This was still not enough. Union Theatres' orientation to the 'better class' product had not changed: not only the subject matter but also the *quality of treatment* had to be approved. A distinction was made between

(i)

"Sir Victor Wilson is Right Man"

says Generalissimo of Movies.

Mr. W. A. GIBSON.

With the appointment of Sir Victor Wilson as President of the Motion Picture Distributors of Australia, a new phase in the industry is entered upon in the Commonwealth and New Zealand.

Hitherto, the industry has conducted its various campaigns in sections. The appointment of Sir Victor, however, has been received so enthusiastically that it is apparent that when the new president takes over his presidential chair in a week or two's time that he will have the full weight and prestige of all sections of the business.

The motion picture industry has fought some mighty battles in the past. Some it won. Some it has lost. But when the tocsin of battle went forth there was always at the head of the forces the Generalissimo of the Movies—W. A. Gibson, O.B.E.

Generally it is invidious to mention names in connection with joint industry efforts.

But none have ever cavilled at the leadership always looked forward to in Mr. Gibson.

Despite the numerous successful enterprises with which the name of Mr. Gibson is associated, this gentleman invariably rallied forces to resist attacks upon the industry or to march forward.

Mr. Gibson is an original member of the Motion Picture Distributors Association of Australia, executive offices of which are located in Sydney. His representatives on the Council of the M.P.D.A., are Messrs Percy Dive (secretary) and L. C. Wicks (sales manager) of Australasian Films Ltd.

When Mr. Gibson was asked his views on the then projected appointment of Sir Victor Wilson, he telegraphed:

"The Right Man For The Right Job."

The judgment of the Generalissimo is seldom wrong.

Which recalls some of the fights that Mr. Gibson headed for the motion picture industry in the past.

Ten years ago, there was the big campaign to remove the heavy film duty placed on by the then Commonwealth Govt. Mr. Gibson from Melbourne headquarters conducted the fight ably assisted by Mr. W. J. Howe (president Federated Picture Showmen) and other leaders in the business.

Two years ago the Tariff Board inquiry was opened into proposed increase in duties, quotas and restrictions. Mr. Gibson's evidence before the Tariff Board was a masterly exposition. The facts he placed before the Board are a Text Book of the Motion Picture Industry.

In the various attempts to impose dual State Censorship in Victoria, Mr. Gibson has been in the forefront—with conspicuous success.

Entertainment Tax too! First there was the campaign to lift it off the lower admissions. Then eighteen months ago the move which resulted in its abolition up to 2/6. Finally there was the recent Senate attempt to double duty. Few outside political circles know of the work and generalship exhibited by W. A. Gibson.

With the experience and knowledge of Mr. Gibson, plus the mobility and ability of Sir Victor Wilson, the industry approaches 1927 in a mood justifiably optimistic. M.C.B.

(ii)

SIR VICTOR WILSON—FILM LEADER.

M.P.D.A. ANNOUNCES ELECTION OF "AUSTRALIAN WILL HAYS."

"Sir Victor Wilson, on October 4, will become President of the Motion Picture Distributors' Association of Australia.

He will be virtually the Will H. Hays of the Motion Picture Industry in the Commonwealth.

During the two years that the M.P.D.A. has been in existence, it has performed wonderful work in building up the industry.

The M.P.D.A. has been the spearhead in all crusades against those who sought to damage the good name of the "movies."

When the industry has been threatened by unfair legislative or administrative Acts of Federal or State Parliaments the M.P.D.A. has been the rallying ground in defence of the rights of all sections in the film field.

THE FILM INDUSTRY'S RED-LETTER DAY.

Every country has its historical places. Every industry has its historical landmarks. And, in the years to come, the future Men of the Movies will toast September 30, 1924, as the Red Letter Day of the Industry.

Two years ago to-day there met at the Film House, Sydney, the following gentlemen:

L. C. Wicks (Australasian Films Ltd.)
W. J. Hutchinson (Fox Film Corp.)
S. S. Crick (Fox Film Corp.)
John W. Hicks, Junr. (Paramount.)
A. Young (Co-operative Films.)
J. Lipman
Ralph Doyle (United Artists)
John C. Jones (United Artists)
F. Holdaway (Universal)
Percy Dive (Australasian Films Ltd.)

They took stock of the situation so far as the film outlook appeared in the Commonwealth.

The industry was then menaced in all directions. In the Federal and various State Parliaments there were threats and rumors of war against the welfare of the motion picture. THEREUPON THE MOTION PICTURE DISTRIBUTORS' ASSOCIATION OF AUSTRALIA WAS BORN.

Mr. Wicks was elected chairman, and Mr. Dive secretary, pro tem.

After two years of joint effort on behalf of all interests in the business, it is a commonplace to-day to find the executives of huge rival organisations sitting at the industry's round table, discussing the consolidation of the business in the public goodwill.

But, the men who came together at that fateful meeting in the Film House were unconsciously recording an historic landmark in the progress of the Motion Picture.

The cinema was a young, vigorous giant. But its force and vigor was being used blindly against its many enemies.

September 30, 1924, saw the force and vigor welded into a fighting machine that was to expand and develop.

To-day, headquarters of the M.P.D.A. house under its roof the Film Renters' Association and the Co-operative Film Insurance.

"Originals" of the M.P.D.A. can look back over two years of strenuous work. There have been many battles. And, in all, the industry has triumphed.

There are two reasons why it won.

FIRSTLY, ITS CAUSE WAS RIGHT. SECONDLY, IT FOUGHT AS A UNIT IN STEP AND NOT AS A FRAGMENTARY ARMY.

On Monday the M.P.D.A. faces the dawn of its third year. It does so under the leadership of Sir Victor Wilson, who will this week take over the Federal Presidency.

While September 30, 1924, was a Red Letter Day, September 30, 1926, marks an Epoch in the history of the motion picture in Australia.

M.B.

(iii)

Film Weekly (i) 23 September 1926, p.5; (ii) 30 September 1926, p.4

A series of editorials in *Film Weekly* illustrates the close collaboration between the trade press, leading exhibitors and the MPDA — on behalf, supposedly, of 'all sections in the film field'. Emphasis on 'progress', Australasian Films' new world of 'civilisation', 'prosperity' and 'advancement'

First in the Flight of Progress!

Capt. Cobham and Australasian Films Ltd.

EVA NOVAK

Two Popular Personalities Arrive in Australia.

CAPT. COBHAM

CAPTAIN COBHAM arrives this week—marking another milestone in the Progress of Aviation.

EVA NOVAK arrived last Saturday—marking another milestone in the Progress of Australian Film Production.

The arrival of CAPTAIN COBHAM and EVA NOVAK in this country is indeed an exceedingly happy coincidence; providing representative events of equal historical importance to the Australian community.

AUSTRALASIAN FILMS LTD.—FIRST IN THE FLIGHT OF PROGRESS!

Everyones 11 August 1926, p.21

the 'rough' old Australian bushranger-convict films and the sophisticated new one, *The Term*. Four distinctions were implicitly drawn in the 11 August article between the crude products *Everyones* was 'really' talking about in its 14 July editorial, and the one Australasian Films was about to produce.

Both Doyle and *Everyones* emphasised from the beginning that *The Term* would be a responsible film which would not sully 'the good name of Australia'. *Everyones* said that the bushranging and convict films, which had been censored 'were inept and at too embryonic a stage'. They deserved censorship for belittling the police and making wrong-doers into heroes; in contrast, Australasian Films, wishing 'to make a picture that will last for all time', would never 'sacrifice ideals for the sake of cheap sensationalism'.[4] Clearly, a precise stage had been reached in that evolution from depravity to civilisation in which a sensibility had been attained which, in *Everyones* opinion, enabled Australasian Films to tell what had never been told before.

Secondly, there was the historical significance of the film, the proud tale of Australia which would rank with Carlyle's *History of the French Revolution* in marking the emergence of a people from a 'dark and awful history' to 'occupy the place in civilistation they have today'.[5]

Thirdly, there was the scale and cost of the project which would put 'Australia motion-pictorially on the map' and employ 'hundreds of Australian artists and artisans'. Scale was emphasised, not simply in the current Hollywood sense of 'bigger is better', but also in the context of Doyle's standard reply to any government 'interference' with the trade: while government threatened Australian enterprise, Australasian Films was going to boost it with investment and employment.

Fourthly, the film would improve the state of the art. Inexperienced Australian directors, actors and other local people would 'learn about the art' from the American 'star and her associates'.

The sheer amount of publicity which attended the making of *The Term of His Natural Life* was not the most significant aspect of it, although the film certainly did receive far more publicity than any other Australian film of the 1920s. Even more significantly, this first article laid down the nature of that publicity: all the subsequent publicity followed the implicit guidelines established in the 11 August article.

Responsibility

The publicity for *The Term* quickly became an exercise in public 'education', using not only the print media but the novel means of wireless. The presentation of Eva Novak's tumultuous arrival in Sydney Harbour, with hooting ferry boats and cheering crowds, was carefully interwoven with the reasons why Americans were needed to boost the local industry. Much publicised stunts like the filming of a ship on fire were alternated with careful exposition of technical studio details, trick photography and the preparation of sets and props. The publicity officer for Australasian Films, Percy L. Curtis, wrote in *Everyones*,

> Instead of publishing a succession of publicity paragraphs to excite the imagination of the picture-folk, they set out to convey a truthful idea of the immensity of the scheme from the many interesting phases of its production.[6]

Listeners to radio station 2BL, for instance, were taken on an aural tour of the new Union Master Studio, No. 2 at Bondi, and given technical details of the means by which 'a picture can be taken, developed, printed and projected on the big sheet within one hour.' Certain items of equipment were said to be in advance of Hollywood,[7] and it was felt that this emphasised the proper professionalism of the enterprise, distinguishing it from cheaper endeavours of the past. Given the gap between 'the morbid evidence' of Tasmania's convict past contained in Hobart Museum, and the seventh wonder of modern civilisation at Bondi, Curtis wondered why the *The Term* could ever have been thought of as 'a bad advertisement for the apple state'.[8]

Historical Significance

Curtis wrote of the film:

> It is in *For The Term of His Natural Life* that Australia reflects on her greatness today. She looks back into the past from which she has emerged a splendid nation and finds even some of the darkest pages of her history illuminated with rare and glorious incidents such as *The Term* portrays.[9]

A good deal of emphasis was placed on the 'realism' with which this epic history was to be conveyed. 'Nothing is being left undone to thoroughly visualise the primitiveness and hardships of the humanity the picture is depicting'[10] The convict labour scenes in the swamp (with artificial logs covered in 'real bark') and the riot scenes were 'of true realism', the latter being 'shot seven times before passing the camera with Dawn's approval'.[11] The prison sets were re-created to the last detail at Bondi and, adding science to history, natural sunlight could be more easily obtained by using '3000 amps at 110 volts' producing 'chemical carbons known as white flame'.[12] An antique expert, Ralph Tyrell, was appointed to provide original convict tools, to restore the Royal Coat of Arms in the court house to its 'original form,' provide 'authentic' old charts and telescopes, and muster 'the whole of the trinkets, furniture and bric-a-brac used in the English and Tasmanian sequences — all genuine articles'.[13] These 'thousands of pounds worth of real antiques' would, it was thought, 'add a touch of realism to the picture as fakes are never so effective as the real thing'.[14] Eager to make up for its bad start on *The Term*, *Everyones* was quick to pat Australasian Films on the back for establishing authenticity in the detail of rings, purses, and even the growth of beards by the cast 'for screen realism'.[15] The result would be 'splendid and epochal history', both in the film itself and in 'the magnitude and national significance of a young and virile organisation's enterprise in answering the Call of Progress with a £50,000 film'.[16]

Scale

The size of *For The Term of His Natural Life*, originally 'one hundred thousand feet of human endeavour' at a cost of about £46,000, was constantly in the public eye — and always in terms of its economic advantages to Australia. The sets may have been vast, but the important publicity was that 'Australia collects £25,000 in local trade for *The Term* — £90 in nails alone — carpenters who cleared £23 a week'.[17] It was considered spectacular that Dawn used six cameras 'to shoot the biggest scene ever taken in Australia', but always in the context of the 500 extras paid at the rate of £1 a day, thus 'absorbing Newcastle's unemployed'.[18] Curtis also pointed out that the Tasmanian newspapers which had 'originally cried loudest against the project' were soon clamouring for production copy when they saw the benefit to the island's economy through the direct spending (£1,000 to the Port Arthur Hotel in three weeks) and in tourist value. He added that this new harmony between the trade and the free press had been forged only through the quality of 'such men who guide the destiny of Australia's own greatest releasing and producing organisation, and who have the good of the entire industry at heart'.[19] What more convincing evidence could there be of the 'good of the entire industry' than the fact that Australasian Films were 'creating employment for thousands every year, beside absorbing hundreds of our own high-class artists',[20] and that 'solely as the result of the tremendous publicity which has attended the making of this picture', several new production companies were in the offing? *Everyones* insisted that 'the whole hope of local production' depended on Australasian Films' enterprise, which, should it meet with the success it deserved, would 'mean the establishment on a permanent basis of motion picture production in Australia' and 'be the means of adding yet another possibility to the many avenues of employment of both manpower and capital in this country of opportunities'.[21]

Art

The trade press, seldom overconcerned with 'Art' in the cinema, suddenly discovered it when talking about the new Hollywood imports. Usual satisfaction with 'types' was gone overnight. George Fisher it was noted, often exhausted himself in his roles:

> it is always so with great artists, who, like George Fisher, have the power to rise out of themselves, for when he acts he is not George Fisher, but Rufus Dawes or John Rex — he lives his part, he feels the emotions of the men he portrays.[22]

Similarly, Eva Novak

> mentally, physically, and spiritually . . . has become the person and the mood required of the scene . . . Rising to an emotional crisis of the highest intensity without real circumstances or provocation to bring it about can only come through *real* art, which all goes to explain why Eva Novak is here'.[23]

She had come to teach Australian players 'that finish and technique . . . that every embryo venture stands in need of':[24] The same was said of the cameraman, though, ironically, when *Everyones* first spoke of the need to harness the practical knowledge of Len Roos, it was specifically to lead Australia away from the bad old days when people filmed the story of Rufus Dawes.[25] When it was announced that this was precisely the subject Roos would be filming, *Everyones* was not perplexed for long. The art of Len Roos, 'ace cinematographer', 'specialist in panchromatic scenic work', and 'member of the exclusive American Society of Cinematographers' would still 'bring to the mute scene a new angle of this country's efforts'.

The way in which the publicity was handled for 'the coming of Norman Dawn, distinguished motion picture director of some forty film successes' provides the most potent example of the *construction* of *The Term* in the context of current political events. The parliamentary attack on Australasian Films had concerned the 'invasion' of Americans, and the displacement of Australia's 'natural' ties with Britain. Leading articles in *Everyones* pre-empted and re-directed this argument. An editorial article on Dawn entitled 'The Invasion?' introduced (from the parliamentary hat) the 'artist'

(i)

ctober 13, 1926 EVERYONES. Page Seven.

Film History in the Making.

Pictorial Reproductions of the Progress of "For the Term of His Natural Life" which Norman Dawn is Producing for Australasian Films Ltd.

Top. Left: Rufus Dawes (George Fisher) urges an attack upon Warder Troke (Arthur Tauchert).

Top. Right: Rev. North (Mayne Lynton) pleads with Warder Troke (Arthur Tauchert) to show leniency toward Rufus Dawes (George Fisher).

Left. Bottom: Mrs. Vickers (Katherine Dawn) and Sylvia Vickers as a child (Beryl Gow) are here seen in a tense moment.

Right. Bottom: Capt. Frere (Dunstan Webb) seen here with Sylvia Vickers (Eva Novak).

Everyones 12 October 1926, p. 7

The Use of Glass in Cinematography.

THE use of glass work, or trick photography has often been referred to in articles recording the progress of a picture. This innovation has, however, never been so explicitly illustrated as it is in the accompanying photograph which was taken during the filming of "For the Term of His Natural Life" in Tasmania by Australasian Films.

It shows Len H. Roos standing on the specially erected platform in the front of which is suspended a sheet of ordinary glass.

In the distance may be seen the ruins of the old convict barracks. The photo shows clearly that the roof is missing from the wing on the extreme left. The centre portion of the barracks is also in ruins.

Just below the camera may be clearly seen how this missing portion has been reconstructed **on the glass.** The camera then photographs through the glass and takes in the actual building, including the missing portion.

In the finished film the reconstruction is perfect and the building appears in its original state.

YULETIDE GREETINGS AND
THE BEST OF LUCK IN 1927

LEN H. ROOS, A.S.C.
BEHIND THE CAMERA

CURRENT PRODUCTION:
"FOR THE TERM OF
HIS NATURAL LIFE"

Everyones 15 December 1926, p.46

Cinematic progress in a consensual world: *Everyones'* greetings from cameraman Len Roos, Christmas 1926

(i) ***The "Dawn" of a New Movie Era.***

The Brains Behind the Production

MR. NORMAN DAWN.

(ii)

AUSTRALIA FACES . . . THE DAWN

UNION PICTURE THEATRES

The Sign of Quality

¶ As the sun rises in a blaze of golden glory in the east, so will the new era—transcending all other epochs of progress—dawn in flaming splendour throughout the Australian realm of motion picture entertainment.

¶ The silent drama is going to occupy a niche in Australia's Pantheon of the arts.

¶ The creation of UNION THEATRES circuit of modern houses in city, suburb and country guarantees to the amusement-loving public the presentation of the works of film genius in an "atmosphere" and environment worthy of their greatness.

¶ There'll be a UNION THEATRE everywhere.

UNION THEATRES'

ALL-AUSTRALIAN CIRCUIT,

Sydney, Melbourne, Brisbane, Adelaide, Perth and throughout the Commonwealth, India, Java, Singapore, Japan and China.

Managing Directors:
EDWIN GEACH, W. A. GIBSON, STUART F. DOYLE.
Member M.P.A.A.

FRANK DUNNE

(i) *Everyones* 3 November 1926, p.39; (ii) *Picture Show* 1 February 1921, p.52

A guided evolution out of the Dark Ages: (i) *Everyones* hails Norman Dawn's arrival in 1926, but (ii) this 1921 advertisement for Union Theatres shows the 'new era' paradigm established long before 'the coming of Dawn'.

(i)

(ii)

(i) National Film Archive; (ii) *Film Weekly* 14 July 1927, p.23

The limited gestural range of Eva Novak, as demonstrated in *The Romance of Runnibede* who, using the same basic materials as 'the indifferent director . . . mixes them with brains', and 'produces superior colours from his paints'. Dawn was unconcerned by the parliamentary rumpus around him, and insisted that if art should be mixed with brains it could not mingle with politics. He ingenuously presented in the article his own highly political creed, of a beneficent Hollywood, melting pot of teachers and pupils, without parochial monopolies (like the Guthrie clique) which could say: 'Stop — this is our business, we created it'.[26]

'The Dawn of a New Movie Era'

Norman Dawn, the article noted, had not come to Australia to seek capital, nor, as a true invader, to exploit the country as a member of any large foreign producing unit. He came as an independent to teach and to create films of quality here. His arrival became 'a peaceful invasion of these shores for the purpose of making an *Australian* motion picture'.[27] In articles with titles like 'And then came Dawn', 'After Dawn — The Sun of Great Promise', and 'The Dawn of a New Movie Era', the final image transition could be made:

> After the expenditure of much money, and effort often misdirected in the pioneering of a new industry, the travail and state of total darkness evident in so many Australian productions is soon to be illumined — invariably the 'darker hour is before the Dawn'.[28]

Dawn, by experience and example, would 'bring the day of the Australian star nearer', and with his 'superb artistic temperament', 'perfection of detail', 'genius on lighting', 'masterly set designing', 'businesslike ability and thoroughness so necessary in high-class production' inaugurate the new birth of 'an industry here that refuses to be an infant any longer'.[29]

It was brazen but clever publicity. The 'coming of the Dawn, vision deflected the 'invasion' paradigm through the notion of 'Art' into something which was once more harmonious and consensual. Instead of the notion of natural Australian evolution destroyed by an alien American culture, there was now implanted the idea of a *guided* evolution out of the 'dark ages' of Australian production into the 'Dawn' of a new era when local films could compete on equal terms with the world. In a characteristic eulogy, *Everyones* announced the coming of Dawn as 'probably the most signficant happening of this generation'.[30]

Aside from all this fanfare, who were Novak, Fisher and Dawn? Eva Novak and George Fisher were what American director Wallace Worsley described as 'second- and third-level' box-office stars who, like Roos, had been associated with Dawn in other productions. Neither Fisher nor Novak (with her limited gestural range) displayed anything of the 'artistry' in breaking down 'types' that Arthur Tauchert and Lottie Lyell had shown years before. In fact, Novak, Roos and Dawn were all remarkably 'typed' in the productions they worked on. Novak had 'attained a distinctive fame of her own'[31] in a series of adventure films of the Canadian snows, like *Lure of the Yukon*, shot by Dawn, and *The Snowshoe Trail*, shot by Roos. Roos had also worked extensively in the snow with features like *Going Up For Ice* and *The Snowshoe Trail*, and Fox Education specials like *Canadian Alps* and *Fur Trapper*, and was 'regarded as an authority on locations in North-western Canada'.[32] Dawn had made no less than five snow country films in addition to others in exotic South Seas locations, and when his Australian venture was over, would return to his theme with Hollywood sound films such as *Trail of the Yukon, Orphans of the North* and *Arctic Fury*.

Dawn was regarded as a director who was 'committed to the policy of attaining realism regardless of production costs'[33] (which in effect meant extensive location work on plots he often wrote himself) long before he made *The Term*. He was particularly proud of having taken his company away for several months to the Aleutian Peninsula to 'face starvation, intense cold, and many hazards' of the Arctic in filming 'what has been called the Epic of Alaska'. Commenting on the 'six steaming volcanoes', many thousands of steaming pits, and hot springs covering some 1,100 square miles' he had filmed, he felt that the 'harzardous journey enabled us to secure the real atmosphere in country much more impressive than *Nanook* (which was made in flat country)'.[34]

His belief that *For the Term of His Natural Life* began 'where *Nanook of the North* finished' indicates what Dawn was aiming for and what his limitations were. Flaherty's film had been a box-office success, opening up a potential market for films in exotic locations; and Dawn had followed it with his own film of the frozen North. Flaherty's next film, *Moana*, was set in the South Seas and released the year Dawn was making *The Term*. Dawn again followed with his own South Seas tale, *The Adorable Outcast*, in 1927.[35]

He was, however, trying to buy into a market rather than imitate Flaherty. In fact Dawn tended to imitate himself. If one compares trade reviews of *The Adorable Outcast* with those of earlier Dawn films, one gets a distinct feeling of *dĕjà vu*. In *The Adorable Outcast* Edith Roberts plays a young woman left to the mercy of the 'island rabble' seeking 'hidden gold' by

(i)

(ii)

National Film Archive

'Spectacle, inexhaustible, lavish and gigantic': shooting (i) *For the Term of His Natural Life* and (ii) *The Adorable Outcast.* Note Dawn's policy of building open sets against scenic background to combine action and spectacle in the tradition of theatrical melodrama the death of her father. She is rescued by the hero in a series of incidents notable for their spectacular quality (such as the attack on the rebels' stronghold) and the 'realism' of the photography. In *The Lure of the Yukon*, Eva Novak plays a young woman left prey to the mercies of men 'of the submerged class' by the death of her father in 'the elusive goldfields of Alaska'. She is saved by the hero in a series of spectacular incidents (an avalanche, the dynamiting of logs in a frozen river) photographed with a realism that 'presents the Alaskan country like no film before it'. *Typhoon Love* was the story of a young woman abandoned by her father in the South Seas and saved by the hero in a story spiced with 'startling shots of a tropical typhoon' and 'the sheering off of an immense cliff face'.

This repetition of action-packed incidents and amazing spectacle reveals less the 'artist' than the successful spectacle-melodrama formula already noted in relation to other film-makers most admired by U.T.–A.F., Beaumont Smith and Frank Hurley. Dawn had an advantage over these lesser rivals, apart from his speciality of glass and matte shots,[36] which was particularly suited to spectacle in that he was said to have been the cameraman on the Italian classic of spectacle-melodrama which had profoundly influenced the development of Hollywood cinema, *Cabiria*. Nicholas Vardac described *Cabiria* as a film which was less a dramatic narrative than a patriotic and episodic spectacle.

> The drama of character-conflict existent in the book may have been buried beneath the continuous surge of scenic glories, but the dramatic impact of the spectacle, inexhaustible, lavish, and gigantic, was overwhelming.[37]

W.A. Gibson told the Royal Commission that the major influence in his choice of Dawn was '*Cabiria*, an Italian film, one of the finest that ever came to Australia'. Gibson knew his man because, whether or not Dawn worked on *Cabiria*, Vardac's description of that film stands, word for word, for the film Dawn shot thirteen years later, *For the Term Of His Natural Life*.

Dawn was invariably praised for his camerawork, which had a quality of expressionism comparable with Lang's *Metropolis*, and criticised for his continuity. *Everyones* said of *The Adorable Outcast* that 'the story is too episodic. That flaw in Norman Dawn's direction was apparent in *The Term*, and it is repeated here'.[38] He is reputed to have ignored a shooting script in making *The Term*, choosing instead to work directly from the novel, and the completed film suggests that this was the case. Dawn adhered with scrupulous care to the more photogenic scenes of the already episodic

(i)

(ii)

National Film Archive

German Expressionist influence: (i) still from Fritz Lang's *Metropolis* (1925-6) and frame enlargements from Norman Dawn's *For the Term of His Natural Life* (1926-7)

(iii)

(iv)

National Film Archive

(i)

(ii)

(i), (ii) *Everyones* 11 July 1928, p.44

'Atmospheric prologues' were a feature of cinema presentation imported from America: (i) the Nine Royal Samoans introduce *The Adorable Outcast;* (ii) Franklyn Barrett now a cinema manager in Canberra, presents *Uncle Tom's Cabin;* (iii) tram display in Perth for *The Term;* and (iv) street float and (v) lobby display for *The Adorable Outcast,* the work of manager Ted Lane for the Tivoli, Brisbane

(iii)

(iv)

(v)

(iii) *Film Weekly* 8 September 1927, p.29; (iv), (v) *Everyones* 11 July 1928, p.10

novel, changing only the spiritually charged death of hero and heroine into a new earthly beginning as Rufus Dawes and Sylvia Vickers bob in safety on a raft after the cyclone has passed.

The emphasis on quality scenic shooting in exotic locations explains why Longford's opinion of him was so different from that of the trade: 'Mr Dawn is not a producer, he is a photographer.' He taught Australians 'how to spend money when we have it. Otherwise Mr Dawn has not taught us anything we did not already know'.[39] On the other hand, Dawn's appeal to Stuart Doyle is obvious. He combined the 'realism' and the melodrama which Doyle had liked in Beau Smith and Frank Hurley but in bigger, better and more dramatic ways. The publicity for *The Adorable Outcast* strongly suggests Hurley:

> hundreds of native outriggers gliding along the ocean with full sail . . . The weird interior of the heathen temple depicted with a realism that establishes a supernatural influence immediately. The great native feast, and dance of the warriors to celebrate victory; the turtle fishers bringing in their big catch.[40]

In contrast, Doyle's presentation of the South Seas tale as a theatrical spectacle with an 'atmospheric prologue' by Nine Royal Samoans was directly in the tradition of Beaumont Smith's Princess Rangiri and her Maori Maidens.

While most of the publicity for *The Term* had concentrated on the arrival of the stars and the production details, for *Adorable Outcast* it was focussed on the Queensland release. Dolls of Eva Novak were dropped from aeroplanes, the hit Parlophone recording of the song was promoted over the radio, fifteen big shop window displays were mounted 'with special island backcloths and sand-strewn floors and cut-outs of Edith Roberts in her native costume',[41] 'educational' talks to schools were arranged on 'Island life, scenery and customs', and extensive street and lobby displays set up.

The Term, described by *Film Weekly*, as 'the great Australian picture which shall show for all time that our writers, artists and photographers can confidently take their place besides the world's best',[42] ran at Union Theatres' Crystal Palace in Sydney for eleven weeks. It was said to have made up to £50,000 throughout Australia and New Zealand. The trade press proudly claimed that this probably put its real revenue ahead of *The Ten Commandments*, and in saying so, contradicted its repeated assertions that Australian films could not recoup costs in the local market. *The Adorable Outcast*, which cost £35,000 to produce, and was described by *Everyones* as 'a material advance on previous Australian-made offerings, running well up to world-market standards',[43] ran for a month in Sydney and was said to have taken £3,000 in its first week in Brisbane. But there the fanfare had to stop. By July 1928 Australasian Films' executives were complaining in the trade press that it seemed remarkable that films like *For the Term Of His Natural Life* and *The Adorable Outcast* 'cannot secure any market at all in the United Kingdom'.[44]

Dawn returned to the United States and tried touring 'the smalls of California and Arizona' with the two films, both heavily cut. *The Term* failed completely, supposedly because of lack of American interest in Australian penal history. *The Adorable Outcast*, with added sound synchronisation of 'South Sea melodies, tribal songs, the mob-cries of the blackbirders' and now retitled *Black Cargo of the South Seas*, apparently did a little better. But, like Eva Novak, Dawn could not find work in America. Like Chauvel, he noted that the 'big interests have so strengthened themselves, either by mergers or sudden growth' that no independent could survive. Hollywood was not an open melting pot after all. Thoroughly chastened, no longer possessing star quality, and suddenly believing that 'no picture made here should exceed a budget of £10,000', he returned quietly to Australia.[45]

From then on the publicity slackened off, except when Dawn could be used as political fodder. In February 1928 *Everyones* fulminated against the idea that the English quota might exclude *The Adorable Outcast* because its American stars were said to have earned £6,000 during the ten-week production — and the English quota prescribed that this should represent no more than twenty-five per cent of the total wages bill. In December, *Everyones* remarked upon 'Australasian Films' abandonment of important production ventures on which the company had embarked',[46] and, amazingly, blamed 'political interference with private enterprise'. The Royal Commission had frightened off investment. *Everyones* continued:

> The irony of the situation is this. The people who promoted the investigation levelled against Australasian Films the charge that the company was strangling Australian production, although in one year it spent £80,000 on two pictures. Having discovered that no strangulation existed, the Federal Government, by its dilatoriness, has applied the stranglehold itself.

For the Term Of His Natural Life had failed, but *Everyones* was snugly back in harness with the bosses of Union Theatres.

Phillips Film Productions

In November 1926 N.B. Freeman of Metro-Goldwyn said that future box office success lay with prestigious outdoor-action pictures. In the same month Fred Phillips advertised a company with a nominal capital of £100,000 in one pound shares, which was set up to make just such films.[47]

Before arriving in Australia Phillips had spent most of his business life in America where he had been imbued, as his co-director Frederick Strack complained, with fierce American 'ideas' of free enterprise. Apart from Gibson of Australasian Films, Phillips was the only producer of the period who strongly rejected government involvement in the film industry. With a supreme confidence in the abilities of his company to create a market through quality alone, he rejected the idea of a quota because it would encourage others to float 'mushroom' companies and produce inferior films. He rejected the idea of a government subsidy 'because I do not believe in government interference with business'.[48] He also rejected suggestions of aid, such as an increased tax on American film imports (even though he was quite aware that huge profits were going back to America disguised as bonus shares and, unlike Stuart Doyle, was prepared to say so) because he feared it would compromise the American market he was aiming at:

> I confess that in this matter I may be somewhat selfish. I am trying to establish an efficient organisation for the making of pictures in Australia for the world's market and naturally I do not wish to see anything done that will antagonise our friends.[49]

With this orientation and ebullient self-confidence, Phillips felt he could float free of petty Australian wrangles. Asked if the existence of exhibitor combines hurt him, he said that the sale of his films in Australia would simply be a bonus since 'I am satisfied that the pictures will show a wonderful profit from abroad'.[50]

Phillips adopted the stance of a visiting prophet from America. He would encourage in Australia the confidence needed to make Australians 'believe that they can do it'. He hit Australia on a broad front, setting up a carpet factory and helping establish a motor credit company. 'Australians believed that we could not make carpets in this country, but we have done so'.[51] He planned to do the same for the film industry, and within a few years expected to have three or four separate film units in continuous production, making up to twenty films a year, thereby reaching the potential Australian quota requirements all by himself. Furthermore, they would be prestigious productions, and Phillips, who had no previous film production experience, disdainfully wrote off Arthur Shirley's efforts to market films abroad with, 'Frankly, what did he know about pictures? I hope you are not putting our company in the same category as his'.[52]

Some of Phillips's flamboyant opinions were, of course, founded on facts: for instance the investment-crippling rumour that Australian films could not secure local release. One of the two areas in which he did accept government intervention was in employing 'a cracker-jack publicity man' to 'educate the public through the press that good pictures can be made here'.[53] The other was to set up a national film studio.

Phillips clearly saw his production company, and its first film, *The Romance of Runnibede* (based on the Steele Rudd novel), as the most important foray by far into Australian film production, not excluding *For the Term of His Natural Life* which had just been completed. Like Shirley, this confidence was based on a careful vetting of the stated needs of the American distributors while he was in the United States, and an attempt to achieve lavish production values on a relatively modest Australian scale. Gayne Dexter, who had been a writer in America, had been told that Australian plots should capture the natural romance of the country — of the outback, of the waterfronts, of the Pacific islands — and it is clear that Phillips had been told the same thing. Wallace Worsley, *Runnibede*'s original director, always argued that 'the splendid dramatic story material of Australia and her mandated territories'[54] would sell well in America because inferior Hollywood copies, bearing as much resemblance to the original 'as a jellyfish does to a shark' were big box office. His idea was that 'the needs of the American market could be met by spending £30,000 on an outdoor story needing few sets, containing 'one or more phases of life in Australia . . . unfamiliar to the American public' and by using an American director, leading American stars and 'a small colony of American technical men'.[55]

Runnibede's second director, Scott Dunlap, showed similar ideas for 'solving Australia's motion picture production problems'. 'With the storied islands of the Pacific practically at your front door, and a world of romance around your waterfronts and in your big open spaces, you have here material which in other countries would have to be counterfeited at tremendous expense.' America was 'crying out for novelties' and Australia had them.[56] The directors whom Phillips imported were relatively big names in America. Worsley was chairman of the American Motion Picture Directors' Association until he left for Australia, and was famous for directing Lon Chaney in *The Hunchback of Notre Dame*. This had brought him a reputation for handling crowds, 'for composition, for mass effect and for the development of drama by purely pictorial methods'.[57] Scott Dunlap was known as a busy producer of Westerns, especially those of Buck Jones, and was late joining the production of *The Romance of Runnibede* 'because of other commitments'. He arrived in Australia with the reputation of being a 'working director', 'at the zenith of his career', 'up to the minute' and not looking for employment like Worsley or Dawn.

Phillips paid his directors and production manager, also American, £200 a week, and another £160 a week went to Eva Novak. He was hoping to cash in on the enormous publicity Novak had received from Australasian Films and the expected success of *The Term* in America. Since, however, the shares of his company were not bought up, he had only £10,000, not Worsley's suggested £30,000, to spend on production — though Victor Longford was to say *Runnibede* could have been made 'for £1,000, exclusive of the expenses of Miss Eva Novak'.[58]

Phillips was criticised from several directions for employing Eva Novak. When the chairman of the Royal Commission said, 'I strongly resent seeing an American star in an Australian picture', Phillips replied: 'May I suggest to you that it is better to produce an Australian picture even with an American star than to buy an American picture'. However, a much more serious and insidious attack came from the pages of *Film Weekly*. The editor, Martin Brennan, warned investors to be very careful before putting money into a scheme 'more in the nature of a stock exchange proposition than in an honest desire to make pictures in Australia from the standpoint of Art',[59] and floated ominous notions of the investors losing all their money if Union Theatres were to close their doors to the company which had pinched Novak. Brennan was sharply questioned by the Royal Commission about the article, which it was felt could be a setback to Phillips's hopes of investment. It was suggested that *Film Weekly* was operating under the influence of the distributors who controlled the journal through their advertising. Brennan did not deny this power in general. But he proclaimed his independence in this matter, saying he wanted to protect prospective investors against a film which carried overheads that were too high to allow any hope of a profit.[60]

Phillips admitted that these overheads were high, but, like the Commission, felt that the article, and others which appeared in the press to the effect that Novak and Dunlap were not returning to Australia, were inspired by interested parties unknown. He said that he was indeed in the business for the sake of profit, not 'Art', but so, too, were the trade

,reetings Which Reflect a Paper's Prestige

Many Happy Returns to Martin C. ,rennan on his 50th Birthday. May "The ilm Weekly" continue to occupy a high lace in the esteem of the Industry, is the ıncere good wish of

JOHN W. HICKS, Jnr.,
Managing Director,
Paramount Pictures.

Many happy returns and best wishes for the future o Martin C. Brennan.

JOHN C. JONES
General Manager,
First National Pictures, Australia.

To Martin C. Brennan and "The Film Weekly." "Continued success to both"—the Industry needs them. Many happy returns on the 50th Birthday of the Editor of "The Film Weekly."

STANLEY S. CRICK,
Managing Director,
Fox Films.

I extend to "The Film Weekly" and its enial editor, the best of good wishes. The ndustry appreciates both. May they rosper with the Industry itself.

HERC. C. McINTYRE,
General Manager,
Universal Films.

To Martin C. Brennan I extend my best wishes on his attaining the half-century. At the same time I would show my appreciation of his value to the Industry by the foundation of a very able and well-conducted paper in "The Film Weekly."

CHAS. E. MUNRO,
Fox Films.

This is the time for congratulations. One o Martin Brennan on attaining the half-century—and he don't look it—the other n turning out such a dignified and informative trade magazine as "The Film Weekly."

(CAPT.) P. F. DAWSON,
General Sales Manager,
Cinema Art Films.

To Martin C. Brennan and his "Film Weekly" I extend sincere good wishes for the future prosperity of both, and appreciate this occasion to wish him "Many Happy Returns."

W. A. GIBSON, O.B.E.,
Managing Director,
Australasian Films Ltd.

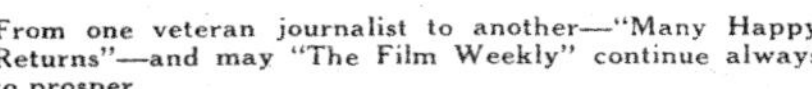

From one veteran journalist to another—"Many Happy Returns"—and may "The Film Weekly" continue always to prosper.

EDWIN GEACH,
Managing Director,
Union Theatres Ltd.

"Many Happy Returns" to Martin C. Brennan, and Good Wishes for the Future of the "Film Weekly."

STUART F. DOYLE,
Managing Director,
Australasian Films Ltd.

Let me add my meed of praise to a tip-top trade magazine and its hard-working and conscientious proprietor-editor.

L. P. HOSKINS,
Managing Director,
Cinema Art Films Ltd.

Martin C. Brennan and "The Film Weekly." Congratulations on your 50th Birthday. Prosperity to both!

RALPH R. DOYLE,
General Manager,
United Artists.

Very best wishes for continued success of "The Film Weekly," and "Many Happy Returns" to its capable editor, Martin C. Brennan, on his 50th Birthday.

E. J. & DAN CARROLL & E. J. TAIT,
Managing Directors,
Prince Edward Theatre Beautiful.

Hearty good wishes for the future of yourself and "The Film Weekly"—read and appreciated everywhere in the profession.

SIR BENJAMIN FULLER,
Managing Director,
Fullers Theatres Ltd.

Film Weekly 22 December 1927, p.7

Big distributors, said to control *Film Weekly* through their advertising, club together to back the editor, Martin C. Brennan, on his fiftieth birthday.

In The Sydney Morning Herald of August 15

there appeared this item of news.

AUSTRALIAN FILMS.

Expanding Production.

PHILLIPS COMPANY'S PLANS.

A notable expansion in the resources of Phillips Film Productions, Ltd., was forecasted yesterday by Mr. Fred Phillips (managing director). Mr Scott Dunlap, supervising director of the company, left for America on Saturday by the Sonoma, in order to complete the arrangements. He has been authorised to purchase a complete studio equipment, including all the latest lighting devices; and these are to be installed in new premises the company will erect for itself in the suburbs.

"Mr. Dunlap's trip," said Mr. Phillips, "is an earnest of the thorough manner in which we intend to proceed with the making of motion pictures in Australia. Already Mr. Del Clausen, one of the foremost cinematographers of Hollywood, is under engagement to us, and is on his way by the Aorangi, and on our supervising director's return in about two months we shall have as complete a unit as any in Hollywood.

"Mr. Dunlap will also investigate and report on several locations which we have in mind for our next production. Locations have been offered us at Pago Pago, but a great deal will depend upon his report as to the suitability of the island for our purpose.

"We look forward to the future of Australian-made films with the greatest confidence. Mr. Dunlap is about to complete arrangements for the American release of all Miss Eva Novak's pictures."

Read it!
It's interesting
and will serve to
contradict several
rumours which have
been floating around.

Mr. Dunlap's trip was hurriedly arranged. In fact, it was not decided that he should make it until Thursday, so there was no time for beg pardons or farewells.

SO THAT'S THAT!

NOW THERE'S SOMETHING ELSE.

When we started out to make Australian pictures, people told us that the Showmen of Australasia did not want to screen the product of their own country. The hundreds of letters we have received enquiring for

"THE ROMANCE OF RUNNIBEDE"

gives this suggestion the lie direct; but here's another way to let us prove it to be wrong without the least shadow of doubt.

We have prepared a beautiful art booklet of sixteen pages, containing photographs of the principals in this picture, together with some beautifully reproduced stills of the main incidents, including the rare scenes of aboriginal rites, etc., which figure prominently in its sequences.

We will send this free to any Picture Showman, or to anyone interested in Australian Motion pictures, on receipt of a post card or letter of request.

As a work of art, it reflects credit on those who produced it: Messrs. Harris & Wagg, who made the blocks, and Messrs. Edward Lee & Co., who printed it.

Now don't rush us. The postman is only a human being, who does his utmost in his 44 hours, but we will work all night to get this handsome souvenir into the hands of all interested parties. **Ladies and Gentlemen: Get to it!**

Address:—

Phillips Film Productions Limited

Metropolitan Buildings, 56 Hunter Street, Sydney, Australia

Cables and Telegrams: Philson, Sydney.

Film Weekly 18 August 1927, p.17

Fred Phillips' advertisement in *Film Weekly*, aimed at the trade rumour campaign journals, except when eulogising *For the Term of His Natural Life* — an A.F. film. The 'knocking' campaign was to dog Phillips throughout his enterprise to the extent that in August 1927 he was driven to take out a full page advertisement in *Film Weekly* to quash rumours that his company was about to fold.

However, he remained convinced of his immunity from the petty politics of the local market, and, throwing off other jibes such as his supposed cashing in on the publicity for local films brought about by Shirley's M.P.D.A. deputation, bought Steele Rudd's as yet unpublished story,[61] and prepared for production.

It is possible that there was conscious manipulation to defeat him. Rudd's son wrote that the company was 'wrecked by the irresistible tide of overseas vested film interests'. And already by mid-1926 the American film industry and Congress were beginning to collaborate in 'counter-action' (discouraging quota legislation, discouraging foreign production) against what they called 'a serious menace to the continued maintenance of the foreign film trade'.[62] Alternatively, Union Theatres may have been heavying this rival in prestigious 'outdoor-action' films. But neither Union Theatres' release of *Runnibede* nor *Film Weekly*'s later praise of it particularly suggests malicious intent. On the contrary, the trade was mainly worried at this time by the local quota emphasis of the Imperial Conference in London, and was arguing that the only way to safeguard shareholders was to employ Americans. Hence Phillips's preoccupation with foreign 'experts' gained considerable sympathy for his enterprise.

The note of Australian 'novelty' that Worsley and then Dunlap chose for their film was Aboriginal culture. Worsley, calling for lavish 'local colour', shot Aboriginal 'war dances'. Dunlap impressed with the wealth of tradition the Aboriginals had retained, despite their association with the whites, shot native black rituals and corroborees 'never before photographed'. The fact that Dunlap found the Aborigines 'the most intelligent bunch I have ever had the good fortune to handle' [63] did not, of course, prevent the directors from casting Dunstan Webb, fresh from the villainous Frere in *The Term*, as the equally villainous witch-doctor, Goondi; nor did it prevent this travesty of Aboriginal customs being hailed by Barambah Aboriginal Settlement, Murgon, as 'true to native life'.[64]

The decision to shoot the film at Murgon, Queensland, where Rudd's novel was set,[65] added considerably to production costs. Although Worsley accused Dunlap of incompetence and inefficiency in spending money, the production was lavish from the start. Rudd had long preceded Phillips in arguing that only the cinema could open up the economic potential of Australia by making its opportunities visible to Europeans and North Americans. He had also invested in the film (money he could ill afford), and had been given a relatively large initial payment on account of £100 for his story, with more to follow — so he had every reason to be excited by the venture. However, no sooner was the company in its Brisbane hotel than he noticed that 'nothing was being spared in the way of lavish living'.[66] The Queensland exhibitor, R.F. Stephens, who was also sympathetic to the film, also observed 'the waste of money . . . I can remember practically a whole week's work occupying but a few feet of film in the story'. Worsley had employed three cameramen to shoot what he regarded as an important comedy scene, but this, together with virtually all the scenes including Nellie Fergusson and the American star, Virginia Ainsworth, and thousands of feet of stockyard shots, were scrapped by Dunlap when he took over. Stephens commented that Ainsworth 'was a member of the company from start to finish yet she appears in the picture for about five seconds.'[67] He also saw considerable disorganisation in the planning of the production by Worsley, followed by chaos when Dunlap arrived and Worsley departed, in anger, 'leaving a picture nearly three-quarters finished in charge of the new director who knew nothing about it'.

The reason for the change of directors in unknown,[68] but the net result, Stephens thought, was that:

> £900 must have been expended in production that a new director thought not up to his standard. Without proper organisation, under directors whose American experience counts not the money cost, Australian production will never be a financial success'.[69]

The production director, Frederick Strack, was also to say:

> 'I fail to see the need for the spending of vast sums of money on Australian pictures. American producers generally have big ideas, and no doubt are responsible for heavy expenditure'.[70]

Other observers noted, in contrast, that since the arrival of Dunlap 'the vast organisation created by this company has assumed shape very rapidly' with a good balance between his efficient supervision and departmental delegation.[71] Also, in fairness to Phillips, it should be remembered that the policy of taking considerable 'local colour' footage in exotic locations prior to a director's arrival and fitting it into a story was a common Hollywood practice.

By the end of June 1927 the location work was over. The few interiors were shot in the very cramped studios of De Forest Phonofilms, and the ballroom scene shot during the early hours of one morning at the Wentworth Hotel. Dunlap was already planning future productions starring Novak, and Steele Rudd was working on a second story. Films were planned depicting the oriental and cosmopolitan mysteries of the Sydney waterfront, a race track story, mining

> and, in fact, every phase of our life will be probed to provide suitable material for the little box office star with the winning smile who is rapidly conquering Australian motion picture fans as she did her American audiences.[72]

All this was remarkably similar to Harry Southwell's plans of just a few months before for marketing *Down Under* internationally, to be followed by 'pictures embracing forestry, mining and pearling'.[73] The results in both cases were nil. In late July Dunlap cabled to Dal Clausen, 'one of Hollywood's leading cinematographers', to come out for the next production, and Dunlap himself was supposedly about to seek out a tropical island to put Novak on for her next film. But in Dunlap's interview with *Film Weekly*, there was already an ominous emphasis on the importance of the Australian market, despite all his talk of an international one. As Frederick Strack was to point out, the American distributing houses were 'not running after our picture, good as it was'.[74] John C. Jones, managing director of First National in Sydney, rejected it on the grounds that 'a good picture cannot be made for £10,000'.[75] Hicks of Paramount said he liked it, but said that it was 'too American' — an opinion shared, according to Eric Davis, Steele Rudd's son, by rather a lot of Australians, but not by *Everyones*. Berating the English quota laws, *Everyones* called it 'the most purely Australian picture Australia has turned out', despite being 'made by an American star, two American directors, an American production manager, an American cameraman and an American-trained assistant director'.[76]

Fred Phillips, however, was still totally confident of the American market and said he was sending Dunlap to the United States to release the film and 'purchase a complete studio of equipment, including all the latest lighting devices'.[77] Exactly the same had been said before about the earlier American imports, Wilfred Lucas in 1920, and then Lawson Harris in 1923 and the result was indeed the same — the film was not sold and Dunlap, as the rumours had predicted, did not return to Australia to make more films.

The Romance of Runnibede was released as a 'floater' by Australasian Films. It opened successfully in Sydney and Tasmania in early 1928. *Everyones* said, 'in production values it is the equal of a good American Western',

The Camera Catches the Exhibitors Exploitation Ideas

This excellent street ballyhoo was used for the season of Australasian Films' "The Missing Link," at the Majestic Theatre, Auckland.

Stage setting, principals and ballet in the presentation for First National's "The Volga Boatman" at the Capitol, Melbourne.

An excellent street parade idea for Australasian Films' "The Romance of Runnibede." It was used by Hall Bros., of the Tivoli, Collie (W.A.) when the picture was screened there.

Manager Doug. Medcraf arrayed himself in naval officer's uniform and decorated his car for the season of Paramount's "The Flag Lieutenant" at the Bungalow Theatre, Maryborough (Q.).

This fine outdoor display was the work of Exhibitor Kenny, of Swan Hill (Vic.), for Australasian Films' "Mademoiselle from Armentieres." Exploiteer Izzy Smith, V.C., is on the left.

This humorous street stunt was put over for United Artists' "Two Arabian Knights" when it was screened at the Haymarket, Sydney, recently.

Everyones 7 March 1928, p.31

Street ballyhoo for *The Romance of Runnibede* and other films of 1928 and saw it as 'one of the three likeliest Australian productions for the world market'.[78] The *Sydney Morning Herald* said that in dramatic power it was 'far and away in advance' of *The Term*.[79] *Film Weekly* praised the film very highly, saying it was 'devoid of senseless exaggeration and shows Eva Novak at her very best'.[80] Steele Rudd's own journal, *Shop Assistants Magazine*, said the film 'will certainly be an epoch-making achievement for Australia' since it had the 'essentials' which earlier productions lacked for gaining a world market.[81]

Bankruptcy

None of this was enough. In April 1928, Eva Novak, pictured by the trade as a heroine who, at great financial cost 'had maintained her faith in the country's possibilities though others came, saw, and hurried away',[82] herself left Australia. Phillips Productions owed Novak £4,240 backlog in salary and W.R. Reed, the production manager, £4,900 so Phillips gave them the American rights to *Runnibede* in lieu. There was still talk of the film selling in England, and of sending 'a troupe of Aborigines abroad to circus the picture as the Red Indians did with *The Vanishing Race* here'.[83] But in August Phillips was declared bankrupt with liabilities of £11,475 and assets of £3,200. He gave two reasons. The first was the loss of a contract valued at £35,000 to sell shares worth £1,000,000 for Motor Credits. The second reason he gave was his attempt 'to promote and pioneer new industries in Australia'.[84] In relation to the film, Phillips argued that despite capacity houses, sixty-five per cent return on the rentals, the 'picture venture was not a success because Australians do not want Australian productions. The people will not put the money in them' with the result that the company was never floated.

How much influence the adverse advice of the trade journals had had on potential investors is impossible to determine. What can be said is that from the time of *Runnibede*'s first screening, *Everyones* continually commented that the film showings 'did not bring out the large numbers of howlers against American films, the loud-mouthed speakers at Loyalty, Empire and Returned Soldiers' Associations, who want to show Empire films'.[85] As so often happened, the affair gave the trade journals the opportunity to play political football with Australian productions — and in this case against *Everyones* particular enemy, Guthrie's followers. *Everyones* advanced the trivial argument that the loyalists should back their mouthings with their backsides on cinema seats to see *Runnibede* without,

How "Odds On" Cost £2000

TELLING how to make an Australian picture for £2,000.... Well, after you've found your story and mortgaged your soul for the cash, you get the wind up, wondering whether you'll take the gamble or play safe on some 5 per cent. bonds. Arthur Higgins must have felt that way before and during the shooting of "Odds On." It's a sure bet that sometime or other he asked himself why he was taking the chance, and what the deuce would happen if "Odds On" blew out to a million to one against.

It didn't; it makes a creditable showing for £2,000, with a better box-office chance than Australian pictures of the last few years that cost anywhere from twice to six times that sum.

How the Cash Was Spent.

FIGURES are interesting, particularly when you can induce the producer to itemise them. Here's how Higgins' budget worked out.

Salaries to players, not including extras	£700
Direction and technical staff	£300
Camera-men, laboratory costs and raw stock	£300
Cost of Romano's for cabaret scenes, including food, tips and motor hire	£100
Transportation and hotel expenses	£175
Studio rent including hire of sets and juice	£80
Payment to jockeys, extras and hire of race-horses and race-course scenes	£180
Editing and titling	£60
Continuity	£50
Trade screening	£35
Publicity	£20

Can't Reckon Cost in Advance.

TROUBLE is you can't reckon expenditure accurately in advance; and the only way to know how much your picture has cost to date is to accept the bank-teller's word on whether there'll be enough to meet the next pay-roll.

The only occasion I can recall that a picture cost less than estimated was four or five years ago when a chap named J. K. MacDonald was producing "Penrod and Sam" in Hollywood with Bennie Alexander as star. MacDonald was given a production budget of 100,000 dollars. Each week his expense reports came up to the New York office, indicating that the finished film would run out at less than 90,000 dollars. In all the company's history such a thing was unknown. Troubled executives held whispered confabs; the Big Boss got heebee-jeebies every Monday morning when MacDonald's report arrived—every expense was lower than estimated. Always under, always under! Then after weeks, when his nerves were frayed, guitar strings, the Big Boss wired MacDonald: "Fod God's sake spend another 50,000 dollars. I can't sleep for thinking how much of my money the other fellows must be wasting."

£3 an Afternoon for Horse and Jockey.

BUT getting back to Arthur Higgins. "Odds On" is the first picture he has directed, although, since "The Fatal Wedding" in 1912, he has cranked his camera on maybe 50 features. Just a matter of swapping lens-lamentations for megaphone-miseries. He doesn't say which was the greater grief.

For his race scenes, he hired 14 horses and jockeys at £3 per horse-and-jock to gallop around the course for as long as he needed them one afternoon. It seemed an easy matter to mount cameras on cars on the inside track, run parallel, and get just what race action was desired. But the track was grass, the cars couldn't keep pace with the gees, and after twice around the jockeys figured they'd earned their money and rode home. That little excursion cost £80 and Higgins used only six feet of it in his finished picture.

Difference Between Hollywood and Here.

WELL, what of it? Over in Hollywood they'll shoot away thousands of dollars and thousands of feet without using even one frame! Quite so; but over in Hollywood they have money to burn; over there, too, a man who at first shot did as many things in one picture as Higgins has done in "Odds On," would eventually find himself a supervisor or director in one of the high falutin' studios.

For "Odds On," Higgins found the money, wrote the continuity, directed the picture, lighted it, did half the camera-work, printed, edited and cut it. After all that, he certainly deserved the satisfaction of seeing the critics O.K. his efforts, and hearing film-men comment: "That little fellow would go a long way if somebody put real money behind him."

Everyones (i) 19 September 1928, p.6

The end of an era: after the failure of *The Term* and *The Romance of Runnibede* the final two years of Australian silent film-making were dominated by 'quota quickies' — films made quickly and cheaply to cash in on the expected quota and Government prize. The best of these was Arthur Higgins' *Odds On*. Meanwhile 'Australian' film was represented by MGM's big budget *The Bushranger*. This included a small part, — a travesty of the great hopes of 1919 — for Snowy Baker's brother.

(i)

Everyones (i) 3 October 1928, p. 16 (ii) 30 May 1928, p.20

(ii) **Australians in Hollywood Hired for "The Bushranger"**

HOLLYWOOD.—A general round-up in Hollywood has practically filled the extra ranks and the list of small-part players with Australians in M.-G.-M.'s production, "The Bushranger."

BESIDES coming from the regular actors, the property-rooms, the assistant-directorial quarters and other unexpected places in the studios have disgorged lean-faced Australians, who will wear the mounted troopers' uniforms and gallop in the tracks of Tim McCoy. Commercial houses and gymnasiums have revealed others. One of the first engaged was Frank Baker, brother of Reg L. Baker, who has been cast as a sergeant, and in the accompanying photograph is shown playing opposite Dale Austen, the New Zealand beauty.

Miss Austen finished "The Bushranger" before returning to Auckland under the terms of the contract with M.-G.-M., by which she came to America.

of course, a shred of statistical evidence. The journal even used the occasion of its review of the film to say, 'While *Runnibede* will win audiences on its merit, here is an opportunity for the "loud-speakers" to display practical patriotism by according a worthwhile local picture their support'.[86]

After Novak's departure, Gayne Dexter carried the message of Phillips's failure under a leading editorial, 'Disconcerting But . . .', in which he said that the £2,000 local return on the film 'stands to the lasting discredit of all those people and associations who have been loudest in their praises for Australian productions. . . the agitators feel they have done enough when they have passed resolutions and gone home'.[87] No mention was made of the huge disparity between that £2,000 and the reputed £50,000 flowing back to Union Theatres from *The Term*, which had rather more to do with the 'floater' status they gave *Runnibede* and the long runs they gave their own film, than with the backsides of any number of Empire Loyalists. In fact, the trade press managed to have it all ways, since Senator Guthrie was also condemned for self-interested and 'deep-laid' schemes when it was thought he had done precisely what the trade press demanded and invested in an Empire film production scheme.

The Romance of Runnibede was accepted as eligible for the British quota, but not before it had provided a further opportunity for *Everyones* to attack the Empire quota supporters, with major articles by Dexter under headings such as 'English Law Can Classify Our Films As Foreign Productions' and 'Does English Bill Block Importation Of Our Film Talent To Train Australians'.[88] Dexter was supporting the two films made by Australasian Films here, since he had argued that local production was most likely 'to be undertaken with any degree of success by a concern already well-established in the exhibition or distribution field' and not 'from public companies floated for production purposes'.[89] *Runnibede* was used as suitable bait in the attack. During these, the last gasps of the 'American invasion' issue, Fred Phillips had, after all, fallen prey to local film politics.

PART THREE

The Bush Legend

National Film Archive

'The drama of man's struggle against nature': Longford's *On Our Selection*

10

A Magnificient Reward: The Australian Legend in the Cinema

The American director Wallace Worsley, who observed the central debate in Australian film production of the 1920s — whether simply to 'make it' in the Hollywood way or to 'make it Australian', said:

> The drama of Australia is not as it is so frequently represented overseas —a drama of an Australian falling victim to the wiles of a native girl . . . or of a white woman living amongst Aborigines, but the drama of man's struggle against nature in the face of great physical and mental hardship, his eventual triumph, and his magnificient reward.[1]

Here was one American who recognised the essential qualities of the Australian legend, especially as located in the more important films of Franklyn Barrett and Raymond Longford.

The relationship between man and landscape first appears as purely an oppositional one: like Barrett's Joe Gallaway, 'a fighter who . . . has pulled through strikes, droughts, bush fires, floods, grasshopper plagues and rabbit plagues till he's got the constitution of a stock horse'; and like the supporting woman, Mrs Gallaway, who endures without yielding, 'a true-hearted woman of the outback whose kindly nature has not been soured by adversities'. The very titles of Barrett's films, *The Breaking of the Drought* and *A Girl of the Bush*, draw on these images of active struggle and passive resistance which were deemed to be permanent features of the lot of men and women in the Australian bush.

But through this initial opposition, the fuller image that the narrative develops is one of fusion of land and people. The process is dialectical, evoking from this proposed antithesis of pioneer and nature a symbiotic dimension. Ultimately the image is of a people, sometimes broken by and sometimes breaking the drought, who by virtue of that toughening contact will open up more land, endure more hardship and develop more resources, endlessly projecting forward an Australian future of spectacular dimension.

This was the hallmark of a dream held by pioneer and politician, artist and worker alike — of a new land, locked away in the the Southern hemisphere, with the potential to be not simply a granary for the world, but the source of a new and purer humanity as well. It was a vision dear to Henry Lawson as it was to the editors of the *Picture Show*, and again, to film-makers like Charles Chauvel: 'A land of hills and plains and rivers running free, a land won by conquering people toughened by adversity'.[2]

The opening titles and shots of *The Breaking of the Drought* evoke a land of extremes: the age-old 'country'[3] notion of a paradise blessed by nature, offering its own fruits, is tempered by the alternative legend of hardship, of working in an inhospitable frontier land to produce the barest living. 'Australia, the land of vivid contrasts . . . From rich pastures literally flowing with milk and honey to outback plains upon which grim drought has laid its devastating hand'. The film now marks the track of this particular discourse in which it is man's moral as much as his physical labour which mediates between the two extreme poles of a potential horizon and replaces an opposition between man and nature with a bountiful communion.

The main narrative begins by showing cracked earth, starving sheep, desperately work-weary men. The combination of images tells a tale of adversity and defines the authentic man in contrast to the degraded city world we will soon confront. The film ends by showing a promised land of richness and plenty, of waving grass and corn husbanded by these same men and their machines. Into this physical trajectory *The Drought* inserts another, which is homologous with it. The breaking of the drought is spiritual as well as physical: the 'city' son of a 'country' father is saved from a life of vice which threatens not only himself but the whole country tradition from which he comes. The film has one final sequence after the 'natural' plenitude of the harvest as the two people who have done most to save him unite in a spiritual fulfilment. Tom and Marjorie are, as the film assures us, two genuine bush dwellers who enter, like Orpheus, the depths of the city to bring back their cherished one. Like him, they falter, but *their* muse, a union of true country love and mateship, is too strong not to prevail.

The Breaking of the Drought invokes much of the Australian legend as Russel Ward has defined it:[4]

That the 'Australian' spirit is derived from the isolated, ordinary people of the bush, in contrast to the fragmenting high-life of the people of the cities.

National Film Archive

The narrative trajectory from lack to plenitude: frame enlargements from *The Breaking of the Drought*

That the land belongs to those who work it, in contrast to the city which belongs to parasites who exploit the bush people.

That the land produces a reasonable living for all, in contrast to the gross divisions and inequities of the city.

That the environmental conditions of the land produce the improvisation, intolerance of conventions and manly independence as well as understanding between employer and employee that signify the true Australian.

Ward rightly points out that the legend was part of a wider Romantic myth that was symptomatic of the expansion of industrial civilisation. This contained three aspects:

1. A symbol of Romantic escape from the drab and constricting urban-industrial society: in Australia this was signified as a movement from Clancy's 'dusty, dirty city' outwards and away from limitations of space and time to 'the visions splendid of the sun-lit plains extended, and at night the wondrous glory of the everlasting stars'.[5]
2. A symbol of compensation and self-justification for the exploitative evils of an expanding imperialism which claimed that its wealth came not from persecuting the natives and taking their land, but from the labour of worthy pioneers: as in those definitive lines from *The Romance of Runnibede*: 'I have cleared every foot of this land and I'm not letting a few blacks drive me away'.
3. A symbol of a new nationhood and identity, forged out of the imputed distinction between the 'eager eyes and greedy cosmopolitanism' of the Old World, and the pioneer life on the frontier.

These aspects of the broader Romantic myth were, of course, as typical of the American frontier as of Australia. What then were the specifically Australian features? And what accounted for the legend's cross-class currency, given that it was generated, according to Ward, by bush workers?

The Romance of the Land

Part of the answer lies in the fact that fiercely competitive European-style cities could do little to provide a specifically Australian identity. Whereas the easy mobility of bush workers, miners, drovers, shearers, selectors and pastoralists alike, all with their own investment in the romance of the land, made the inland an 'effective melting pot for ideas, and matrix for the Australian legend'.[6] But these are no more than permissive reasons.

The very nature of that fusion, the coding of its elements, the inflecting of its core structure, are not explained.

The potency of the legend depended on the fact that it was a *lived* legend — lived at one time or another by almost every section of the Australian community. Different social groups and classes placed emphasis on different aspects of the legend. The squatters emphasised the manly independence and fortitude which had transformed a wasteland into a pastoral paradise and provided a staple which secured a world market for Australia. The farmers emphasised the property which they felt was rightly theirs by dint of labour, and, as they built churches and provided schools, epitomised their status as the moral as well as the economic backbone of a country fast expanding away from the eastern city vices. The selectors emphasised the purifying ritual of seasonal hardship. For many of these men there had been two or three defeats and migrations: from English country to English city to colony. The price of moderate success for some was the loss of everything for many more — and that made the adherence to a final identity on the land so much stronger.

Even in the nineteenth century, however, the bush ethos was a city legend too, and one for all classes. The new capitalist class used it to oust the 'monopoly' power of the squattocracy. They argued that 'free trade in land' (though not too free), secured by 'iron ways' into the bush, would produce wealth for all and establish democracy as the handmaiden of Australian civilisation. And as the land settlement acts came through, protecting the squatters' rights at the cost of indebtedness to the city banks, the new financial and urban élite could grow strong on the fruits of the land, while stridently protesting against its monopolisation by the old ruling class. The radical working class, at the other end of the city spectrum and in the face of mass unemployment, called for free selection of land as a panacea. As Buxton has pointed out, the 'dream of a verandah, pipe and the fruit of the vine as wilderness blossomed as the rose'[7] was, for much of the nineteenth century, a working-class dream as much as that of any other social group. It may be, as historian T.H. Irving has argued, that for many a worker 'land hunger meant in actuality no more than a slab cottage and vegetable garden on the edge of town',[8] but his devotion to the bush dream was no less powerful for that.

By the 1870s most Australians, as a result of the isolation and international ineffectiveness of the country, were looking inward rather than abroad for their national identity, and were finding it in a broadly accepted equalitarian social doctrine. As the nineteenth century came to a close, that ideal was located even more securely in the bush legend, not only by the 'bush' literature of Lawson, Paterson, Furphy, Steele Rudd and others promoted by the *Bulletin*, but also by the severe depression of the 1890s. The historian B.K. deGaris points out that:

> the spectacular growth of the major colonial capitals had been a striking feature of the boom and when the crash came critics were quick to lay the blame at their door; the wasteful and vulgar ostentation of city life was unfavourably contrasted with the simple rural values of the bush. Fossicking for gold provided a living for quite a few in New South Wales and Victoria. Moreover the discovery of rich goldfields in Western Australia came at just the right time to serve as a form of large-scale outdoor relief for the eastern colonies'.[9]

Not for the first time, nor the last, governments adopted the panacea of 'putting men on the land' by establishing cooperative agricultural settlements.

The bush dream was maintained right into and throughout the period this book covers, and so was the predominant rural economy. Despite setbacks and the considerable urban and industrial growth of the early twentieth century, Australia remained primarily dependent on her rural industries until well after the end of the period of Australian silent cinema.[10] There was renewed interest in the 1920s in what the historian, Heather Radi has called the bewitching Australian vision of water flowing in a dry land.[11] Not only was this vision supported in every way by the heads of the cinema industry (in their support, for instance, for the 'Million Farms for a Million Farmers' scheme), but the bush-pioneering paradigm became the focus for the ideological constructions of what was by now an American-dominated industry. The welding of this American present with its 'rain' of Hollywood films and the staple-producing rain of the Australian legend is especially clear in an editorial of Paramount's film magazine, *The Exhibitor*, entitled, 'The Farmer, The Grazier, The Orchardist and The Exhibitor'.[12]

> Four men of National Importance met in a Great City during a Time of Great Significance. Said the Farmer, 'This has been my most prosperous year.' 'I have never known conditions better,' said the Grazier. The Orchardist announced, 'My fruit this year has been fuller and richer than I have ever known it before.' And the Exhibitor said, 'I have finally solved the problem of knowing exactly what it is that my patrons want.' '. . . 'Rains brought to my orchard by the irrigation scheme of man's inventing have ensured its being a success for all time,' said the Orchardist. 'Well,' said the Exhibitor . . . 'I am, of course, vitally interested in this rain of which you speak because it means prosperity to your district and of course

> that brings more patrons to my theatre. It is, however, more of the rain of good pictures for showing on my screen that I am concerned with . . . I took the powerful precaution of taking out a Paramount contract. Which means, that like you chaps, I have located my means of livelihood so that it will best be served, all the year round, by the vital rain from whence springs all prosperity.

By then the agrarian dream had been bolstered by events which were emphasised by a different film magazine, *Picture Show*. The reputation of the Anzacs at Gallipoli and European trenches was instantly incorporated into the traditional values of the Australian bush. When the historian Ian Turner recently pointed to the image of the traditional enemy, death, which the Anzacs were said to face with humour and endurance, his reference to the bush legend was the same as Longford's in the deaths of Dennis's *Ginger Mick*. Turner noted that not only did the Australian soldiers pioneer a new 'bushman' style of fighting, but the Australian performance was judged to be distinctively within the bush traditions — of high physical fitness, ability to adapt to unusual conditions, respect but not class servility before officers, and that bush blend of individualism and cooperation, 'independent judgment and readiness to self-effacement in a common cause'.[13]

The Anzacs refurbished the bush legend powerfully, at just the time that the Australian film industry was trying, most self-consciously, to get off the ground, which accounts for the prescribed concatenation of bush, Anzacs and cinema found in the *Picture Show*, and which in film probably existed most poignantly in the lost *Ginger Mick*. The historian Heather Radi has said, 'the new story of the Anzacs bridged the gap between the pioneering past and the urban present by giving the people of the city the right to the qualities of the outback'.[14] But exactly the same could be said of the pioneer myths of the new cinema moguls.

In one way the soldier-settlers were 'luckier' than the film-making pioneers. As Radi remarks, 'Profitability was hardly discussed in soldier settlement, the ideal seemed so natural.' Schemes for irrigation, the setting up of dairy industries and land clearance therefore forged ahead at the expense of the more necessary but mythically dull notions of providing water, electricity, sewerage, transport and educational services for the massively developing cities. In place of these urban services there was of course the cinema — and that supported the bush myth. But for the cinema there were no government schemes in the 1920s to subsidise the bush legend, despite Prime Minister Bruce's assurance that film was the most potent means of attracting attention to 'the greatest country in all the world lacking but the means of development'.[15] In the absence of government support, profitability certainly was discussed, endlessly in the case of the Australian film producers, though even this was systematically collapsed into the master terms of 'individualism', 'enterprise' and 'initiative' which had had such a different meaning among the original bush workers.

The bush legend, which was so consistently a part of Australian silent film production, was by no means, then, a 'dead' myth. The legend was still part of the construction of Australian reality for very broad sections of the public. This is not to suggest that the legend was 'natural', either in a sense that it was an uncoded, direct representation of Australian 'reality', or in the sense that it arose naturally or spontaneously from an entire community. On the contrary, it can be argued that the bush legend was consistently manipulated (as in the case of the Paramount editorial) as part of a hegemonic ideology; and that as an ideological communication the legend has been consistently structured toward a preferred interpretation, one sympathetic to the current ruling faction.

There are two things to consider here: the first is the way the bush values were structured thematically — that is, in what systematic ways they were put into tales of heroes and villains; the second is to ask which social group was most powerful in manipulating these themes.[16]

In the late nineteenth century there were a number of versions of the bush ideal competing for hegemony. The squatters' identity lay with imperial Britain, both culturally (in terms of their furnishings, their daydreams and, if they were sufficiently educated, their art and reading), and economically, through the whole apparatus of expanding technology and finance. They despised Jefferson's 'small landholder' ideal as they did Locke's belief that property rights should depend on the labour a man put into the land. On the contrary, they tended to regard selectors as a 'horde of thieves' incapable of the *civilisation* the squatters had imported and painstakingly rekindled in a hostile land. The fight with selectors over the land led to heavy debt and a one-sided dependence on the city banks which was an early and potent reason for the fostering of the 'urban parasite' critique. The squatters saw themselves as defending a patriarchal civilisation, based on notions of responsibility and deference, against the urban *divisiveness* of 'class' legislation which sought to establish a new, urban-based, ruling class. In the last resort, the squatters defined their position as the civilising centre between the wasteland they had found and the new threat of the cities.

The class that they rightly saw as most threatening to their traditions was that of country-town entrepreneurs (storekeepers, millers, newspapermen, professionals) led by the metropolitan middle class of the capital cities. There were the adherents of the age of reason — Locke's ideas of labour, desire for mobility, belief in science, technology, the survival of the fittest, civilising the land by settlement, individual self-improvement, progress, moderate egalitarianism and religion. The urban agrarians argued that it was the squatters with their caste-like plantation economy who widened class divisions, and they fought for the application of science ('iron rails' through the bush), egalitarianism (land settlement acts) and self-improvement to bring about a more consensual community. On the other hand they were also afraid of working-class 'divisiveness' (meaning aspirations to social mobility similar to their own). As Waterson notes, having destroyed the squatters' power, they protected themselves against the bush workers and proletariat beneath them, and by the 1890s their radicalism was a thing of the past. So these, too, saw themselves as the civilising mediating point between two extremes: in this case the colonial caste system and proletarian revolution.

The urban middle class provided the strategies of the civilising consensus: labour, self-improvement, progress, religion, school, the home. But it was the farmers who provided its Australian content. Waterson notes that the importance of the family to this group was utterly functional — without free family labour no selector could hope to succeed. Because of this a crucial link between the notions of family and those of labour and a yeoman colony were forged. Though farmers were in effect 'small businessmen in an age of rapidly expanding capitalist enterprise' their *local* dependence (on miller and storekeeper) for credit, and their relative autonomy in terms of what they did on their own land, enabled the farmers to deny the larger connection with a world capitalist system, and replace it with an opposition: the purity of country family labour against the banks and other city parasites. It was easy for farmers to believe, in the good times, that their success depended on their efforts alone, and in times of depression to blame the banks which appeared, in moments of imminent failure, 'as soulless and merciless as bloodsuckers'.[17] Paradoxically, then, both the squatters and their enemies the selectors promoted the notion of the city as a vampire through their necessary ties with finance capitalism. For the selector, that apparently self-dependent family farm and home was an oasis of purity between rapacious squatters on the one side and parasitic financiers on the other.

The successful hegemony of the new capitalist class was based on its ability to delude possibly itself and certainly the farmer-selector and working classes that the authentic Australia was a new popular-consensual civilisation in which class (defined as monopoly) was a thing of the squatter past.[18] And the settler's dream of a piece of land, a home and a working family became the key icon in the hegemonic myth.

It is also indicative of the power of this ruling that even after the 1890s, when interest politics at last became overt and institutionalised with the depression, the shearers' strikes, the rise of the Labor Party and the Farmers' Alliances, that the organic, anti-divisive community continued to be valorised by the vast majority as the key to civilisation. The middle-class belief that what was good for one section was good for all, combined with fervent hostility towards the idea of class or sectional parties, continued to dominate the broader public mind. Certainly the 'harmony of interests' assumptions were weakened, first by the class warfare of the 1890s and later by the widespread conflicts generated by the First World War. But significantly, the main planks of both the new Labor and Country parties derived a great deal from the consensus legend. The capitalistic Labor Party was dedicated, like the various anti-squatter interest groups of old, not to class war, but against monopoly of land, to which it had added monopolies of financiers and big business. The Country Party, which both ideologically and tactically[19] rejected sectionalism, preferred the familiar displacement of class opposition into the opposition of city and bush, in which real economic interests (shorter working hours in the cities, complaints about more being spent on city and rural transport and facilities) were absorbed into (hidden beneath) the old image of the 'soft-life' cities sucking, vampire-like, the country's economic blood from its heart — the labour on the land.[20]

From this brief historical survey of the generation and maintenance of the bush legend we can draw certain facts crucial to our study of Australian cinema:

1. That the key opposition was that between the 'naturally' organic, and democratic civilisation on the one hand and the divisiveness of class and urban-industrial society on the other.

2. That the struggle for progress was not thought of in terms of class struggle but was aimed against 'unfair' monopolies.

3. That the structure of the various rural groups' legend was the same in each case, even though the content was different. The organic consensus was defined as a place of mediation and synthesis between barbarous forces on either side. Thus:

Squatters' legend
wilderness/ patriarchal civilisation/ urban divisiveness

Urban-agrarian legend
caste system/ rational civilisation/ proletarian revolution

Selectors' legend
squattocracy/ privatised farm civilisation/ city rapacity

4. That the hegemonic fraction which emerged by way of the bush legend and which was well established by the beginning of the twentieth century, was the country-city entrepreneurial group.

Each of these aspects of the bush legend was significant for the Australian film industry in the 1920s.

1. The most systematic strategy of the cinema industry in protecting and promoting its 'pioneering' status was the populist consensual politics adopted by *Picture Show* in 1919. This strategy, though becoming more cynical and manipulative as time went on, was always premised on the 'natural harmony of interests' of public, trade and industry against ignorantly divisive and rapacious external forces, such as the trade unions, governments and pressure groups.

2. The major obstacle to the development of the Australian production industry was seen by some to be unfair monopoly, the American 'octopus', rather than the systematic workings of national and international capitalism; and by others to be the 'monopolies' created by government legislation, union organisation, or the independent exhibitors' buying circuits, whenever these threatened the status quo.

3. The central thematic structure which generates the narratives, in all their diversity, of Australian silent cinema is this one of antithesis and synthesis:

under-cultured (nature)/country culture/over-cultured (city)
The structure is homologous, in its mediation of the true 'bush' between country barbarity and city rapacity, with each of the bush legends we noted above.

4. It was still, in the cinema of the early 1920s, the urban entrepreneurs who manipulated the consensus in the interests of their own hegemony. The parallel between the entrepreneurial professionals of the late nineteenth century and the dominant circle around Stuart Doyle, W.A. Gibson and their peers at Hoyts was close in a number of important ways:

First, the core values of the nineteenth-century hegemonic group of 'improvement—progress—settlement' (by which was meant the transformation of wilderness into commerce) were also the core values of Doyle and Gibson.

Second, the entrepeneurs' place in the system of social stratification, as originally a service group who were seeking to become masters, was similar.

Third, as in the nineteenth century, the cinema élite of the 1920s manipulated values associated with 'democracy' and the 'working class' against the conservative, British-Imperial oriented upper-middle class, while at the same time stopping the push for an 'open market' once they had attained a monopolising position.

Fourth, the cinema élite used the Australian producers in the same way that the earlier entrepreneurial élite used the selectors: to continue the myth of a 'magnificent reward' through pioneering struggle, individual initiative and perseverance long after it was possible. Waterson says of the rural middle class who achieved affluence by 1900 that, once secure:

> they could afford to cultivate their now irrelevant myths to conserve what had been won . . . Physical toughness, strong muscles, perseverance, faith in nineteenth-century work values, religious justification for economic success and tremendous pioneer belief in progress — these values saturated the social and mental climate.[21]

With the exception that they no longer used religious arguments, that quotation could apply virtually word-for-word to the cinema élite of the 1920s. Yet in any situation of impending quota legislation, producers were suddenly no longer pioneers but city vampires sucking cash out of the country where, as the editor of *Everyones* put it, 'in the past, rich squatters have proved easier victims than Macquarie Street doctors to the film promoter's guile'.[22]

Finally there is one more significant parallel. Waterson speaks of farmers and country entrepreneurs as:

> pathetic marionettes dancing on imperial strings, mere extensions of mowing machines cutting grain to provide Europe with cheap raw material. The metropolis won, but for a while . . . hard work and ambition obscured this fact.[23]

As the 1930s were to show, Doyle's empire was by no means autonomous either, and he and his Australian peers were also seen to be marionettes providing easy profits to a foreign metropolis, only now the empire was American and the financial strings increasingly held, not by London banks, but Wall Street.

11

The Legend: Films of the Bush

In *The Breaking of the Drought* the metropolis does not win. To ask why this is so, is not simply to ask what elements of the bushworkers' legend the film invokes but, in the light of the last chapter, which central elements of the history behind the legend it represses.

Three repressed elements in that history are particularly significant — the role of country towns, class hostility, the dominance of non-family life — and they are integrally related in generating the ideological closure of the 'bush' films.

1. As we have seen, the role of country-town entrepreneurs was central in the struggle for dominance. Yet the historian D.W. Meinig has rightly described the country township as the 'forgotten feature of the frontier'.[1] Country towns did not appear after the pioneers, but were an integral part of the whole frontier process. Indeed, in many cases the country town preceded the selectors, since they often came on to the scene to service the needs of the squatters who were already there. The functional reasons for the importance of the country town are however less important than their ideological significance, since it was here that the legend of a 'true' Australia, 'new granary of Empire, farmed by yeomen and supplied by respectable shopkeepers representing the very vanguard of Progress'[2] was forged.

Yet this location (the kernel of ideological production of the legend) is missing from Australian 'bush' films. Unlike towns in the American Western, the Australian country town is seen neither as a centre of power nor as a source of community feeling. Where the town exists at all, it tends to signify that even the country villain is really not of the bush since he drinks there, and drink is located icongraphically as a thing of the cities in Australian silent films. Country towns act as places of purgatory for heroes in transition, as in *The Man From Kangaroo* or *A Girl of the Bush*, from the city to a true country identity. Unlike the more complete purging in nature, as in *The Breaking of the Drought*, their purgatory is rather a matter of temporary suffering, of mistakes which complicate the progress of the narrative, and which draw on the country town's ambivalence as a place between country and city. Just occasionally, as in *A Girl of the Bush*, there is a hint of the monopoly rapacity of the country storekeeper. But it is never generalised and quickly forgotten. More often than not, the country town is suppressed altogether.

2. Ward points out that there was class hostility between pastoral workers and their employers in the nineteenth century, and yet the conditions of labour and natural hazard tended to repress their hostility except against absentee landlords. *The Drought*, in its overt theme, exploits this ambivalence, asserting at its start the truth of bush cooperation in the face of natural hazard, exploiting in its narrative development the half-truth of cooperative community gathered around the family of the station owner, and concluding with the untruth that in the country nature bestows its gifts without favour of class. What is suppressed, is the question of theft of one man's labour by another.

Yet theft *is* a recurring theme in Australian films; indeed it is the principal theme of the two main generic variants of the bush subject: the bushranger film and the bush–city film. Australian cinema began and prospered with films about bushrangers and had nothing to say (apart from passing dismissive comment in *The Drought*) about shearers' strikes. This is not surprising, given that the late nineteenth-century bushranging theme was locked into the opposition of farmer (and pastoral worker) to the monopolist squatters, an opposition which we have seen to be a key but not radical strategy of that time.[3] In contrast shearers' strikes represented a genuinely radical threat which disturbed farmer and country entrepreneurs alike. Neither is it a coincidence that at the time when the cinema entrepreneurs were establishing themselves in monopolies as strong as the squatters had ever been, bushranging films, too, declined. Bushranging themes may have displaced class-theft on to individual exploitation, but always with a degree of sympathy, even identifying the hero as one of the oppressed — and this lingered uncomfortably close to the original mark of social exploitation. The more typical displacement of the 1920s was also a safer one — the projection of theft onto the city. This symbolically evoked the larger myth, encompassing more social groups, of the vampire quality of the city in stealing the country's wealth. In Barrett's *A Girl of the Bush*, cattle duffing itself is transferred to the mores of the city: the work of a 'typically' degenerate city man.

3. Sexual promiscuity, gambling and larceny were extraordinarily rife in the country; yet in Australian films they have become icons of city life. The effect of this 'emptying' of country history is to leave a space — which

is systematically filled, not by the history and mores of Ward's rural proletariat (whose outback 'vices' these were), but of the farmer and urban agrarian — the history of family, home, and self-help in the improvement of the land. Taken together these three repressions precipitate the modern Fall: from pristine rural to degenerate urban-industrial society — a myth which, as British cultural historian Raymond Williams has said, is difficult to underestimate in modern social thought:

> It is the main source for the perpetual retrospect to an 'organic' or 'natural' society. But it is also the main source for that last protecting illusion that it is not capitalism which is injuring us but the more isolable, more evident industrial civilisation.[4]

Specifically, in the Australian context, the effect of these three repressions is to hide the site of hegemonic struggle, and therefore negate the notion of 'ideology' for that of simple representation of the 'true country' order; to displace class hostility onto the city–bush opposition; to displace valued communal action from class consciousness (or the equally problematical country-town consciousness) to the more 'natural' community: the family.

The Breaking of the Drought

Joe Gallaway, veteran fighter of strikes and droughts, has a son Gilbert and a daughter Marjorie who symbolise the only contradiction in a homogenous world: between the city and the country. Marjorie, as we first see her, is a smiling woman, equally at home herding cattle on horseback as she is in the more 'feminine' delight of 'tending a garden which seems so out of place in all this drought-striken area'. From the beginning she is the sign of the bounty (amidst a 'sea' of cattle, in a beautiful garden) which human labour (herding, tending) can extract from arid nature. She is the sign of *culture* — and that culture is located in the country: as she later tells her father, 'I have no desire for city life. My place is here with you.'

'Here' — country life — as the following sequence shows us, is defined as the proximity of two 'types'. Tom Wattleby,[5] who signifies the active male force transforming the natural wattle paradise into a *productive* storehouse for the world (Tom sells Australian horses to India); and Mrs Gallaway, the passively resistant female force who invests the doorway of their country home with her 'true heart' and blesses this young couple with her smiles while telling them of the tradition they will inherit — of her 'fighting' husband.

There is an immediate cut to Gilbert Gallaway who, unlike the first shot of his sister, is neither smiling nor in the country — nor, despite the university background, at work. The titles inform us that he is studying 'medicine — and other things in Sydney'. As with his sister, the first shots show him quickly mobile, but compared with Marjorie's working horse, here a chaffeur-driven car symptomises his effete life. He is taken by an 'all-round blackguard', Varsey Liddleton, to the apartment of Olive Lorette, 'a woman of pleasure', who 'surrounds herself with many luxuries at the expense of the young and foolish'.

So, as in the preceding sequence, a threesome is established in which the young receive 'tradition' from the older. But this is a very different tradition, signified by Olive, the degraded physical object passed on by Varsey (in contrast to Mrs Gallaway's spiritual gift to Tom and Majorie). The opposition is over-emphasised by the iconography: the outdoor country freshness and natural flowers of Marjorie against the opulent potted ferns and vased flowers of Olive: her lapdog against Tom's work-dog and horse. The city vampires are about to suck the country's lifeblood — and the seduction begins with another iconographic sign. In the bush genre the pipe *always* connotes bush fortitude and purity (Gilbert only smokes one when he has defeated the city vices and, as a sundowner, boils his billy on a country road); the cigarette *always* connotes the city of vice and seduction. Olive lights a cigarette, puts one into Gilbert's mouth, and brings her luscious mouth close as she lights his cigarette with hers. White smoke bursts from this coupling like semen: the city seduction is complete.

The film continues with the systematic juxtaposition of these character-actants, spaces and values. First, the city penetrates the country, as Varsey persuades Gilbert to take him home to Wallaby. This 'reconnaissance of the villain'[6] has several important narrative values. In terms of plot development it 'naturalises' (via, for example, human actants, psychological motivation) the mythical disunity, city exploitation of the country, of which Varsey signifies the representative figure: the absentee landlord who sucks the real country workers dry from a distance. At the same time it establishes the two characters who learn of the deception, Marjorie and Tom, in the narrative role of 'helper',[7] which they will carry through to the end of the film: the woman with passive horror, the man with active financial support.

Secondly, the insertion of a *moral* dearth within a physical drought is established for the first time as the camera tracks ahead of Gilbert and Varsey riding while, intercut, we see naturalistic representations of the

(v)

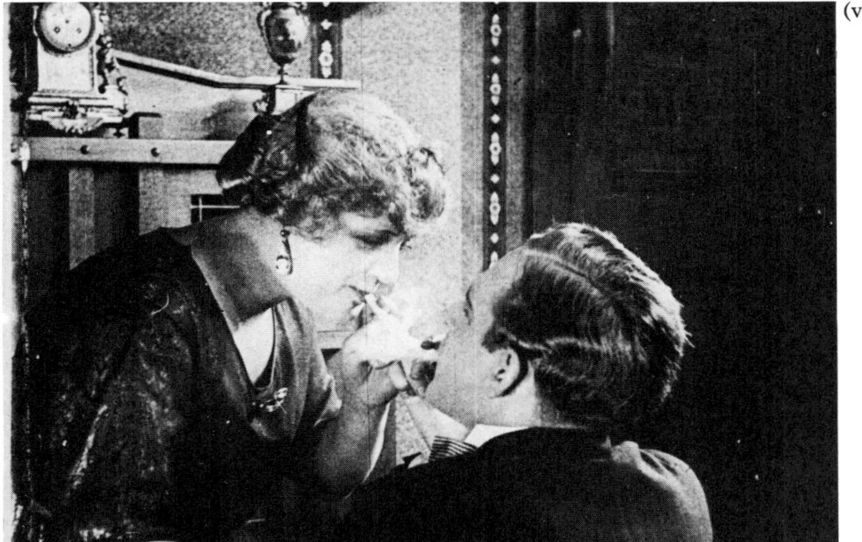

(vi)

National Film Archive

Gestural and iconographic codes of melodrama: the cigarette and city seduction, the pipe and country authenticity. Frame enlargements of Olive and Gilbert in *The Breaking of the Drought*

(i)

(ii)

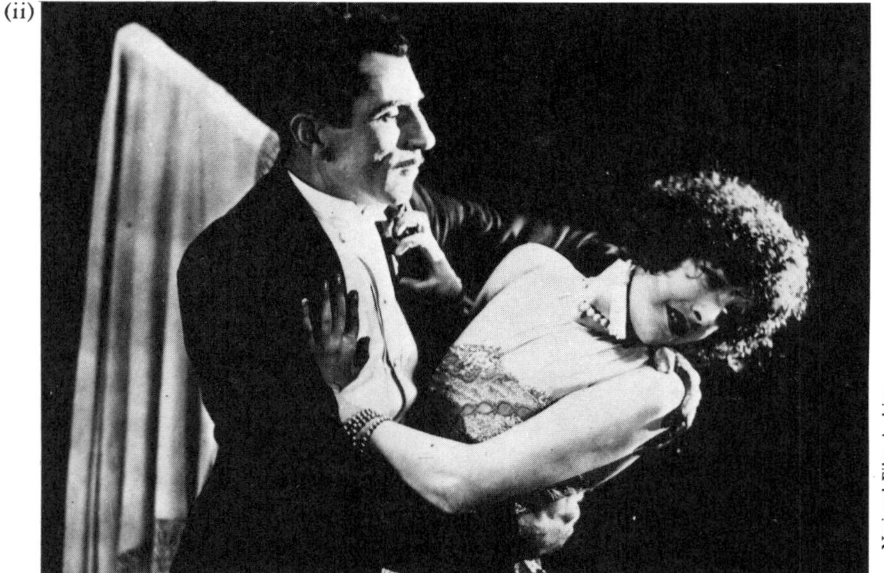

National Film Archive

(i) The city villain and vamp and (ii) the city villain and heroine. The latter's very different gesture tells us she will end up happily married in the bush. Frame enlargements from *Sunrise*

(i)

(ii)

National Film Archive

Flowers of the bush and city: (i) Marjorie and (ii) Olive, frames from *The Breaking of the Drought*

(i)

(ii)

National Film Archive

Essential bush and city social gatherings: Molly breaking in a wild brumby and Marjorie on the road to hell, 'Let's be merry tonight!': frames from *The Breaking of the Drought*

drought: a man feeding grain to the starving sheep, the empty dam, skeletons of sheep covered with black crows. Gilbert, unconsciously, unites the natural (crows ripping sheep), personal (Varsey exploiting him) and social (city exploiting country) as he tells Varsey: 'Our lean times are fat times for those', pointing to the black birds.

Thirdly, a generic staple of the Australian bush film is introduced: the independent woman, Molly Henderson, breaking a wild pony in the stockyard. Watched by the two city men, she calls this 'fun'; and we are reminded of the contrast with city women's fun as Gilbert tells Varsey: 'Rather a different sort of girl from our city friends.' The latter cynically replies, 'My dear Gilbert, there are two sorts of women: good ones and bad ones. The bad ones are never found at home, and the good ones are never found out'. In the city 'out' invariably means the 'bohemian' dance — champagne, cigarette smoke, male voyeurism, jazz and frenetic coupling — where Marjorie later will nearly lose her soul as she drinks 'to the Pursuit of Pleasure'.

The night-time dance is the essentially urban social gathering; the corresponding event for the country is the day-time brumby breaking. The dance and the horse-breaking are paired 'figures' which, as the narrative theorist A.J. Greimas has pointed out,[8] are stable units of content that invest the formal narrative structure with semantic meaning. The dance, which is a central 'figure' in literature and film, is a unit of the narrative which contains several permanent 'semes'.[9] (i.e. minimal units of meaning at a given level). Thus as Greimas notes, the dance implies:

1. 'temporality', in so far as it is a reunion which lasts a certain length of time: (e.g. 'While his friend was at the ball, he went . . .');
2. 'spaciality', in so far as a dance is at a place ('Crossing the ballroom she noted . . .');
3. 'gesturality', in so far as dancing is an action that takes place ('Because the ball had tired her, she . . .');
4. 'sociality', in so far as the dance brings people together ('The ball gave her a chance to forget her loneliness');
5. 'Sexuality', in so far as the dance calls into play male—female relationships: (as in Marjorie's comment later to her brother, 'You've had your fling, Gilbert. I'm going to have mine').

These sets of semes are, as it were, the formal kernel of a figurative unit, and each is capable of being realised in action variously according to context. It is clear, for example, that the dance in John Ford's western films has exactly the same kernel of semes as it has in Barrett's *The Breaking of the Drought*, or in Fritz Lang's *Metropolis* (1927) but these are actualised in a very different way. In Ford, dances are signs of legitimate 'frontier' familial sexuality. They are civilised social gatherings carved out of a wilderness by pioneering endeavour, gestures of vigour and perseverance, both spatially related to and temporally threatened by the rigours of the desert beyond. In *The Breaking of the Drought* and *Metropolis*, by contrast, the sexual presentation of women dancing in front of a primarily male audience marks in that separation between a mere body (woman) and a voyeuristic eye (man), the divisiveness of an urban–industrial civilisation which has shattered the 'natural' organic wholeness and community of pre-industrial society.[10] The lightly clad woman dancing 'La Sheila' at the Hurricane Club later in *The Drought* prefigures the near-naked Maria's dance at Yoshiwara in *Metropolis*, just as Marjorie's 'If Hell claims us at dawn, at least let us be merry tonight' prefigures Maria's 'Dance, dance, dance . . . Let's watch the world going to the devil'. In both films the time is insistently located as the modern one (the 1920s, the jazz age, flapperdom) of surface sensation and spiritual loss; the space — a fragile lighted chamber of frippery that masks a monstrous urban ghetto; the gesture — an aimless dash as jigging couples trip in and out of frame before a determinedly static camera; the sociality — (hollow) and masking a real sexual division and exploitation.

However, what marks the Australian bush film as a distinct genre is that the dance figure is inflected in relation to the figure of the stockyard. From the example of these films we can extend Greimas's argument to suggest that figures present themselves in opposed pairs, a structural relationship in which one semantic unit is defined in terms of another. Thus:

Stockyard		*Dance*	
Temporality:	traditional/authentic (day)	Temporality:	modern/inauthentic (night)
Spatiality:	country openness	Spatiality:	urban claustrophobia
Gesturality:	functional, productive	Gesturality:	frenetic, cosmetic
Sociality:	natural, equal, motivated by ability	Sociality:	artificial, divisive, motivated by wealth
Sexuality:	independent	Sexuality:	exploitative

The sequence then, in which Varsey and Gilbert watch from the stock-rails as Molly Henderson, champion horsewoman, masters a pony which few others can even hold relates to the sequence later on in which Varsey and Gilbert again watch a woman perform — when it is the other 'innocent

(i)

(ii)

National Film Archive

The function of women: the city, dancing for men — surface sensation and spiritual loss *(The Breaking of the Drought)*; the country, sexuality displaced onto productivity *(A Girl of the Bush)*

(i)

(ii)

National Film Archive

Paired 'figures' of melodrama: (i) the stockyard (*The Breaking of the Drought*) and the city dance (*The Shattered Illusion*)

(i)

(ii)

National Film Archive

Dances in city and bush: (i) as in *The Breaking of the Drought* the city *mise-en-scène* of *The Romance of Runnibede* heavily emphasises exotic and artificial ferns and flowers. Compare (ii) the humorous functionality of mateship in the (missing) shearer's ball sequence from *The Man from Kangaroo*.

National Film Archive

Spectacle melodrama: Gilbert purged by his survival of a natural country hazard, the bushfire: *The Breaking of the Drought* country miss', Marjorie, who risks at the dance a spiritual loss as great as Molly's physical gain.

Fourthly, this section of the film introduces us to an attenuated representative of the labouring class: Damper, whose very name depends on the baby-talk of his master's children. Damper has a number of functions. First, and typically for films of this period, as a member of an inferior class, caste or race, he provides the film with its rather studied humour (falling over suitcases, dressing as a maid,[11] cheeking hotel doormen in a caricature of class consciousness, and being appropriately dim-witted). Second, as a member of the working class eager to try the temptations of the city, his failure there combined with his country 'wit' and perspicacity, function, rather as in Molière's servants, to comment on the traumas and follies of his betters. It is Damper who remarks on the 'peroxided, powder-faced, portable fairies' that are the bane of his master Gilbert's city life. In action as well as in name, Damper keeps a space open in the foul and threatening air of the city for basic country qualities when the 'real' country people, the squatters, are symbolically threatened with extinction. As the down-and-out Joe Gallaway tells him later in their city tenement, 'Damper, the sight of you brings back memories of the dear old bush, with the scent of gum leaves and wattle blossom all around.' So it is appropriate that it is Damper who carries their bush salvation, as the supposed donor of Tom's secret gift. Appropriate, but also a cynical reversal of history as the real theft of labour becomes, in this film, no more than the *apparent* bestowal of property on the squattocracy by the rural working class.

A fifth operation which the 'reconnaissance of the villain' establishes is the only real puzzle of the narrative: what is the youthful mistake which prevents Tom from proposing to Marjorie? As Roland Barthes[12] has pointed out in *S/Z*, the code of puzzles (or hermeneutic code) is crucial to the narrative syntax, in that a story exists only in the fact that, having begun *actions*, it raises puzzles, imposes barriers to the answering of those questions via the use of lures, traps and equivocations, until at last all is resolved and the narrative ends. The code of action (proairetic code) is less or more deeply immersed in the hermeneutic code; with the murder mystery being close to complete immersion in so far as the major action — the murder — has already taken place before the story starts, or at the very beginning, while the resolution of the puzzle takes up the entire plot. However, *The Breaking of the Drought* is not a murder mystery. The murder of Olive is not really a feature of the hermeneutic code at all — there is no puzzle about it — but relates symbolically to what Barthes calls the 'cultural code', the system of social values drawn on by the film text to give it meaning — in this case, the country–city opposition. The mystery in *The Breaking of the Drought* is consequently a much weaker device than both the main action, which is always entirely explained to us by the inter-titles, and the symbolic reference. In fact, the central puzzle of the film is developed so weakly that it operates as a direct feature of the cultural code. We later learn that the 'youthful mistake', was Tom's seduction by the city marriage to the self-same Olive Lorette. Tom tries to buy his freedom, but melodrama intervenes and Olive is murdered by Varsey. With considerable moral dexterity, Tom abandons his materialistic attitude to Olive for a spiritual one: 'Poor frail piece of clay! Your mad race on the road to ruin is ended. May God forgive you, as I do.'

Textually what occurs here is the complete domination of the hermeneutic code by the modal *form* of melodrama, which, in its simple assertion of good and evil, asserts the cultural code *par excellence*. Beyond the universalised purity–vice signification there is also a socially and temporally specific one, marked by the gap between Tom's 'youthful folly' and his later 'saintliness' in saving Gilbert, Marjorie and the Gallaway home and way of life. Tom's early folly generalises Gilbert's seduction as the mark of a certain kind of society — the city — and a certain era. And Tom's spiritual regeneration equally parallels Gilbert's when he is purged, not so much by his experience in the city, but by his survival of a *natural* country hazard — the bush fire. We can be sure, because of Tom's example, that Gilbert's spiritual resurrection will be both personally complete and *socially* transformative: that the tradition of the past is safe in the future of Australia's country youth — in other words, that the current city malaise *can* be cured. The resolution of Tom's puzzle is so overladen with this cultural signification as to virtually sink from sight as a syntactic device in the narrative of the film.

The 'reconnaissance of the villain', the penetration of the country by the city, thus sets in motion a number of syntactic, semantic and iconographic devices which the second part of the film, the penetration of the city by the country, does much to resolve and close off. Gilbert's degree is completed, but instead of working, he uses his parents' money to set Olive up in an expensive flat, which is endlessly populated by bohemian bludgers who are thus subsidised by Varsey's continuing exploitation of country money and labour. Class differences (marked by Damper becoming down-and-out while Gilbert lives the high life) are displaced onto urban divisiveness — city temptations are the cause of both their falls. The *economic* myth (of the city vampire sucking the country's hard-earned wealth) is naturalised by its representation as *sexual* exploitation (the country man's physical potency sapped by a horde of city women). All this provides a perfect alibi for the hidden face of that economic myth: the myth of country classlessness. Physical exploitation is not supposed to happen in the country where people work together; they add to each other socially and economically rather than physically taking away.

At the same time the film's conflation of social and natural threats devalues the social divisiveness of class conflict. If strikes and drought are of one category, then the natural response to both is seen to be mateship and communal opposition. The effect is a strongly ideological statement under the guise of 'natural' law: man's organic cooperation in the face of adversity (a *male* principle) will easily offset his selfish lusts (subject to an unfettered *female* principle). The real 'sin' of the city is that, in its relation to the manly country, it asserts itself in the vamp role, instead of accepting the 'natural' female role of dependence. The city, then, must be turned from its exploitative role into a suitably subordinate one; and it *will* be so reformed because of the natural superiority of male mateship in the country to female seduction in the city. That, in the end, is the process of natural selection through which the true Australian environment will raise a superior breed of men to the whole city-born civilisation of the old world. And that, ultimately, is the point of juxtaposed 'droughts' of city and bush which the film systematically presents until its closure.

The degradation of Damper and Gilbert is intercut with the rotting bones and carcasses of the country. 'Lean steers upon the cattle camp and in the yard . . . Battle days and hungry days and hard.' The result of Gilbert's sinking in the town, is that his father sinks in the country: 'friendly possession' is taken of his property by a monopolising pastoral company. But while the natural drought works to intensify the moral one, it also contains a difference. Because, as well as 'hungry days' there are 'battle days', and as well as the 'dreariness' of drought there is also the 'sweat'. The difference is carried iconographically by the semantic location of horses. They mean 'work' as Joe and Marjorie Gallaway battle for survival with the cooperation of their men; but 'idleness' in the following sequence at Randwick racecourse where 'the worship of the horse . . . Australia's favourite idolatry' marks the site of mass voyeurism and private speculation.

From this point to the end of the film there are three sequences of high melodrama in the city, each an intense elaboration of the social drought. Each is intercut with a crippling natural hazard, and yet in every case the latter opens out to a physical and moral regeneration. The first occurs after the Gallaway family are confronted with Gilbert's 'city' inhospitality and

(i)

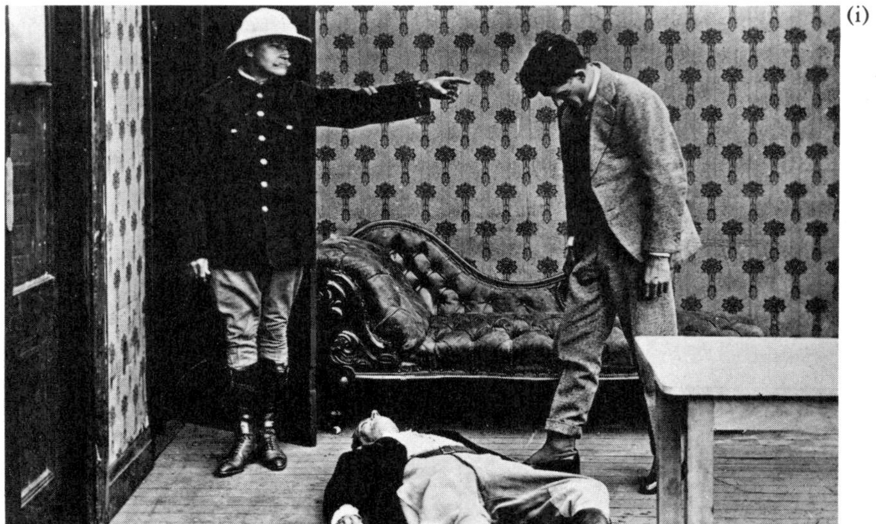

(ii)

National Film Archive

Melodrama and naturalism: (i) the arrest of Tom in *A Girl of the Bush;* and (ii) one of the previously unfilmed areas of Sydney where Joe Galloway struggles with the lowest of jobs in *The Breaking of the Drought* debauchery. The sequence rises in melodramatic intensity as Marjorie, impelled by 'love for her weak-willed brother' warns him that his evil ways have been discovered, and Gilbert grasps a pistol. The rich set erupt into the house and are stunned into immobility by the sudden entrance of Joe Gallaway, arm erect to heaven: 'I'm the father of the lad you all helped bring to ruin. It was on such as you he has wasted the money that should have kept his mother in comfort when I take the last track'. The detective seizes Gilbert's shoulder with melodramatic composure, and the scene ends with Marjorie and her mother saving Gilbert from the law. A cut moves from this atmosphere of moral intensity to the country where 'the hot air scorched like a furnace blast from the very mouth of hell to a blinding dust storm Back 'o Beyond'. We see mirages which mock with promises as empty as those of Varsey, Olive and the Bohemian set. But the hope that lies in the action of the two country women at the end of the previous sequence is matched here: some graziers do survive, and we see, as a token of the film's ultimate endorsement of plenty, fat sheep in rich pastures. Then follows the narrative device which will bring the Gallaways back to those pastures: Tom Wattleby with his horses, his successful return from India, and his redeeming plan put into action.

The second sequence of grand melodrama then begins. Mother sews desperately in a city slum apartment; Joe struggles with the lowest of jobs; Marjorie returns exhausted from seeking work. They comfort each other in despair and desolation, and Joe, stretching his arm out in supplication, complains: 'The drought of misfortune, will it ever break?' Enter 'millionaire' Damper, and Joe is right to scent in him the purity of the 'dear old bush' because he is the agent of Tom, the country man whose *work* profits will bring them home.

In the next major sequence Tom saves Marjorie from the Hurricane Club; this is followed by the third sequence of high melodrama, as Olive is strangled by Varsey. Tom breaks in and Varsey leaps to his death from the window. The film cuts to the bush where Gilbert, 'relieved of his evil genius . . . seeks to expiate his follies and sins in the clear bracing air of the Outback'. Caught in a raging bush fire which follows the natural drought as naturally as Gilbert's purgation follows the urban one, he, like everyone else, is saved by Tom. Only one action is needed now to break both natural and social droughts: Gilbert is received back into the family by his father and at once the rain comes, 'The drought is broken', and half the screen shows the abundance of water while the other half makes the spiritual connection plain:

'Every drop a golden rhyme is
Every shower a stanza strong
And each day of raining time is
Canto time of God's great song'.

Natural and human abundance, as a result of all this adversity, combine and 'God's great song' is in effect that of the humble old rural worker who comes to his door, with arms stretched high: 'Won't the boss be pleased! One shower of rain makes the clip worth double'. Slow pans and tilts reveal the natural abundance as 'cattle and sheep wax fat in luxuriant pastures', horses pull carts filled with happy children through lush fields where we see workers sewing bags of wheat 'There's a record harvest of the golden grain.'

It is man's labour that has harnessed the extremes of the Australian climate. This notion of a *humanised* and *cultured* nature is marked at the beginning of the film by Marjorie, her hair flowing free, tending her garden in the midst of the wilderness, and at the end by the close up of a little girl (we do not know whose child she is and it does not matter) tending a baby lamb. Such spiritual fulfilment brings the film to its close: Tom and Marjorie, united, going forward, on their horses, into the future of the bush.

> 'Here's to the man Back O' Beyond. May his horse be sure, and his pipe well lit, for he's the backbone of our grand Commonwealth. The drought is broken. The land is green again'.

The Breaking of the Drought, like most narratives, traces a course from an initial lack to the final fulfilment, from the cracked earth, starving sheep and desperate men to the overflowing water casks, rich pastures, fat animals and productive work of people in a sun-kissed land. But in this particular film that final plenitude is dense and over-determined. The film poses parallels, relations and oppositions between natural and social affairs. There is a relation of implication established by cross-cutting between human (urban) and natural drought; and there is a causal relationship, premised as 'work', between natural and social fulfilment. The narrative establishes the veracity of the opening shots: Australia is indeed a land of extremes. But it has located them in a human landscape. Separated, man and nature are harsh and solipsistic: drought and dust storms in the country, depravity and exploitation in the city. Together, man and nature produce a fulfilment which is both spiritual and physical.

	Lack	*Plenitude*
Natural:	Drought	Harvest
Domestic:	Divided family	United family
Social:	Country community threatened	Country community restored
Moral:	Gilbert depraved, thus threatening the dignity of his father, the courage of his mother, the virtue of his sister	Gilbert reformed; dignity, courage, virtue upheld.
Economic:	Property threatened	Property restored
Historical:	Old tradition lost	Regenerated tradition

Thus whereas the *separation*:

Natural landscape (harsh, exacting)	(Urban) man (selfish, solipsistic)

produces droughts both physical and moral, the *connection* of man and landscape produces the synthesis which we know as the bush legend: hardened by the adversity of the land, man forges a new civilisation through work and mateship.

A Girl of the Bush

'After unsuccessful prospecting trips, Keane and Denver had 'selected' a strip of country on the 'edge of civilisation', calling it Kangaroo Flat'.

It is a feature of the structure described above that 'the edge of civilisation' is a significant figure, or location of meaning, in Australian films, mainly because it is a narrative space which can be inflected with emphasis on either the toughening, purifying *edge* of culture, or on the *civilising* quality of human society in the wilderness. Australian bush films play backwards and forwards between these two emphases while pretending not to, pretending in other words to a semantic *essence* of the 'bush'.

The first inter-titles suggest, as did the opening shots of *The Breaking of the Drought*, the romance of a new country, a land of choice, potential and contrast — the terrain of droughts and rains which marked the beginning and the end of the earlier film. But the titles also suggest two other things: the small man—pioneer—settler clinging to life on the inner edge of the 'Never-Never'; and the farm station representing culture on the outer edge of civilisation.

The first visual of the film establishes the pioneering *edge* of civilisation: a station in a wilderness, a few trees, rough tracks, burning white roofs, and, as we iris out of this image and into the next, the harshness of that edge is revealed: the crippled Jim Keane. The Never-Never is quickly balanced, however, by the valorisation of culture: despite his horseriding accident Jim still controls the work of the station, and the cultural icons support that comforting notion of purpose and control: the moustache, the pipe that he lights. The next iris-in continues this theme as the notion of dominance and control is given a generational inflection: the smiling, competent horsewoman, Jim's adopted daughter, Lorna Denver.

As in *The Drought*, we are introduced successively to the old pioneer, who will decline as the film continues, and then to his 'flower of the bush', the independent daughter. On each occasion the process of continuity is established and valued in the same way: a smiling girl, a horse, the herding of cattle and sheep. The shots of Jim and Lorna establish parameters of control and confidence with a substance yet to be filled in, and there follows one of the more potent images of natural–cultural plenitude in Australian silent cinema: a solitary horseman and a multitude of sheep which flows across a track and round a lone tree — and, before we iris out to something very different, there is a shot of Lorna riding, a woman who, by her labour and independence, is *part* of this wealth. Jim Keane is crippled on the edge of the Never-Never; Lorna, as these shots of human cultivation show, is a pioneer on the edge of civilisation. That is the mark of generational change and progress.

The fact that Keane is a cripple enables Lorna to appear strong from the start, which raises a key problem of the Australian 'bush' genre. On the one hand it borrowed the cross-cultural narrative root: woman as a weak victim of the villain of melodrama. On the other hand it sought to assert its own Australian inflection: the independent woman. Keane's incapacity enables this ambiguity to be resolved on the surface more easily than in *The Drought* where Marjorie's independence (horsewoman, saviour of her brother) is more ambivalent and, once in the city, decidedly threatened. In *A Girl of the Bush*, Barrett handles the problem with more dexterity. We have (i) Lorna the victim of melodrama, desired by the villain as *property*; and (ii) Lorna the dynamic overseer, representative of *work*.

This familiar opposition between ascribed and achieved qualities complicates the characterisation of Lorna, and is itself carried by an opposition between modal forms — those of melodrama and naturalism. As one resolution to this problem there is another narrative embedded within the main development, incorporating an alternative female discourse — the

(i)

(ii)

National Film Archive

(i) Flowers of the bush; (ii) the bush, natural-cultural plenitude. Still and frame enlargement from *A Girl of the Bush* tale of the seduction and death of a country girl, Mary Burns, at the hands of a city bounder, Oswald Keane.

Jim Keane is a pioneer cripple, a working cripple, not a cripple from birth. In contrast, his nephew Oswald is a moral cripple who does no work. As in our first view of Lorna, we iris-in on Oswald and find him smiling, next to a horse. But the iconography, the social relations and the cultural implications are different. In place of Jim's pipe there is Oswald's small cigar; in place of Lorna's work, Oswald stands idle while a groom labours for him; in place of Lorna's stockhorse, there is the gambling implication of Oswald's racehorse, Moonlight (while the inter-titles carry the familiar city iconography: racecourse, bottles, glasses, dice).

The character Oswald Keane is quickly filled up with a density of semes: he hates the country, does no work, bludges on its men, is a voyeur and seducer of its women (both black and white), can't fight, can't shoot, lies, opens other people's mail, is a rotter, a thief. The function of character is to naturalise the cultural values and meanings from which these emblems derive, in the sense that dominant values (the puritan ethic, the productive country, the vampire-like city and so on) are displaced, re-appearing as individual actions and motivations (this bludging villain, this wholesome working woman) on which the entire narrative is enacted. In melodrama, however, this gathering together of semes is less to do with creating psychologically dense characters than it is in more 'realistic' modes. Melodrama has a representative quality, in which what are so often taken to be stereotypical characterisations are in fact representations of more universal qualities. The clustered semes defining a character are not only one-dimensional (the hopelessly bad villain, Oswald Keane) but are also frequently *metaphors for one another*, part of one paradigm. The 'vampire-like' relation of city to country can thus be represented in a number of ways:

1. Economically: the man of the city bludges on the people of the country — first Jim Keane, and then, after his death, the new owner of the station, Lorna Denver. The typical two-shot is of Lorna working while Oswald sits and watches.
2. Sexually: Oswald seduces the country girl, Mary Burns, and seeks to do the same with Lorna.
3. Perceptually: Oswald is a voyeur of other people's actions, turning the natural country wholesomeness of two women swimming naked at a waterhole into a city-type spectacle. In an important sense this voyeuristic relationship both weakens and defiles the country, stripping its women

of the formless clothes which signify their independence, in the same way that the financier strips the country of its wealth.

4. Culturally: Oswald's inability to shoot or fight are semes defining precisely the parasitic city in terms of the absence of central bush qualities. The city *quality*, in the absence of these skills, is theft — hence the displacement by the film of cattle duffing (from its historical location generated by the rural class system) to the city via Oswald Keane.

5. Phatically: the film repeatedly insists on the importance of communication to the country. 'Mail day is looked forward to by lonely outback people'; 'Twice a week the mail coach supplies a link between civilisation and the settlers on the edge of the Never-Never.' We see the mail going out to that *edge*, and the grain sacks which establish *civilisation* coming back in return. Historically, the expansion of pioneering and country production *was* inseparably related to the development of communication;[13] here again the melodrama converts systematic economic relations into individual actions which themselves are metaphors for universal qualities. It is the breakdown of the telephone which later puts Tom (and therefore the continuance of an entire country order) at risk as he is tried for his life. It also motivates the cross-cutting finale as one group of men round a table (the station hands) seek to communicate Sing Lee's evidence to another group round a table (the jury). Communication in its different forms (telephone, coach and languages — Chinese, English) is seen as the very essence of country life and continuity. This makes Oswald's act of cutting off the mail especially heinous, and it occurs immediately after we see communication operating effectively as the top wire of the boundary fence carries news of the death of Mary Burns to the police: 'Hating work, Oswald attended to the mails — which may be why Lorna received no letters from Tom'. The man who hates work is, of course, also the thief, and here the city's vampire-like interference with the communicative lifeblood of the country enhances the possibility of theft in a very real way. Oswald threatens the potential marriage of Lorna and Tom, which would restore the country patriarchy that the death of Jim Denver has endangered. By intercepting Tom's mail to Lorna, Oswald is able not only to separate them through the suppression of news of the survival of Mary's baby, not only to offer himself as an alternative, but also to create the future physical isolation of Tom which will find him alone, without alibis, over Oswald's dead body.

The city's relation to communication is (quite unhistorically) one of deceit (Oswald's letter to Mary carries false promises of a 'little home' in

(i)

(ii)

National Film Archive

Visual metaphors for the city-as-vampire: bludging in the bush and city — Oswald and Lorna in *A Girl of the Bush*

(i)

(ii)

National Film Archive

Voyeurism in the bush: frames of nude bathing sequence in *A Girl of the Bush* the city) and dependency. The letters which Oswald receives in the city point to the typically degenerate existence there (unpaid bills, solicitors' letters); the letter carrying news of Lorna's successful country inheritance is, in context, simply further evidence of the city's moral poverty as it drops into his drink-sodden tenement room, since it motivates his villainous desire to marry her.

Each of Oswald's 'competences'[14] in villainy is, then, a potential for further action which will be derived from the same paradigm: the parasitic dependence of an effete city on a productive country. The quality of the melodramatic narrative film is therefore its ability either to repeatedly alternate metaphors within this paradigm or to focus the entire paradigm on the screen with great force and economy. This occurs in Barrett's striking shot of the idle Oswald return from the city: we gaze at his back through one window of his carriage as he spies on the quiet communication of Tom and Lorna through the other.

However, the potency of individual images can create difficulties for the text which it has to work hard to overcome. In the sequence that follows the opening one of Lorna and Oswald, Bill Tressle's story of his discovery of Oswald stealing cattle is recounted in flashback to Jim. What we see is Bill, hiding behind a tree, and a shot of what he is looking at: the cattle duffers driving the herd across a creek. The polysemic quality of the image allows alternative decodings, and, given the negative definition of voyeurism which the film will seek to establish, the text now works to establish its own preferred positive reading of this *countryman's* voyeuristic act. First, Bill encounters this scene in the process of his work, in contrast to the later shot of Oswald watching the naked bathers (the relating of two acts of a man stumbling inadvertently upon, and then looking secretly and fixedly at, prized objects — women, cattle — is marked). But the objects Bill contemplates are associated with production, not pure spectacle. Secondly, as though this coding were not enough, the text introduces an inter-title so markedly 'buttonholing' as seriously to risk its interpretation (presumably even in the 1920s) as 'propaganda'. Over a sketch map of Australia, the titles inform us that 'Australians have a great aversion to "putting a man's pot on", but Bill Tressle has a duty to perform'. Immediately following Oswald's kissing of Lorna, and preceding his cattle duffing, the titles act as a link associating the desirable properties of 'Lorna' and 'cattle'. Bill's 'duty' is, implicitly, to warn of the sexual as well as economic theft lurking in the city–bush relation, thus confirming the association already established between country woman and country plenitude. It establishes also, in terms of human motivations, the association

(i)

(ii)

National Film Archive

Bad and good voyeurism: Oswald watches the lovers and (ii) Bill Tressle about to catch Oswald cattle duffing. Frame enlargements from *A Girl of the Bush* between sexual and economic threats to the country (since sexual interference with Lorna will cut off the pure generational progression of the country).

The confrontation between Jim and Oswald that follows confirms the connection, as Jim remarks that he has twice saved Oswald: firstly, from his economic activities (he has paid off his gambling debts); secondly, from his sexual activities (he has saved him from the Aborigines' revenge for interference with their women). Drawing on the mythical placement of the bush as a synthesis between nature and civilisation, the text devalues Oswald for his attachment to the ways of the under-cultured (the Aborigines) and to the ways of the over-cultured (the city).

The attitude to blacks here is a paternalistic one. The history of the white man's exploitation of the blacks' land is displaced onto Oswald. The process of scapegoating leaves a space open for the other white men (the bushmen) not to steal a land, but to create one through their labour. The projection of the city onto the landscape of imperialistic theft, purifies the bush (the true Australia) of the stain of exploitation, and opens the way to the alternative paradigm: the productive country.

Here the melodrama again displaces socio-economic relations by representing them as the suffering of character types who stand for universal qualities: the evil city white man who exploits the primitive blacks, who in turn revenge themselves on the passive, white countrywoman Mary Burns. Thus Mary is twice wronged by the villain: in the loss of her purity, and in the loss of her life. In contrast, true country people mediate between the blacks and the city people, as Jim does, and later as Lorna does in bringing up the child-victim of those two wrongs: of the city which produced a deserting father, and of the blacks who killed its mother.

The double displacement of economic onto sexual relations (in which the city now becomes the scapegoat for imperialistic capitalism) emphasises the centrality of sexual exploitation as a melodramatic representation.[15] This doubling of the seme 'rape' (innocent blacks/innocent women) is marked by the fact that the sequence which introduces Mary Burns immediately follows the story of Oswald's seduction of the gins. Oswald, a thief sexually as well as economically, is located for the first time as 'voyeur', as he waits watching from a distance for Mary's father to leave his home unprotected. The 'reconnaisance of the villain' is followed by deception of the victim as Mary succumbs to his tale of marriage and a city home.

There is a further doubling here: the link, via Oswald's embraces, of Lorna with Mary, which raises the question, beyond that of role duplication referred to earlier, of the rhythmic variation of the central female roles. And this leads beyond the foregoing analysis of *The Drought* and the first few sequences of *Girl of the Bush* which emphasised their ideological conventionality, to questions about the subversive potential of Barrett's films.

Bush Films: from Convention to Subversion

The film theorist Geoffrey Nowell-Smith has pointed out that melodrama differs from tragedy in two fundamental ways: as a mode of address, and in the representation of the hero(ine). Both of these have profoundly to do with sexuality.[16]

Whereas the tragic mode is about kings and princes, and is mainly the address of court intellectuals to lower social orders, melodrama is a mode of address by, to and about the middle class. Like realism (and it is this similarity which allows the conflation of naturalism with melodrama in Barrett's films), melodrama is based on a notion of a world of equals and is addressed to an audience which sees itself as neither possessing power nor dispossessed of power.

> The characters are neither the rulers nor the ruled, but occupy a middle ground, exercising local power or suffering local powerlessness, within the family or small town. The locus of power is the family and individual private property, the two being connected through inheritance.

In a world of such localised proportions, patriarchal right is of central importance, and it is this which provides the main narrative design. Thus: either

(a) the son has to emulate his father in order to inherit his property and his status within the community: for example, in *The Breaking of the Drought* in which the son's *social* regeneration is not enough — only an ordeal by *nature* will enable him to truly emulate and therefore be worthy of replacing his father.

or

(b) a woman inherits, but the question is posed: which man can she rightly pass the property on to by marriage? This is the central device of *A Girl of the Bush*: not only must the girl be pure (hence the ritualised acting out of the results of country impurity in the Oswald—Mary subplot, and hence, too, the apparently absurd textual emphasis on the 'illegitimate' baby separating the 'impure' Lorna from the 'pure' Tom), but the man she marries must be pure too (Tom is strongly associated with country work, visually associated, via the most 'scenic' of all the location shots, with country purity. In addition, the melodramatic device of the false murder charge projects the matter of his purity as a major narrative development). The man she marries must also have a status in the community commensurate with that of the father ('Tom was very popular in the district': the court sequence establishes not only his innocence but also his social standing).

or

(c) the father is evil and the son must grow up different from him in order to justly re-distribute the property. This is *never* a variant in the bush stories (except in a displaced and ambivalent form in bushranging films, such as *Robbery Under Arms*), but for obvious reasons is confined to the city (for example, the two unworthy fathers — one upper class, the other working class — in *Sunshine Sally*).

This familial—patriarchal emphasis means that the central question of law and legitimacy in tragedy: 'Has this man a right to rule over us?', is turned inwards in melodrama to become: 'Has this man a right to rule over a family like ours?'

It is worth noting that both the Barrett films which trace the decline of a patriarchal order conclude with the embryonic marriage of the patriarch's independent daughter and his proven worthy successor. Sexuality, sanctified at last, will work to preserve the right and proper socio-economic order.

Nowell-Smith, in examining melodrama's representation of heroes and heroines, points to the separation, since the romantic period, of 'action' from 'passion' (suffering), with the result that, broadly speaking, the active hero becomes the subject of the Western, and the passive or impotent hero (or more often, heroine) becomes the subject of melodrama. Similarly, another film theorist, Thomas Elsaesser argues that Oedipal and other conflicts in action genres push 'the protagonists forward in an unrelenting linear course' into external actions, 'a jail-break, a bank-robbery, a Western chase or cavalry charge, and even a criminal investigation', all lending themselves to 'psychological, thematised representations of the heroes' inner dilemmas'. In the domestic melodrama, however, 'the range of "strong" actions is limited. The tellingly impotent gesture, the social gaffe, the hysterical outburst replaces any more liberating or self-annihilating action'.[17]

Nowell-Smith and Elsaesser's formulation of the hero(ine)'s representation is particularly helpful in enabling us to understand the peculiarly mixed mode of Barrett's films. While it is certainly the case that in *The Breaking of the Drought* Gilbert's melodramatically impotent gestures, social gaffes (refusal to give hospitality to his family) and hysterical outburst (attempted suicide) are internalised responses to his symbolic 'castration' at the hands of the city vamps, it is also true that his purgation is the result of external action (returning to the country, the bushfire). It is equally the case that the internalised connotations of purity and impurity (generating the actants 'Lorna' and 'Mary') which are symptomatic of melodrama, are at the same time externalised in *A Girl of the Bush*, precisely in one of Elsaesser's 'criminal investigations'. Hence, Nowell-Smith's further elaboration of his argument is both true and not true of these Australian films. He argues that unlike the Western, where the hero is male and the woman only a receptacle (or occasionally a surrogate male), in melodrama a woman is often the protagonist, and where man is a central figure he is often severely impaired (thus Lorna/Gilbert). The reorganisation of the heroic 'space' to allow a greater place for women in melodrama, and particularly to include their 'passion', creates new problems for the text. 'In so far as activity remains equated with masculinity and passivity with femininity the destiny of the characters remain unrealisable'. Each can do no more than live out his or her impairment ('castration').

The problem for women in melodrama, however, is even greater than for men. In what *terms* can they suffer and be active? The suffering and impotence of men (Gilbert in the city) is seen in unproblematical terms, since the definition of masculinity exists (the virility of the bushman). But the suffering and impotence of women (Mary Burns for example) is also seen in masculine terms (desertion of the passive woman by the potent male), a failure to be male which is only redressed by the vengeance of her father. And that, as murder, is itself far more problematical than Gilbert's assertion of masculinity. Mary Burns's problem is in fact doubly located: as a woman and as the daughter of a prospector who does not know when to stop chasing the elusive gold. Jim Keane gives up prospecting, recognising that there is a time to settle down (civilisation); but Mary's father is a 'hatter' (and therefore prone both to low social status and mistakes) because he chooses not to settle down.

Yet this double location of Mary as 'woman' also gives a clue as to how *A Girl of the Bush* resolves the problem of locating the woman of action, Lorna. It is significant that the sequence immediately following Mary's succumbing to Oswald forms the most sustained assertion of country plenitude in the film. In this sequence wealth = work. Lorna in contrast to Mary, is actively involved. *This* is the plenitude which Mary's father neglects and which Mary wishes to leave in favour of the city. This is the authentic civilisation; he lives beyond one edge of it, and she, prey to the

(i)

(ii)

National Film Archive

(i) Country vigour: station and hand at work; (ii) city vigour: Oswald escapes the police. Frame enlargements from *A Girl of the Bush* city vices, is beyond the other edge. This is the synthesis, the place of nature and culture (where clothed black men act as outriders to white men's produce), of tradition and contemporaneity.

The quality of frame composition and naturalistic action in this sequence draws attention to itself, and is typified by an enormously active shot of one worker, on foot, driving sheep which break around him like a heaving ocean, as slow pans and still shots allow maximum movement within the frame. Powerful visuals confirm the richness the titles assert ('658 million pounds of Australian wool annually'). The sequence begins with the profile of a proud ram leading a multitude of sheep over a creek, with cuts to further 'wealth' shots which strongly emphasise multitudinous movement across and within the picture frame. The sequence continues with sustained shots that are emblematic of cultural control, as men force that 'wealth' into enclosures through the narrow hole of a nearby closed gate, next to where Lorna is standing. The sequence concludes with Lorna working (in control of the men) shearing, dipping sheep, until a cart, piled high with bags, crosses the creek accompanied by a black outrider.

The dynamism of this country sequence is maintained in the gambling scene that follows it, establishing the bush-city opposition as a matter of stylistic vigour. Lively cuts between middle-shots, close-ups and extreme close-ups of feet, thrusting hands and two-up action, fill the frame but are contained by the seated circle of men that anchors the movement. The scene explodes outwards as the cops arrive and a contrast is established between the flat-lit police and the silhouetted, strong diagonal of men escaping down corridors and into the open. The following escape is a strongly verticalised image (long windows, drain pipes, buttresses of adjoining walls —but all are slightly tilted). Small figures in an urban landscape are chased down and off sloping roofs by huge energetic policemen who loom suddenly into frame from beneath, the camera holding long enough for these to become small running figures in a landscape too. Men are chased out to the right of the yard, down diagonal shutes, into alleys, forcing the pell-mell movement either directly away from or directly into the camera. There is constraint as one of the gamblers is caught in an alley, humour as a policeman sees feet protruding from under sacking. An unusually strong shot looks down on the taut crouching back of a policeman who, with his feet splayed, head hidden in a white helmet, is looking up, waiting for a man to drop. Finally the heads of Oswald and his friend shoot up over a roof-top wall with two strong diagonals tilting the frame. They escape to Oswald's room for a drink, and the sequence ends.

Counterpoint: Music, Sexuality; Naturalistic Mise-en-scene

Visually, these two sequences provide the strongest oppositions of the film, and they do so by asserting a *naturalistic* mode which acts as rhythmic counterpoint to the seduction melodrama. Elsaesser has argued that melodrama, fundamentally defined, is as much a matter of syntactic variation as of simple thematic continuity. Just as music can be both an element of the theme (belonging to the expressive content) and of the form (acting in some cases as an ironic counterpoint to the highly moralising action), so too can the black-and-white characterisation act as both elements of content and form. On the one hand it can present polar 'stereotypes' of vice and virtue; yet on the other undermine that clear contrast with ironic parallels of characterisation. (Consider, for instance, the voyeuristic parallel between hero and villain in Pakula's *Klute*, or between Oswald and Bill in Barrett's *A Girl of the Bush*.) If developed in a consistent way these 'rhythmic variations' can establish a counter-movement to the main theme.[18]

Elsaesser's interest in melodrama is largely concerned with its potential (especially in American cinema) to 'subvert' the conservative theme, by means of musical and dramatic counterpoint, conflicting *mise en scène*, and so on. Nowell-Smith's interests are the same when he argues that the tendency of melodrama to culminate in a happy end is not unopposed:

> The happy end is often impossible, and, what is more, the audience knows it is impossible . . . The laying out of the problem 'realistically' always allows for the generation of an excess which cannot be accommodated . . .The undischarged emotion which cannot be accommodated within the action, subordinated as it is to the demands of family/lineage/inheritance, is traditionally expressed in the music, and in the case of film, in certain elements of the *mise en scène*.[19]

Australian silent films were, of course, always accompanied by music, thus exemplifying Elsaesser's definition of melodrama as 'a dramatic narrative in which musical accompaniment marks the emotional effects'. In rare instances, the musical scores of these films still exist, as in the case of *The Sentimental Bloke* and *For The Term Of His Natural Life*, but we do not know what music was used for Barrett's films. It is possible to work out the principles involved in its selection, however, by considering the ideas of leading cinema musicians of the day, and there is no doubt at all that accompanying music was seen to have a purely expressive function.

In 1921, the year in which *A Girl of the Bush* was released, Fred G. Mumford, musical director for Harry Musgrove's First National—Tivoli circuit, argued that 'dramatic music' comprised many different movements

> known to the profession and stage directors as Plaintives, Agitatos, Hurrys, Mysteriosos, Themes, Melo-dramatic, and by other titles . . . The greatest effect is got by humouring the situation and closely watching the titles on the screen.[20]

Mumford expressed considerable indignation when a truly subversive accompaniment was heard in a country cinema. *From Manger to Cross* was being screened and as Jesus walked on the water, the pianist struck up with 'A Life on the Ocean Wave'! Another musical director was appalled at the playing of 'A Life on the Ocean Wave' at a death-bed scene. Accompanying music had to be 'suitable'. Thus the 'Plaintive' was music

> for use to describe love and devotion, and is used for dying scenes and all such scenes of tense feeling and poignant grief, and will always be found to be played in a major key . . . The 'Agitato' is a style of music that at once suggests coming trouble of any description, and is usually started very softly and worked to business. This music is always in the minor key and of special character. Then comes 'The Hurry'. Good composition is always minor, and is good for fights, fire, and mob scenes, storms and all situations that require weight behind them . . . The 'Mysterioso' is composed to denote stealthy movements, such as burglary scenes, creepy business, uncanny situations, haunted houses . . .

Thus, to accompany 'a Chinaman of peculiarly sneaky habits and a most unreliable and treacherous nature', Mumford fitted an 'Oriental' theme into a 'Mysterioso' movement, so 'telling the story of the Chinaman's character at once'.

Some sense of how this operated can be seen from the musical synopsis accompanying *For The Term of his Natural Life*, of which the following are extracts from the 85 sequential musical pieces accompanying 111½ minutes of film:[21]

Minutes		*Number*	
1	North End House	3	Rustic Revels
½	Mrs Vickers	10	Chatterbox
½	The convict prison between decks	12	Notte Mysterioso
1	Prisoners talking (overheard plotting by Dawes)	16	Burglar or Spy: Mysterioso
1	The prisoners fight	24	Mysterioso No. 5
1	Two prisoners in saloon (threatening Mrs Vickers and Sylvia)	25	Dramatic Hurry
2	Mother and Daughter (kidnapped) taken ashore by escaped convicts	36	Hurry (I) Arncliffe

Minutes		*Number*	
1	Dawes on island (a time of unusual serenity and fulfillment for him)	37	Poesia Pastorale
2	While at Port Arthur . . .	38	Agitated Hurry: Berge
1	Mrs Vickers's illness (dies)	39	Rhapsody Appassionato
2	John Rex approaches Dawes in prisoner's dock	45	Treacherous Knave
2	Sylvia struggles to remember a great injustice	46	Mysterious Nights
3	Dawes's sensational escape forgotten	50	Dance (Alberts)
	Sylvia outside: Dawes approaches	51	A Love Scene
1	Sylvia's 'Monstrous ingratitude'	52	Dramatic Adagio
3	Sylvia goes on board ship (Storm)	82	Furioso (1)

From this it is evident that though music could be used to prepare audiences for characterisation ('Chatterbox' for example, for the first appearance of Mrs Vickers) and could also be used subjectively ('Love Scene' for Dawes's infatuated approach to the terrified Sylvia, followed by 'Dramatic Adagio' on his rejection), it was always used expressively. This was laid down in terms of 'three fundamental principles':

> 1. Music and pictures should be similar in emotional characteristics.
> 2. The music should be on the same plane of artistic merit as the picture.
> 3. There should be a continuity of musical idea which will create an emotion rather than disjointed and meaningless short sentences which may be supposed to follow the exact action of the picture.[22]

The object of the first principle

> is obvious and generally recognised. If the character and emotional content of pictures and music do not agree the effect of each is to hamper the other, whereas agreement will intensify the effect of both.

The third principle opened up the only dispute about musical accompaniment at the time: whether music should express *every* changing emotion rather than a general mood.

The second principle is the most interesting, since it suggests that far from being used in any 'subversive' way, it was very much part of the move to attract the patronage of a 'better class'. On the principle that 'a picture on a low-art level will draw its own audience', this was an appeal for 'master' music' to capture the elite. As one of Union Theatres' musical directors said, speaking in the tone of his boss Stuart Doyle:

'Love Scene': Dawes' infatuated approach to the terrified Sylvia in *For the Term of His Natural Life* (ii) Vamp in the bush, the iconography of horses and baggy riding breeches: modes of female sexuality in *The Man from Snowy River*

(i) National Film Archive; (ii) *Picture Show*, 1 July 1922, p. 41

> The wonderful advance in presentation has attracted to the picture theatre an entirely new class of audience, which is either the outcome of better pictures or better music, or possibly a combination of both'.[23]

As Barrett's two bush melodramas were screened by Union Theatres, and he himself received his original initiation into the Australian cinema industry as a musical director, we can be sure that music was not used in a syntactically counterpointing way in his films.

But what of the other modes of potential subversion raised by Elsaesser and Nowell-Smith — rhythmic variation via a paralleling of roles and *mise en scène*? Syntactic variation in cinema melodrama is often associated with 'undisplayed emotion' and sexuality, and it is the case that Australian bush films of this period find sexuality a problem. Foregrounding the 'independent woman' made this likely but the contrast of country-pure independence with the sexuality of the city vamp made it certain. In Barrett's films this excess of sexuality is channelled through a process of counterpointing which works both via the *mise en scène* and the paralleling of roles. Woman's sexuality is relocated in a number of ways:

1. First by separating woman's power from woman's sexuality. In both Barrett films there are subordinate female characters who, in different ways, parallel Marjorie Gallaway's and Lorna Denver's roles. Molly Henderson, featured forcing down and vanquishing a wild brumby between her thighs, exemplifies the displacement of sexuality onto power, labour and athleticism which is the major aspect of Marjorie's and Lorna's presentation (consider the shot of Lorna dominating a male worker at his machine once she has taken over the property). This displacement of active female sexuality behind the iconography of horses and baggy riding breeches is so controlled, and becomes so expected that the discarding of both by the women at the bathing hole comes especially as a shock. For a moment the two 'rhythmic variations' on the heroine's characterisation (the active woman of power, the passive, sexual woman) are uncomfortably juxtaposed, drawing attention to the dominant variation on Lorna's role (the passive woman seduced: Lorna/black gins/Mary) and therefore to the text's work to counter the active female 'sexuality' it has foregrounded. The counterpointing of female vigour (power, labour) and female passivity (voyeuristic spectacle) — contained, for instance, in the single shot of Lorna, sheep and the constricted gate opening — is a tension the text never resolves, despite the conservative narrative closure.

2. This is mainly because of the extraordinarily dynamic investment in the naturalistic *mise en scène* which critics then, as now, saw as distinctly 'Barrett'. The naturalistic discourse is dominated to an unusual extent by women, and it is the power of the *mise en scène* rather than physical features, idiosyncrasies or mode of performance of the actress which provide the 'independent women' with their potency (as is shown again by the shots of Lorna and the milling sheep).

3. The effect of the covert introduction of active female sexuality (via displacement and the *mise en scène*) is a considerable subversion, in so far as sexual excess is associated with social and economic excess. The virile woman stands visibly at the heart of the 658 million pounds of Australian plenty, threatening the bush genre's association of female vigour with the city/vamp and its project of asserting the 'natural' superiority of male (country/productive) mateship. It is, in particular, the potency of the sequences of women working in the stockyard, the emphatic moments of men being dominated by women, which attain an almost metaphoric presence, holding us out and away from the linear narrative development. They are iconographic moments, perhaps of women as spectacle, but if so as *working* spectacle.

What is especially fascinating here is the way in which the adopted mode of naturalism, which is basic to melodrama, itself exposes the fissures and potential discontinuities of this hybrid form. The tendency of cinema on the one hand towards the 'transparency' of window-on-the-world verisimilitude, and on the other to the melodrama of unlikely events, had not been seen as a contradiction by cinema audiences because this combination had already become conventional on the popular stage where naturalistic spectacle was no more than a passive *mise en scène,* a supposedly neutral background for heroic male protagonists. In Barrett's films, however, the naturalistic discourse threatens the preferred reading of the narrative, thus opening up a potential subversion embryonic in the melodramatic form itself. Both films *also* attempt to re-stitch what has been separated — for instance in their penultimate sequences (Gilbert struggling for his life through a bushfire; Tom's life at risk in the crowded court room). These sequences depend on a determinedly protracted cross-cutting of naturalistic scenes (the stagecoach turning in the tree-scattered bush; human figures and horse insignificant against cliffs and water) with others acted in tones of high melodrama (Gilbert staggering through the trees; the entry of the station hands with Sing Lee providentially at the moment of pronouncement). This attempts to return naturalism to its conventional form as passive support for male-dominated melodrama. It is only because the attempt to contain the excess it has generated elsewhere fails that we know these texts by the signature 'Franklyn Barrett', marking them as distinct from other bush films of the period which have an essentially similar ideological project.

12

The Legend: Films of the City

By the late nineteenth century another master image of community had joined that of the 'country' in Western culture: the figure of the family hearth. Originally defined in early capitalist production as an economic unit of work, by the nineteenth century the family was defined rather in its distinction *from* work: a place of spiritual repose. Then, as commodity capitalism advanced, it became increasingly a place where one purchased one's leisure. Both these aspects — a place of spirit and a place of leisure — were important.

The Victorian critic John Ruskin wrote of the home:

> It is the place of peace; and shelter, not only from all injury, but from all terror, doubt and division . . . So far as the anxieties of the outer life penetrate into it . . . it ceases to be a home.[1]

As a place of the spirit the family home was a precious and fragile thing to the Victorian bourgeoisie, a 'tent pitch'd in the world not right'.[2]

As a place of leisure the privatised family home grew as part and parcel of the enormous technological and social change carried by industrial capitalism. As such it benefitted from the greater affluence and more ordered working days the new system brought with it. The home could become a place with possessions, no matter how minor, which distinguished it from every other place. It became associated with off-work hours over which it had sovereignty to an extent never possible in an agrarian society.

These two features of 'home' were structurally related. The privatised home depended for its greater affluence, and the degree of control of its inner rhythms of space and time, on its subservience to the economic system 'out there'. It was *because* of its irredeemable attachment to a greater, harsher and more incomprehensible system that the home, particularly among the bourgeoisie, became a place of retreat and recuperation, where some kind of 'culture' could alleviate the economic manners of the working day. But the anxieties of the outer world did pentrate: the family was part of the economic system as a market for its commodities and a place for the reproduction and socialisation of its labour force.

Raymond Williams has remarked on the new structure of communications which emerged from this situation, in which men and women stared from windows (that is, through the developing channels of the media) in their new homes, waiting anxiously for messages to learn about forces 'out there'. This structural opposition, of the gentle domesticity of the private home threatened and penetrated by far greater forces from the outside world, became the defining opposition of a new movement in cinema. The horror genre, in its archetypal form, had its passive and pure-white heroine locked fast at her window, staring out while the monstrous black vampire clawed and fluttered to get in.

The horror film works at the heart of this structure, but other films, such as Barrett's *The Breaking of the Drought* and *A Girl of the Bush* or Dunlap's *The Romance of Runnibede*, draw some of their energy from it too. Families are threatened, the next generation 'castrated', women are stripped of their productive independence and reduced to spectacles for the voyeuristic city or Aboriginal gaze. In this context the organic nature of the home stands in a fascinating relation to the bush ethos. On the one hand, the 'home' is homologous with the 'bush' in that each attempts to fix the present in a moment of nostalgia against encroaching urban forces. Each secures its definition as a location of pure essence — spirit — in opposition to the divisive pressures of materialism. Each is most acutely threatened, most dramatic, when the separation fails, and the outside forces penetrate. Each sublimates its own sexuality and projects it *outside*, onto the alien power, thus displacing real economic relations with sexual ones.

On the other hand, the bush genre emphasises the very thing the home hides from: production. That is its alibi which protects in a way that is stronger than anything the home can produce — man's work in nature is the plenitude of the bush. In contrast, the home, as film theorist Andrew Britton has remarked, is *threatened* from the very centre of its plenitude — the mother. Britton has noted that family (and its extension, the small town) melodrama have worked within a debased pastoral convention, sublimating sexuality and projecting it outwards. The original paradigm of threat in the pastoral mode — sexuality—the devil—the darker nature of the forest — has become, in the American context — libido/wilderness/Devil/Indian. In this form, however, the attempt to repress sexuality has failed. The development, from Melville's novels to recent American horror films like *The Exorcist* and *Carrie*, has been one in which sexuality has burst out *inside* the home, in its women. Though order is always restored in these films and the anarchy exposed by the de-repression of female sexuality is found to have too high a cost, the potential and the potency remain: 'Regression to home and mother — to home *as* mother — contains the possibility of refinding mother's body, of ending up "inside" with a vengeance'. The bastion and outpost of civilisation, the home, the family, the small town, 'created and consecrated in the name of woman, has actually taken the serpent to its bosom. Satan has not been expelled to the wilderness at all. The guardian of the "vestal temple" herself contains the forces which continually threaten to destroy it'.[3]

A safer solution seemed to be to take the boy children out of the home, away from compromising sexuality and into frontier and exotic locations, as in Ballantyne's *Coral Island*, where repressed energies could be unleashed as boyhood games and imperial endeavour, or, as with Dickens's circus people in *Hard Times*, to recreate in the present the spontaneity, face-to-face relations, wholeness which was thought to have existed in the agrarian past — to establish an urban village. But the disruption of this comfortable organic closeness was always threatened by the elements of stratified conflict — race, class and (especially dangerous because so near the surface) sex. We have seen how *The Breaking of the Drought*, for instance, attempts to exorcise the problem by conflating sexuality and class, and then explaining each of them, not as irreconcilable contradictions of a capitalist structure, but as unnatural growths of the cities; and how *A Girl of the Bush* goes one stage further by conflating sex, class *and* race.

The point is that this search for organic essence was not confined to pastoral retreatism — nor was it in Australian cinema. Tal Ordell's *The Kid Stakes*(1927) is in fact premised on two myths of organicism: the isolated world of childhood and the urban village. There is a central meeting point of the two myths, out of which the main trajectory of the film is generated. The 'urban village' is founded on a particular inflection of liberal capitalist ideology which emphasises the values of community bonding and a non-destructive healthy competiveness which safely contain any sexual and class excesses.[4] Similarly, the sublimation of class privilege and sexual threat within healthy (sporting) competition was a central strategy in the élite English private school.

The Kid Stakes

The great Public School tradition was acted out for over a century in little 'organic' communities located generally in the country. They trained their (boy) children for leadership in the world of industrial exploitation that spread from just beyond the trees outside the dormitory windows and, ultimately, across an Empire. In *The Kid Stakes* essentially the same project

(i)

(ii)

National Film Archive

(i) Myths of organicism in *The Kid Stakes:* the isolated world of childhood and the urban village.
(ii) Children and the urban village: Yvonne Pavis in *Sunshine Sally*

is presented, except here the location is at the other end of those lines of force, the Australian colonies, and the group of children comes mainly from the subordinate, not the ruling class. But the central constituent — the sublimation of sex and class in the competiveness of sport — is the same, and the tradition is still European, blending Romanticism's world of pure childhood with that other Romantic notion of the authentic urban 'outcast' found in Dickens's circus people and carried through a whole line of outsiders, artists, bohemians and harlequins in nineteenth and early twentieth century literature and art.

Critics have pointed to the potency of children in cinema in subverting the family bastion from its position of ultimate economic strength — the place of social reproduction.[5] *The Kid Stakes* avoids that peril by taking the children *out* of their families (like the English Public Schools), and into their own peer-group community. The avoidance of sexuality in Fatty Finn's community is at the same time avoidance of class. All are welcome to this working-class children's world which is one of honest competition (in comparison to that of its enemies), density of social experience (incorporating several nationalities), and good fun without deprivation (there is always money to pay for broken windows). In contrast, the upper-class life is not attractive. It is a life of isolation (the lone boy from Potts Point) and divisiveness (the rejected lovers from Potts Point), which its 'better' elements want to leave for Fatty's community. But they can only do so, like new private school boys, by means of rituals which establish both the undefiled purity and the organic solidarity of the Woolloomooloo community.

The narrative opens with one child's fantasy, as a boy competes and wins in an adult's world of sport; it ends with a community of children competing and winning in a child's world *served* by adults. The transformation from the initial situation to the final fulfillment is a significant one, since it is precisely the movement from an adult world (associated with speed, the jazz age, divisiveness) to a child-centred one which is the film's project. Woolloomooloo is a child's eye view of a social structure in which the world is ordered by adults, but activated by children. When the good adults try to activate it, they are clownish (the policeman and the cricket match, the aeroplane pilot and the goat, the Italian neighbour, the woman hanging out washing, the bill-poster). These are, of course, kids' eye views of adults straight out of comic strips;[6] but that does not mean they are ideologically innocent. As in the later sound film, *Harmony Row* (again the organic, urban village connection), the policeman is valued,

(ii)

(i)

National Film Archive

Organic solidarity: Fatty Finn's world faces (i) the bad working class and (ii) the effete upper class however clownish, via his association with these healthy deviants. And through him, the state order is legitimated as being, at heart if not always by rule, on the side of the underprivileged. In contrast, sectional groups (working-class gangs/ upper-class individuals who monopolise property and swimming pools) are devalued.

If Woolloomooloo is basically a child's world where adults are spectators, Potts Point is an adult's world — of the orchard over the high wall variety — which children invade. In contrast to the communal competiveness of the children's sport, the emptiness of upper-class life is marked by divisive social relationships and the ostentatious pool, which, unlike the healthy democracy of the kid stakes, is set apart from the world like a fetish, until sent up by a row of working-class backsides.

The other inauthentic group — Bruiser's gang — is adult too, but in a different way. It emulates the contemporary, 1920s adult world through smoking, make-up, flapperdom and ruthless ambition. The upper-class world is condemned for witholding property (its by inheritance not labour) as well as keeping Fatty's goat from healthy competition. The working-class gang is condemned for *taking* property (its by theft not labour). Appropriately, just as the characterisation of the upper class is marked by being silly, asexual and effete, the 'bad' working class is characterised as threatening, violent and sexual. However, Fatty's 'good' working class children effect a synthesis of classes which combines for victory in the fair market competition of the race. A world of separation, in which upper-class adults chase children and working-class gangs bully them, is contained, and replaced by a community in which adults serve children and proper use is made of upper-class wealth (planes, pools, cars) and labour on behalf of the natural consensus.

As in *Sunshine Sally*, the proper role of the 'good' working class is here one of mediation, extracting a healthy civilised vigour out of the brutality of *under-civilisation* (the gang) on the one hand, and the vapidity of *over-refinement* (the upper class) on the other. The inflection of *Sunshine Sally* is different from *The Kid Stakes* in that the devices of mediation in the narrative are women, not children.[7] Men are characterised by competitiveness and ambitious action which frequently leads to community division and trouble.[8]

Sunshine Sally

Nevertheless the major strategies of the film are the same. In its first titles *Sunshine Sally* evokes the urban village:

> Paris has its Montmartre; London its East End; New York its Bowery. Sydney its 'Loo . . . And it is in this oft heard but little known district of Woolloomooloo that the events portrayed in this photoplay take place.

These titles offer a reading while asserting it as 'reality' — and the naturalism of the photography in the Woolloomooloo sequences carries this strategy through the film. *This* film, it promises, will fill in the 'little known', will show you the reality of Woolloomooloo. But in fact it offers a *preferred* reading: the context — Montmartre, East End, Bowery — a world of flower girls, artists, the colourful, cheeky characters evoked by popular cultural images — a dense, closely-knit world of the demimonde — the urban village.

Sunshine Sally, in contrast, initially presents a world of exploitation (the Chinese laundry), yet one which generates a feeling of community. The exploitation is not of class against class, as the oppression of Sally by her working-class family (in contrast to Mrs Stanton's beneficence) quickly shows. Nor is there any suggestion that upper-class wealth is based on the labour of the working class: Stanton *finds* his wealth, in the ground overseas.

The narrative of *Sunshine Sally* begins with a situation of fullness, a plenitude (the spontaneous urban community) which the first visuals of the Chinese laundry both affirm (Sally's comradeship for Tottie) and deny (their exploitation by the manager, followed by Sally's expulsion by her depraved family). And it is the task of the film to restore a plenitude — in this case a wider one: the restoration of community *within* classes (the Stanton family re-united; a new, happy and responsible Smith family); and *between* classes (Sally united to Basil, and all the working-class folk acceptable at Potts Point and Bellevue Hill). A Woolloomooloo *vigour* (as established in the most visually striking scene in the film: the cart race) is united with a Potts Point *compassion* for the less fortunate. In contrast, what is defeated in this synthesis are the inauthentic 'city' features: theft and drink among the urban working class, overweening material ambition in the upper-middle class.

It is no accident that the two early sequences which denote 'lack' (the tryannical and depraved Smith home, and the fatherless Stanton home) are placed between the two which carry the most life and spontaneity in the film: the cart race, and the working-class picnic. Spud and Skinny *own* their carts and, rampant on them, are as emblematic of virility as any stockrider. Tracking shots and graphic photography proclaim the 'Loo: in 'bush' terms a place of energy, independence, spontaneity, idiosyncracy, vernacular humour and open air — in contrast to the exploitative closure and ubiquity of the Chinese laundry from which the women have just escaped. The shots of the picnic add another component: the childishness of the urban village in the bush on its 'perfect day'. There are swings, happy waving, puerile fights, fun and games as they dance in circles. The film draws a lot of its presence from the comedy of these and the following boxing scenes, which establish the working class as subordinate figures of fun, yet possessing an authentic vigour derived from the continuing vernacular and simple customs of the urban village. Sally herself is an emblem of this community of children whom we see surrounding her outside the terraces of Woolloomooloo, to the titles: 'Both young and old alike bask in the radiance of Sally's sunshine'.

Sunshine Sally resembles *The Kid Stakes* in drawing much of its power from the myths of childhood and the urban village, and in locating them as authentic points of mediation and purification between the under-civilised world of the 'bad' working class and the divisive world of the upper class. The thematic structure of both films, based on antithesis and synthesis, of under-cultured/cultured/over-cultured, is the same as that of the bush films analysed earlier.

That the urban films of the 1920s, like the bush melodramas, valued organic consensus and the healthy competition of sport against sectionalism and 'party-mindedness' is not surprising. The 1920s was a time of 'old-fashioned consensus', and it would be wrong, perhaps, to expect a glimmer of radical working-class vision in the commercial cinema when there was none in the official Labor Party. Relative affluence, lack of class solidarity and a deep public hostility to strikes and unions generated a desire, in the working class no less than in the middle class, for leisure rather than confrontations with the contradictions of a country about to enter the Depression.[9] The sport and healthy competitiveness at the centre of *The Kid Stakes* and *Sunshine Sally* was symptomatic:

> in the absence of dynamic class traditions, Australians found their identity in the assurance that life was like that of their fathers in sport, and in the final area of pioneering, the sky, while life-saving was a heroic alternative to urban tameness. . . 'The champion' was a category created in the cities, their substitute for the real challenge of the bush'.[10]

In this context we should remember not only the sporting events which are the beginning, ending and narrative design for *The Kid Stakes*, but also the racing, boxing and prolonged life-saving sequence of *Sunshine Sally*. There were many potential carriers for the traditional bush ethos which entered the cinema in the next few years — sport, life-saving, aviation, the army. In one way or another all of these new myths sought to reconcile and synthesise (just as the scheme to put war heroes on the land had) the *best* features of the new and old cultures.

An Urban Village

Yet it remains true that *The Kid Stakes* is satisfying in a way which other films sharing its organicist values are not. In attempting to account for this the usual answer emphasises Tal Ordell's outstandingly naturalistic direction in his handling of the children. While this is true in a limited way, it does not explain why naturalism was so important to the project of *The Kid Stakes*. Another explanation is that the film authentically represented Australian inner-city settings with an innovative 'neo-realism' which unaffectedly presented the 'rundown back streets by the wharves' of Woolloomooloo.[11] However, the fact that critics in the 1920s praised the film for its similarity to the American Jackie Coogan *Our Gang* films should make us cautious of the 'authentic Australia' interpretation.

A third answer might be that the consensualist theme of the film is subverted by self-reflexive formal devices. As evidence for this one might first cite the 'framing device' of an artist creating Fatty Finn on his drawing board. The reference here is not only to the fact that the actants who animate the narrative are 'constructed' rather than 'real', but that there is a major subversion of the main discourse of the film. The view of a world in which adults are there to serve children is undercut at the very beginning, where an adult 'creates' a child to work for him. Secondly, the inter-titles speak directly to the audience, cracking jokes which exist only in the mode of direct address; and in addition, by sometimes preceding the images and narrative events referred to, have the effect of undercutting the transparency of the narrative. Thirdly, *The Kid Stakes* is an over-fantasised world which occasionally draws attention to itself *as* fantasy — as for example, in the sequence of the goat falling from an aeroplane.

This kind of interpretation is attractive to the contemporary theorist but it is, I think, wrong because it entirely ignores the vitality of the film which, through standard processes of identification, narrative hermeneutic and closure locates the audience thoroughly within the organic world of the children. The Syd Nicholls sequence is not a framing device, but a prologue, not so very different in kind to that of C.J. Dennis at the beginning of *The Sentimental Bloke*, and it was quite common for films of this period to draw attention to their literary sources, without in any sense destroying the illusion.

National Film Archive

Adult control: the artist summons up Fatty Finn at the beginning of *The Kid Stakes*

Most important of all, the self-reflexive reading totally ignores the *allegorical* mode of the film, for it is here that its unique quality in blending naturalism and Romanticism lies. There is continuous play between the child's eye and the adult view of the world. After the opening device of an adult manipulating a child, we expect a comic book story to start. Instead we see 'documentary' footage of a car race, which is anchored by an intertitle evoking the age of speed, faster love, divorce and so on — in short, the contemporary jazz age from an adult's viewpoint. Next, in triumphant finale, a child wins the race in an adult world — an archetypal comic book perspective. However, that event is immediately established as fantasy (from an adult's point of view) by visual cues: the sound of the band at the race track was 'really' the sound of a street band passing the sleeping child, and his 'dream' was motivated by the poster of motor racing. Yet, by the end of the film that fantasy has become reality — of a kind that the film offers for adult emulation. Moreover, different social groups locate and solidify these alternative perspectives. The upper-class world is, as suggested earlier, seen from a child's position, 'scrumping apples over the orchard wall'. The working-class gang on the other hand depends for its resonances on an adult's knowledge of flappers, faster divorce and the jazz age.

Put another way, there are two modes of address, or discourses, in *The Kid Stakes*. The address of one is outward to a contemporary adult world of speed, sexuality and so on; its mode is referential, documentary and analytical. The address of the other is inward to popular culture (comics/film) and its mode is fantasy. Thus, as above, we have:

1. artist/child — reference to the conventions of comics and cinema (e.g. the cinematic effect of the comic filling in itself).
2. 'world of speed' — reference to the transparency of film as a document on reality.

There is a continuous tension in *The Kid Stakes* between evocation of a children's world (separate not simply as location, but also as discourse) presenting a fantasy world of spontaneous community, and the referential contemporary world of speed and divisiveness. The skill of the film lies in its location of that childish world *both* as fantasy *and* as potential reality. On the one hand we have the signification: all is fantasy in the hands of the adult artist who manipulates and motivates the children's world. On the other we have the signification: fantasy is potential reality as adults (the present) are manipulated by children (the future) who, however, resonate with all the best qualities of an authentic bush tradition.

The ambiguity depends on a formal one which is central to allegory as an artistic mode. As the literary theorist Todorov has pointed out,[12] allegory is a proposition with a double meaning in which the literal meaning is indicated as the less important. Allegory depends on a process of continuous metaphor — the very elaboration of which points to an 'intention to speak of something else besides the first object of utterance'.[13] In other words, the double meaning is indicated explicitly in one way or another within the text: there must be some process or device which alerts the reader or viewer to an allegorical meaning amongst all the other possible interpretations. This is, of course, the point of the first inter-title of *The Kid Stakes*, which otherwise seems so out of place in a comic-book fantasy.

The problem with allegory, however, is that by pointing to its own intention, its concern that a reading should proceed in this way and not in that, the second level of allegory threatens to reveal its own status as *discourse*. Perhaps in those centuries when allegory was most prolific readers saw no contradiction between the Creator's discourse and the universal 'truths' carried by allegory.

Yet modern allegory is by no means in decline. The literary critic Angus Fletcher has pointed out[14] that the matrices of 'cosmic hierarchy' on which allegory depends to locate its 'truths' have not disappeared but have simply been changed. Whereas truth was once to be found in God's revealed will, it has, in the last two centuries been found instead in the notion of scientific progress. In each case the dominant discourse has had the status of 'objective knowledge'. But the old allegorical ideal of perfecting the individual by providing the correct spiritual reading has become much grander. 'Now whole societies, whole technologies, whole cultural ideals are seen developing in a progressivist vision'.[15]

It is not at all surprising, therefore, that successful allegory has frequently drawn upon the world of childhood in our time. This is partly because Romantic conceptions of childhood set up alternative images of potential purity and perfection in the agonies of an industrial age, and partly because children as a *social group* offered to the artist convenient and isolable images of what man could become. Groups of children could be presented through their natural and potential modes of interaction 'realistically'; but at the same time, through the artificiality of their isolation as a spotlit social group, could carry metaphoric meaning without undue emphasis.

Ordell's film *The Kid Stakes* and Golding's novel *Lord of the Flies* are two works which, though presenting the social world from opposite sides of the Freudian divide, nevertheless try to counter the contradiction of modern allegory in essentially the same way. Though in *The Kid Stakes* social order is authentically a matter of regenerative community and in *Lord of the Flies* it is a matter of murderous and implacable divisiveness, they both try to present their allegorical (and ideological) message as the pure world of reality. They do this, first of all, by a locational and stylistic density which draws attention away from the allegorical towards the literal meaning (*this* is the significance of the naturalistic acting of *The Kid Stakes*); and secondly by drawing on, and inflecting topically, the conventionally accepted myth which valued the world of childhood for its purity, spontaneity and healthy competitive creativity. *Lord of the Flies* draws on our expectations of the Romantic myth only to subvert it, and replace it with a 'modern' interpretation. *The Kid Stakes* augments the myth by filling it out with a bush sense of community which was perfectly compatible because itself a Romantic legend. Each inflection is successful as 'realism' because so soundly based on the living myths of the time: 'pioneering' competitive optimism in Australia in 1927, and post-Freudian, post-nuclear pessimism in England in 1954.

In *The Kid Stakes* the film-maker's discourse, re-presented as that of the artist at the beginning, is further displaced and subsumed as Fatty Finn and his friends become the marks of inventiveness and creativity within the fictional world. Hence the contradiction between the adult control at the beginning of the film and the adult subservience at the end is, in terms of the legend, no contradiction at all. The adult world at the beginning is that of individual labour, inventiveness and Romantic tradition (signified here as 'art'); the adult world at the end is the world of spectatorship, impotence and contemporaneity (signified here as 'media'). The ability to create, to produce, to compete, to succeed now belongs to Fatty, and as always this is the defining term in the distinction between his authentic 'culture' and the worlds of brutality and impotent spectatorship that surround him. Whereas in *Lord of the Flies*, Golding writes desperately against the grain of the allegory, so that the moment when story and symbol come closest together in the martyrdom of the saintly Simon is also the moment of the most intense aestheticism on the part of the artist,[16] in *The Kid Stakes*, the representation of childhood authenticates the Romantic myth of creativity.

And yet, this conflation of so many aspects of the Romantic myth has its potential contradictions. *The Kid Stakes* has removed the children from the home, but not from the sense of escape, from threatening outside forces. The scope of the children's world, from secret societies to back-street cricket, is essentially home grown. The private world of the home is only displaced and, not surprisingly, sexuality obtrudes insistently in *The Kid Stakes*, as much in its overt repression in Potts Point as in its deviant emphasis among the gang. The competitive virility of the goat race, in which the rewards are actually women won and lost, effectively contains the problem of sexuality only until the race's end, and the last shots of the film, when Fatty wards off Kitty's kiss, disclose the real meaning of the race.

It is precisely because allegory does not suppress sexuality but codifies it in new ways, that it is such a perfect form for this theme. In the sense that asceticism generates desire, or more exactly is *defined* by desire, the natural theme of allegory is temptation. Allegory relocates human ambivalence by allowing 'a degree of certainty in a world of flux'[17] and projecting outwards onto separate personifications of good and evil, emotional states and psychological dispositions which are internal and inseparable. Historically, allegory has been made up of two ritual modes: the consummate battle between forces of evil and good; and the 'progress', which is a quest, a journey toward a desired and 'authentic' goal. Very frequently, as in *The Kid Stakes*, the allegory is made up of both (the quest for the object of desire, and victory via the object of desire); and what is at the primary level simply a tale of children and their animals takes on, if we read allegorically, a talismanic quality in so far as this lost object carries with it a concentrated history. It is a token of a culture, a way of asserting a fair, honest manhood in a world which seeks to deprive it.

But whether protagonists of battle or quest, heroes of allegory differ from those of 'realist' representation by a self-proclaimed lack of complexity. They are fated, as agents of abstract ideas — virtues, vices, chivalry, heroically competitive manhood — to an extreme simplification of character, where all doubt and ambivalence are eliminated. Heroes of the grail, like Fatty Finn, would be compromised by their sexuality, and villains of city melodramas are caricatures of sexual and economic vampirism. Sexuality is not suppressed so much as displaced onto other characters in parallel situations. Allegory, as Fletcher points out, works not by probability (goats fall out of aeroplanes and live) but by its own 'magical' principles of causation. For instance, the imitative magic of doubled plots where one plot is generated by another on a principle of similarity (the hero desires a woman; the villain also desires the woman), and the second plot recreates the first with greater coherence or force, pointing to its underlying logic. This allegorical symmetry may be of various kinds: it may be the see-saw of battle between two perfectly matched opponents; or, more appropriately to the picaresque nature of 'progress', there may be double plots involving different levels of society.

hero desires a woman; the villain also desires the woman), and the second plot recreates the first with greater coherence or force, pointing to its underlying logic. This allegorical symmetry may be of various kinds: it may be the see-saw of battle between two perfectly matched opponents; or, more appropriately to the picaresque nature of 'progress', there may be double plots involving different levels of society.

In *The Kid Stakes* the doubling works both in terms of the battle and the 'progress' which discovers and highlights different social orders. In either case character development is not in terms of psychological growth, maturity or density ('realism'), but rather a matter of acting out the logical implications of different aspects of the hero's 'soul' by their individual displacement onto other characters. Fatty's potential sexuality is displaced onto Bruiser, and the potential *impotence* which remains is projected onto Horatio. By becoming characters in narrative, Bruiser and Horatio safely release the tensions, complications and ambiguities in the hero's innermost being (and, through him, the social order he represents — 'pioneering' capitalism), leaving Fatty 'pure' in his healthy competitiveness. Bruiser acts out the brutality that 'healthy' capitalist competitiveness must include; Horatio stands for its impotence deprived of patriarchal dominance; and Fatty lives its 'pure' ideology.

Because narrative development cannot depend on psychological development and motivation, it takes place via magical agencies: the lustful enemy of the hero takes some personal possession of his — an article of clothing, a fingernail, a lock of hair, a precious possession, and in this film, a goat — which will lessen the hero's virility, thus giving his enemy control. In the context of sexual debate, Fatty's loss of the goat to his enemy is a symbolic loss, a threatened impotence which adheres to the logic of the division of heroes into 'pure' and 'lustful' stereotypes. The mechanism of control is a magical contagion, whereby there is a relation of metonymy between the lost object and the hero: and casting a spell over it will hurt the hero at a distance. Further, the allegorical villain is himself metonymically related to the hero, a contiguous part of him, in the sense that a virus is related to a healthy organ, and merely projected outward for the purpose of the narrative.

Proximity with this opposite, which *must* be allowed for meaning to exist, offers the risk of endless contagion, which is the reason why the topographical isolation of the hero is a principal constituent of allegory. The holy mountain, the sacred city, the walled garden, the town in the wilderness, the family hearth, the island, are examples of a cosmic centre of absolute purity and therefore 'reality' in the history of allegory, as too are topographical personifications such as the Christian community of believers, the Romantic world of childhood, or the science-fiction world of isolated space travellers.

A mark of Golding's considerable subversion of conventions in *Lord of the Flies* is that he takes two of these most potent centres — the island and the world of childhood — and turns them from places of pure essence, and security from contagion, into the historical and biological centre from which the hellish adult world of war beyond the island arises. *The Kid Stakes* also conflates, for greater potency, two topographical centres: the world of childhood and the organic world of the urban village, but the treatment is conventional. Unlike *Lord of the Flies*, it works toward an authentic rescue at the end. The grail of authenticity — mateship, competitiveness, and the refusal of divisions of class, race or sex — is attained, and the necessary repressions laid out allegorically as sub-plots.

Allegory often functions in a syncretic way by reconciling different world views and systems of belief. Fletcher points to the compromise between medieval morality and Renaissance humanism in *The Faerie Queen,* and critic William Empson to the accommodation of class conflict with social mobility in the pastoral, as courtiers become shepherds and shepherds courtiers.[18] *The Kid Stakes* is also an allegory of accommodation, not only in the obvious sense of reconciling classes, but also in that a dream of authentic urban living is fused with the mythical structures of the bush. This attempt was to become increasingly familiar in the 1930s, but never with the same success. The quality of *The Kid Stakes* lies, in no small degree, in its precise inflection of a form adapted to just this social function. By converting ideological ambivalence into *narratives* where the complexity of uncertainty is re-coded as a compulsive struggle between forces of good and evil, allegory is, as Fletcher says, the mode which 'monumentalises our ideals' and yet does so by way of 'rattling good stories', warmth and exuberance as well. By investing its ambivalences in characters in the narrative, by locating these characters in class terms, and by proposing (in opposition to these 'inauthentic' *differences* of status and discourse) a cosmic and undifferentiated centre where white and black, male and female, lower and upper class relate naturally, *The Kid Stakes* represents cultural contradictions as children's fantasies, and at the same time contains them.

Notes

Chapter 1

1. *Picture Show*, 1 November 1919, p.57.
2. *ibid.*, 2 August 1919, p.13.
3. *ibid.*, 10 May 1919, p.31.
4. *ibid.*, 24 May 1919, p.10.
5. *ibid.*
6. *ibid.*, 11 October 1919, p.1; and 18 October 1919, p.1.
7. *ibid.*, 11 October 1919, pp.1–2.
8. *ibid.*, 18 October 1919, pp.1–2.
9. *ibid.*, 12 July 1919, p.1.
10. *ibid.*, 5 July 1919, p.1.
11. *ibid.*, 26 July 1919, p.1.
12. *ibid.*, 14 June 1919, p.1.
13. *ibid.*, 19 July 1919, p.1.
14. *ibid.*, 26 July 1919, p.14.
15. G.L. Buxton, '1870–90', in F.K. Crowley, *A New History of Australia*, Melbourne, 1974, p.172.
16. *Kine Weekly*, 23 September, 1920.
17. *Picture Show*, 1 April 1921, p.33.
18. *Bioscope*, 23 September 1920.
19. *Picture Show*, 1 April 1921, p.32.
20. *ibid.*, 1 April 1920, p.45.
21. This thesis and some of the ideas that follow are valuably elaborated in Richard Dyer, *Stars*, London, 1979, pp.24ff.
22. e.g. Alexander Walker, Edgar Morin, cited in Dyer, *op. cit.*, p.24.
23. Richard Schickel, cited in Dyer, *op. cit.*, p.24.
24. Cited in Dyer, *op. cit.*, p.25.
25. *ibid.*, pp.28–9.
26. *ibid.*, p.38.
27. *ibid.*, pp.30ff.
28. *Picture Show.*, 1 February 1920, p.51.
29. *ibid.*, 25 October 1919, p.7.
30. *ibid.*, 19 April 1919, p.9.
31. *ibid.*, 10 May 1919, p.12.
32. *ibid.*, 27 September 1919, p.20.

33. *ibid.*, 25 October 1919, p.10.
34. *ibid.*, 1 November 1919, p.4.
35. *ibid.*, p.39.
36. *ibid.*, 2 August 1919, p.17.
37. *ibid.*, 24 May 1919, p.32.
38. *Sun*, 18 April 1915, p.14.
39. *Picture Show*, 17 May 1919, p.32.
40. *ibid.*, 1 December 1919, p.29.

Chapter 2

1. *Picture Show*, 23 August 1919, p.11.
2. *ibid.*
3. *ibid.*, 6 September 1919, p.21.
4. *ibid.*, 24 May 1919, p.13.
5. *ibid.*, 11 October 1919, p.11.
6. *Photoplayer*, 15 December 1923, p.27; see also William K. Everson's discussion of Hollywood vamps in *The American Silent Film*, New York, 1978.
7. *Picture Show*, 4 October 1919, p.11.
8. *Everyones*, 22 December 1926, p.3.
9. *ibid.*, 27 March 1929, p.20.
10. *ibid.*, 11 May 1921, p.3.
11. *ibid.*, 7 October 1925, p.3.
12. *Picture Show*, 1 December 1919, p.61.
13. Raymond Longford in Report of the Royal Commission into the Moving Picture Industry in Australia 1927–28, Evidence (R.C.E.), p.156.
14. R. Sklar, *Movie Made America*, New York, 1975, p.103.
15. *Picture Show*, 27 September 1919, p.17.
16. *ibid.*, 7 June 1919, p.32.
17. Lucas used three different reflector screens, blue, silver and gold, with, it was said, remarkable lighting effects.
18. *Picture Show*, 18 October 1919, p.23.
19. Cited in *Picture Show*, 1 March 1922, p.62.
20. Cited in National Library notes to accompany screening of *The Man From Kangaroo*, 25 March 1974.
21. *Picture Show*, 1 March 1922, p.62.
22. *ibid.*, 1 March 1920, p.33.
23. *ibid.*, 1 January 1920, p.21.
24. *ibid.*, p.51.
25. *ibid.*, 1 June 1920, p.49.
26. See First National's criticism of 'exclusive' scenarios, *Picture Show*, 1 March 1923, p.21.
27. *Picture Show*, 1 April 1920, p.57.

28. *ibid.*, 1 July 1920, p.49.
29. *ibid.*, 1 August 1920, p.43.
30. *ibid.*, 1 November 1920, p.29.
31. *Everyones*, 11 August 1920, p.11.
32. *Picture Show*, 1 November 1920, p.29.
33. *ibid.*, 1 September 1920, p.30.
34. *ibid.*, p.38.
35. *Everyones*, 16 March 1921, p.15.
36. *Picture Show*, 1 December 1921, p.22.
37. Both American and Australian reviews of the first of these, *His Last Race*, suggested that he had neither forgotten nor changed much: an American critic applauded his death-defying stunts and a sequence of horsemanship so unprecedented on the screen 'that they leave one convinced that Baker could ride a cannonball or comet should he so desire'.
38. *Picture Show*, 1 September 1920, p.38.
39. *ibid.*, 1 May 1921, p.42.
40. Ramée had played vamp in *The Throwback* as well as having fifteen years' stage experience.
41. *Picture Show*, 1 April 1922, p.66.
42. *Everyones*, 10 May 1922, p.18.
43. *Picture Show*, 1 June 1922, p.67.
44. *Everyones*, 14 June 1922, p.12.
45. *Picture Show*, 1 July 1922, p.61.
46. *Everyones*, 24 May 1922, p.3.
47. *Picture Show*, 1 December 1922, p.13.
48. *Everyones*, 30 August 1922, p.10.
49. *Picture Show*, 1 October 1922, p.66.
50. *ibid.*, 1 December 1922, p.13.
51. *Everyones*, 15 November 1922, p.4.
52. This would avoid the 'unwarranted interference from Government, mission and other sources' which tended to meet film companies shooting in Papua or the South Sea Islands — including Frank Hurley later on.
53. *Everyones*, 24 January 1923, p.10.
54. *Picture Show*, 1 February 1923, p.57.
55. *Everyones*, 27 March 1923, p.25.
56. *ibid.*, 6 May 1925, p.10.
57. R.C.E., p.798.
58. *Circumstance*, which cost something over £700, brought in only £40 from the Haymarket first release.
59. R.C.E., p.674.
60. *Picture Show*, 1 April 1920, p.38.
61. *ibid.*, 1 November 1920, p.37.
62. *ibid.*, 1 April 1920, p.51.

63. It is not altogether clear which of Southwell's Kelly films was banned. *Everyones* says the first one, *Picture Show* the second; Eric Reade in the *Australian Screen* says the first (p. 111), Ina Bertrand in *Film Censorship in Australia* says the second (p. 111). Probably both were: in 1926, *Everyones*, referring to the 'disrespect shown the police' in *The Kelly Gang*, said that 'the film was immediately withdrawn, and some years later, when a more complete version of the picture was suggested, leave to make it was withheld'. Bertrand suggests that *The Kelly Gang* was prohibited in South Australia, and *When the Kellys Were Out* in New South Wales.
64. *Everyones*, 16 July 1924, p.5.
65. In contrast to his Australian experience, Southwell commented on the considerable help he received from the authorities and police in letting him shoot in forbidden places, lending him a squad of mounted police, and rounding up 2,500 Arabs for the epic crowd and battle scenes.
66. Cited in *Everyones*, 8 October 1924, p. 10.
67. *ibid*, 7 October 1925, p. 16.
68. W&F handled the Snub Pollard and Harold Lloyd films in England as well as the important British Gainsborough productions.
69. *Film Weekly*, 27 January 1927, p.27.
70. *Everyones*, 6 March 1929, p. 18.
71. *Film Weekly*, 7 March 1929, p.8.
72. *Exhibitor*, 7 November 1923, p.6.
73. Longford in his evidence to the Royal Commission, for instance, argued that *For The Term Of His Natural Life* should not be exported because it belonged to 'a chapter in our history that we want the world to forget'. R.C.E., p. 167.
74. *Everyones*, 14 July 1926, p.4.
75. *ibid.*, 31 October 1923, p.5.
76. *ibid.*, 16 December 1925, p.3.
77. See Diane Collins, *Cinema and Society in Australia 1920–1939* (unpublished PhD thesis, University of Sydney, 1975), Part 4.

Chapter 3

1. According to Barrett this was the basis for the 'first direct natural colour movies', relying on the projection at twice normal speed of alternate red and mixed yellow and blue frames.
2. *Picture Show*, 1 December 1919, p.37.
3. *ibid.*, 1 February 1920, p.39.
4. *ibid.*, 1 July 1920, p.50.
5. These succeeded avoiding clichéd shots to the extent of puzzling critics where they were taken.
6. *Everyones*, 10 December 1930, p. 14.
7. *ibid.*, p. 12.
8. *Picture Show*, 1 February 1920, p.39.

9. *ibid.*, 1 March 1920, p.35.
10. *ibid.*, 1 July 1920, p.50.
11. *ibid.*
12. *Everyones*, 20 December 1922, p.3.
13. *ibid.*
14. *Theatre Magazine*, 1 January 1917, p.14.
15. *Picture Show*, 1 December 1920, p.67.
16. *ibid*,1 March 1921, p.33.
17. *ibid.*
18. *ibid.*, p.34.
19. *ibid.*, 1 May 1921, p.61.
20. *ibid.*, 1 November 1921, p.42.
21. *Everyones*, 7 September 1921, p.18.
22. *ibid.*, 10 December 1930, p.14.
23. *ibid.*, 24 May 1922, p.4.
24. *ibid.*, 11 December 1929, p.116.
25. *ibid.*, 13 December 1933, p.11.
26. *ibid.*, 18 February 1925, p.6.
27. *ibid.*, 18 March 1925, p.6.

Chapter 4

1. The Newcastle enterpreneurs who controlled the Palace Theatre, Sydney.
2. The only journal which gave the case prominence, The *Theatre Magazine*, according to Longford, backed off when its advertising was threatened.
3. Stuart Doyle said he paid a total of £576 for screening *The Sentimental Bloke* at the Lyceum, Lyric, King's Cross, Majestic, Empress and Rialto theatres, Sydney.
4. *Picture Show*, 18 October 1919, p.17.
5. *ibid.*, 25 October 1919, p.8.
6. R.C.E., p.158.
7. *ibid.*, p.157.
8. *Picture Show*, 1 August 1920, p.43; 1 April 1920, p.44.
9. *ibid.*, 1 April 1920, p.44.
10. *ibid.*, 1 April 1921, p.33.
11. *ibid.*, 25 May 1921, p.9.
12. *ibid.*, 1 March 1921, p.64.
13. *ibid.*, 1 June 1921, p.40.
14. *ibid.*, 1 October 1921, p.32.
15. *ibid.*, 1 November 1921, p.31.
16. *ibid.*, 1 October 1921, p.40.
17. *Everyones*, 9 November 1921, p.6.
18. *Picture Show*, 1 December 1921, p.40.

19. *Everyones*, 9 November 1921, p.6.
20. *ibid.*, 2 November 1921, p.4.
21. *ibid.*, 4 January 1922, p.11.
22. *Cows and Cuddles* was handled by the Carrolls, as was *Silks and Saddles* which Dan Carroll boasted of selling in England for a good price, but there was a plethora of poor production at this time to back Carroll's argument.
23. *Everyones*, 4 November 1925, p.8.
24. *Picture Show*, 1 September 1922, p.70.
25. The Carrolls had just abandoned Waverley to Jeffree and Bruce who did the major cinematographic and laboratory work in Australia for Paramount.
26. Cited in *Everyones*, 23 January 1924, p.5.
27. *Everyones* was at that time changing over from a mainly theatrical to a mainly cinema paper, and rapidly becoming the mouthpiece of the trade.
28. *ibid.*, 3 May 1922, p.4.
29. *ibid.*, 27 April 1922, p.11.
30. *ibid.*, 2 March 1922, p.11.
31. *ibid.*, 4 May 1921, p.11.
32. *ibid.*, 31 August 1921, p.8.
33. *ibid.*, 14 September 1921, p.3.
34. *ibid.*, 13 December 1922, p.15.
35. *ibid.*, 1 August 1923, p.13.
36. This included A.F. who regularly gave out what purported to be 'true' histories of the rise of and justification for American dominance — see, for instance, W.A. Gibson in *Everyones*, 31 October 1923, p.5.
37. At the Royal Commission Longford said, 'as an incentive to securing a release from the combine, I employed their cameraman' (though an alternative explanation is that Arthur Higgins has already contracted himself to the new Harris—Pavis venture after the failure of the Carrolls). Likewise, Longford associated himself with Howe.
38. R.C.E., p.716. The company refused an offer of £65 for the South African rights; and Howe argued that this contemptuous offer proved that the ideal of a necessary and sufficient Empire market for Australian productions was a pipe dream.
39. *Everyones*, 5 November 1924, p.7.
40. *ibid.*, 8 October 1924, p.23.
41. *ibid.*, 8 April 1925, p.4.
42. Everson, *op. cit.,* p.218.
43. They did, however, receive £500 for selling the English rights.
44. *Everyones*, 20 May 1925, p.5.
45. Ironically, again, on the same bill as the latest Eva Novak film.
46. *Everyones*, 20 May 1925, p.5.
47. *ibid.*, 17 June 1925, p.30.

48. Longford had already filmed unusually heavy snow at Katoomba for *The Blue Mountains Mystery*.
49. *Everyones*, 3 November 1926, p.33.
50. There is another inconsistency in Longford's position at the Royal Commission here, as elsewhere he argued that the subject matter of *The Term* was unsuitable for the overseas market.
51. *Everyones*, 21 October 1925, p.3.
52. *ibid.*, 14 October 1925, p.16.
53. R.C.E. p.161.
54. *Everyones*, 19 August 1925, p.5.
55. Sklar, *op. cit.*, p.217.
56. *Everyones*, 26 August 1925, p.5.
57. Stuart Doyle was to implicity admit the force of control over the media through advertising when he told the Royal Commission that as Union Theatres spent almost nothing on advertising in the *Sydney Morning Herald* he could not be accused of influencing what it had to say about Australian cinema.
58. See Beatrice Tildesley, 'The Cinema in Australia', *Pan Pacific Womens' Conference — Proceedings,* No. 2, 1930, p.70. In June 1929, Union Theatres gained joint control of the new Australian Broadcasting Company with Fullers Theatres Ltd and J. Albert and Sons.
59. R.C.E., p.383.
60. *Everyones*, 19 August 1925, p.7.
61. *ibid.*, 14 October 1925, p.16.
62. *ibid.*, 21 October 1925, p.10.
63. He had already begun to collect an Australian cast led by Frank Harvey and Jack Gavin for a production that was to cost £15,000.
64. R.C.E., p.152,159.
65. See notes to chapter 5, p.60.
66. *Everyones*, 16 February 1927, p.6.
67. *ibid.*, 2 November 1927, p.7.
68. *ibid.*, 27 March 1929, p.6.
69. *ibid.*, 12 February 1930, p.6.
70. *ibid.*, 4 June 1930, p.7.
71. *Melbourne Herald*, 10 October 1976.
72. *Sunday Telegraph*, 26 June 1955, p.15.

Chapter 5

1. Smith had set up the *Gadfly* with C.J. Dennis and Archie Martin in 1905 after failing as a suburban journalist in Adelaide. He later joined the Sydney *Bulletin*.
2. *Everyones*, 18 November 1925, p.6.
3. *ibid.*, 10 December 1930, p.70.

4. This was in emulation of Hollywood, and was supported by American director Wilfred Lucas who said Lupino was a 'comedian with the biggest screen chances he had ever met'.
5. *Picture Show*, 1 November 1919, p.7.
6. *ibid.*, 1 May 1920, p.48.
7. Smith, ever the entrepreneur, intended to sell this lighting in Australia as agent for the company, and also brought back 12,000 feet of film of anecdotal material concerning 'leading screen people'. This he intended to release throughout Australia and New Zealand accompanied by lectures.
8. Mackay had also worked for Smith on the stage, as well as having film producing and acting experience before the war.
9. Cosgrove had also had very early film experience, producing and acting in some crude films with Frank M. Clarke in one of the first picture shows in Australia. Apart from his work for Smith, he wrote the scenario for and acted in *Silks and Saddles*, and himself produced the burlesque *Guyra Ghost Mystery* in 1921. It only cost £100, but he still lost money on the production.
10. R.C.E., p.158.
11. *Picture Show*, 1 April 1920, p.38.
12. *Everyones*, 20 May 1925, p.3.
13. *ibid.*, 16 February 1927, p.6.
14. Noting this of *Barry Butts In*, *Picture Show* added that this pace was the feature of all Smith's productions.
15. *Film Weekly*, 25 November 1926, p.27.
16. *Everyones*, 14 July 1920, p.10.
17. *ibid.*, 8 September 1920, p.11.
18. *Picture Show*, 1 September 1920, p.72.
19. *ibid.*,1 September 1921, p.34.
20. *ibid.*, 1 August 1920, p.44.
21. *ibid.*, 1 September 1921, p.34.
22. *ibid.*, 1 October 1921, pp.26-7.
23. Henry Lawson was reported to be afraid that amateur city bushmen would ruin his tale, 'that swags would be incorrectly rolled, and that the forked stick and cross-piece of convention would be used to suspend the billy over the fire'. Ironically, that is just what we see in the advertisement for the film.
24. *Picture Show*, 1 December 1920, p.41.
25. *ibid.*, 1 February 1921, p.21. There was much emphasis on the use of reflecting screens to overcome the problems 'the dark skins of the Maoris have always given photographers'.
26. *ibid.*, 1 March 1921, p.38. *Picture Show* noted that at last local film-makers were showing 'the good old surf'. The other was P.J. Ramster in his comedy, *Jasamine Freckel's Love Affair*.
27. Vardac, *op.cit.*, p.43.

28. *Picture Show*, 1 October 1921, p.39.
29. It had been given seven earlier performances at Mittagong, Moss Vale and Bowral, where it was shot, in late December.
30. *Everyones*, 26 April 1922, p.11.
31. *ibid.*, 13 December 1922, p.57.
32. *Picture Show*, 1 January 1923, p.55.
33. As a further source of depression, the *Kinematograph Weekly* had panned *The Man From Snowy River*, a very different treatment from that received by Longford.
34. Smith did import an 'Irish Village' show, but showed little profit.
35. An earlier Smith film, *Gay Paree*, was screened in Melbourne in February, but this seems to have been an anecdotal documentary, comparable to the one he brought back from America in 1920.
36. *Photoplayer*, 30 June 1923, p.15.
37. *Everyones*, 16 May 1923, p.5.
38. *ibid.*, 27 June 1923, p.24.
39. *ibid.*, p.27.
40. Smith had been refused permission to shoot the Artists' Ball at Sydney Town Hall.
41. *Everyones*, 28 November 1923, p.21.
42. *ibid.*, p.17.
43. *Photoplayer*, 17 November 1923, p.16.
44. *The Digger Earl* was sold to independents in South Australia.
45. *Everyones*, 27 August 1924, p.18.
46. Very few of the cast had been in Australian films before; most had extensive stage and some overseas film experience.
47. *Everyones*, 5 November 1924, p.13.
48. *ibid.*, 20 May 1925, p.8.
49. *ibid.*, 26 November 1924, p.26. Doyle argued that any criticisms came from producers lacking the 'ability, experience and efficiency' to make worth-while films — he presumably included in this category the Longford—Lyell films which were not gaining a ready release from Union Theatres.
50. *ibid.*, 18 February 1925, p.6.
51. *ibid.*, 29 April 1925, p.8.
52. *ibid.*, 24 November 1926, p.5
53. *ibid.*,27 May 1925, p.5.
54. *ibid.*, 20 May 1925, p.3.
55. *ibid.*,24 June 1925, p.24.
56. *ibid.*, 17 June 1925, p.3.
57. *ibid.* 29 July 1925, p.23.
58. *ibid.*,15 July 1925, p.6.
59. *ibid.*, 18 November 1925, p.3.
60. The relationship between Union Theatres and J.C. Williamson Ltd. is a complex one and difficult to be clear about. In February 1920 *Picture Show*

announced an 'amalgamation of interests involving the investment of a capital considerably over £1,000,000' between Union Theatres/Australasian Films and Electrical Theatres Ltd. (incorporating J.C. Williamson Films Ltd.). In November 1926 *Everyones* announced the amalgamation, with capital of £3,500,000, of Hoyts and the J.C. Williamson group whose directors Sir George Tallis, F.W. Thring and J.H. Tait would join Griffith and Challingworth of Hoyts on the new board. Since at that time J.C. Williamson was still handling Hurley's films for Union Theatres, and there is no mention of any break-up, we can assume a tie-up between Hoyts and U.T.—A.F. via J.C. Williamson. At the Royal Commission, W.A. Gibson of U.T.—A.F. was asked to explain his firm's connection with J.C. Williamson. He replied, 'I am J.C. Williamson Films'. The following day he said he was not J.C. Williamson Ltd but J.C. Williamson Films Ltd. Asked to explain, he said, 'The J.C. Williamson Films Limited was a separate organisation created by J.C. Williamson Limited and Mr Thring. It carried on business for some time until we purchased its film business'. (This was presumably the 1920 deal; the company set up by Williamson, Thring, Tallis and Tait in November 1925 which Beau Smith joined was called J.C. Williamson Pictures Ltd.). Gibson concluded, 'but we have nothing to do with J.C. Williamson Limited'. It is not surprising that the commissioners found his explanations 'pretty difficult to follow'. When they pressed the matter further by asking him whether Union Theatres and Hoyts were connected, Gibson said, 'No. They are in opposition to each other.' When the commissioners suggested that 'there have been directors from each organisation sitting on a certain board . . . interested in suburban shows', Gibson replied, 'Not from Hoyts, but from J.C. Williamson Ltd, Electric Theatres, and Associated Theatres . . . J.C. Williamson Limited and Associated Theatres came together. Never at any time were Hoyts' directors connected with the organisation with which I am associated', The fact is, though, that Frank Thring was working with Gibson in Melbourne for Union Theatres only a month before news of his association with Williamson and Smith in November 1925, and, of course, he had also worked for J.C.W. before that. Two directors of J.C. Williamson Ltd, Theodore Fink and F.J. Smith were also directors of companies that were part of the Union Theatres combine. Gibson's attempts to deny a link between Hoyts and Union Theatres depended on the argument that the Hoyts Group was not a 'combine' but, in Thring's words 'a cooperative amalgamation formed not only for mutual protection but for the assistance of all those associated in the ever growing business of moving picture presentation'. The same kind of thing was said about the M.P.D.A. — but this never prevented the associated companies from breathing unanimously whenever their interests were threatened.

61. Moreover, he kept his own film exchange, releasing through it his own and other Australian films.

Chapter 6

1. *Picture Show*, 1 May 1920, pp.26-7.
2. *Everyones*, 21 July 1920, p.11.
3. *Picture Show*, 1 June 1921, p.41.
4. *ibid.*,1 September 1921, p.44.
5. *Everyones*, 13 December 1922, p.53.
6. *ibid.*,24 January 1923, p.10.
7. *ibid.*, 12 November 1924, p.18.
8. *ibid.*, 3 September 1924, p.26.
9. *ibid.*, 25 March 1925, p. 14.
10. *ibid.*, 21 January 1925, p.3.
11. *ibid.*, 18 February 1925, p.5.
12. *ibid.*, 18 March 1925, p.4.
13. *The Mystery of a Hansom Cab* was advertised as 'Australia's Greatest Picture', and *The Sealed Room*, not as the greatest Australian picture, but 'greater than *The Mystery of a Hansom Cab*'!
14. *Everyones*, 11 March 1926, p.29.
15. *ibid.*, 5 August 1925, p.6.
16. R.C.E., p.70.
17. *Everyones*, 30 June 1926, p.36.
18. *ibid.*, 7 July 1926, p.37.
19. For a discussion of the consensual basis of conspiratorial thinking and its application in the cinema see J. Tulloch, *Conflict and Control in the Cinema*, Melbourne, 1977, pp.253-72.
20. *Everyones*, 7 July 1926, p.10.
21. *Film Weekly*, 2 September 1926, p.16.
22. *Stage and Society*, 17 June 1926, p.8.
23. *Everyones*, 5 September 1928, p.5.
24. *ibid.*, 24 May 1922, p.19.
25. *ibid.*, 9 May 1923, p.166.
26. *ibid.*, 22 August 1923, p.5.
27. *ibid.*, 9 April 1924, p.7.
28. *ibid.*, 1 April 1925, p.24. The forthcoming Pauline Frederick tour saw the temporary return to Australia, as her manager, of Snowy Baker. She did not however, act in an Australian film.
29. *ibid.*, 2 September 1925, p.12.
30. *ibid.*, 9 December 1925, p.6.
31. *Trooper O'Brien* would have cost Hoyts £1,500 for five copies of the film and screening rights in Australia and New Zealand.
32. R.C.E., p.670.
33. *ibid.*, p.669.
34. New South Wales Government Inquiry Into The Film Industry: Evidence

of Stuart F. Doyle, Managing Director of Greater Union Theatres, 12 January 1934, pp.1-2.
35. R.C.E., p.799.
36. *Everyones*, 19 November 1924, p.10.
37. R.C.E., p.669.
38. *ibid.*, p.670.

Chapter 7

1. This was the thinking behind his often quoted remark to the Royal Commission, 'The only way in which we can give an Australian picture international appeal is to make it Australian.'
2. *Picture Show*, 1 April 1922, p.37.
3. Baker snapped cigarettes out of his mouth and lighted candles off his head with a stockwhip.
4. *Picture Show*, 1 November 1923, p.34.
5. *ibid.*
6. He argued that this led to inefficiency and increased costs since in Hollywood there was a streamlined department to handle each of these areas.
7. For instance, with the replacement of Kleig lights by incandescent ones his ideas on make-up were also very out of date.
8. *Picture Show*, 1 November 1923, p.34.
9. While this changeover was under way, he argued that the path was open for 'typical, local color' Australian silent films to exploit the American States' rights circuit which was still largely unwired for sound.
10. The company had a nominal capital of £50,000, of which 38,000 £1 shares were offered to the public and 1500 fully-paid shares to the promoter.
11. Ironically, Hassell was to say years later that he never saw anything in these Australian films, and far preferred the American ones.
12. *Sydney Mail*, 24 March 1926, p.3.
13. *Everyones*, 16 September 1926, p.15.
14. *ibid.*, p. 26.
15. Elsa Chauvel, *My Life With Charles Chauvel*, 1973, p.23.
16. R.C.E., p.203.
17. *Everyones*, 8 December 1926, p.10.
18. *Film Weekly*, 24 March 1927, p.6.
19. R.C.E., p.370.
20. *Everyones*, 16 February 1927, p.4.
21. Elsa Chauvel, *ibid.*, pp.25-6.
22. R.C.E., p.201.
23. *ibid.*
24. *ibid.*, p.227.
25. *ibid.*, p.201.

26. Kerr read a number of exhibitors' letters to the Royal Commission pointing out that they were already too over-stretched in terms of screening nights by their contracts with the major distributors to take the Chauvel films; R.C.E., p.225.
27. See, for instance, R.C.E., p.289, p.226.
28. It was not till 1933 that Chauvel put a heavy emphasis on quotas.
29. *Everyones*, 3 April 1929, p.24.
30. *ibid.*, 12 May 1926, p.5.
31. *ibid.*, 19 August 1925, p.3.
32. *Picture Show*, 1 October 1922, p.70.
33. *Photoplayer*, 29 September 1923, p.16. Both this film, which Hurley shot with a special light-weight camera personally given to him by Stuart Doyle, and *Pearls and Savages* were generally noted for their blend of 'beautiful scenic studies' and 'many adventurous exploits . . . replete with incident'.
34. *Everyones*, 19 May 1926, p.26.
35. *ibid.*, 19 December 1923, p.20.
36. Hurley told the Royal Commission that he personally could never have handled the lecture tours throughout America which were necessary to the film. This led him to change his format from the documentary/lecture to the documentary/narrative films of the years ahead.
37. *Everyones*, 3 August 1925, p.19.
38. Transport costs were considerably increased in the event of Hurley having to change his shooting location because of hostility from the New Guinea government at a film mixing white and black actors.
39. The first production, *Jungle Woman*, was a joint Hurley-Stoll production, which gave the 'Pearls and Savages' company a greater stake in it than *Hound of the Deep* — and the advertising of the later film, although still good, reflected this situation.
40. Made safe by having the black heroine played by an Australian actress and telling the audience in advance that the love is not consummated.
41. *Everyones*, 5 May 1926, p.8.
42. *ibid.*, 26 May 1926, p.16.
43. *Film Weekly*, 9 September 1926, p.27; *Everyones*, 15 September 1926, p.46.
44. *Everyones*, 10 November 1926, p.31.
45. R.C.E., p.168.

Chapter 8

1. Australian Film Institute: Report for 1978.
2. *Cinema Papers*, June/July 1976, p.37.
3. Reps., 2156, 19 October 1978.
4. The *Sydney Morning Herald*, scourge of so many Australian (and indeed Hollywood) film-makers, did call the sisters' first film, *Those Who Love*, 'palpably

an experiment, a rather timid imitation of the American movies', but made up for it with the review of *The Far Paradise* which it said showed decision in every detail and was 'a distinct advance upon most of its predecessors'.

5. *Everyones*, 27 October 1926, p.32.
6. *ibid.*, 14 July 1926, p.6.
7. *Everyones*, 22 December 1926, p.3.
8. *Film Weekly*, 1 November 1926, p.26.
9. *Everyones*, 22 December 1926, p.3.
10. Isabel noted at the Royal Commission that *Those Who Love* would have cost far more than its £1,000 if 'we had hired a studio and engaged leading actors and actresses'. Ross Cooper has also noted (*Cinema Papers*, July 1974, p.261) that their class background led 'to an easy informality of approach with high officials' who gave them special privileges, such as access to state institutions and the use of the Governor's train (the Governor's daughter had a small part in the film). This aspect of the McDonaghs' activity bears comparison with that of their mentor, P.J. Ramster, from whom film historians seem eager to dissociate them.
11. *Everyones*, 12 March 1930, p.5.
12. Cooper, *op. cit.*
13. Interview with Graham Shirley and Pat Lovell, *Cinema papers*, June/July 1976, p.89.
14. *Everyones*, 27 October 1925, p.23.
15. *ibid.*, 22 December 1926, p.3.
16. *ibid.*,11 August 1926, p.6.
17. *ibid.*, p.13, and 22 December 1926, p.3.
18. R.C.E., p.952.
19. *Film Weekly*, 25 November 1926, p.27.
20. *Everyones*, 15 December 1926, p.20.
21. R.C.E., p.927.
22. *Film Weekly*, 11 November 1926, p.26.
23. *ibid.*, 16 December 1926, p.6.
24. *ibid.*, 11 November 1926, p.26.
25. *Sydney Morning Herald*, 20 June 1928, p.12.
26. *Everyones*, 15 December 1926, p.20; 22 December 1926, p.3.
27. *Film Weekly*, 18 November 1926, p.5.
28. R.C.E., p.724.
29. The mystery is, who were Greater Australasian Films Ltd? In 1927 W.A. Gibson was asked at the Royal Commission whether it was true that contracts had been made between Australasian Films and another company 'whereby they take over your picture-producing studio and assets, and you cease production'. Gibson said the matter had been discussed, but 'nothing has been done so far'. In February 1929 *Everyones* announced 'the happiest news this journal has broadcast . . . that Australasian Films is not to die', since 'W.A.

Gibson, O.B.E., who has fathered Australasian Films as he has fathered the whole industry . . . has now chosen John C. Jones to carry on'. Greater Australasian Films was supposedly independent, but Jones had come from First National which had recently concluded a five-year exclusive supply deal with U.T.—A.F. His replacement as manager of First National, Leslie Wicks, had moved from A.F., taking many colleagues with him. Now it was announced that Jones would levy on First National for these same men in staffing the new company, and that First National would vacate its offices to him. Concerning the joy of *Everyones*, we should perhaps note the rumour mentioned at the Royal Commission that '*Everyones*, which recently published such eulogistic interviews with Stuart Doyle of Union Theatres, and with Mr Jones of First National, is controlled by First National'. Gibson said he did not think this was true; but it is an interesting fact that Gayne Dexter had been publicity manager for First National in the United States before suddenly returning to Australia and becoming part owner and editor of *Everyones*. Another possible tie up between Greater Australasian Films and an American company was with the fast-rising Columbia Pictures. Announcing the new company, *Everyones* said that Columbia had made strenuous efforts to secure Jones as managing director for Australia 'to establish a new exchange system here'. A month later the journal announced a big supply tie-up between Columbia and Greater Australasian Films which involved 'the permanent establishment of Columbia here . . . The name of the company will be changed to Greater Australasian and Columbia Films Ltd'. This may have been similar to the deal between Musgrove, as an independent, and First National earlier in the decade; but given the change of company name, it may have been the first penetration of American money directly into the Australian film trade, some time before the well-known Fox takeover.

30. *Everyones*, 11 December, 1929, p.12.
31. *The Cheaters* was placed second to *Fellers* in the long delayed £10,000 Film Contest, but neither was considered good enough. *Fellers* received third prize money, *The Cheaters* nothing.

Chapter 9

1. *Everyones*, 18 August 1926, p.4.
2. *ibid.*, 15 September 1926, p.4.
3. *ibid.*, p.23.
4. *ibid.*, 18 August 1926, p.14.
5. *ibid.*, 11 August 1926, p.25.
6. *ibid.*, 3 November 1926, p.9.
7. The 'big advance' over America, which it was to the 'credit of Australian brains and initiative' to have achieved, was the heating system of the boiler!
8. *Everyones*, 22 September 1926, p.7.

9. *ibid.*, 19 June 1927, p.7.
10. *ibid.*, 8 September 1926, p.48.
11. *ibid.*, 15 December 1926, p.55.
12. *ibid.*, 22 September 1926, p.8.
13. *ibid.*, p.20.
14. *ibid.*, 18 August 1926, p.36.
15. *ibid.*, 22 September 1926, p.3.
16. *ibid.*, 3 November 1926, p.9.
17. *ibid.*, 23 February 1927, p.7.
18. *ibid.*, 15 December 1926, p.55.
19. *ibid.*, 3 November 1926, p.9.
20. *ibid.*, 6 October 1926, p.7.
21. *ibid.*, 16 December 1926, p.19.
22. *Film Weekly*, 18 November 1926, p.14.
23. *Everyones*, 25 August 1926, p.7.
24. *ibid.*, 4 August 1926, p.7.
25. *ibid.*, 27 May 1925, p.11.
26. *ibid.*, 2 June 1926, p.3.
27. *ibid.*, 9 June 1926, p.5. My italics.
28. *ibid.*, 28 April 1926, p.10.
29. *ibid.*, 12 June 1927, p.7.
30. *ibid.*, 9 June 1926, p.5. There was even talk of a second Hollywood being established at Maroubra 'where space is limitless, and the atmosphere ideal'.
31. *ibid.*, 21 July 1926, p.57. She had supposedly impressed 'the hardy mining people of the Yukon river' by her ability to 'drive a dog team with the best of them'.
32. *ibid.*, 28 April 1926, p.10.
33. *ibid.*, 27 October 1926, p.45. He had insisted, for instance, on shooting *Typhoon Love* at the Pacific Islands when 'it was entirely practical to film this story of the South Seas in Southern California'.
34. *ibid.*, 28 April 1926, p.10.
35. Indeed the advertising Paramount gave to the Flaherty film, 'the love life of a South Sea siren', would have been better applied to Dawn's film.
36. For a full description of these processes, see R.E. Fielding, 'Norman O. Dawn: Pioneer Worker in Special-Effects Cinematography', *Journal of Motion Picture and Television Engineers*, vol. 72, no. 1, January 1963, pp.15-23. While giving a clear exposition, the article's claims about Dawn's 'pioneering' status need to be taken with caution. For instance, a photo showing Dawn using a glass-shot set-up in front of the ruined Tasmanian convict barracks, which was taken in 1926, is used as an example of a pioneering glass-shot in *1908*!
37. Vardac, *op.cit.*, pp.213-14.
38. *Everyones*, 26 December 1928, p.8.

39. R.C.E., 149,160.
40. *Film Weekly*, 19 January 1928. Interestingly, at the Royal Commission Hurley, who thought highly of Dawn, claimed the two typical Dawn locations — the Arctic and the South Seas — to be 'uniquely' Australian.
41. *Everyones*, 11 July 1928, p.10.
42. *Film Weekly*, 30 June 1927, p.6.
43. *Everyones*, 26 December 1928, p.8.
44. *ibid.*, 4 July 1928, p.10. Critical comments of a minor kind began appearing in *Everyones*: from a Brisbane journalist who complained about poor imitations of Hollywood (25 July); from a Hollywood actor who said they could not hope for a world market because 'they lack typical Australia' (29 February 1929); etc.
45. Where he made the cheap early sound review. *Talkie Mad*, for J.C. Williamson.
46. *Everyones*, 12 December 1928, p.86.
47. *ibid.*, 24 November 1926, p.6.
48. R.C.E., p.660.
49. *ibid.*, p.661.
50. *ibid.*, p.659.
51. *ibid.*, p665.
52. *ibid.*, p.667. Ironically, though, he had the same propagandist ambition as Shirley, to help make Australia flourish by attracting immigrants with films which gave the right impression of 'this great country'.
53. R.C.E., p.665.
54. *Everyones*, 4 September 1929, p.18.
55. R.C.E., p.719.
56. *Film Weekly*, 14 July 1927, p.4.
57. *ibid.*, 27 January 1927, p.5. Worsley was unemployed at this time, due, American writers claimed, to the invasion of Hollywood by 'inferior' European directors.
58. R.C.E., p.768.
59. *Film Weekly*, 11 November 1926.
60. Because of the number of men touring the country canvassing shares.
61. Even this was subject to the knocking campaign: *Everyones* had criticised the 'ridiculously inadequate' offer of a £150 scenario prize by Phillips.
62. Eric Davis, *The Life and Times of Steele Rudd*, Melbourne, 1976, p.182; and R.C.E., pp.26-7.
63. *Film Weekly*, 30 June 1927, p.20.
64. *ibid.*, 19 January 1928, p.36.
65. Rudd had helped prepare the shooting script himself.
66. Davis, *op.cit.*, p.180.
67. *Everyones*, 1 February 1928, p.22.

68. Phillips' only comment to the Royal Commission about this was that Worsley did some shooting in Queensland for him while waiting for the arrival of Dunlap.
69. *Everyones*, 18 January 1928, p.14.
70. R.C.E., p.834.
71. *Film Weekly*, 7 July 1927, p.12.
72. *ibid.*
73. *Everyones*, 17 November 1926, p.6.
74. R.C.E., p834.
75. *ibid.*, p.758.
76. *Everyones*, 18 January 1928, p.4.
77. *Sydney Morning Herald*, 15 August 1927.
78. *Everyones*, 22 February 1928, p.23.
79. *Sydney Morning Herald*, 30 December 1927.
80. *Film Weekly*, 8 September 1927, p.10.
81. *Shop Assistants Magazine.*
82. *Everyones*, 18 April 1928, p.5.
83. *ibid.*, p.7.
84. *ibid.*, 15 August 1928, p.6.
85. *ibid.*, 8 February 1928, p.20.
86. *ibid.*, 22 February 1928, p.23.
87. *ibid.*, 9 May 1928, p.4.
88. *ibid.*, 22 February 1928, pp5,6.
89. *ibid.*, 9 May 1928, p.4.

Chapter 10

1. *Everyones*, 28 December 1932, p.4.
2. Chauvel's *The Rats of Tobruk.*
3. Raymond Williams has traced this concept back to Virgil in *The Country and the City* (London, Chatto and Windus, 1973).
4. Russel Ward, *The Australian Legend*, Melbourne, 1958.
5. 'Banjo' Patterson, 'Clancy of the Overflow'.
6. G.L. Buxton, '1870-90', in F.K. Crowley (ed.), *A New History of Australia*, Melbourne 1974, p.198.
7. *ibid.*, p.172.
8. T.H. Irving, '1850-70', in Crowley, *A New History of Australia*, p.156.
9. B.K. de Garis, '1890-1900' in Crowley, *op.cit.*, p.226.
10. Until 1939 the gross product from rural industries, without including mining, was still considerably ahead of that of manufacturing, and less than five per cent of export income came from the sale of manufactured products.
11. H. Radi, '1920-29', in Crowley, *op.cit.*, p.381.

12. *The Exhibitor*, 9 December 1925, p.3.
13. I Turner, '1914-19', in Crowley, *op.cit.*, p.349.
14. Radi, *op.cit.*, p.395.
15. *The Exhibitor*, 7 May 1924, p.3.
16. For the nineteenth century, D.B. Waterson's thesis on the Darling Downs in *Squatter, Selector and Storekeeper: A History of the Darling Downs, 1859-93*, Sydney, 1968, is invaluable, and I shall draw on it for some of the following.
17. Waterson., p.177.
18. Irving points out that the urban radicals' belief in popular democracy and their fervant anti-monopolistic stand 'did not prepare them for the metamorphosis of businessmen from an economic interest into a new ruling class — they believed that all except the squatters had an equal interest in building a new society, and that classes were relics of the old world'.
19. As a matter of its own numerical support.
20. Frank Crowley (*op.cit.*) has pointed to the important role of country newspapers in continuing this myth, and remarks that it was very rare for anyone in the first years of the Twentieth century to defend city growth on the grounds of the necessary economic symbiosis between country and city within the capitalist system.
21. Waterson, *op.cit.*, p.278.
22. *Everyones*, 12 December 1934, p.18.
23. Waterson, *op.cit.*, p.279.

Chapter 11

1. D.W. Meinig, *On the Margins of the Good Earth*, Adelaide, 1962, ch. 8. The townsman was, as Meinig notes, no less a pioneer than the farmer, and where frontier expansion was planned, as in South Australia, a policy of building towns to serve a five mile country radius was part of the pioneering programme.
2. Waterson, p.67.
3. R. Ward, *op.cit.*, pp.174-7.
4. R. Williams, *op.cit.*, p.121.
5. We note the name, and that of Barrett's dedicated Australian company, Golden Wattle.
6. See Vladimir Propp's theory of narrative in *Morphology of the Folktale* (Austin, 1975). The reconaissance of the villain is one of the early functions in Propp's syntagmatic narrative structure, and as such motivates the key function of the narrative, 'villainy'.
7. The sphere of action of the helper is one of seven which define the seven dramatis personae of the fairy-tale, according to Propp. I am using it here, however, in the broader motion of Claude Bremond, where the helper, together with

victim and villain, is one of only three central characters in the tale. See C. Bremond, 'The Morphology of the French Fairy Tale: The Ethical Model', in Heda Jason and Dimitri Sigal (eds.) *Patterns in Oral Literature*, The Hague, 1977, pp.49-76.

8. A.J. Greimas and J. Courtés, 'The Cognitive Dimension of Narrative Discourse', *New Literary History*, v.7,n.3, 1976, p.446.
9. Minimal units of meaning at a given level.
10. Elsewhere I have analysed this organicist position in *Metropolis* in terms of the ideology of a downwardly-mobile élite group in Germany during the period of industrialisation. See J.C. Tulloch, *Conflict and Control in the Cinema*, ch. 3.
11. He replaces the real maid who, with an immorality reserved only for the working class in the country, has run off with a boundary rider.
12. R. Barthes, *S/Z* (London, 1975).
13. Particularly the railways and telegraph, to the extent of these being essential pioneer tools rather than the intruders of Lawson's 'mighty bush with iron rails . . . tethered to the world' image.
14. For elaboration of this concept and the narrative relation of 'competence' to 'performance' see Greimas and Courtés, *op.cit*.
15. See Thomas Elsaesser, 'Tales of Sound and Fury. Observations on the Family Melodrama', *Monogram*, 4, 1973, pp.2-15. Elsaesser sees sexual exploitation and rape as central metaphors for class conflict in melodrama. In contrast I see them as *displacements*, directing the narrative away from class analysis — at least in Australian cinema.
16. G. Nowell-Smith, 'Minelli and Melodrama', *Australian Journal of Screen Theory*, 3, 1977, pp.31-5.
17. Elsaesser, *op.cit.*, p.10.
18. Bill Tressle's 'voyeurism' breaks down the simple opposition between 'production' and 'spectacle' — which I would argue it has to do, since so much of the effect of the bush films depends on the spectacle they present of rural plenitude: slow pans of plentiful cattle, luscious countryside, and so on.
19. Without being as confident as Nowell-Smith that we can easily know *what* the audience (particularly an audience in the past) knows, and while being more than doubtful about his assumption that the audience will decode any film in one, unanimous, way, it does seem the case that this kind of analysis of melodrama is fruitful in helping us understand Barrett's films, at least in terms of their popularity today.
20. *Everyones*, 11 May 1921, p.18.
21. Musical Synposis for *For The Term Of His Natural Life*, National Library of Australia, National Film Archive.
22. W.J. Bellingham, in *Everyones*, 23 April 1924, p.4.
23. E. Aarons, in *Everyones*, 29 April 1925, p.8.

Chapter 12

1. Cited in Andrew Britton, '*Meet Me In St. Louis*: Smith, or the Ambiguities' *Australian Journal of Screen Theory*, 3, 1977, p.7.
2. Eli Zaretsky, *Capitalism, The Family and Personal Life*, cited in Britton, '*Meet Me In St. Louis*', p.7.
3. *ibid.*, p.13.
4. *ibid.*, p.9.
5. *ibid.*; and also Robin Wood, *Personal Views: Explorations in Film* (London, 1976), ch.3.
6. Fatty Finn was a long running cartoon character in the *Sunday News* drawn by Syd Nicholls.
7. Sally as mediator at the robbery, Mrs Stanton linking the classes by inviting Sally to her home, Mrs Smith's story which re-unites the family.
8. Spud and Skinny who have a penchant for racing and fighting, and end in gaol; the laundry manager who exploits Sally and Tottie; Mr Stanton who searches for diamonds at the expense of his family.
9. See Heather Radi, *op.cit.*
10. *ibid.*, p.390.
11. Sylvia Lawson, 'Good Taste at Hanging Rock', in J.C. Tulloch, *op.cit.*
12. T. Todorov, *The Fantastic*, Ithaca, 1975, ch.4.
13. *ibid.*,pp.62-3.
14. A. Fletcher, *Allegory; The Theory of a Symbolic Mode*, Ithaca, 1964.
15. *ibid.*, p.239.
16. For instance, his description of Simon's body floating out to sea.
17. Fletcher, p.344.
18. W. Empson, *Some Versions of Pastoral*, Norfolk (Conn.).

Notes on Terms

Definitions are given here only of terms which are not to be found in a dictionary or which differ from their standard dictionary definition. Terms which are defined either in the body of the text or in footnotes are not included.

Actant. In his theory of narrative, Vladimir Propp distinguishes between the names/attributes of the dramatis personae in a tale and their actions/functions. In one tale a dragon may kidnap a king's daughter; in another a whirlwind takes away a farmer's golden apples; in another a sorcerer makes a peasant's wife disappear. In each case the names and attributes of the cherished object (princess, golden apples, wife) and the villain (dragon, whirlwind, sorcerer) are different, but their function in the narrative (the disequilibrium caused by the loss of a precious object: i.e. the act of villainy) is the same. Because a tale may attribute identical actions to various personages, narrative analysis proceeds according to the identification of 'actants' (eg. 'the villain') and their functions, rather than through a consideration of individual persons or things.

Combine. The term 'combine' meant different things to different people in Australia in the 1920s. To Raymond Longford 'combine' connoted the amalgamation of interests between Amalgamated Pictures Ltd, J.D. Williams' Greater Amusement Company, Spencer's Ltd, West's Ltd, Electrical Theatres and J.C. Williamson Films within the organisation of Australasian Films and Union Theatres Ltd. To others the 'Australian combine' also included the imputed link-up between the two dominant exhibition chains, Union Theatres and Hoyts (see chapter 5, note 60). In the reference on p. 144 Barrett was following the Guthrie-ites and the terms of reference of the Royal Commission in defining 'combine' as the supposed American 'Octopus' with many apparently independent arms (First National, Selznick, Paramount, etc.) but with one body which, after 1924, was organised by the M.P.D.A.

Discourse. A term deriving from linguistics. It has been used to attack the 'scientific' notion that there is an order of reality which legitimises or validates a theory or explanation of the world. In contrast with such notions, discourse analysis takes the approach that the limits of explanation are not set by nature, but merely by the problems which the practice of theoretical or explanatory work sets itself in terms of producing definite effects, such as articulating, criticising and solving problems. Explanation of the world, whether, for instance, contained in Christian allegory about the problem of 'sin', in Marxist theorisation of the nature of 'exploitation', or scientific theories of natural/social 'order' and 'disorder' is always a matter of social intervention, not of natural or transparent 'truth', and therefore is deeply implicated in ideology. For recent consideration of the term within the field of film theory, see for instance Colin MacCabe, 'Realism and the Cinema', *Screen,* Vol. 15, 2 (1974), pp.7-27, and 'The discursive and the ideological in film', *Screen*, Vol. 19, 4 (1978/9), pp.29-43. There is also in use the more specific sense of a 'discourse shared by a socially constituted group of speakers or particular social practice' — for instance, a female discourse in a film which is carried not simply by women characters, but potentially by any of the aesthetic, semantic, ideological and social codes which intersect in the film text. By and large the discourses of subordinate (sexual, class and racial) groups are explained and thus controlled by the discourse carrying the dominant ideology. This 'meta-discourse' confers on the spectator 'true' knowledge about these inferior groups, and this unity of the 'knowledge' of the narrative and the spectator's knowledge at the end of the film is its most profound 'plenitude' (see below). But occasionally subordinate discourses may escape the dominant discourse through (as I have argued in this book) devices such as counterpointing and contradiction in music, *mise-en-scène*, parallelled characteristion etc. The potential for subversions of this kind depends, of course, on the work of feminist criticism, itself a discourse, which produces meanings that would have been impossible prior to the development of feminist theory. See Christine Gledhill, 'Klute', in E.A. Kaplan (ed.) *Women in Film Noir,* London, 1978, pp.6-21.

Hegemony. The term as developed by Gramsci, goes beyond the (Chambers) dictionary definition of 'leadership; preponderant influence' to a notion of control which is neither a matter of direct coercion nor merely a matter of conscious, manipulative, and fully articulated ideological control. Hegemony is more than either of these: it involves the penetration of the relations of domination and subordination in a society as far as the taken-for-granted, internalised and 'common sense' assumptions of most people's everyday lives. Because it translates social, economic and cultural relations into the transparent common sense of 'experienced reality' it represents human exploitation as 'facts of nature', difficult or impossible to change. The notion of the 'hegemonic' also includes the idea of process, of a complex system of domination which has constantly to be defended by renewal and recreation, so that oppositional forces generated by changing historical circumstances are neutralised or incorporated, as for instance in the mobilisation of the bush legend on behalf of urban entrepreneurs in the nineteenth century, or American capital in the twentieth century, discussed in chapter 10. The further aspect of the concept of hegemony, that even alternative and oppositional forms must, in so far as they cannot avoid the 'lived experience' of society, be tied to the hegemonic, is of particular relevance to Russel Ward's original thesis of the bush legend as, on the one hand, the world view of a rural proletarian group, and on the other hand, an aspect of imperialist Romanticism. For further discussion of the concept see, for instance, Raymond Williams, *Marxism and Literature,* Oxford, 1977, Part II chapter 6.

Narrative. The classical narrative, as defined by theorists such as Propp and Todorov, is a tale beginning with a stable situation that is disturbed by some power, often a force of evil, which it is the task of the text to redress. The narrative thus ends in a state of restored equilibrium, though this will not be identical with that of the initial situation. Thus, in Propp's example, in the initial situation the king has a beautiful daughter; this equilibrium is then disturbed when a dragon takes the princess; and the task of the narrative is to restore her through the actions of a hero, whose reward is her hand in marriage. The princess begins as daughter and ends as wife. A narrative may begin with the misfortune (or 'lack') but will, classically, always end in the fulfillment (or 'plenitude') of repose at the end. Some brief notes on the notion of narrative as discourse, on which I had intended a chapter (see Preface) are contained under *Discourse.*

Phatic. A term emphasising the significance of the communicative act itself (for maintaining social interaction, order, consensus) rather than the meaning a communicative act conveys.

Plenitude. See *Narrative.*

Romantic. The term, as used in the Longford chapter, suggests the notion of the complete and autonomous individual, the creative artist of genius struggling against oppressive social forces (whether the entire industrial civilisation or, more specifically in Longford's case, the 'combine'), and yet able to surmount social conditioning in his/her personal vision. The term is given a broader social focus within the ideology of imperialism in Chapter 10.

Self-Reflexive. The term is normally applied to devices which oppose the claims of film (whether documentary or narrative) to verisimilitude, or to reflect the world transparently and without mediation. Hence self-reflexivity is defined as 'any aspect of a film which points to its own processes of production: the conceptualisation of a film, the procedures necessary to make the technology available, the process of filming itself, editing to construct a single presentation from separate segments of image and sound, the desires and demands of marketing the film, the circumstances of exhibition.' (J. Allen, 'Self-Reflexivity in Documentary', *Cine-Tracts,* 2, p.37).

Picture Show, 1 September 1921, p. 27

See Chapter 5, note 23

Index